ABOUT THE AUTHOR

Mark Blake is an acclaimed music journalist and author. A long-time contributor to the UK's biggest-selling music magazine, *Mojo*, and former assistant editor of *Q* magazine, Blake has written for many high-profile publications including *Rolling Stone, Classic Rock* and *Billboard*.

Among his previous books are the bestselling *Pigs Might Fly: The Inside Story of Pink Floyd* and *Bring It On Home: Peter Grant, Led Zeppelin and Beyond*, which was listed as a 'Music Book of the Year' by *The Times*, the *Sunday Times*, the *Daily Mail* and the *Daily Telegraph*.

Blake has also worked on official projects for Queen, Pink Floyd, the Who and the Jimi Hendrix estate. He lives just outside London with his wife and son.

Magnifico!

THE A TO Z OF
QUEEN

MARK BLAKE

NINE
EIGHT
BOOKS

NINE
EIGHT
BOOKS

NEB 002

First published in the UK in 2021 by Nine Eight Books
An imprint of Bonnier Books UK
4th Floor, Victoria House, Bloomsbury Square, London, WC1B 4DA
Owned by Bonnier Books, Sveavägen 56, Stockholm, Sweden

 @nineeightbooks

 @nineeightbooks

Hardback ISBN: 978-1-7887-0478-6
Trade paperback ISBN: 978-1-7887-0479-3
eBook ISBN: 978-1-7887-0572-1
Audio ISBN: 978-1-7887-0484-7

A CIP catalogue record for this book is available from the British Library.

Publishing director: Pete Selby
Senior editor: Melissa Bond

Cover design by Lora Findlay
Cover image © Look Press/Avalon
Typeset by IDSUK (Data Connection) Ltd
Printed and bound in Great Britain by Clays Ltd, Elcograf S.p.A

1 3 5 7 9 10 8 6 4 2

Picture credits: pp. 13, 98, 252/253 – Michael Ochs Archives/Getty Images; p. 40 – Dave Hogan/ Getty Images; pp. 57, 68, 213, 224, 405 – Koh Hasebe/Shinko Music/Getty Images; p. 84 – Mark and Colleen Hayward/Redferns/Getty Images; p. 90 – Artips/Alamy Stock Photo; p. 124 – Fox Photos/ Hulton Archive/Getty Images; p. 134 – Ben Stansall/AFP/Getty Images; pp. 154/155 – Michael Montfort/Michael Ochs Archives/Getty Images; p. 178 – Phil Dent/Redferns/Getty Images; pp. 192/193 – FG/Bauer-Griffin/Getty Images; p. 258 © Mark Blake; p. 277 – Michael Putland/ Getty Images; p. 289 – Ian Dickson/Redferns/Getty Images; p. 299 – Richard Creamer/Michael Ochs Archives/Getty Images; p. 310 – Colin Davey/Evening Standard/Getty Images; p. 336 – Jack Garofalo/Paris Match/Getty Images; p. 344 – Ferdaus Shamim/WireImage/Getty Images; pp. 360, 374 – Mick Hutson/Redferns/Getty Images; p. 394 – Anthony Harvey/Getty Images

Every reasonable effort has been made to trace copyright-holders of material reproduced in this book. If any have been inadvertently overlooked, the publisher would be glad to hear from them.

Nine Eight Books is an imprint of Bonnier Books UK
www.bonnierbooks.co.uk

CONTENTS

FOREWORD

'Thank you, God bless and sweet dreams, you load of tarts!'
– Freddie Mercury, 1986

In the 1980s, Queen were the only band I ever saw who made me laugh for the right reasons. Other groups and lead singers took themselves too seriously. Queen and Freddie Mercury were the exception.

Queen's music could be smart, shameless, funny, fearless, complex and disarmingly simple – sometimes all in the course of one song. Making this music was a serious business and Queen sweated blood in the studio. But, on stage, they were entertainers, and Freddie Mercury always made the audience feel like they were in on the joke.

This is partly why Queen are even bigger this century than they were in the previous one when Mercury was still alive. There's been less of a Queen revival in recent years and more of a second coming.

Inside are 132 stories, anecdotes and observations, each based on Queen's music and on three decades' worth of original interviews with their gatekeepers: guitarist Brian May and drummer Roger Taylor. This Queen alphabet shines a light on the band, its members, their hits, their misses and those characters, places, inspirations and random objects that have contributed to their never-ending story.

'When I'm dead, who cares?' said Freddie Mercury once.

How wrong he was.

ALTERNATIVE BAND NAMES

Because Queen nearly weren't called Queen

It was Freddie Mercury's idea to call the band Queen. Not everyone was on side. 'I didn't like the name originally,' said Roger Taylor, 'and neither did Brian, but we got used to it.'

Just as well, as the other contenders included:

- Build Your Own Boat
  Named after a book Brian May saw at a friend of Roger Taylor's house in Cornwall. In 2011, Taylor rediscovered his diaries from summer 1970: 'We were nearly called Build Your Own Boat. I'd actually drawn a logo for it. Oh dear . . .'

- Great Dance
  Named after a phrase in author C. S. Lewis's 1943 book *Perelandra*, the second novel in his science-fiction Space Trilogy. Both May and Taylor were avid fans. 'I was always reading,' said Taylor. '*Lord of the Rings*, of course, Heinlein, Asimov, C. S. Lewis's adult sci-fi.' This prospective band name was also remembered by some contemporaries as the Grand Dance.

- Rich Kids
  Origin unknown, but name may have been wishful thinking on Freddie Mercury's part. In 1977, ex-Sex Pistol Glen Matlock used the name for his new, short-lived group.

'ANOTHER ONE BITES THE DUST'
Queen's boogie night

The 'disco sucks' campaign is one of the more depressing episodes in American music history. In 1978, DJ Steve Dahl was fired by a Chicago radio station, WDAI, after it switched formats from rock to disco. (The *Saturday Night Fever*-inspired dance craze had prompted sweeping changes at stations across the US.) Dahl was later hired by a rival and started protesting on air about his former employers and their new format.

However, what began as the actions of an aggrieved disc jockey soon snowballed into a backlash against an entire musical genre. Dahl's campaign hit a new low in July 1979 with Disco Demolition Night. The event saw 50,000 people arrive at Chicago's Comiskey Park stadium with disco records that would be ceremoniously blown up during the half-time break of a Chicago White Sox game. Many of the records weren't even disco, but by black artists, adding an uneasy, racist edge to the protest. It was an extreme reaction, but also emblematic of the tribal nature of fandom. For a while, 'disco sucks' badges even started appearing in the UK, worn on leather jackets by partisan punk and heavy-metal fans.

It was into this divisive world that Queen released 'Another One Bites the Dust' a year later – a single that attracted a new audience, alienated some of the old and split opinion within the group.

Among the first victims of Dahl's campaign was the American R&B band Chic. Spearheaded by guitarist Nile Rodgers, Chic's golden streak ended with summer 1979's 'Good Times'. 'Our career was cut dramatically short due to the backlash,' said Rodgers. 'Chic never had another hit.'

Chic, however, played a part in Queen's unexpected foray onto the dancefloor. That same summer, John Deacon visited New York's Power Station Studios where Chic were recording 'Good Times'. He returned to Munich's Musicland Studios with a bassline remarkably similar to theirs and a song idea unlike any in the Queen catalogue.

'We didn't have a clue what Deaky was up to when he started "Another One Bites the Dust",' said Brian May. This wasn't unusual, though, as Deacon kept his own counsel. Indeed, producer Reinhold Mack even nicknamed him 'Ostrich' because of his ability to remain silent before laying 'a perfect egg'.

With his bandmates still none the wiser, Deacon asked Roger Taylor to muffle his drums before they recorded the backing track. This was the antithesis of how Taylor liked his instrument to sound, but Deacon wanted the dryness he'd heard on the Chic record. 'I remember Roger didn't want to play drums that way,' May said. 'He stuck blankets in them. But he played the pattern John wanted him to and made the drums sound very R&B or disco. He did a brilliant drum loop.' To this, Deacon added rhythm guitar, piano and handclaps, with May supplying 'the dirty guitar stuff' in the middle.

'We were being coerced in a direction Roger and I probably wouldn't have chosen to go in,' admitted the guitarist. But Deacon had an ally in fellow dance music fan Freddie Mercury. Deacon wasn't a singer, so Mercury became his interpreter and sung the vocal with such aggression that his throat bled. It's Mercury's voice that helped distinguish Queen's song from other disco records. There's none of the smoothness of Chic's 'Good Times' in his delivery; he spits the lyrics out like broken teeth.

The song was a daring move for Queen, especially in the contemporary musical climate. 'Roger hated it,' May said in 2008. 'He didn't want Queen to become funky.'

'I did not hate it,' Taylor insisted. 'I was never opposed to the song; I just didn't think it would be a hit.'

In July 1980, when Queen played four sold-out nights at the LA Forum, Michael Jackson and his brothers came backstage to see the band. 'They were in the dressing room and going on and on about "Another One Bites the Dust",' recalled Taylor. Queen maintain it was the Jackson 5 who persuaded them to release the song as a single, although Queen's road crew insist it was them. 'But we were told to mix some more cocktails,' quipped one.

Either way, Queen gave in and an early pressing of the single was soon being played on black stations, including New York's WBLS. Queen went disco at the worst time commercially, but had a hit nevertheless. The song reached number seven at home and number two in the *Billboard* soul and disco charts, with some unexpected consequences. 'A lot of people bought the single and came to our shows thinking we were a black act,' said May, 'and suddenly realised we weren't.'

Chic's bass guitarist, Bernard Edwards, died in 1996, but always insisted he had no problem with Queen co-opting his bassline. His grievance was with critics, ignorant of the chronology, accusing Chic of copying Queen. 'It was inconceivable to these people that black musicians could be innovative,' he protested. 'It was just these dumb disco guys ripping off this rock 'n' roll song.'

The song also came close to being used in a Hollywood block-buster. In 1982, actor/director Sylvester Stallone approached

Queen's management to use the song in *Rocky III*, the latest instalment of his boxing movie franchise. An early cut of the film even included 'Another One Bites the Dust', but no deal was ever struck. Instead, unknown American soft-rockers Survivor were asked to provide a replacement and wrote 'Eye of the Tiger'. 'Thank you, Queen!' said co-writer Jim Peterik after the song became a top-ten hit in nineteen countries.

However, 'Another One Bites the Dust' would be Queen's last US hit for more than a decade. In America, Queen were still perceived as rock with a capital 'R'. The song, coupled with Mercury's shorn hair and newly cultivated moustache, confused those who expected their rock groups to look and sound like Van Halen or a variation thereof.

In 2012, medical professionals revealed how 'Another One Bites the Dust' was being used as a training aid in cardiopulmonary resuscitation. Apparently, the song's 120 beats per minute are ideal for timing chest compressions.

'It still surprises me it was a hit, though,' said a baffled Roger Taylor. 'But it just goes to show: what do I know?'

AUSTIN, MARY
The wife's tale

Freddie Mercury never changed a plug or a light bulb. And he never learned to drive either. Through most of the 1970s and beyond, these tasks fell to his partner and dearest friend, Mary Austin. Even after Mercury embraced his true sexuality, the pair remained inseparable.

Mary remembers meeting Freddie in either late 1969 or early 1970. At the time, she was living with her widowed father (who, like her late mother, was deaf) in a small, terraced house in Fulham. Mary had left school at fifteen and trained as a secretary before landing a job at Biba, the glamorous Kensington clothes store. This was heartland Smile territory – near both Imperial College and Mercury and Roger Taylor's market stall.

One afternoon, Freddie and Roger swanned into Biba together. It took Mercury several months to ask her out (she went on dates with Brian May in the meantime). In summer 1971, Freddie and Mary went to see Mott the Hoople at the Marquee. Mercury could barely afford to buy a drink, but charmed her nevertheless. 'Freddie was like no one I had ever met before,' she said. 'He was super confident, almost to the point of arrogance.'

Mary later took him to meet her father, but hadn't warned him how unusual her boyfriend looked. The neighbours' curtains twitched as the self-professed 'Persian popinjay' tottered down the garden path, all skinny trousers, tonged black hair and big teeth. 'It must have been quite a shock for my dad,' she allowed. Father and daughter communicated in sign language. Freddie smiled sweetly and wondered what they were saying.

Five months after their first date, Mary and Freddie were living together in a bedsit at 2 Victoria Road, Kensington. Mary usually paid the rent (£10 a week) as Freddie was penniless. Two years later, they moved into a slightly bigger flat at 100 Holland Road, which they shared with their two cats – Tom and Jerry – and Freddie's upright piano.

The rent was £19 a week. The apartment was decorated with colourful throws, feathers, fronds and ornaments, and visitors were served tea in china cups. But the couple could barely afford to feed themselves. 'We had so little money then, we could only afford one pair of curtains, so we hung them in the bedroom,' Mary recalled. 'We shared the kitchen and bathroom with another couple.'

Mary later said that it took her three years to fall deeply in love with Mercury. During this time, she realised that his supreme confidence concealed a deep shyness and insecurity. Queen were making more money, but were mistrustful of their management company. This made Freddie suspicious of people and their motives, though never of Mary. 'We knew we could trust each other and would never hurt each other,' she said.

'Mary was a sweetheart of a girl,' said musician and ex-Kensington Market stall holder Alan Mair. 'She was practical, earthy and no-nonsense. She was very beautiful with a lovely way about her.'

However, after 1974, Mercury's life became a dizzying merry-go-round of tour dates, recording sessions and press interviews. 'He was Freddie Bulsara when I met him,' said Mary. 'But now he was Freddie Mercury.'

Mary helped to run her partner's new life by taking care of his day-to-day business. Outwardly, they were still a couple. Mercury even asked Mary to marry him and bought her an engagement ring – a beautiful Egyptian scarab. Having proposed, though, he never mentioned it again. Privately, he was struggling with his sexuality. 'There was something he was hiding and I don't think it made him feel very good, lying to himself,' she said.

The tipping point was 'Bohemian Rhapsody'. Brian May and others have suggested that its lyrics were coded references to Mercury's private life. But the song's success also boosted his confidence and self-belief. In 1976, Freddie told Mary that he was bisexual. She told him that she thought he was homosexual.

Mary moved out of their Kensington duplex and into a flat nearby. Freddie paid for it with his publishing royalties. After moving, Mary realised she could see Freddie's flat from her bathroom window. The nature of their relationship changed, but their friendship remained the same. Mercury's boyfriends came and went, but – in the words of one Queen familiar – 'Mary was the rock base of Freddie's life.' And his muse, too. It is widely believed that he wrote the ballad 'Love of My Life' for her, although Freddie, coy as ever, never confirmed this.

In 1980, Mercury asked Mary to find him somewhere new to live. She found Garden Lodge – a beautiful Georgian town-house in Logan Place, Kensington. Later, Mary's tasks involved ensuring Freddie's staff were paid. This included his boyfriend, Jim Hutton, who was nominally employed as his gardener. The pair of them – the ex-'wife' and the boyfriend – cared for Mercury during his final years.

However, being Mercury's wife in all but name brought challenges. After his death, Mercury left Garden Lodge to Mary, along with a huge percentage of his sales and publishing income. By then, she'd married painter Piers Cameron, with whom she had two sons, Richard and James. Mercury, who was godfather to Richard, wanted his old house to become a family home.

However, Mary's marriage to Cameron ended in 1993. In the interim years, Mary dealt with her own grief, but also the legal and personal fallout from Freddie's death. In addition to Jim Hutton, Peter Freestone (Mercury's aide) and Joe Fanelli (his chef) had lived with Freddie and cared for him at Garden Lodge. While Mercury left them all a sizeable amount of money in his will, there was some reluctance to give up the lavish home.

Mary took over Garden Lodge, but it was three years before she could bring herself to go into Freddie's old bedroom. She moved on with her life, but it wasn't easy. Her second marriage – to businessman Nicholas Holford – ended in divorce in 2002. To the public and to some in the Queen camp, she would always be Freddie's widow.

For many years, the gates and walls surrounding Garden Lodge were covered in graffiti – messages of love and condolence left by fans from around the world. Then, in 2017, the walls and gates were cleaned and repainted and warnings were posted outside, leaving many fans outraged. 'Some even told me I was only the keeper of the house,' she said.

Mary Austin's life with Freddie Mercury was recreated, with great dramatic license, in the movie *Bohemian Rhapsody*. Their love affair became the spine of the story: how Mary accepted Freddie's sexuality and encouraged and nurtured him. The real Mary has yet to comment publicly. 'She is very private,' said the movie's producer, Graham King, 'and we want to respect that.'

'Ours is a pure friendship and a friendship of the highest standard,' said Mercury once when asked about the love of his life. 'Mary is my common-law wife. To me, it was a marriage – and what is a marriage anyway?'

BAKER, ROY THOMAS

The fifth cock

Queen's co-producer Roy Thomas Baker was fascinated by sound from a young age. He still remembers walking into his parents' bathroom, aged five, and realising that there was more echo when he was naked than when he had clothes on. 'And that intrigued me,' he said.

Born in Hampstead, north London, in 1946, Baker grew up loving pop music. However, when he listened to records on the Tamla Motown and Stax labels, he wanted to know why they sounded better than their British counterparts.

Baker started to discover why with a job at Decca Studios, aged fourteen. He studied under future Elton John producer Gus Dudgeon and, as a foretaste of life with Queen, helped engineer the D'Oyly Carte Opera Company. By 1970, Baker was working at Trident Studios in Soho. There, he was recruited to help remix 'All Right Now', a single by blues rockers Free. It was a hit for Island Records, but, as Baker was moonlighting from Trident, his name was missing from the credits. 'We had to sneak him in,' recalled Free's bass player Andy Fraser. 'Poor Roy was so nervous . . .'

Nerves were rarely an issue for Roy after that. Baker first encountered Queen in winter 1971 when visiting De Lane Lea Studios in Wembley: 'I was checking out the studio and this unknown band had done a deal to play while the engineers made sure everything was working.' The first song Baker heard was 'Keep Yourself Alive'.

'I totally forgot about the studio,' he said. 'I was very, very impressed.'

Baker had already formed a production company, Neptune, with fellow Trident producers John Anthony, who had previously worked with Smile, and Robin Geoffrey Cable. All three of them wanted to sign the new group. Baker went on to co-produce Queen's first four albums and 1978's *Jazz*.

Right from the beginning, Baker and the group bonded over their shared ambition. 'Queen had all these musical ideas they wanted to put on a record and I had all these production ideas,' he explained. 'They were also bolshie, over the top and aggressive.'

Freddie Mercury once compared Queen to 'four cocks fighting'. Baker was the fifth cock then. Unlike actor Tim Plester's portrayal of a downtrodden yes man in *Bohemian Rhapsody*, the real Roy was as forthright as his clients. He and Queen ruffled each other's feathers, but there was a mutual respect.

'Whenever Fred and I worked together, we had this unspoken thing where I wouldn't sit behind the recording console, but between the console and the window,' Baker recalled. 'Freddie could then tell from my facial expression if I thought a vocal was good enough.'

On *Queen II*, an LP Baker nicknamed the 'kitchen-sink album', they threw everything they could into the mix: phased vocals, backwards gongs, multiple overdubs, 'virtuoso castanets'. It was a band and producer striving for digital sounds in the analogue age. 'Roy brought great perfectionism and a flawless technical approach,' said Brian May. This mutual admiration society lasted for two more albums, *Sheer Heart Attack* and *A Night at the Opera*. 'But, by then, Roy's ego was exploding,' suggested a Queen insider.

Baker disappeared to the States to make records with other artists. It was an excessive time. He blew the record company's budget trying to make a hit of Dusty Springfield's *It Begins Again* album, while Ian Hunter's *Overnight Angels* LP was a litany of disasters. (The album's personnel racked up fourteen car accidents between them and their residential studio in Quebec caught fire. Baker had to jump, naked, from an upstairs window into a snow drift and was later treated for frostbite.) During this period, however, Baker finessed his sound. It was no longer necessary to use everything including the kitchen sink. In February 1978, he produced the debut album of Boston new-wave group the Cars. He did so in three weeks and without virtuoso castanets. The LP and its hit singles went platinum.

Shortly after, Baker was invited back to the mothership (as Queen called themselves) to co-produce *Jazz*. He considered the project a success ('I thought we all had a lot of fun'), but it was the last time he and Queen worked together.

Baker thoroughly embraced the 1980s. It was the era of big bands, big images and even bigger productions. With his shaggy locks, permanent shades and gated Hollywood mansion, Roy looked and behaved more like a rock star than some of his clients did. He made hit-and-miss records for Journey, Cheap Trick, Foreigner and Alice Cooper and became senior vice president of A&R at Elektra.

In 1982, Motley Crüe, an up-and-coming glam-metal group, asked Baker to remix their debut LP. They wanted him because he'd worked with Queen. Motley Crüe nicknamed him 'RTB' and hung on to his every word.

'I learned a lot by watching him work,' recalled producer Tom Zutaut in the Crüe's raucous memoir, *The Dirt*. 'After the band spent the day in the studio, Roy would usually invite them up to his house where they'd be snorting cocaine off his Plexi-glass piano while he told them about the time Freddie Mercury wrote "Bohemian Rhapsody" at that very piano while getting a blow job.'

Not true, of course. But Baker understood the importance of the legend. It would sustain him all the way through to the current century.

In 2005, he produced the album *One Way Ticket to Hell... and Back* for British band the Darkness, whose witty pomp-rock owes much to Queen. The Darkness wanted the Roy Thomas Baker of '70s Queen fame – and he did not disappoint. Their album incorporated custom-made panpipes, 1,000 tracks on one song alone, and lead vocalist Justin Hawkins singing into a Champagne bucket. Freddie surely would have approved.

The royal court: Roy Thomas Baker (far right) with Queen, Mott the Hoople's Ian Hunter (in sunglasses) and friends, Montreal Forum, 1977.

13

'BICYCLE RACE' AND 'FAT BOTTOMED GIRLS'

Queen's guide to sex

In July 1978, cyclist Bernard Hinault, nicknamed 'The Badger' and 'The Boss', won the esteemed Tour de France race. As Hinault received his coveted yellow jersey and 10,000 francs in prize money, he had no idea that he and his fellow riders had just inspired one of Queen's greatest hits.

Queen had just started work on their *Jazz* album, split between Mountain Studios in Montreux and Super Bear Studios in the foothills of the Alpes-Maritimes. Roger Taylor recalled Freddie Mercury watching the Tour de France cyclists and feeling inspired, presumably by the blur of pumping thighs and Lycra. 'He was gazing with absolute amazement and I think it triggered something in his imagination,' Taylor said.

Regardless of how or when inspiration struck – Super Bear was actually four or five hours away from the cyclists' route and Queen may have been in Montreux when the race took place anyway – Mercury wrote 'Bicycle Race' in honour of the Tour de France.

It's a strange song. At times, the stop/start rhythm is less suggestive of a racing bike speeding through the French Alps and more of a penny-farthing with a puncture, wobbling down a cobbled street. But it works brilliantly.

'Then Freddie told us there would be a bicycle-bell solo in the middle,' said Taylor.

'And every cycle shop in the Montreux area was scoured in order to build a collection of various tones and actions of bell,' recalled road manager Peter 'Ratty' Hince.

In October 1978, 'Bicycle Race' was released as a double A-side single with 'Fat Bottomed Girls'. Any pop song beginning with the word 'bicycle' sung three times in a barbershop quartet style is guaranteed to grab attention. Then the lyric drops the names of two topical blockbuster movies, *Jaws* and *Star Wars*, plus the Vietnam War and Mercury's drug du jour, cocaine. After that comes the fifteen-second bicycle-bell solo. By then, Mercury has also announced the arrival of 'fat bottomed girls', inviting listeners to flip the record over and play the other side.

Brian May's 'Fat Bottomed Girls' says a lot about Queen and sex in that it's not terribly sexy. Today, its lyrics would provoke a sharp intake of breath. The song's hero has seemingly been corrupted by 'a naughty nanny' who made 'a bad boy' out of the 'skinny lad' in her charge. Its composer has claimed the song was inspired by the band's most devoted fans rather than by sex. 'It's about a community of people,' said May. 'The people you see in your line of sight when you're playing. It's a song about them and they don't have to be the most beautiful girls or the prettiest of men, but their hearts are in it.' Soon after the single's release, those same fans May referenced started bringing bicycle bells to Queen concerts.

The title of the song itself has had a wider influence, too. Michael McKean, who played 'Derek St Hubbins' in the 1984 'rockumentary' *This Is Spinal Tap*, confirmed that Queen's song was the inspiration for the spoof rockers' 'Big Bottom'.

'Get on your bikes and ride!' implores Mercury at around the 3:25 mark of 'Fat Bottomed Girls'. It was all very meta: two songs namechecking each other on opposite sides of a single. But everything about those two songs, from their provocative titles to their self-referential lyrics, reeks of confidence. Queen sound utterly assured of themselves here.

That same confidence tipping over into arrogance also inspired the promotional video for 'Bicycle Race'. It showed Queen performing, spliced with footage of nude female models peddling bicycles around the track at Wimbledon Stadium. According to unconfirmed EMI gossip, Queen had to pay the hire shop to replace the bikes' saddles after the owners discovered the riders had been naked.

In 1978, the video was deemed far too racy for broadcast, but the single still reached number eleven in the UK chart. Today, it all looks terribly tame; more *Carry On Camping* than *Emmanuelle*, with nary a glimpse of nipple or pubic hair. 'In our music, sex is either implied or referred to semi-jokingly,' said Brian May. 'But it's always there.'

BALI
John Deacon's great vanishing act

Making 1984's *The Works* album was not a pleasant experience for Queen. Everyone was jockeying to get their songs on the record; three members of the band were smarting about Freddie Mercury's lucrative solo deal; their personal relationships were in jeopardy.

John Deacon certainly felt the stress. He later admitted to 'being really bored and depressed' during the lay-off between the Hot Space Tour and *The Works*. But his state of mind didn't improve when making the album.

In autumn 1983, after two months recording *The Works* in Los Angeles, Queen returned to Munich's Musicland Studios and the city's familiar distractions: men, women, alcohol, drugs and the Sugar Shack nightclub. Then, at five o'clock one morning, roadie Peter 'Ratty' Hince heard a knock on his hotel room door. It was the boss. Deacon said he needed some money as he'd booked a flight to the Indonesian island of Bali and was taking off in a few hours' time.

'When are you back?' asked Hince.

'Dunno,' Deacon replied. 'I'll call you. I need a break. I'm fed up with all this. You'd better tell the rest of the band please.'

In his memoir, *Queen Unseen*, 'Ratty' recalled getting Deacon his money (which was hidden in a flight case at Musicland), driving him to the airport and putting him on the plane. He broke the news to the rest of Queen in the studio. Mercury immediately leapt on a table and began singing 'Bali Ha'i' from the musical *South Pacific*: 'Bali Ha'i may call you,' he crooned, grinning toothily, 'any night, any day . . .'

'We were okay about it as we were all going mad as well,' said Brian May, who also claimed Deacon left a note – 'Gone to Bali' – on his bass. Hince insists this isn't true.

Nobody has divulged why John Deacon needed a break and why, specifically, he chose Bali. 'It was for personal reasons,' Hince said. A week later, though, Deacon phoned 'Ratty' and asked him to book another suite at the Munich Hilton. He was on his way back.

Hince collected Deacon from the airport. Nothing more was said and the recording sessions picked up where they'd left off. The only significant difference was that John was extremely sunburnt and flaking skin all over the studio. Mercury coined yet another nickname for him. From now on, Queen's elusive bass player was John 'Snakeman' Deacon.

'BIG SPENDER'
Queen on Broadway

Queen signed their first management deal partly thanks to 'Big Spender'. Freddie Mercury adored Welsh diva Shirley Bassey's

1967 hit and Queen had been performing it since they began. On 24 March 1972, they played a nursing college dance in Forest Hill, south London. In the audience was Trident producer John Anthony, who was accompanying the studio's co-owner Barry Sheffield.

At the time, Sheffield and his brother, Norman, were undecided as to whether to take on Queen. However, when Brian May started grinding out the riff to 'Big Spender', Sheffield turned to his producer, laughing, and said, 'Right, that's it. We're signing them.'

'Big Spender' was composed for *Sweet Charity*, Cy Coleman and Dorothy Fields' Broadway musical about the romantic misadventures of a New York dancer (though the character was a prostitute in the original story). The song became a universal striptease anthem after the 1969 film version starring Shirley MacLaine in the lead role.

Queen's version was heavier than Bassey's or the movie's – imagine Black Sabbath playing in a pole-dancing club – but it was an anomaly at a time when progressive rock was king. 'I listen to all kinds of music, from Hendrix to Liza Minelli, all the way back to Mae West,' explained Mercury. 'Big Spender' epitomised Queen's ability to poke fun at themselves and confound expectations. They still performed part of it during their last UK tour with Freddie Mercury in 1986. 'It was fun,' said Roger Taylor, 'and it was funny to see people's faces in the audience when we started playing it.'

Shirley Bassey has never commented on Queen's version, but she later recorded two of their songs. In 1995 and '96, Bassey turned 'Who Wants to Live Forever' and 'The Show Must Go On' into lung-busting Broadway-style show tunes. Queen's world had come full circle.

BIRMINGHAM TOWN HALL

When Queen gigs went wrong, part 1

Birmingham Town Hall on the city's Victoria Square was built in the 1830s, modelled by architects on the Temple of Castor and Pollux in ancient Rome. Fittingly, there was something gladiatorial about Queen's first performance there.

It was 27 November 1973 and Queen were supporting Mott the Hoople, whose audience was in no mood for anything but Mott the Hoople. The gig started poorly when Freddie Mercury's 'Hello, Birmingham!' was greeted with a heckle of 'Fuck off, ya cunt!'

'Charming,' Mercury grimaced.

According to one eyewitness/audience member, this was standard behaviour at the Town Hall. A week earlier, Roxy Music's support, singer-songwriter Leo Sayer, had shown up on stage dressed as Pierrot the clown, prompting one disapproving Roxy fan to urinate off the balcony in Leo's direction.

Five songs into Queen's set, though, the single 'Keep Yourself Alive' won over some of the disbelievers. Then Mercury slipped and landed on his arse. He carried on singing, despite being clearly winded, and pretended it was all part of the act. Sadly, the doubters turned on him again. During the final song, 'Jailhouse Rock', a half-eaten hot dog torpedoed from the crowd and hit Freddie in the face, smothering him with Frankfurter and tomato ketchup.

Undeterred, Queen risked being thrown to the lions again and played the Town Hall the following year. By then, they were headlining and the gig passed without heckles, flying food or public urination.

BOGIE, DOUGLAS

Queen's bass player, no. 2.5

In spring 1980, Scottish guitarist Douglas Bogie was at London's AIR Studios making an album with his new group, RAF. Suddenly and quite unexpectedly, he spotted Brian May in the corridor. Bogie felt awkward, but relaxed when May recognised him and started chatting. The reason for his unease was that Douglas had once been Queen's bass guitarist, but was fired after playing just two gigs.

His RAF colleagues were astonished when their guitarist introduced them to his old bandmate. 'I was embarrassed about being dumped by Queen,' Bogie said. 'So I never went on about it. I thought people might think it was a bullshit fairy story.'

In February 1971, Douglas Bogie was an eighteen-year-old trainee telephone technician when he answered an advert in *Melody Maker* that read: 'A fabulous new group, looking for a bassist.' Queen had problems hanging on to their bass guitarists. They'd already had two by that point: Mike Grose and Barry Mitchell.

Bogie auditioned at Imperial College and made his Queen debut supporting '60s agit-rockers the Pretty Things at Hornsey Town Hall on 19 February. There were apparently fewer than ten people in the audience. The next evening they played to a much larger crowd, opening for prog-rock royalty Yes at Kingston Polytechnic.

Bogie thought both shows went well and later said that he'd expressed his enjoyment by 'leaping about' on stage. In the van after the Kingston gig, though, Freddie Mercury declared Queen a waste of time, claimed the whole world was against him and said he didn't want to be in a band any more. By the end of the journey, Bogie was convinced Queen had just broken up.

He now believes it was an elaborate ruse to let him down gently and get him out of the band. His animated performance had upset the others. In a 1991 interview, Queen were asked about a mysterious ex-bassist remembered only as 'Doug' and the best Brian May could manage was that 'he jumped up and down in a manner most incongruous'.

'I wish they'd said something at the time,' said Bogie, not unreasonably. 'No one told me they didn't like it.' Five months after his departure, Queen replaced him with John Deacon.

In 1980, Bogie's new band's name, RAF, stood for 'rich and famous'. The irony was not lost on him and he later remarked, 'RAF made two albums so hugely successful we were never asked to make a third . . .'

Douglas Bogie went on to own a television production company and is happy to talk about his brief time in one of the world's biggest rock bands.

'BOHEMIAN RHAPSODY'

Queen's biggest hit in six acts

ACT I
'Is this the real life . . .'

The first fourteen seconds of 'Bohemian Rhapsody' are sung a cappella. The intro and outro were recorded at Rockfield Studios in Monmouthshire, juggling with the restrictions of 1975 technology to find space for piano, lead vocals, backing vocals and more backing vocals.

The intro evoked the Beach Boys in their magisterial 'God Only Knows' phase. Brian Wilson, principal Beach Boy, later said that Queen's song terrified him. 'There's a group called Queen,' he excitedly told *Creem* magazine in 1976. 'They made a record, "Bohemian Rhapsody", which to me was a fulfilment and an answer to a teenage prayer of artistic music.'

Wilson became very animated at this point. 'I studied the record,' he continued. 'I became very familiar with it and I'm very, very fond of it and I'm scared of it at the same time. Oh, it's the most competitive thing that's come along in ages! It's just totally amazing what people do when they lose their noggins, when they lose their heads and they go in there and freak. That's what Queen did. They'd had enough of what was happening and, by God, they went in and did their thing and stomped!'

Wilson eventually stopped talking about 'Bohemian Rhapsody' and the interviewer changed the subject.

ACT II
'Mama, just killed a man . . .'

The first verse proper introduces the story: an admission of murder followed by regret. It's a literary device used in Greek tragedies, Shakespeare, Dickens and even the present day, but the piano intro would trouble Mercury for the rest of his Queen career.

'Freddie never claimed to be a great pianist,' wrote his former personal assistant, Peter Freestone. 'In fact, he absolutely dreaded "Bohemian Rhapsody" in performance in case he got the run-up on the piano wrong.'

He felt more confident about the words, though. 'The first thing Freddie played us was "Mama, just killed a man,"' said Roger Taylor. 'I thought, "Oh, that is just a fantastic verse." It's a typical libretto. He's going to be executed for murder and he regrets it. But, in the end, he's philosophical about it, I think.'

Nobody in Queen is sure. According to one man, this opening line is older than the band. In 1969, Mercury and his friend – Smile's ex-keyboard player and fellow art student, Chris Smith – spent their lunchtimes trying to write songs in the college music room.

'Fred had a thing we called "The Cowboy Song",' Smith said. 'The opening line was "Mama, just killed a man." That was all he had. That was it. When I heard "Bohemian Rhapsody" years later, I thought, "Oh, Fred's finished the song."'

'"Bohemian Rhapsody" was really three songs and I just put them together,' said Mercury. 'I'd always wanted to do something operatic. I just wanted it to be opera in the rock 'n' roll sense. Why not? I went as far as my limited capacity could take me.'

It wasn't the first or last time Queen mentioned a matriarch in a song. See also Brian May's 'Tie Your Mother Down' and 'My Fairy King', on which Freddie sang, 'Mother Mercury (Mercury), look what they've done to me.'

'Oh, Mother's in the audience tonight,' Mercury used to tell his bandmates whenever Jer Bulsara attended a Queen show. 'I must throw in some swear words.'

'Freddie's mother was always wonderful to him and he was terrified of her,' said Taylor.

John Deacon later suggested 'Bohemian Rhapsody' was too wordy a title and they should call the song 'Mama' and be done with it.

ACT III
'Scaramouche! Scaramouche! . . .'

Roy Thomas Baker remembers Mercury playing him an early version of the song on piano. 'Then he said, "And here's where the opera section comes in." I started laughing.'

The opera section was constructed at London's Scorpio Sound Studios. It grew and grew and required so many vocal overdubs (as many as 180, though some say less, some more) that Queen almost wore through the tape. This story has acquired the same air of urban mythology as the cocaine-carrying dwarves, but it's true.

The lyrics meshed Italian, Iberian, Islamic and Hebrew phrases with imagery that reappeared later in the catalogue. 'Scaramouche' is from the Italian 'scaramuccia', meaning 'little skirmisher'. He's a stock clown in *commedia dell'arte* – a genre of early Italian theatre big on pantomime and masked characters.

Queen had a thing for clowns. 'It's a Hard Life' lifted a melody from Ruggero Leoncavallo's nineteenth-century opera *Pagliacci*, which is about a heartbroken clown. A clown/jester also appeared on the cover of *Innuendo*. The image was adapted from French caricaturist J. J. Grandville's artwork *Juggler of Universes*, which appeared in his book *Un Autre Monde*. The book's title translates as 'Another World' – later the title of Brian May's 1998 solo album. So clowns everywhere . . .

'Will you do the fandango?' Mercury asks his Scaramouche, splicing *commedia dell'arte* with a traditional form of Spanish and Portuguese dance performed with guitars, castanets and hand-claps. (Queen also stuck a fandango in the middle of *Innuendo*'s title track, played by Yes's guitarist Steve Howe, with Queen presumably on castanets and handclaps.)

Mercury stages another bid for European unity in the following line – 'Galileo, Figaro!' – with 'Galileo' being Galileo Galilei, the sixteenth-century Italian mathematician and astronomer who fell afoul of the Catholic church with his scientific discoveries, and 'Figaro' being the troublesome Spanish barber in the operas *The Barber of Seville* and *The Marriage of Figaro*. 'Magnifico' comes next – an Italian word for a Venetian nobleman.

The word 'Bismillah!' puts another spin on the song. 'Bismillah' or 'Basmala' translates from Arabic to mean 'in the name of Allah'. It's a word used in everyday Muslim life – in prayers and before preparing halal food – and is recited in every chapter of the Qur'an, except the ninth.

Mercury, Zoroastrian by birth and irreligious by nature, would have heard the word growing up. Zanzibar had a Muslim population dating back to the tenth century. Mercury revisited Islamic culture on Queen's 1978 song 'Mustapha', mixing English, Arabic and pretend Persian words. In concert, Mercury sometimes preceded the line 'Mama, just killed man' with a lyric from 'Mustapha': 'Allah, we'll pray for you.'

The opera section's final pay-off – 'Beelzebub has a devil put aside for me' – revived an alternative word for Satan first used in the Hebrew Bible. Although Queen were once a heavy-rock band, they usually left the occult to Zeppelin, Sabbath and the Stones. After all, Mercury seemed more interested in Jesus, hence the song of the same name on *Queen*.

'Could you explain to me what the "mama mia"/"Galileo"/ "Scaramouche" part is about?' a radio interviewer asked Brian May in 2010.

'Of course not,' he laughed. 'Because I didn't write it.'

'What does it mean, Brian?' he was asked again in 2012.

'I have my own ideas,' he replied. 'But I'm not going to talk about it. We never discussed what our songs meant. It was an unwritten law in Queen that there would be things in some songs that were personal. But you wouldn't ask the person who wrote it what it meant.'

'What does it mean, Brian?' probed music magazine *Mojo* in 2020.

'I think there is a lot of autobiography in the way Freddie wrote it,' May allowed. 'By then, Freddie was getting braver in expressing his inner emotions.' This suggests that the story was a metaphor for Mercury coming out as gay, especially to his partner, Mary Austin, which he did soon after the song's release in winter 1975.

'"Bohemian Rhapsody" is fairly self-explanatory, with just a bit of nonsense in the middle,' suggested Roger Taylor mischievously.

ACT IV
'So you think you can stop me . . .'

The galloping finale suggests Mercury challenging his accusers and fighting his way out of his physical or metaphorical prison. Perhaps. Like the denouement of Led Zeppelin's 'Stairway to Heaven', it sounds very grand and meaningful, even if it isn't. The song ends with the line 'Any way the wind blows . . .', as though Freddie has found some peace and redemption.

The last sound heard, however, is Roger Taylor's gong. Queen transported this ungainly instrument around the world for it only to be used once a night in 'Bohemian Rhapsody'.

'For one moment in a song, it's a very big flight case,' said Taylor. Nowadays, Queen don't bother with the gong. It's an ornament in Taylor's back garden, gathering moss alongside his statue of Freddie Mercury.

ACT V
'Like being run over by a truck . . .'

Queen's early mentor, Ian Hunter of Mott the Hoople, remembered hearing 'Bohemian Rhapsody' for the first time in the studio. 'I couldn't make head nor tail of it all,' he admitted. 'It was like being run over by a truck. It finished and Fred said, "What do you think?" I didn't have the faintest idea. He was like, "Did you not hear the third harmony in the second voice? There's a slight variation there." I just looked at him aghast and said, "Give me a break."'

Hunter wasn't alone. Queen's then-manager, John Reid, played his client and boyfriend Elton John an early pressing.

'I shook my head, incredulous,' wrote Elton in his 2019 memoir, *Me*. 'You're not actually going to release that, are you? It's the campest thing I've ever heard in my life and the title's ridiculous as well.'

Even John Deacon wasn't sure. 'I remember John saying, "I'm sure this could be a hit, but it does need to be simplified,"' recalled May. 'John said, "Let's cut it down and it'll play nicely on the radio."'

Queen's paymasters, EMI, agreed with Deacon. They didn't want 'Bohemian Rhapsody' to be released as a single. It was Mercury's friend Kenny Everett, a Capital Radio DJ, who helped convince EMI. Everett played a test pressing of the song repeatedly over one weekend.

On the first morning, Brian May was in bed in his flat, having been up all night mixing *A Night at the Opera*. He was fitfully dozing when he heard the unfinished 'Bohemian Rhapsody' on his upstairs neighbour's radio and wondered if he was having a bad dream.

'Bohemian Rhapsody' was released as a single on 31 October 1975. It entered the UK chart at number forty-seven. Ten days later, it was in the top twenty and then the top ten. Queen hired director Bruce Gowers to make a promo video. They already knew they couldn't perform the whole song live; the opera section had to be on tape, 'allowing us the chance to go backstage and change our frocks', said May.

Gowers' film was created in just four hours at Elstree Studios. In keeping with the song itself, Queen's singing heads and *Doctor Who*-style special effects were guaranteed to provoke a reaction. On 21 November, Queen saw the finished video for the first time on a hotel TV in Taunton. 'We thought it was wonderful,' said Taylor. Four days later, Queen were in Southampton when they learned the song had topped the chart. Taylor's mother, Winifred, had been to the band's show at the Gaumont Theatre the night before. Roger came down to breakfast in their hotel and said, 'Alright, Mum, we're number one.'

ACT VI

'Taking a wizz on a Picasso . . .'

In 1991, *Saturday Night Live* comedian and writer Mike Myers phoned up Brian May. He wanted to use 'Bohemian Rhapsody' in his new movie. *Wayne's World* was a goofball comedy about a couple of small-town Illinois rock fans. Myers had scripted a scene in which his character, Wayne, and a bunch of like-minded friends listen to 'Bohemian Rhapsody' while cruising in their so-called 'Mirthmobile'.

Although the director and producer of *Wayne's World* had other ideas (they wanted to use a song by Guns N' Roses, the biggest band in the world at the time), Myers threatened to leave the film unless they let him have Queen.

However, Myers needed Freddie Mercury's permission to use the song. So, in autumn 1991, May visited Mercury with a tape of the movie. Mercury was very sick by then, but the pair watched the scene together.

'I think I'll go with a little "Bohemian Rhapsody", gentleman,' says Myers' 'Wayne', inserting a cassette into the car's tape deck.

'I see a little silhouetto of a man,' he booms, singing along.

'Scaramouche! Scaramouche!' reply his passengers, before trading 'Galileo's back and forth. The song's big finale is accompanied by synchronised headbanging, air drumming and air guitaring. Myers later revealed that he and his friends used to do the same as teenagers while listening to 'Bohemian Rhapsody' in his brother's 'vomit-stained Camaro'.

Mercury and May loved the scene. They could also see the commercial potential. Queen had lost the US after 1982's

Hot Space. 'And I remember Freddie saying, "This film might do for us what nothing else would do,"' recalled May. Mercury's parting words stayed with him: 'Freddie joked, "I suppose I have to fucking die before we ever get big in America."'

Mercury died on 24 November 1991. *Wayne's World* arrived on 14 February 1992. 'Bohemian Rhapsody' was re-released the same month and a new video was issued, splicing together Bruce Gowers' original and the headbanging scenes from *Wayne's World*. Mike Myers was appalled and likened it to 'taking a whizz on a Picasso'.

Queen disagreed. *Wayne's World* reintroduced them to America. 'Bohemian Rhapsody' went to number two in the States, five places higher than it had in 1975. Freddie Mercury's prediction had come true. In 2018, the producers of *Bohemian Rhapsody* asked Mike Myers if he'd make a cameo appearance in the film. He didn't need to be asked twice.

Myers played 'Ray Foster', a composite of all the EMI executives who'd told Queen that 'Bohemian Rhapsody' could never be a single. Myers adopted a dour northern accent for the role. 'It goes on for ever, six bloody minutes,' he grumbles after listening to the song. 'What on earth is it about anyway? Bloody Bismillah?'

'True poetry is for the listener,' replies Rami Malek's 'Freddie'.

Foster starts suggesting other songs for Queen's next single. 'What about "I'm in Love with My Car"?'

The band all groan, apart from Ben Hardy's 'Roger Taylor'.

'"I'm in Love with My Car!" That's the kind of song teenagers can crank up the volume in their car and bang their heads to,' enthuses Foster. '"Bohemian Rhapsody" will never be that song.'

BOHEMIAN RHAPSODY

Thirty-six observations about Queen's big box-office hit

1. In the movie's opening scene, Rami Malek's 'Freddie' is seen waking up on the morning of Live Aid. A portrait of actress Marlene Dietrich, taken for her 1932 movie *Shanghai Express*, is hanging on the wall. This was the picture the real-life Freddie asked photographer Mick Rock to replicate for the cover of *Queen II*.

2. There are five cats in Mercury's house. In real life, between 1970 and 1991, he owned ten: Dorothy, Tiffany, Tom, Jerry, Lily, Goliath, Miko, Oscar, Romeo and Delilah (the last of which he wrote a song for on Queen's *Innuendo* album).

3. Unlike in the film, Freddie never carried a bottle of Stolichnaya vodka or a packet of Consulate cigarettes in his microphone case. He smoked Silk Cut in real life anyway. 'Naturally, he never bought his own,' recalled former roadie Peter Hince. Like John Deacon, Freddie only started smoking in the early 1980s.

4. Freddie walks to the Live Aid stage as another band, meant to be U2, are shown walking back down. The group that preceded Queen at Live Aid was actually Dire Straits.

5. Freddie writes the lyrics for 'Liar' sat a bus stop. This was one of his first pre-Queen compositions, originally known as 'Lover'. (His mother, Jer Bulsara, recalled finding scraps of lyrics stuffed under his pillow at home. 'Don't throw them away, Mum,' he'd tell her. 'It's very important.')

6. Freddie attends a Smile gig in 1970 and orders a pint of lager. The real Freddie rarely drank beer, though, and even cautioned others against it for the 'sake of your waistline'.

7. Freddie introduces himself to Smile after the show. Their frontman, Tim Staffell, has just quit and Freddie offers his services. He'd actually already known the group for almost two years, though.

8. 'Not with those teeth, mate,' responds Ben Hardy's 'Roger'. 'I was born with four additional incisors,' Freddie replies loftily. After seeing the film, the actual Tim Staffell was shocked by Malek's performance. 'He got some of Freddie's mannerisms,' he said. 'Like pulling his front lip over his teeth like a nervous tic.'

9. Actor Gwilym Lee captures Brian May's voice and pensive manner, particularly his trademark head tilt. 'He's right there with the body language,' agreed the real thing. 'He fooled my kids. They genuinely thought I'd dubbed my voice over his.'

10. 'Roger' isn't quite so well observed. 'Ben did a wonderful job,' said the real Roger, 'but some of the clothes were things I'd never have worn. They also didn't get my hair quite right.' (In 1982, Freddie flew his and Roger's barber, Denni Godber, from London's fashionable Sweeny's salon all the way to Germany for a haircut.)

11. Lucy Boynton's 'Mary Austin' mimics the real Mary, with shades of Paul McCartney's ex, lapsed celebrity cake-maker Jane Asher. When Freddie meets up with her in the Biba clothes shop, she encourages him to try on make-up and women's trousers. 'I love your style,' she tells him. 'We should all take more risks.' Mary was actually Brian's girlfriend when she first met the singer.

12. Bassist John Deacon is already in the band when Freddie plays his debut gig, but really Queen's original bass player, Mike Grose, was still with them at this point. The frontman confidently parades around the stage, but messes up the words to 'Keep Yourself Alive'. (In May 2020, Brian discovered a cassette of one of Queen's early gigs and, upon being asked

whether Queen would release it, cautiously replied, 'Freddie had all the will and charisma and passion, but he didn't have the opportunity to harness that voice yet, which makes me hesitate because I'm not sure Freddie would be that happy hearing himself at this stage.')

13. In one scene, Joseph Mazzello's 'John Deacon' is shown changing a tyre on the band's van. John is the most believable tyre-changer in Queen.

14. In the studio recording of Smile's fictional album, Roger is seen cosying up to a dark-haired woman in hot pants. Roger is the most believable ladies' man in Queen. ('Oh God, am I a cliché?' the real Roger once asked an interviewer.)

15. Freddie and Mary's bed has an upright piano doubling as a headboard. He plays the intro to 'Bohemian Rhapsody' upside down. In truth, the piano was near the bed, but not part of it. As the real Freddie recalled, 'I woke up in the middle of the night and a song just wouldn't go away, so I got up and dragged my piano over to the bedside so I could reach the keyboard.'

16. During Freddie's birthday tea with the Bulsaras, the rest of Queen discover his real name is 'Farrokh' and he comes from Zanzibar. 'I thought Freddie was born in London,' says John. 'Oh, he was – at the age of eighteen,' replies Priya Blackburn's 'Kashmira', Mercury's sister. The real Freddie would often brush aside questions about his pre-Queen life: 'So long ago, during the Boer War.' Sadly, this charming soirée never actually happened. ('No,' confirmed Roger in 2019. 'We never all went round Fred's house for tea.')

17. 'We're four misfits playing to all the other misfits,' Freddie tells their manager, Aiden Gillen's 'John Reid'. 'That's true,' said the real Roger. 'I remember roller-skating nuns and all sorts of exotic people turning up at our first American shows.'

18. Freddie's rabbit-fur blouson, as worn on *Top of the Pops* in 1974, is a perfect replica. As is his Zandra Rhodes-designed satin tunic from that year's tour. 'I always hated *Top of the Pops*, though,' grumbled the drummer.

19. Queen are seen performing 1978's 'Fat Bottomed Girls' in the American Midwest in presumably 1974 or '75. Purists, including Brian May, winced. 'I remember making a fuss about that,' he said. '"No, it's the wrong song for that time!" But I sat down with the film company and they explained that's what you have to do if you want to tell the story.'

20. 'You're the love of my life,' Freddie tells Mary in a post-coital scene. 'Will you marry me?' A few minutes later, he's sloping off into a truck-stop lavatory for sex with a trucker (played in a lovely bit of meta casting by Queen's guest singer Adam Lambert). It's all implied, though; no intercourse is shown. 'There's people who say we didn't go far enough with the film in addressing Freddie's sexuality,' conceded Brian. Previous 'Freddie' actor Sacha Baron Cohen quit the production in 2013 complaining that the script whitewashed Mercury's homosexuality. 'We wanted it to be a family film, something everybody could see,' insisted Roger. 'Sacha wanted . . . buggery.'

21. Adam Lambert's truck has the word 'Mack' emblazoned across its hood, after the Mack trucking company of Greensboro, North Carolina. It's also the surname of Queen's long-suffering German co-producer, Reinhold Mack (known by all simply as 'Mack'). Deliberate or a happy accident?

22. Mike Myers' cameo as fictional EMI executive 'Ray Foster' acknowledges the role his 1992 movie *Wayne's World* played in reviving 'Bohemian Rhapsody'. Foster is an amalgam of several real-life record label naysayers, including Paul Watts, the general manager of EMI's international division at the time. 'When they first played me "Bohemian Rhapsody",' said Watts, 'my reaction was "What the fuck's this? Are you mad?"'

23. In one scene, Freddie sings 'Love of My Life' at the piano in Rockfield Studios. It's a sterling performance, merging the voices of Malek and the real Mercury. Other vocal recordings in the film were augmented by Marc Martel of official tribute band the Queen Extravaganza. ('I was in the room with Marc and had my eyes closed and I could have been in a room with Freddie,' said Roger. 'It must be genetic. Maybe he has the same oral cavities.')

24. Freddie's 1980s party scene crams in as much Queen trivia as will fit. There are transvestites, a dwarf (sans cocaine on head) and Freddie wearing a crown, as well as two women in their underwear peddling stationary bikes (in honour of the 'Bicycle Race' video), which looks like the least fun thing to be doing at a party. There's also a crystal chandelier, but, disappointingly, Freddie doesn't swing from it as he allegedly did at Roger Taylor's twenty-ninth birthday party.

25. Freddie's Machiavellian manager Paul Prenter (well portrayed by *Downton Abbey* actor Allen Leech) is shown pouring Champagne for the boss, but ignoring the rest of the band – a metaphor for him trying to entice Mercury away from Queen. (Prenter's family later complained about his portrayal in what the *Daily Mail* called 'the hurtful blockbuster'.)

26. At the end of the party, Freddie chats up liveried waiter Jim Hutton (played by Aaron McCusker). In real life, Mercury met Hutton – a barber at the Savoy Hotel – in a London nightclub in 1983. They became a couple two years later. According to Mercury's biographer Lesley-Ann Jones, Freddie's opening line was 'How big's your dick?' This line is absent from the film, though. ('That script went through seventeen rewrites,' said Roger.)

27. Queen are seen recording 'We Will Rock You' with their contemporary wives/girlfriends stamping their feet on a studio podium. None of the wives/girlfriends really stamped

on the song, though; it was actually the band members, roadies, engineers and studio tea lady Betty.

28. Freddie's moustache is chronologically wrong, but cinema-goers/normal people don't care. 'It's not a documentary,' Brian explained. 'It's an attempt to portray Freddie Mercury as a musician and a human being, so any argument about whether he should have a moustache at a particular time is a waste of breath.'

29. During a row about 'Another One Bites the Dust', Freddie and Roger start pushing each other – 'Let's see how good a boxer you are!' shouts the drummer – but physical fights in Queen were rare in reality. (Though they came close when Roger accidentally sprayed Brian in the face with hairspray.)

30. The 'I Want to Break Free' video is hilariously recreated, with Ben Hardy as convincing a schoolgirl as the real Roger. They even have the flying ducks on the wall.

31. In the scene in which Freddie announces his departure from Queen, John's body language makes up for the fact that this incident never happened. 'The guy playing John was tapping his foot and shaking his leg nervously,' said Queen's official photographer, Neal Preston, 'and I remember Deaky doing that all the time.'

32. Mary gives Freddie a good talking-to about all the drink and drugs he's taking, after which he phones up Queen's new manager, Jim 'Miami' Beach (played by a slightly too urbane Tom Hollander), and asks if he can rejoin Queen to play the 'Africa concert'. In real life, Mercury was still in Queen at the time, but had to be persuaded to perform at Live Aid. In the ensuing reconciliation scene, John's new perm looks like it has its own eco system, but, disappoint-ingly, Roger is dressed like a Miami coke dealer. And his hair is still wrong.

33. Freddie learns that he is HIV-positive in a poignant, understated scene soundtracked by 'Who Wants to Live Forever'. He didn't take the test before Live Aid in real life, though. 'To tell it the way it happened would have taken another hour of screen time,' said Brian. 'So we took liberties – or rather the film-makers did.'

34. Live Aid is recreated with great period detail, down to the correct number of cups on top of Freddie's Steinway and the crack in his voice during 'We Are the Champions'.

35. The real Brian is apparently reduced to tears after watching a friends-and-family screening of the biopic. 'It was quite overwhelming,' he said. 'Emotionally devastating. Even traumatic.'

36. *Bohemian Rhapsody*, released in October 2018, wins twenty-two industry awards – including seven BAFTAs, four Oscars and two Golden Globes – and goes on to gross over $900 million. 'A rock slog with a moralistic subtext,' complained *The Guardian*. 'Fuck you,' responded the real Roger when asked about the reviewer's comment a year later. 'Fuck you all the way to the bank.'

BOWIE, DAVID
A hero

Queen's relationship with David Bowie was mutually appreciative, highly competitive and extremely difficult – often all at the same time. It also pre-dated their 1981 hit collaboration, 'Under Pressure'.

Freddie Mercury first met his future singing partner while he was still a student at Ealing Art College. It was 29 April 1969 and Bowie was booked to play a lunchtime gig in the college refectory. After several flop singles, the career of the singer born David Jones had stalled and his breakthrough hit, 'Space Oddity', wouldn't be out for another two months.

Not that this deterred Freddie, who'd appointed himself Bowie's roadie and was waiting for him outside the college gates. This was one of Freddie's regular ploys to meet musicians and he'd already welcomed blues revivalists Chicken Shack and Marc Bolan's Tyrannosaurus Rex in the same way. Once they were in his clutches, Freddie would question them about writing songs and playing live – anything to broaden his knowledge of the music business.

That morning, 22-year-old Bowie drove up in his modest Citroën with an acoustic guitar, tape recorder, mic stand and PA in the back. Mercury helped unload the gear and escorted him to the refectory. Bowie was unimpressed. 'There's no stage,' he complained. Freddie and his friend – fellow student and ex-Smile keyboard player Chris Smith – quickly built a rostrum from canteen tables. The show must go on . . .

The gig passed without incident, but the singer and roadie didn't meet again until 1971 when Mercury was working on musician Alan Mair's shoe stall in Kensington Market. Bowie showed up one afternoon and recognised Mair, who'd once played bass in '60s group the Beatstalkers. Mair's handmade boots were popular with the rock-star set – Santana had been photographed wearing them – and Bowie wanted a pair.

Bowie tried on the footwear as Mercury fussed around him. 'Bowie said he liked the boots, but had no money,' recalls Mair. 'I was surprised as he'd just had a hit single, but he blamed it on the music business. Years later, I thought it funny that Freddie Mercury once tried to sell David Bowie a pair of my boots.' In the end, Mair let him have them for free. It's likely Mercury told

Bowie he played in a band, but less likely he mentioned their earlier encounter at the art college.

David Bowie made Queen very nervous. The band were experimenting with fancy stage costumes, but Bowie had gazumped them by wearing a dress on the cover of his recent LP, *The Man Who Sold the World*. On 25 September 1971, Brian May and Roger Taylor saw Bowie play at Friars Aylesbury. Bowie arrived on stage sporting a woman's jacket, billowing black culottes, bright red platform boots and a big floppy hat. 'Brian and I looked at each other and thought, "Oh no, he's beaten us to it,"' said Taylor.

On 24 December 1972, the pair were at London's Rainbow Theatre watching Bowie and his band unveil their alien alter egos: Ziggy Stardust and the Spiders from Mars. 'I thought, "Oh God, he's done it again,"' recalled May, having glimpsed the silhouette of Bowie's carrot-hued mullet.

This uneasiness continued in the months ahead. Queen recorded their debut album at night in Trident Studios; Bowie was there producing Lou Reed's *Transformer* LP during the day. When *Queen* was released in July 1973, Mercury waspishly told *Melody Maker* that they'd been 'into glam rock before the Sweet and Bowie'.

A pecking order still prevailed, though. The following year, Bowie turned down a coveted spot on *Top of the Pops* because the video for his latest 45, 'Rebel Rebel', wasn't finished. Queen were rushed to the studio to mime their upcoming single, 'Seven Seas of Rhye', instead.

Queen and Bowie spent the rest of the decade orbiting each other before finally colliding in Switzerland in 1981. The results were explosive. 'Under Pressure' gave Queen a number-one hit and helped reboot Bowie's career.

'We always looked up to the Who, Led Zeppelin and Bowie,' Roger Taylor said in 2019. Mercury also regarded Bowie as a kindred showman and show-off. 'Look at us! Look at David Bowie! People want to be entertained,' he said. But niggling competitiveness lingered. Queen and Bowie's mutual friend, Elton John, visited Mercury when he was dying. 'He was too frail to get out of bed, he was losing his sight, his body was covered in lesions,' Elton wrote in his memoir, *Me*. 'Yet he was gossiping away, completely outrageous: "Have you heard Mrs Bowie's new record, dear? What *does* she think she's doing?"'

Queen and Bowie's paths finally crossed again at the 1992 Freddie Mercury Tribute Concert. At the televised show from Wembley Stadium, Bowie duetted with Annie Lennox on 'Under Pressure', performed 'All the Young Dudes' and 'Heroes' and then dropped to his knee to recite the Lord's Prayer. TV cameras captured the bemused look on Roger Taylor's face, though Freddie Mercury would have applauded such a preposterous gesture.

Like Mercury, Bowie retreated from public life in the years preceding his death, leaving rumours about his health to circulate in his absence. There were other parallels between the two performers, too. In 1991, audiences had been shocked by Mercury's skeletal appearance in Queen's video for 'These Are the Days of Our Lives'. But, while that song and video played like a fond, teary farewell, the promo for Bowie's final single, 'Lazarus', was harrowing. A wizened Bowie was shown lying in bed, his eyes swathed in bandages, before climbing backwards into a wardrobe as a parting gesture.

'What a talent,' said Roger Taylor. 'I don't think anybody had been that graphic about their own death . . . It was really quite something.' Bowie released his last album, *Blackstar*, two days before his death from liver cancer on 10 January 2016. Twenty-four hours afterwards, Taylor described him on Twitter as 'the cleverest and most brilliant man of our time'.

Boys keep swinging: David Bowie with Brian May, Roger Taylor and the Prince and Princess of Wales, Live Aid, 1985.

'BRIGHTON ROCK'

Queen's greatest non-hits, no. 1

'Brighton Rock' was once known as 'Happy Little Fuck'. Queen's engineer Mike Stone had a bunch of working titles for *Sheer Heart Attack*'s opening track (others included 'Southend Sea Scout' and 'Bognor Ballad').

Brian May's composition had its roots in a Smile song, 'Blag', which had used a similar multi-tracked guitar solo. May went for the same effect later when performing Queen's 'Son and Daughter' on stage. Then came 'Brighton Rock' . . .

A woozy-sounding fairground organ set the scene, before May's bouncing riff cut through the candyfloss and kiss-me-quick hats. Freddie Mercury played two roles: one was 'Jenny'; the other was her adulterous lover 'Jimmy'. In the song, the couple spend a secret bank holiday weekend together. Mercury pitched his voice higher pretending to be Jenny ('Oh no, I must away, to my mum in disarray'). It's unintentionally funny, but somehow doesn't derail the song.

Forty-three years after *Sheer Heart Attack*, 'Brighton Rock' appeared, twice, in the 2017 car chase movie *Baby Driver*. The film's director, Edgar Wright, had previously brought 'Don't Stop Me Now' back from the grave in his black comedy *Shaun of the Dead*. 'The main reason for using ['Brighton Rock'] is that it's Brian May's greatest guitar solo,' Wright told *Variety*.

May's solo utilised an Echoplex tape delay unit to make it sound like there were two Brians in the studio. In concert, 'Brighton Rock' became May's showpiece. While the other Queens changed their costumes or had a drink in their side-of-stage hideaway (known as the 'tent' or the 'doll's house'), May would noodle away for ten minutes or more. Even after 'Brighton Rock' was retired from the set, his solo remained. 'I certainly had a lot of fun with it,' he said.

Not all of his bandmates agreed, though. One night on the 1982 Hot Space Tour, Mercury was slumped in the 'tent', a towel draped around his neck, listening to May's solo. With each passing minute and flurry of notes, his face fell further. Suddenly, Freddie exploded. 'For God's sake!' he roared. 'Let's go shopping! Get me out of here!' Brian's 'Happy Little Fuck' was just too much.

CABALLÉ, MONTSERRAT

A night at the opera

On 27 November 1991, Freddie Mercury's coffin disappeared at West London Crematorium to a recording of Montserrat Caballé singing Verdi's *D'amor sull'ali rosee*. The Spanish soprano had been one of Mercury's favourite singers and they had collaborated on the 1987 song 'Barcelona', though it was actually a misheard comment in a Spanish restaurant that led to this unusual pairing and one of Mercury's biggest hits.

In August 1986, Queen were touring Spain when a TV reporter asked Mercury about his favourite Spanish performer. He named Montserrat Caballé. Spain had just been announced as the host nation of the 1992 Olympic Games and Queen's promoter, Pino Sagliocci, was organising a televised music festival to celebrate the news. Sagliocci phoned Caballé's manager immediately: he wanted these two great divas to perform together.

While his solo album, 1985's *Mr Bad Guy*, hadn't been a huge hit, Mercury was already planning a second. He had also contributed songs to *Time*, the West End musical by his friend Dave Clark. The soundtrack was produced by Mike Moran, who had worked on several film scores and performed 'Rock Bottom' – a duet with singer Lynsey de Paul – at the 1977 Eurovision Song Contest.

'Fred said, "I've got Town House Studios booked for a year,"' Moran recalled. 'He said, "I don't know what I want to do, but I don't want to be sitting around on my arse doing nothing. Shall we write something together?"'

Their first project was Mercury's cover of the Platters' 1955 hit 'The Great Pretender'. During a late-night mixing session, Moran realised they didn't have a B-side. 'Freddie said, "Oh, stuff it! Just go and do some of your flashy piano-playing and we'll make something up." I started to play something a bit classical and a bit Manfred Mann and Freddie started to sing in a falsetto voice, just "oohs" and "aahs", no words.'

Within two hours, they'd recorded 'Exercises in Free Love'. It's A-side, 'The Great Pretender', would become a top-five hit in February 1987. Soon after, Mercury received a phone call from Montserrat Caballé. She was intrigued by Sagliocci's idea and had sent her assistant out to buy Queen's albums. 'Montserrat wanted Fred to meet her in Barcelona,' said Moran. 'And he told me I was coming with him.'

Mercury was nervous about meeting a huge star from a different musical genre and he didn't want to go alone. The pair flew to Barcelona for lunch with Caballé in a private room at the Ritz hotel. 'She arrived like the Queen of Sheba,' said Moran. 'Everybody started bowing and scraping and suddenly Freddie wasn't the biggest person in the room.'

'I didn't know how to approach her or anything,' Mercury admitted. 'You have this sort of idea of a super diva walking in, but she really made me feel at ease.' Buoyed by several flutes of Champagne, Mercury told Caballé he'd recorded a song in her honour and proceeded to play her 'Exercises in Free Love'.

'This is me pretending to be you,' he announced.

'Montserrat got the wrong end of the stick,' revealed Moran. 'She thought he had said, "I have written something for you." She sat there, eyes closed, giving it her full attention, and said, "I love it! I will give it its world premiere at Covent Garden in three weeks' time."' She then grabbed Moran's arm and told him he would accompany her on piano.

After the Covent Garden performance, Caballé and Moran joined Mercury at home in Garden Lodge. More Champagne was consumed and Freddie began calling her 'Montsy'. He was in awe of her voice and she was fascinated by the fact that Freddie could compose music without knowing how to read it. At around 3 a.m., with Caballé booked on a flight to Buenos Aires in a few hours' time, she suggested Mercury and Moran try to write a song for her.

'This predated the Three Tenors and Alfie Boe, so we didn't have a clue,' said Moran. But they agreed to do it anyway. Mercury and Moran established two ground rules: 1) Mercury wouldn't attempt to sing opera; and 2) Caballé wouldn't try to sing rock 'n' roll. Between them, they composed 'Barcelona', a love song about 'two people meeting and getting carried away with each other'.

Mercury sent Caballé a demo of the song. She loved it. It was at this point that they agreed to make an album together. 'The record company had no idea about any of this,' said Moran. 'And we were completely making it up as we went along.'

It was a revelation for Caballé to be creating music instead of interpreting other people's music and lyrics. For Mercury and Moran, though, it was a challenge. The pair conjured up an album's worth of arias and ballads, with help from West End lyricist Tim Rice, but Caballé's schedule meant she and Mercury couldn't record together. Instead, they couriered cassettes – on which Freddie had improvised her vocal parts – to hotels around the world.

'Barcelona' was heard in public for the first time in May 1987. Pino Sagliocci's wish had come true. Freddie and 'Montsy' mimed the song at Ibiza's Ku Club for the promoter's Ibiza 92 festival. Mercury was clean-shaven and wearing a dinner suit. It took about a minute for him to start showboating: arms outstretched, fists clenched, right leg twitching up and down like it did on stage with Queen. But the great opera star matched him for melodrama, with Caballé's final vocal segueing into a fireworks display. The duo received a standing ovation.

Backstage beforehand, Mercury had taken special care with his appearance. He'd used make-up to disguise a Kaposi's sarcoma discoloration on his cheek – a symptom of HIV. Mercury had been diagnosed HIV-positive just weeks earlier, though some claim he'd already been told by doctors that he had contracted AIDS. Faced with a potential death sentence, Freddie was determined to keep working.

After months of swapping tapes, Montserrat finally flew to London to record her vocals. Ahead of her visit, Mercury investigated the women's lavatory at Town House Studios and was appalled. He demanded the room be redecorated and filled with flowers before Caballé's arrival. 'He did not want it looking like a rock 'n' roll toilet,' said Moran.

'Barcelona' became a top-ten hit in October 1987; the album of the same name went into the top thirty a year later. The only downside for Mike Moran was his appearance in the song's video. Moran was seen conducting an invisible orchestra with a lightsaber/baton. He had long, permed hair at the time and was mistaken by some for Brian May.

On 8 October 1988, Mercury and Caballé performed together once more. They mimed three songs outside Barcelona's Montjuïc Castle. The show celebrated the handover of the Olympic flag from South Korea and the audience included King Juan Carlos. Once again, Mercury wore his dinner suit and gave it his all, but he kept his twitching leg under control on this occasion. It was the last time Freddie Mercury ever performed on stage.

Montserrat Caballé died in October 2018. By then, she'd been an opera star for over fifty years, but it was her collaboration with Queen's lead singer that had brought her greater fame. The odd musical couple complemented each other: 'Montsy' gave Mercury credibility outside the world of rock 'n' roll and he gave her freedom. 'With Freddie, I finally had the chance to create,' she said.

CELEBRITY MASTERMIND
Champion of the world

In December 2010, the comedy writer and actor Rhys Thomas won a celebrity edition of BBC quiz show *Mastermind*. His specialist subject: Queen. Thomas had previously appeared in the sketch shows *Star Stories* and *The Fast Show*. Behind the scenes, he'd also produced several DVDs for Queen and would go on to direct the documentary *Freddie Mercury: The Great Pretender*.

Thomas was raising money for the Mercury Phoenix Trust and clearly meant business. He turned up in a replica of Mercury's 1977 harlequinade catsuit, making his fellow contestants, including *Gardener's World*'s Toby Buckland and TV presenter Kirsten O'Brien, look positively underdressed.

Once in the famous *Mastermind* chair, Thomas proved unstoppable, like a shooting star leaping through the sky or a tiger defying the laws of gravity etc.

He won the show after correctly answering twenty-one of the twenty-two questions below:

1. Who was the last of the four members to join the band, doing so in 1971?
2. What is Freddie Mercury doing when he first appears on the video of 'I Want to Break Free'?
3. In 1973, just before the band's first album was released, under what name did Freddie Mercury release a cover of the Beach Boys' 'I Can Hear Music'?
4. Which member of the band wrote their 1984 top-ten hit single 'Radio Ga Ga'?
5. In October 1984, Queen were heavily criticised for playing a series of concerts in which venue?
6. In which year did 'Bohemian Rhapsody' first top the UK singles chart? It reached number one again after Freddie's death in 1991.
7. What song did the band perform on their first appearance on *Top of the Pops*?
8. Who co-produced some of the band's earlier albums, including *Sheer Heart Attack* and *A Night at the Opera*?
9. Which guitar did Brian May use on 'Crazy Little Thing Called Love' instead of his usual homemade one?
10. In 1978, which song was released on a double A-sided single with 'Fat Bottomed Girls'?
11. Which album was launched at a notorious party in New Orleans on Halloween 1978?
12. EMI released 'Bohemian Rhapsody' as a single partly in response to the audience reaction after a DJ played it on his radio show. Who was the DJ?
13. In 1980, Queen wrote and performed the soundtrack for which film, directed by Mike Hodges?

14. The track 'Sheer Heart Attack' does not appear on the album of the same title. On which album did it first appear?
15. Where in London did the band perform a free open-air concert in September 1976?
16. Queen's 1981 UK number-one hit, 'Under Pressure', was a collaboration with which singer?
17. The band played a concert in which Eastern Bloc country in July 1986?
18. Which song gave Queen their last number-one hit single during Freddie Mercury's lifetime?
19. With which former Free and Bad Company vocalist did Roger Taylor and Brian May perform as Queen from 2004 onwards?
20. Which festively titled single did Queen release in December 1984?
21. What is the title of Queen's 1979 live album?
22. 'Bohemian Rhapsody' reached number two in the US singles chart in 1992 after the song appeared in which film?

COLLINS, PHIL

Great Queen rumours, part 1

In 2009, a rumour circulated that Freddie Mercury and fellow pop superstar Phil Collins had once jammed together as unknown teenagers in west London. This tale originated with one of Mercury's first friends in England, but it had been told to him by a friend of a boy who'd witnessed the encounter.

The musical love-in (with Collins playing drums, Mercury singing and an unnamed third party on guitar) supposedly took place at a house on Martindale Road, Hounslow, in the mid-1960s. At the time, Phil Collins' childhood home was a five-minute drive away on Hanworth Road.

In 1966, seventeen-year-old Freddie Mercury had tried to put a group together while studying at Isleworth Polytechnic. He'd plastered posters around the college and at neighbouring schools and several musicians showed up to audition. That same year, fifteen-year-old Phil Collins formed his first band, the Real Thing, and started playing gigs. 'But not much further than Acton,' he said. On paper then, it could have happened – couldn't it?

Before Collins joined Genesis, the band actually offered his job to Roger Taylor. 'But it was a bit too prog for me,' Taylor said. After joining Genesis, Collins continued to play sessions at Trident Studios and ended up drumming on *The Man from Manhattan* – an album by Mercury's protégé, singer-songwriter Eddie Howell. Collins and Queen both performed at Live Aid, too, where Collins was permitted to use Mercury's grand piano. This was 'an unprecedented act', according to one insider. Mercury mentioned Collins once in an interview, saying that they were both workaholics ('Phil Collins is a prime example') and Collins briefly described Mercury as a 'one-off'. That was it, though.

However, the rumour of the mystery jam at Martindale Road refused to die. In the end, Collins' publicist was asked to pass on a message, so that music critics could separate fact from fiction. The 'Dear Phil . . .' email mentioned Martindale Road, Hounslow, Freddie's poster campaign . . .

Collins replied just twenty-four hours later: 'I have no recollection of this at all,' followed by a kiss.

❦ —— ❦

THE COSMOS ROCKS

Lost in space

In his knockabout memoir *Going to Sea in a Sieve*, the broadcaster Danny Baker wrote about an early encounter with Queen. In 1973, Baker was working at One Stop Records in London's West End when Queen arrived bearing copies of their freshly minted first album.

Apparently, Queen were a little tipsy and high on their own brilliance. Freddie Mercury demanded Baker play the record and boozily declared Queen were going to be 'bigger than fucking Led Zeppelin!' Baker did as he was asked and 'Keep Yourself Alive' blasted out the shop speakers.

Baker's boss, One Stop's manager, told Queen that their song sounded like Deep Purple and he couldn't stand it. Queen were outraged. 'Fuck you!'s were exchanged and, on their way out, one band member ('Let's say Roger,' wrote Baker) grabbed a handful of LP sleeves and let them drop on the floor. It was vandalism at its most polite.

Who could've predicated that, decades later, Roger Taylor would once again find himself angry in a record shop? It was winter 2008, Queen + Paul Rodgers were touring Europe and Taylor couldn't find a copy of their new album on sale anywhere. 'I remember being furious,' he said, 'and thinking, "Why did we make this fucking record?"'

Others asked the same question. Still, Queen's reasons for recording *The Cosmos Rocks* were valid. Paul Rodgers had been the sinewy, soulful voice of Free's 'All Right Now' before fronting platinum-selling, double-denim rockers Bad Company. What started as an after-show 'hey, let's do something together'-type conversation with Brian May in 2004 had turned into a money-spinner.

Queen + Paul Rodgers were now filling sheds across the US, where Queen hadn't toured since 1982. But, over time, they'd started playing less Free and Bad Company and more Queen. But only the Queen songs that bluesman Rodgers fancied singing. Two years on and Taylor was worried. 'We have to stay valid or we will turn into our own tribute group,' he said.

Work on *The Cosmos Rocks* commenced in August 2007 at Taylor's home studio in Surrey. The trio worked with three co-producers, but Taylor, May and Rodgers played everything themselves, including keyboards and bass. Paul Rodgers also had the advantage of not having pickled his larynx in alcohol or unmentionable substances, so anything he sang usually sounded halfway decent. But *The Cosmos Rocks* was perfunctory at best.

While every track was credited to all three, it transpired that Taylor had composed six of the album's thirteen songs, while Brian May only wrote three. The guitarist had been busy completing his PhD thesis and co-writing books about astronomy. 'It was tough,' Taylor admitted. 'Brian was having a fairly non-productive period.'

The album's first taster was the single 'C-lebrity', on which Taylor railed against hopeless fame-chasers. It was a lazy target, especially considering the early Queen's hunger for success and the fact that the song's composer was a multi-millionaire living in an eighteenth-century priory.

However, the biggest issue with *The Cosmos Rocks* was that it didn't sound like Queen. Freddie Mercury's absence was unavoidable, but the album also missed John Deacon's nuanced bass-playing and the group's collective idiosyncrasy. Even when they were composing hits to order on *A Kind of Magic* or *The Miracle*, they still found room for some peculiarity. *The Cosmos Rocks* had none of that.

May's contributions were typical of the problem. 'Still Burnin'' sounded like a Bad Company song onto which Queen had grafted some textbook harmonies, though it was better than the handwringing 'We Believe'. 'There's a time for peace and a time for understanding,' implored Rodgers unconvincingly. 'It's a sort of statement song,' suggested Taylor diplomatically. May's moping ballad 'Some Things That Glitter' was a slight improvement.

Meanwhile, Taylor did his best with limited resources. He delivered a sweet, flag-waving ballad called 'Small' and a bigger flag-waving ballad called 'Say It's Not True', as well as 'Surfs Up . . . School's Out!' with Foo Fighters' Taylor Hawkins on backing vocals – a song that briefly lifted the album out of the doldrums.

Rodgers' contributions were mostly workaday blues-rock numbers. 'Time to Shine' was blustery and grand, while the stripped-down 'Voodoo' could have dropped off one of Bad Company's later LPs. But most of these songs sounded like solo Paul Rodgers; only the occasional burst of Taylor's gravelly voice or May's pealing Red Special proved that Queen were there.

The Cosmos Rocks was released in September 2008. It made it to number five in the UK, but was brutally panned by critics, with one suggesting the album was 'like the Jimi Hendrix Experience without Jimi Hendrix'. The band stuck to the party line, though.

'Brian and Roger are a revelation when it comes to harmonies,' said Rodgers. 'They've kicked me up the arse.'

'Paul's spontaneity was great, very refreshing,' countered Taylor.

Only Brian May went rogue. 'Did we have arguments making this record?' he said. 'Some discussions . . .'

He paused, then sighed. 'No, I'll be honest, there were some arguments when we all had to go off and have a think.'

What drove Taylor to anger in a continental record shop, though, was EMI's failure to promote the record. EMI had recently been acquired by private equity firm Terra Firma, headed up by financier Guy Hands. The clash of cultures – of art versus 'The Man' – was immediate and dramatic. Paul McCartney foresaw the changes and left EMI before Hands arrived. Radiohead and the Rolling Stones soon followed.

The Cosmos Rocks was a poor album, but it was still a Queen album. At a time of widespread piracy, EMI's failure to see the value of a fanbase still willing to pay for music was baffling. They should have made more of a fuss and floated giant statues of Taylor and May down the Thames as CBS had done for Michael Jackson's *HIStory* (perhaps with a smaller statue of Paul Rodgers in a dinghy behind).

The impact of *The Cosmos Rocks* was less of a big bang and more of a whimper. 'EMI were fucking useless,' Taylor said. 'The album came and went. It was almost as if it was invisible.'

But was it any good?

Long pause. 'It's got its good bits,' he replied.

'CRAZY LITTLE THING CALLED LOVE'

Freddie takes a bath

For Queen, the 1980s began early – in summer 1979, to be exact – at the Munich Hilton hotel. It was there where Freddie Mercury wrote the song that would reboot the band for the new decade.

Queen had booked Munich's Musicland Studios and producer Reinhold Mack almost on a whim. They craved a change of scene and personnel, but weren't sure they wanted to make a new record. Mercury was luxuriating in his hotel suite bath tub when inspiration came. His personal roadie, Peter 'Ratty' Hince, suddenly heard the boss shouting out chords and calling for his guitar: 'Fred came dashing out in a towel; I handed him his acoustic and he began humming and picking out the notes.'

Mercury didn't want to lose the moment, so Hince drove him straight to Musicland. The rest of the band were there, except Brian May. Reinhold Mack was impressed by Freddie's enthusiasm and amused by his instruction to record the new song 'now, before Brian arrives'. Mercury played him the chords to what would become 'Crazy Little Thing Called Love'.

Mack recorded Mercury's first run-through without telling him. When Freddie asked him to run the tape, Mack responded that he already had. This was a new way of working for Queen – simple and spontaneous – and it suited the song. 'Crazy Little Thing Called Love' had taken Freddie ten minutes to write and was a fun rock 'n' roll number – something Elvis could have serenaded his love interest with in one of his early movies. 'If I'd known too many guitar chords, I might have ruined it,' suggested Mercury.

Mack soon discovered why Mercury was keen to get the song done without Brian. When May turned up, there was nothing for him to do but add a solo. He wasn't impressed. Even less so when Mack told him to try a Fender Telecaster rather than his trusty Red Special. 'I wanted to give it that old-fashioned rockabilly sound,' Mack explained.

But this wasn't how May worked. 'I really kicked against it,' he admitted, 'but eventually I saw it was the right way to go.' 'Crazy Little Thing Called Love' was the first song Queen recorded in Munich and it signposted a new musical approach. 'Rhythm and sparseness. Never two notes played if one would do.'

EMI smelt a hit and rushed it out as a single in October. The video also unveiled a new-look Queen in black leather jackets, sunglasses and, in Mercury's case, skateboarder knee pads. It was like a camper version of the 'Greased Lightning' scene from the hit movie musical *Grease*. But everything about it seemed to wave goodbye to the big, bombastic Queen of the '70s.

'Crazy Little Thing Called Love' reached number two in the UK and became Queen's first US number one. It helped change the way Queen recorded their music and, in doing so, changed their audience.

'All of a sudden,' said May, 'there were a lot of younger people turning up at our concerts.'

'CRAZY SHOPPING'
Queen's personal retail therapy

When Queen first played Japan in April 1975, the phrase 'crazy shopping' was coined to describe the band's impressive spending sprees. Tokyo was a consumer's paradise and the Akihabara shopping centre, nicknamed 'Electric Town', was the perfect place to acquire digital watches, radios, super-8 movie cameras and the first Sony Walkmans (before they were even called Sony Walkmans).

Every band member indulged, but none with as much gusto as Freddie Mercury. 'I walk around Tokyo like the Pied Piper with hordes of people following me, shouting out, "You crazee shopping!"' he said. Employees at Queen's management company, Trident, remember Freddie returning from that first trip laden with kimonos, jewellery, lacquered trinket boxes, dolls, a samurai sword and the first of many Japanese woodcuts.

Spending money was an addiction, a release and a source of comfort. Having finally received his royalties for the hit 'Killer Queen', Mercury had started arriving at the studio weighed down with shopping bags from trips to Harrods and the King's Road. 'Some days, when I'm really fed up, I just want to lose myself in my money,' he admitted. His spending increased the wealthier he became. 'I love going to auctions and buying antiques at Sotheby's and Christie's,' he divulged. 'The only thing I'd really miss if I left Britain would be Sotheby's.'

Mercury's spending was often extravagant and spontaneous. He bought his first car, a Rolls-Royce Silver Shadow, in 1977, but never learned to drive. 'Darling, I'll always be driven,' he explained. But there was also a deeper psychological reason. On Queen's first South American tour, Mercury's Argentinian bodyguard was shocked to see him purchasing twenty identical pairs of trousers and T-shirts. Mercury told him he'd never been allowed to wear what he wanted as a boy and was making up for it now.

For all his overindulgence, Mercury always enjoyed showering friends and lovers with gifts. Elton John visited Freddie in the final weeks of his life and was amazed to find him sat up in bed with a Japanese furniture catalogue on his lap, bidding by phone at an auction.

On Christmas Day 1991, three months after Freddie's death, Elton received a seasonal gift wrapped in a pillowcase. It was a male nude watercolour by one of his favourite artists, the English impressionist Henry Scott Tuke. The accompanying note read: 'Darling Sharon, thought you'd love this, love Melina . . .'

Mercury had gone 'crazy shopping' for a Christmas he knew he'd never see.

Spend! Spend! Spend!: rampant consumerists Queen, Tokyo, 1976.

CRITICS

What the papers said

'Unless you actually listen to their first album, it doesn't sound too bad at all.'

— *NME*, review of *Queen*, January 1974

'Has all the demented fury of the Balham Amateur Operatic Society performing *The Pirates of Penzance*.'

— *Melody Maker*, review of 'Bohemian Rhapsody', November 1975

'These Limey lads are effete, flaky and fey.'

— *Circus*, review of *A Day at the Races*, November 1976

'If only Freddie Mercury weren't such a screeching bore (even his cock-rock, like 'Don't Stop Me Now', is flaccid).'
  – *Sounds*, review of *Jazz*, November 1978

'The whole thing makes me wonder why anyone would indulge these creeps and their polluting ideas.'
  – *Rolling Stone*, review of *Jazz*, November 1978

'A colossal mountain of unmoveable mediocrity.'
  – *Sounds*, review of *The Game*, June 1980

'It's narcissism of a decidedly tongue-in-bum cheek style.'
  – *Sounds*, review of *Hot Space*, 1982

'It quite upset my afternoon.'
  – *NME*, review of 'Radio Ga Ga', January 1984

'The album is absolutely bankrupt of gauche imagination.'
  – *Rolling Stone*, review of *A Kind of Magic*, June 1986

'The only strong emotion Queen now evoke in me is a fervent wish that Brian May would cut his hair.'
  – *Record Mirror*, review of *A Kind of Magic*, June 1986

'You will find nothing bohemian and precious little that's rhapsodic here.'
  – *The Guardian*, review of the musical *We Will Rock You*, May 2002

'Pretentious and insultingly simple-minded.'
  – *The Observer*, review of the musical *We Will Rock You*, May 2002

'The story of the rock band Queen, as imagined by a particularly uninterested toddler.'
  – *The Times*, review of the movie *Bohemian Rhapsody*, October 2018

DEACON, JOHN

The bass guitarist's tale

John Deacon's hotel aliases in Queen:
Judge Dread, Jason Dane

John Deacon's answers in a *People* magazine interview, 1974:

My idea of beauty:
Scotland

My favourite flower:
Rose

My favourite colour:
Brown

My favourite place:
England

My greatest happiness:
Gigs

My greatest misery:
Loneliness

My favourite amusement:
TV

My favourite song and composer:
'Paperback Writer'/Lennon and McCartney

My present state of mind:
Happy

My motto:
'Keep yourself alive'

Five things the rest of Queen have said about John Deacon:

Freddie Mercury:
'He's sort of quiet. But don't underestimate him. He's got a fiery streak underneath.'

Brian May:
'John was never very impressed by things.'

Roger Taylor:
'I think John was slightly more fragile than the rest of us. Not as mentally rugged as we were.'

Brian May:
'He wants to be private and in his own universe.'

Roger Taylor:
'I haven't heard a squeak from John for years. Not a single guttural grunt.'

John Deacon used to bring an inflatable airbed on tour with Queen in the 1980s. It was kept in the backstage tuning room. He needed somewhere to take a nap and just get away from the others. Deacon left Queen in 1997 and is now further away from them than ever.

Still, Queen's continued existence has meant the publication of several 'Whatever happened to John Deacon?' stories. The most recent was in March 2021 when *The Sun* ran paparazzi photos taken near Deacon's home in south-west London.

Unlike Brian May clinging to his signature hairdo or Roger Taylor wearing sunglasses indoors, John Deacon was photographed pottering about in a bobbled fleece and shapeless jeans, puffing on a cigarette wedged in his mouth. 'The musician is worth an estimated £105 million,' wrote *The Sun*, implying that this wasn't how a musician worth £105 million should look.

By leaving the band and disappearing, though, Deacon has become more interesting than ever. Journalists now want to know what the man nicknamed 'Deaky' does all day.

'Does he play golf?' Roger Taylor was once asked.

'I don't know what John does,' Taylor replied wearily.

This much we do know: John Richard Deacon was born on 19 August 1951 and grew up in Oadby, near Leicester. He presumably still has a Leicestershire accent and softly pronounces his 'r's as 'w's', like he once did in TV and radio interviews. 'Joe Mazzello, who played John in *Bohemian Rhapsody*, nailed his mannerisms,' Taylor said, 'but made him slightly too posh.'

John was the eldest of two children born to mother Lillian and father Arthur. 'I remember my first musical instrument,' Deacon said in 1975. 'It was a plastic Tommy Steele guitar when I must have been about seven.' Music and electronics were his childhood hobbies. When he wasn't playing guitar, 'Deaks' (as friends called him) was tinkering with a ham radio set and a reel-to-reel tape recorder. He told everybody he wanted to be an engineer when he grew up.

Arthur Deacon, a Norwich Union insurance clerk, died when his son was just eleven. 'It was rough,' understated John. 'Not easy growing up without a dad.'

Deacon started playing in groups after joining Beauchamp Grammar School in Oadby and spent several years performing pop and soul covers with local band the Opposition. Apparently, Deacon kept his own counsel even then.

'John was stoic,' remembered one ex-bandmate, who compared Deacon to his half-namesake and fellow bassist, the Who's indomitable John Entwistle. Deacon and bandmate Dave Williams both loved the Who and soon became mods with parkas and mirrored scooters. Williams said that the only time he saw Deaky visibly upset was when he crashed his Vespa 180. 'There was a lot of blood,' he recalled, 'and he was pretty stressed out.'

The Opposition shed several singers and guitarists, but Deacon remained with the band until he left Beauchamp Grammar in summer 1968. With his three A levels, he was accepted to study engineering at Chelsea College, London.

It was a year before he picked up the bass again. Deacon is supposed to have played one gig with a couple of university friends in autumn of 1970. They couldn't think of a name and called themselves 'Deacon' just before going on stage. They never played together again. Instead, John started answering 'musician wanted' ads in the music press, though he was sometimes too nervous to show up for auditions. In the summer holidays, he took a job as a tea boy at the British Tourist Authority.

Deacon saw Queen play a show in Kensington ('But I don't remember much about it') before being introduced to May and Taylor at a college disco in spring 1971. Queen had been through two bass players already – two and a half if you include Doug Bogie, who'd lasted just two gigs – so Deacon was offered the job after just one audition at Imperial College. Besides being a gifted bass player and rhythm guitarist, he'd also built his own amp and later graduated from college with a first-class honours degree in electronics. Deacon was younger than the others (by five years in Freddie Mercury's case) and – appropriately for a man who told

People magazine that his favourite colour was brown – came across as quiet and unassuming.

'In the early days, I used to be very quiet because I felt like the new boy,' he explained. 'But I think I fitted in because of that. I was alright because I wasn't going to upstage Brian or Freddie.'

The back cover of *Queen* listed him as 'Deacon John' because the others thought it made him sound more exciting. But Deacon insisted that his name be properly rendered on *Queen II*, so the sleeve was sent back to be printed correctly. John could be pushed, but only so far.

His musical tastes were eclectic. He liked Tamla Motown, the Beatles and solo McCartney, but also arty prog-rockers Yes. One of his favourite bass players was Rory Gallagher's unassuming sideman Gerry McAvoy.

Deacon was never a showman, but he was consistently, infuriatingly brilliant. He came up with two world-famous basslines – for 'Another One Bites the Dust' and 'Under Pressure' (though he tried to claim that David Bowie wrote the latter) – and he left his mark all over the rest of Queen's catalogue: driving the Wagnerian grand finale of 'Bohemian Rhapsody'; chasing Brian May's guitar around on 'Killer Queen'; and grounding Roger Taylor's drums on 'A Kind of Magic'.

The first thing Deacon ever wrote for Queen was 'Misfire', which appeared on 1974's *Sheer Heart Attack*. Originally titled 'Banana Blues', it was a sunny pop song at odds with the rest of the LP. Though Deacon wasn't a prolific writer, he had an uncanny knack of composing hits – and the sort of hits that people didn't associate with Queen.

In 1975, Deacon's 'You're My Best Friend' was considered rather lightweight, but it gave the band a US hit. Five years later, 'Another One Bites the Dust' challenged the popular notion of a 'typical' Queen song. And, while Deacon never wished to upstage the others, he did try to ban May from playing guitar on his R&B songs on *Hot Space*.

Many later interpreted Queen's 1984 hit 'I Want to Break Free' as Deaky's cry for help or liberation. It wasn't the first time he had written about wanting to be free either. 'Monday, the start of my holiday / Freedom for just one week,' begin the lyrics he composed for *Jazz*'s 'In Only Seven Days'. The song's protagonist then falls for a mystery woman on a beach and ends up heartbroken.

In real life, though, Deacon met his wife, Veronica Tetzlaff, when she was studying at the Maria Assumpta Teacher Training College in Kensington. The pair married in January 1975 when Veronica was three months' pregnant with the first of their six children.

However, Deacon's transition from ordinary Leicestershire lad to global rock star wasn't without moments of unwitting comedy. In 1974, he told a journalist that he was thrilled to be able to afford his first car – an Austin Mini he'd nicknamed 'Silver Bullet'. 'I only paid forty quid for it,' he revealed.

A few years later, however, his tastes had become more expensive. One evening, Deacon arranged to meet his friend, ex-Opposition drummer Nigel Bullen, for a drink. John insisted on going to a quiet country pub near Market Harborough, but was surprised when some of the patrons started asking for his autograph. Then again, he had zoomed into the car park behind the wheel of a Jensen Interceptor and was wearing a satin tour jacket with 'QUEEN' emblazoned across the back.

As Queen became bigger, John became increasingly unpredictable. He started smoking cigarettes at the age of thirty-six; he permed his hair so that it was even bigger than Brian May's and looked like an exploding bath sponge; and he disappeared to Bali, without telling the others, in the middle of making *The Works*.

'John could be wonderfully unpredictable,' said May. 'Very quiet and shy, but then suddenly he'd break out and you didn't know what he was going to do next.'

Sometimes his behaviour was self-destructive. In San Diego, he punched a plate-glass window and had his hand patched up before the show. During Queen's Magic Tour, he smashed his bass after a gig in Spain and then threw his spare into an amp on stage at Knebworth. The general consensus was that Deaky had had enough.

His one musical handicap was that he couldn't sing, despite appearing to do so in the video for 'Bohemian Rhapsody' and on stage (the faders on his mic were always kept low). This frustrated him, especially when Queen weren't working. During downtime, he drifted between projects: playing bass for Mercury and Montserrat Caballé; producing for Hot Chocolate singer Errol Brown; and recording on Elton John's *Ice on Fire* and *Leather Jackets* albums. 'Elton reckoned [Deacon] was one of the best bass players he ever worked with,' said former roadie Peter 'Ratty' Hince.

In 1986, Deacon co-wrote a jaunty pop song, 'No Turning Back', for the movie *Biggles*, starring Peter Cushing. He recorded it with a group called the Immortals, but the song and film tanked.

A year later, with Queen off the road, comedian Tony Hawks met Deacon on a Virgin airlines press junket to Miami. Hawks' comedy troupe, Morris Minor and the Majors, performed on the plane and then spent the weekend drinking with Deacon. John also had a walk-on part in the video for their single 'Stutter Rap (No Sleep 'til Bedtime)' – a laboured spoof of the Beastie Boys' 'No Sleep 'til Brooklyn'. Deacon wore an electric-blue wig and mimed a bad guitar solo.

'John struck me as someone who'd become a rock star by accident and who may well have been happier doing something else, in spite of all the benefits,' Hawks later told *Q* magazine.

Apparently, Deacon was also a worrier: he worried about record sales, ticket sales and every aspect of Queen's business affairs. 'John keeps a close eye on our business affairs,' said Mercury in the '70s. 'The rest of the group won't do anything unless John says it's alright.'

'After they left Trident, he took on the task of seeing where the money goes and put an awful lot of energy into the contracts,' said Peter Hince. 'He was instrumental in keeping the band aware because Freddie was not interested in that stuff.'

Deacon was so disgusted by their early management company, Trident, that he won't even discuss the subject this century. In 2007, Trident engineer Ken Scott saw Deacon at Heathrow Airport and said hello, but John was in no mood for conversation. 'He said, "I know who you are, but I have nothing whatsoever to do with any of that any more,"' Scott recalled.

Deacon had something else to worry about, too: Freddie Mercury's health. During Queen's final years, Deacon let May and Taylor promote the albums and answer the awkward questions about their lead singer. There were also rumours that Deacon was embarrassed by Mercury's behaviour. 'I think we might have all been embarrassed by Freddie's antics at some time or another,' May conceded. 'I don't know about Deaky any more than the rest of us.'

'When Freddie died, John took it badly; he was very affected by it,' revealed Peter Hince. 'I think he thought that was the end of the road.'

Deacon did his last major work with Queen on 1995's *Made in Heaven*. He sent the band a letter of resignation two years later, thereby beginning decades of speculation among fans and journalists alike. 'The pressure of being in Queen affected John,' one ex-Queen employee suggested. 'But it had absolutely nothing to do with drugs or alcohol. It was just the pressure of being in one of the biggest bands in the world – writing hit record after hit record, being responsible for some of that financial stuff – and still loving his family.'

Deacon retired completely. When asked why, he told people that he was 'busy with his children'. He didn't even attend Brian May's wedding to Anita Dobson in November 2000. Nevertheless, he has allegedly retained an anonymous internet presence, showing up in Queen fansite forums under various pseudonyms. Deacon was also a regular visitor to the celebrity gossip site Popbitch in the 2000s. When the site asked if any of its readers had ever masturbated in a famous person's house, Deacon emailed back revealing that he had – but it was his own house.

Deacon's disappearing act was rudely interrupted in 2005, though, when the *Mail on Sunday* claimed that 'Queen's boring bassist' had been driven 'into the arms of a lap dancer'. The newspaper reported how a depressed Deacon, seeking solace at Sophisticats strip club in London's West End, had met 25-year-old dancer Emma Shelley, who was working under the name 'Pushbar'.

Maybe he was just missing Queen's famously excessive parties – the snake-charmers, the mud-wrestlers, the fictitious dwarves with bowls of cocaine on their heads – but Deacon took Shelley to restaurants, paid for her to go on holiday and even bought her a flat in Croydon, paid for in cash. No sooner had the newspaper exposed the affair, Shelley claimed she 'didn't know John was a family man'. A spokesman said that Deacon had 'absolutely no comment to make'.

'You could say John kept his mystery,' joked Roger Taylor at the time, 'though I don't know where he's keeping it right now.'

Deacon made a few sporadic public appearances after leaving the band. In 2004, he surprised Taylor by turning up to see *We Will Rock You* at the Dominion Theatre. A year later, he asked to be put on the guest list when Queen + Paul Rodgers played Hyde Park, although the gig was postponed after a terrorist attack in London.

'John would never stop us using the Queen name,' said Taylor in 2005. 'We wondered if he would when we started the musical, but John told us he liked it, he approved.' Not everything met with his approval, though. He publicly denounced Queen + Robbie Williams' version of 'We Are the Champions' and has yet to comment on the band's collaboration with Adam Lambert.

The new boy: John Deacon, 1976.

All of Deacon's communication with his ex-bandmates is conducted via a lawyer or accountant. Yet Queen + Adam Lambert's existence and *Bohemian Rhapsody*'s box-office success continue to affect his life – and his bank balance.

John Deacon resigned his directorship of three Queen-related companies in 2016, but he remains a director of another four, including Queen Music Ltd and Queen Productions Ltd. Though he doesn't play a note any more, he still makes money from the brand. Perhaps 'Jason Dane', aka 'Judge Dread', is the smartest Queen of all.

'DEATH ON TWO LEGS'

Freddie bears a grudge

'This is about a *beep beep beep*.' Freddie Mercury's introduction to 'Death on Two Legs' is censored on Queen's in-concert album, *Live Killers*, but the lyrics are still sufficiently scathing. In the song, Mercury ranted about 'an old barrow boy', 'a misguided old mule' and 'a sewer rat', as well as suggesting that the object of his ire consider suicide.

Mercury was singing about Queen's first manager, Norman Sheffield ('This is about a real motherfucker of a gentleman').

'We had our differences, of course,' said Brian May after learning of Sheffield's death in 2014. 'But, in the grand scheme of things, all the water had long since flown under the bridge.' It was a different story in the '70s, though, and Queen's bitter dispute with Sheffield hung over them like a storm cloud for years.

Norman and his brother, Barry Sheffield, had been around Soho and the music business since the 1950s; Norman briefly played drums for one of Mercury's early idols, Cliff Richard. In 1968, the brothers acquired Trident Studios in St Anne's Court, converting it into a state-of-the-art facility with a top-of-the-range mixing desk. Its reputation spread. Soon after, the Beatles recorded 'Hey Jude' at Trident, with Paul McCartney playing the studio's Bechstein grand piano. 'The Beatles, George Harrison, Bowie did *Hunky Dory* there – it was the place to go,' explained Roger Taylor. The Sheffields also formed a production company, with a video offshoot to capitalise on the growing medium.

Queen signed to Trident Audio Productions in summer 1972. The company then paid for new equipment, stage clothes and lighting, the recording of *Queen* and *Queen II* (which were then licensed to EMI), and the band's promo videos and extensive marketing. In 2009, Norman Sheffield claimed that Trident had 'ploughed over £200,000 into Queen'.

The drawback was that Trident handled every aspect of Queen's affairs. In December 1971, Queen had signed a song publishing deal with Feldman Music, so their publishing then became a joint venture between Feldman and Trident. Trident also licensed their music, effectively making them Queen's record company, and even oversaw their management. Norman Sheffield hired a manager, Jack Nelson, to take care of Queen day to day, but Nelson still reported to the brothers. It was a huge conflict of interest. 'Trident were wearing at least three hats,' said May. 'It was not an ethical situation and they took incredible advantage of that.'

Mercury took his first pot-shot at Queen's handlers on *Sheer Heart Attack*'s 'Flick of the Wrist', but that one snuck under the radar. When band and boss fell out irreconcilably a year later, it was all over money. *Queen II* and *Sheer Heart Attack* had both been UK top-five LPs, while the singles 'Seven Seas of Rhye', 'Killer Queen' and 'Now I'm Here' had made the UK top fifteen, but Queen were still waiting on their royalties.

During their first Japanese tour in April 1975, they were mobbed at Tokyo's Haneda Airport by adoring fans, sold out the 10,000-seater Budokan concert hall and were unable to leave their hotel without security. 'They came back from Japan thinking they were superstars,' Sheffield said, 'and that's when the problems really started.'

Queen were still on wages and yet to see royalties because they still owed Trident for all the money the company had spent on them. 'Our accountants explained we were heavily in debt and it put us under incredible pressure,' said May. 'It started to affect our private lives.'

John Deacon, who was due to marry his girlfriend, Veronica Tetzlaff, requested £4,000 for a deposit on a house (Sheffield claimed he'd asked for £10,000). Veronica was pregnant and John was still living in a tiny apartment. Norman refused the money: 'I told him, "I know I'm your mother and your father, but I'm not your bank." As you can imagine, that went down like a lead balloon.'

Then Mercury asked Trident to pay for a grand piano. 'We had a great row about that,' recalled Sheffield. 'I said, "What can you do with a grand piano? It won't fit in your flat."' But Freddie said he'd buy it as a publicity stunt and have photographers there while he handed over the cash in Harrods. I said no for tax reasons.'

Norman Sheffield insisted Queen's big royalties pay day was due in winter 1975. 'I said, "Boys, just wait, it's coming." But Freddie was too impetuous and too impatient. He was bloody ungrateful.'

It also irked Queen to see the brothers visibly enjoying the perks of their success. 'They were running around in stretch limos,' huffed Roger Taylor. 'You'd think, "Hang on, there's something not right here."'

Queen started looking for a way out and new management. On their spring '75 US tour, they met with Black Sabbath's manager, Don Arden (father of Sharon Osbourne). Back in England, they had meetings with 10cc's Harvey Lisberg and Led Zeppelin's Peter Grant. 'I was sorry it had come to this,' said Sheffield. 'But I also knew it was coming.'

Then came Queen's next album, *A Night at the Opera*, and its opening track, 'Death on Two Legs'. Norman heard the song before the LP was finished, while Queen and Trident were still in negotiations. 'It was a nasty hate mail from Freddie,' he said.

'It was the most vicious lyric I ever wrote,' admitted Mercury. 'It's so vindictive, Brian felt bad singing it.'

Sheffield attempted to sue EMI and Queen for libel and failure to correctly publish the product (EMI had been legally obligated to show Trident the lyrics beforehand). The case was settled out of court.

In August 1975, Queen's lawyer (and future business manager), Jim Beach, of law firm Harbottle & Lewis, officially extricated Queen from their contract with Trident and signed them with Elton John's manager, John Reid. Under the terms of the new deal, Queen's publishing became the responsibility of EMI Publishing, while their record deals (EMI in the UK; Elektra worldwide) were no longer processed through Trident.

Naturally, it came at a price. Trident Audio Productions received severance pay of £100,000 (covered by an advance from EMI Publishing) and retained the rights to 1 per cent of royalties on the band's next six albums. This meant Queen weren't completely free and the Sheffields continued to earn out of the band until 1982's *Hot Space*.

'It was no more than we deserved,' Norman insisted. 'Queen owed us.'

DEATH SCRABBLE

Sex, drugs and word games

An 'en' is a typographic unit and half the width of an 'em'. Freddie Mercury, a former graphic design student, once confounded his bandmates by using both words in a game of what Queen called 'Death Scrabble'. This was Queen's fiercely competitive version of the standard word game. The rules were simple: dictionaries were banned (it was still the 1980s, there was no such thing as Google) and players fought to the bitter end.

Some of the toughest battles took place in Munich's bunker-like Musicland Studios. 'Fred and I could play for hours, especially if the others were doing something else,' said Taylor. Sometimes the band should have been doing something else, but the game came first, despite mounting studio bills. One bout lasted all night and came to a crashing halt at six the following morning.

Mercury, who had honed his skills playing against an aunt in Bombay, described himself as 'a demon' at the game. But Brian May claimed the greatest victory. 'Brian got the biggest single Scrabble word – 156 points for "lacquers". It was a triple-word score,' recalled Taylor.

'Freddie never forgave me,' admitted May. *Innuendo*, Queen's last album during Mercury's lifetime, was named after one of his favourite Death Scrabble words. 'It's the perfect title,' he claimed.

DESERT ISLAND DISCS
Brian May is Robinson Crusoe

The BBC broadcast the first episode of its flagship radio show *Desert Island Discs* in 1942. The format has barely changed since then. A famous guest is marooned on an imaginary island with only *The Complete Works of Shakespeare* and a Bible (or comparable religious/philosophical text) for company. They are then asked to pick another book, one luxury item and eight songs, explaining their choices in the process.

Brian May was cast away on 15 September 2002. He told host Sue Lawley that he'd bring a copy of C. S. Lewis's *Out of the Silent Planet* and his beloved Red Special in addition to the following pieces of music.

Gustav Holst, 'Saturn, the Bringer of Old Age'

From Holst's 1916 orchestral suite, *The Planets*. The young Brian used to play this on the family record player while reciting a monologue about outer space. Listen closely and there are shades of its broody melodrama in 'Who Wants to Live Forever' and 'The Show Must Go On'.

Buddy Holly and the Crickets, 'Maybe Baby'

A 1957 hit for the bespectacled rock 'n' roller. Brian heard this on late-night Radio Luxembourg via a crystal set hidden under his bedspread. Holly showed that geeks could be pop stars, too. The song contains killer harmonies à la the future Mercury/May/Taylor triumvirate.

Smokey Robinson and the Miracles, 'The Tracks of My Tears'

Sixteen-year-old Brian was devastated when he split up with his first girlfriend. This Motown hit helped him 'feel comfortably sorry' for himself while mooning around Imperial College.

Mercury and John Deacon later went through a Motown sound-alike phase. See: 'Pain Is So Close to Pleasure'.

The Babys, 'Back on My Feet Again'

This 1980 anthem by soft-rockers the Babys was all about having pride after a fall. Brian used to play it in his roadie's car while being driven back from Munich's Sugar Shack nightclub. It was motivational therapy before another recording/sparring session on *The Game*.

Anita Dobson, 'To Know Him Is to Love Him'

The future Mrs May's reboot of the Teddy Bears' 1958 hit is notable for Brian's very Queenly guitar solo. It was recorded in 1988, just before the couple went public with their relationship.

Rainbow, 'Since You've Been Gone'

More manly rock for troubled times in Munich. This 1979 hit by former Deep Purple guitarist Ritchie Blackmore's group welds a big fat chorus to a big fat riff. Very 'Hammer to Fall', in hindsight.

AC/DC, 'Highway to Hell'

Brian once said he wished he could be in monster Aussie rock band AC/DC. They were uncomplicated, unpretentious and had a guitarist who dressed as a schoolboy and was more famous than the lead singer. The band's 1979 journey into Hades has a hot, spacey sound with barely a note wasted.

Queen, 'We Will Rock You'

Brian joins a select group of BBC castaways who've chosen their own music for the desert island. See also: funk royalty Nile Rodgers, who selected five songs he had either composed or produced himself. Brian told Sue Lawley, 'I wasn't going to put anything of our own in, but it does seem like a good idea.'

DOBSON, ANITA

She wants it all

It's May 1987 and Anita Dobson, the star of TV soap *EastEnders*, is making her debut as a pop singer. Anita has just released a single, 'Talking of Love', and is being interviewed by the music magazine *Smash Hits* alongside the song's composer, Brian May.

The pair chat to writer Chris Heath about several topics: how Brian's wife persuaded him to start watching *EastEnders*; how Brian and his wife bumped into Anita at a film premiere; how Brian invited Anita to a Queen concert at Wembley Stadium; and why he has now written a song for her.

The newspapers are already full of stories about the two of them supposedly having an affair, suggests Heath.

'We just laughed,' replies Anita dismissively.

'It was such an obvious thing for them to say,' shrugs Brian.

Brian May and Anita Dobson finally wed in November 2000. Their relationship had fascinated the press for several years and inspired May to write two Queen singles.

In 1985, over 30 million viewers watched the Christmas Day episode of *EastEnders*. Dobson, playing fiery pub landlady Angie Watts, was served divorce papers by her on-screen husband, Den. ''Appy Christmas, Ange,' Den hissed as she stared back at him disbelievingly – a riot of bouffant hair and black eyeliner.

With those viewing figures, Fleet Street realised soap stars would sell newspapers, just like pop stars. The royal coupling of Queen's lead guitarist and the queen of soap was irresistible. And, as journalists pointed out with wearying regularity, the couple had similar hairstyles.

Apparently, Anita attended both of Queen's shows at Wembley Stadium in June 1986, after which she and Brian began a clandestine affair. 'We've been kind of together since 1986, a little bit off and on,' confessed Brian on ITV's *Loose Women* chat show in 2012.

'You've been together since 1986?' reiterated the show's co-host and *Sun* columnist Jane Moore, 'and you got divorced from your first wife in 1988?'

'Did I?' replied Brian. 'Is that right? I'm not good on dates.'

'There was some overlap, not proud of it,' said Anita. 'We tried very hard not to be together.'

But the couple's relationship spelled the end of Brian's marriage to his first wife, Chrissie. 'I thought it would never happen to me,' he admitted. 'I kicked and screamed against it. But you grow, the people you're with grow, and sometimes you don't grow together.' Although, to begin with, few in the Queen camp expected Brian and Anita to last: 'My manager said, "Marrying an actress? You must be kidding?"'

The late 1980s were a tempestuous time. Brian's marriage finished, his lead singer was terminally ill and his new partner wanted it all. 'When I met Anita, she had a zest for everything,' he said. 'She wanted it all at once and said, "I want it all and I want it now." A bell went off in my head.' May wrote Queen's 1989 hit 'I Want It All' and gave his girlfriend a framed gold disc inscribed with the message: 'Thank you to Anita Dobson for inspiring this song.'

It wasn't the only Queen single to acknowledge Brian's private life. The lyrics to 'Scandal' that same year criticised the tabloid frenzy accompanying his and Anita's relationship. Brian found the scrutiny unbearable: 'It screwed me up completely. For nearly a year, I was incapable, so depressed.'

Anita's pop career was short-lived. She quit *EastEnders* in 1988 and has refused numerous offers to return. While Brian spent the '90s making solo records and trying not to talk about Queen, Anita worked in theatre and TV, determined to lay the ghost of Angie Watts to rest.

The couple split for a few months when the press revealed Brian's affair with his PA, Julie Glover, but May later checked into a private clinic in Arizona to be treated for depression and credited Anita for aiding his recovery. They married soon after at Richmond register office and have been together ever since.

In 1987, Anita told *Smash Hits* how much she adored the pop group Curiosity Killed the Cat; Brian said he preferred Def Leppard and Bon Jovi. At the time, the couple seemed as surprised by their relationship as the press was. 'It's an odd pairing,' said Brian, who was supposed to be talking about music. 'But I think it's going to work.'

'DON'T STOP ME NOW'

'Brian's favourite'

In April 2005, viewers of the BBC's *Top Gear* programme voted 'Don't Stop Me Now' the greatest driving song of all time, over-taking Meat Loaf's 'Bat Out of Hell' and Steppenwolf's 'Born to Be Wild'. After announcing the winner, host Jeremy Clarkson informed viewers that Brian May had turned down the programme's offer of an award 'because he says he doesn't like that song'.

Instead, Clarkson's co-presenter James May (no relation) flew to Sardinia and presented a tacky trophy to Roger Taylor on his yacht. 'It really was the cheapest, nastiest one they could find,' Taylor said. 'I should have thrown it into the sea.'

Brian May's snub illustrated his difficult relationship with 'Don't Stop Me Now', a song Taylor teasingly refers to as 'Brian's favourite'. May first made his feelings known in 2008. 'Lyrically, it represented something that was happening to Freddie, which we thought was threatening him. I thought the song was fun, but I did worry about Freddie.'

The 'real good time' Mercury was singing about reflected his private life: a heady blur of nightclubs, cocaine and multiple sex partners. On 'Don't Stop Me Now', Freddie compared himself to an unexploded atom bomb, a shooting star, a racing car and a rocket ship on its way to Mars. But really it was a song about taking lots of drugs and having lots of sex.

'Spot on,' confirmed Taylor. 'I know Brian's not so keen, but those lyrics don't worry me in the slightest. I think they're brilliant – "They call me Mister Fahrenheit" – really original and very tongue in cheek.'

May also considered the music a tad lightweight. This was a year or so before 'Crazy Little Thing Called Love' and 'Another One Bites the Dust'. On 'Don't Stop Me Now', Mercury's piano did all the work and there was a noticeable absence of noisy lead guitar. 'I remember thinking, "I'm not quite sure if this is what we should be doing,"' said May.

'Don't Stop Me Now' was released as a single in January 1979, scraped into the top ten in Britain, but died in America. It was long forgotten by the time of Queen's last tour with Mercury and missing from the setlist at the Freddie Tribute Concert.

Then came 2004's cult horror comedy *Shaun of the Dead*, which used the song in a scene where a pub's patrons attack a marauding zombie with pool cues. Cover versions by the boy band McFly and American punk-poppers the Vandals, among others, also followed, introducing the song to new generations and reminding the older ones of Queen's lesser-known hit. And then came *Top Gear* . . .

Roger Taylor had good reason to look perplexed when James May presented him with the trophy. 'It was a medium hit that only just made it into the top ten,' he said. Taylor was surprised again when, in 2012, he saw presenter Chris Evans singing the song on his TV show *TFI Friday*. 'I remember wondering what on earth made him choose it. But I think he tuned into something other people have now tuned into. It's a party song.'

The afterlife of 'Don't Stop Me Now' shows no sign of ending. It's now a karaoke-machine staple and a go-to number for contestants on reality-TV talent shows. In 2009, Essex pop hopeful Olly Murs performed it live on *The X Factor*. May and Taylor showed up beforehand to offer some avuncular advice. 'The song suits you a lot better than I ever would have imagined,' May told Murs. But it's still difficult not to regard 'Don't Stop Me Now' as a Trojan horse: a celebration of cocaine-snorting sexual excess smuggled onto prime-time TV by young pop innocents. 'Yes,' laughed Taylor. 'These people don't know the darkness behind it.'

Brian May's attitude to 'Don't Stop Me Now' has also softened. 'There was a definite feeling we were losing Freddie, which affected the way I perceived it,' he said in 2019. 'I probably thought it was a bit frivolous as well . . . but I've gotten over that now.'

The PRS and MCPS statements must have helped, too. Besides numerous appearances in TV shows and films, Queen's minor hit has been used to advertise Cadbury's Dairy Milk chocolate, Visa bank cards, La Redoute women's apparel, Toyota Camry motor cars, L'Oréal skincare products, Silk almond milk, online retail behemoth Amazon etc.

'I think it's going to end up as the biggest song Queen ever did,' said Roger Taylor. 'I find that fascinating.'

EALING ART COLLEGE

School of rock, no. 1

It's over half a century since Freddie Mercury left Ealing Art College. Today, the London School of Film, Media and Design at the University of West London regularly pays tribute to its former student, though fellow ex-pupils Pete Townshend of the Who and Ronnie Wood of the Rolling Stones barely get a mention. In Mercury's honour, the UWL's Students' Union bar is named 'Freddie's' and, for a time, there was an annual scholarship, 'Freddie's Fund', awarded to 'a student demonstrating outstanding creativity, resilience and ambition'.

Mercury was certainly creative, resilient and ambitious, though not necessarily in pursuit of his diploma. He enrolled on the fashion design course in autumn 1966, one of two male students in a class of thirty. Much of the course was taken up with textile printing and pattern design. His tutor, Althea McNeish, later worked for the Dior fashion house and designed an outfit for the Queen. In 1967, she taught Mercury to tie-dye and helped him make a fashionable batik T-shirt.

Those who knew Mercury back then remember him as shy and even withdrawn. 'He was nothing like the strutting peacock he later became,' said one. Nevertheless, the other male student on the course, Mark Malden, recalled that they both worked as nude life models for the school's evening classes. 'Freddie was doing it first and told me about it,' he said. 'You posed for little old ladies. It was £5 for a couple of hours, enough to buy a pair of Levi's.' Presumably, then, somebody's grandmother has or once had a life drawing of a naked Freddie Mercury?

The first inkling his classmates had of any musical gift was at a lunchtime college gig by the blues group Chicken Shack. After their performance, Mercury snuck onto the stage, sat down at the piano of future Fleetwood Mac member Christine Perfect and began tinkling Beethoven's *Für Elise*. Friends remember him stopping suddenly as if to say, 'Look, see what I can do. But that's all you're going to get . . .'

Everything seemed to change with the arrival of Jimi Hendrix. Mercury's obsession was such that he skipped classes to go to Hendrix's gigs and was threatened with expulsion. Instead, he switched courses to graphic design, insisting it better served his creative interests.

There was another reason for the swap. Mercury had met a group of graphic design students who shared his passion for music. These included Tim Staffell, the vocalist in 1984 (Brian May's group), and Chris Smith, Smile's future keyboard player.

Their second-floor art studio became a musical salon. New songs and LPs were discussed in forensic detail. Mercury, Staffell and the others later made a group pilgrimage to see the Who perform *Tommy* at the London Coliseum. Mercury also had a habit of stopping work to entertain the others with a blast of imaginary Hendrix, wielding his draughtman's yard stick or T-square like a makeshift guitar. 'It could be quite annoying sometimes,' Chris Smith later said. 'One minute you're having a normal conversation, the next he's playing "Purple Haze".'

When 1984 split, Tim Staffell formed Smile. Mercury became their number-one fan and occasional, albeit hopeless, roadie; he was rarely seen carrying anything heavier than a cymbal stand. His earlier shyness was gone and the peacock had emerged. He began a relationship with another art student, Rosemary Pearson, and, by summer 1968, was promenading around Ealing dressed like a pop star.

'He was the centre of attention in whatever group he was with,' recalled fellow student and future rock photographer Derek Ridgers. 'I think he was one of the few students bold enough to wear white flares, always a risky business at an art school, where there's liable to be still-wet paint or printing ink in all sorts of unlikely places.'

'Freddie baby' – as some called him – was also telling everyone he was going to be a mega-star. 'What? Bigger than Hendrix?' asked Chris Smith. 'Oh yes,' he replied. He continued working, nominally, towards his diploma, but focused more attention on what Smile were doing. His friends were writing songs and that's where his ambition lay.

Chris Smith soon split with Smile, but was working towards a part-time music degree and had the keys to the art school music room. He and Mercury would go there at lunchtimes to try to write songs on the piano. 'Freddie used to say, "Tim and Brian can do this, they can write a song, so why can't I?" I was vaguely interested, but he was passionate about it.'

If Mercury had a musical idea, it was imperative he acted on it immediately. 'He'd say, "Quick! Quick! I've got a bit of a song! But I need a guitar." If there wasn't a guitar around, we'd go to one of the music shops on Ealing Broadway. They got fed up with Freddie taking a guitar off the wall, playing a bit and then walking out after buying a plectrum. He was in there doing it every week.'

Mercury joined a band, Ibex, later renamed Wreckage, who made their inauspicious debut in the art school common room in October 1969. 'He was doing all the posing and strutting,' said Smith, who saw the group around this time. 'But I'm not quite sure it worked.'

By then, though, Mercury's frequent absences from class had become a talking point. 'The running joke was "Where's Freddie?",' said one ex-student. 'Because that's all you ever heard from the tutors. He'd usually be off playing the piano somewhere.'

Mercury left Ealing Art College in 1970. A question mark lingers over whether he passed his Diploma in Art & Design. Queen say he did. He certainly had a graduation show, based on the images and lyrics of Jimi Hendrix and illustrated in the style of the American contemporary artist Shepard Fairey. His ex-girlfriend Mary Austin apparently owns one of Mercury's Jimi artworks.

'It was pretty cursory, not particularly good,' said Derek Ridgers in 2011. 'I remember thinking, "If it wasn't for the fact that he was such a popular guy, he most probably would never have been allowed to get as far as having a degree show and graduating."'

Are you experienced?: Freddie Mercury daydreaming of Hendrix and playing his imaginary guitar, Ealing Art College, 1968.

Years later, Mercury supposedly said that, feeling intimidated by his bandmates' degrees, he'd invented one for himself. However, during his time at Ealing Art College, he did demonstrate outstanding creativity, resilience and ambition, worthy of the modern-day Freddie's Fund.

EVERETT, KENNY
The DJ's tale

Kenny Everett was once the *enfant terrible* of British radio. His crazed humour and disregard for broadcasting protocol brought him big ratings and sometimes even bigger trouble. In 1970, Everett was fired from the BBC for jokily claiming that the transport minister's wife had bribed her driving test examiner.

Four years later, Everett was hosting the breakfast show on London's Capital Radio when he first interviewed Freddie Mercury. Everett was drawn to flamboyance and eccentricity. He and Freddie saw aspects of their vivid personalities reflected in each other. Everett, like Mercury, was also living with a woman (his wife, former pop singer 'Lady Lee') and hiding his homosexuality. Over time, Kenny and Freddie became friends.

In October 1975, Everett attended a playback for *A Night at the Opera* at Camden's Roundhouse Studios. According to Queen legend, the DJ purloined a master tape of the album, though others say that he was given a copy by producer Roy Thomas Baker, having promised not to broadcast it.

Either way, Everett played 'Bohemian Rhapsody' fourteen times over the next two days. 'Dig this, listeners. This is so fab and groovy,' he implored. 'I promise you've never heard anything like it.' Capital's switchboard was besieged by listeners wanting to know when the song was out. The early promotion helped 'Bohemian Rhapsody' become a Christmas number one.

A year later, Everett interviewed Mercury again – this time, about Queen's new album, *A Day at the Races*. Their conversation was camp and drily witty. 'You've bought Champagne with you,' Kenny purred. 'But of course, dear,' Freddie replied. 'It travels everywhere with me.'

By the end of the '70s, Everett had become a TV star. *The Kenny Everett Video Show* featured zany animations, a host of comedy characters (including sex-mad Hollywood diva 'Cupid Stunt') played by Everett himself, and pop-star cameos from the likes of Rod Stewart and David Bowie.

Freddie Mercury made his appearance on 18 February 1980. Queen were off the road and Everett told him to come on the show and 'do something, do anything'.

Kenny sauntered into view first, wearing a leather jacket and a biker's cap in the guise of hapless punk rocker 'Sid Snot'. It was a tame, schoolboy parody of a fictitious Sex Pistol.

''Ello, all you friends of Dorothy out there,' Everett drawled in faux cockney. 'This is Sidney Aloysius Snot here to introduce a very important day in the social calendar of our great nation here. As you know, upcoming is the British Eurovision Violence Contest and here, ladies and gentlemen, may I introduce to you your British contender in said contest: Freddie . . .'

Mercury strolled on from the left in a leather cap, leather jacket and red PVC trousers, with a pair of handcuffs dangling from his belt. Before Everett had finished talking, Mercury had emptied a can of beer over the host's brothel creepers.

'Good start,' quipped Everett. ' . . . Mercury! Ladies and gentlemen, do your stuff, Freddie.'

Mercury then launched himself at Everett with remarkable speed, clamped his arms and thighs around the host's torso and pulled him to the floor. The camera cut away as Mercury forced Everett on to his back as if to straddle him. Kenny was shocked yet delighted by this spontaneous act of violence.

The pair's friendship wouldn't survive the rest of the decade, though. Later, Everett and Mercury were both having sex with the same man – a former Red Army soldier named Nikolai Grishanovich. It was just a fling for Freddie, but Kenny was besotted with the Russian.

They were also taking a lot of drugs. Kenny accused Freddie of snorting his cocaine and never sharing his own. 'Freddie couldn't believe his ears,' wrote former aide Peter Freestone. 'The boot was on the other foot and it was Kenny who was always appropriating anyone else's stash other than his own. They never spoke again after Christmas 1980.'

Everett's now ex-wife, Lady Lee, insisted Kenny and Freddie did speak again, but only after both men had been diagnosed with HIV. Everett wanted to make his peace with Mercury. They never resumed their friendship, though.

By the time Mercury died in 1991, Everett was seriously ill. He didn't attend his old friend's funeral. He told everybody he didn't like funerals and it wouldn't be any good because Freddie wasn't there. Kenny Everett died of an AIDS-related illness on 4 April 1995. He was fifty years old.

'THE FAIRY FELLER'S MASTER-STROKE'

Queen commit murder

Queen's song 'The Fairy Feller's Master-Stroke' has its roots in Victorian England. On 28 August 1843, the feted artist Richard Dadd and his father, pharmacist Robert, were taking a late stroll through Cobham Park, Kent. The pair had been drinking in a nearby tavern and Robert stopped to urinate in a bush. This was his son's cue to punch him in the head, slash his throat and stab him to death with a sailor's knife.

Dadd left his father's body in the undergrowth and fled the country on a boat to Calais. He was soon apprehended. In court, he claimed the Egyptian god Osiris had ordered him to murder his father. Dadd had been experiencing paranoid delusions and, during an earlier trip to Rome, had plotted to attack Pope Gregory XVI. He was declared criminally insane and committed to London's Bethlem Royal Hospital and, in 1864, to Broadmoor Criminal Lunatic Asylum.

Richard Dadd had previously been a promising star at the Royal Academy of Arts and one of an elite group of young painters known as the 'Clique'. He continued pursuing his art in hospital and spent six years creating his most famous work, *The Fairy Feller's Master-Stroke*. This devilishly intricate painting was inspired by a scene from *Romeo and Juliet* and depicts Shakespeare's fairy feller poised to make his master-stroke: hewing in half a chestnut, with which to build a carriage for the fairy Queen Mab.

The tableau was completed by a cast of nymphs, centaurs, gnats and a trumpet-playing dragonfly, with Dadd's singular use of perspective giving it a distorted, otherworldly aura. But he always insisted the painting was incomplete and even wrote a long poem, *Elimination of a Picture & Its Subject*, to explain it all.

Richard Dadd died of tuberculosis in 1886. His great nephew later gave the painting as a wedding gift to First World War poet Siegfried Sassoon, who donated it to the Tate Britain. It was there where Freddie Mercury's fascination took hold, inspiring Queen's song of the same name.

In 1974, Mercury spent many a Saturday afternoon at the Tate. One friend recalled him returning with a postcard of *The Fairy Feller's Master-Stroke*, only to utter a cry of disgust when he discovered the image had been printed in reverse. From now on, said Freddie, only the real thing would do . . .

While plotting Queen's second album, Mercury escorted both Roger Taylor and producer Roy Thomas Baker to the Tate to gaze upon his favourite painting. Freddie had written a song inspired by the work, but wanted the whole album to be equally dense and cinematic. 'He wanted it to be over the top,' said Baker.

Taylor spoke about the song in 2016. 'Where the hell did that come from?' he marvelled. 'It was full of these mystical references. I never once saw Freddie with a book. But he had all these words about this painting. Fred was like a magpie. He had this very sharp brain, but he was not what you'd call a well-read man.'

Queen bought the artwork to life, though. Mercury's lyrics – with vocabulary including 'ostler', 'dragonfly', 'pedagogue', 'tatterdemalion' and 'junketer' – borrowed from Dadd's poem, while his harpsichord panned from speaker to speaker in what Taylor called 'our biggest stereo experiment'.

Is this just fantasy?: *The Fairy Feller's Master-Stroke*
by Richard Dadd.

'The Fairy Feller's Master-Stroke' is also one of a select number of rock songs to feature the word 'apothecary' (others include Scritti Politti's 'Philosophy Now' and Elbow's 'My Sad Captain'). Yet, unknown to its composer, the tiny apothecary holding a pestle and mortar in the top-right of Dadd's painting was actually a miniature portrait of his father, Robert. Who knew that the poor pharmacist, stabbed to death by his son while peeing in a bush, was reincarnated in a Queen song?

FLASH GORDON

Queen go to the movies

In August 2020, Brian Blessed told *The Guardian* that *Flash Gordon* was the Queen's favourite film. Blessed, who'd played Prince Vultan in the movie, didn't divulge when Her Majesty told him this, only that she had.

'She watches it every Christmas,' he claimed. 'She said, "If you don't mind, I've got the grandchildren here, would you mind saying, 'Gordon's alive!'?"' Blessed could hardly refuse and bellowed *Flash Gordon*'s famous line of dialogue, presumably to the delight of young William and Harry.

This wasn't *Flash Gordon*'s first royal connection. There was also Queen's soundtrack. In 1980, a rock group had never scored a whole film that wasn't about rock music. 'And we wanted to be the first,' said Roger Taylor.

Flash Gordon began life as a 1930s comic strip about a college football hero sent to outer space to battle invading aliens. The strip had been spun off into three wartime serial movies before the 1980 remake by director Mike Hodges and producer 'Dino' De Laurentiis. Queen weren't Hodges's first choice; he'd asked Pink Floyd, but they were busy with their own film, *The Wall*. Meanwhile, De Laurentiis, the sixty-year-old auteur of Italian cinema, wasn't up on British pop culture. 'Who are the queens?' he asked Hodges.

Queen were shown twenty minutes of footage at Shepperton Studios and asked to demo some ideas. Hodges had zero experience of making science-fiction movies; he'd made his name with the 1971 gangster film *Get Carter*. But he envisaged a kitsch adventure romp, to which Queen responded in kind.

Di Laurentiis wasn't convinced, though. 'Dino made giant epic movies like *King Kong*,' said Brian May. 'He saw *Flash Gordon* as serious and dramatic and thought the music we'd written was too comic-book.' But Hodges assured him Queen were heading in the right direction and insisted they carry on.

Queen created their bespoke soundtrack at the same time as finishing their new album, *The Game*. Elton John's string arranger, Paul Buckmaster, was hired to score orchestral links, but failed to deliver. His replacement, Howard Blake (who'd later compose the soundtrack for Christmas movie *The Snowman*), was given ten days to complete the project. Three days before the deadline, he collapsed with stress-related bronchitis. Some of his orchestral score was then reproduced on Queen's new toy: the Oberheim OB-X synthesiser.

The whole thing was created on the fly and, with deadlines looming, Brian May took the reins. May spent hours in a film studio with a guitar, a synth and an amp, composing to clips playing on a screen. 'Today, it seems like an incredibly old-fashioned way of working, but that's how it was then. The music for *Gone with the Wind* was done the same way.' May and his co-producer, Reinhold Mack, finished *Flash Gordon* at London's

Town House and Advision Studios, while the rest of Queen completed *The Game* in Munich.

Flash Gordon opened in cinemas in December 1980. Hodges had stayed true to the original comic strip, but given it a knowing, post-*Star Wars* makeover. Flash, played by blond, square-jawed Sam J. Jones, archvillain Ming the Merciless (Max von Sydow) and Princess Aura (an often underdressed Ornella Muti) all looked as though they'd been drawn in an artist's studio. It's also the only film to star a future *Blue Peter* presenter (Peter Duncan) and a future James Bond (Timothy Dalton). Apparently, Brian Blessed dislikes *Flash Gordon* being described as camp. But wearing shiny wings and armour-plated bikini shorts while shouting 'Gordon's alive!' somewhat undermines his argument.

Three years earlier, *Star Wars* had brought subtle humour and elements of pastiche to the genre. *Flash Gordon* took this further, but without tipping over into complete parody. 'You were never quite sure what was serious and what was not,' suggested May. 'The film defined its own area.' Much like Queen and their music.

Britain was in on the joke and *Flash Gordon* became a UK box-office hit. America didn't get it, though. While Queen eventually won over De Laurentiis with their score, it created friction within the band. John Deacon was uncomfortable about May and Mack taking over and surprised when *Flash Gordon* was released as a new Queen album barely six months after *The Game*. It made the UK top ten but missed out on the American top twenty.

The soundtrack also confused those who'd recently discovered Queen via 'We Will Rock You' or 'Another One Bites the Dust'. It only included two conventional songs, 'The Hero' and future hit single 'Flash's Theme'. In contrast, 'Execution of Ming', 'The Kiss (Aura Resurrects Flash)' and 'Arboria (Planet of the Tree Men)' wove together wordless chants and Spaghetti Western-style guitar, ambient synths and classical orchestra. There's much to recommend and compare to critically revered scores by John Williams, John Barry and, later, Vangelis, although Queen's Oberheim OB-X now sounds as antiquated as 1981's Donkey Kong arcade game.

Besides making Queen the first rock group to score a non-rock movie, *Flash Gordon* broke new ground by splicing music with dialogue. This was Brian May's idea. Two years later, Vangelis's *Blade Runner* soundtrack did the same and then director Quentin Tarantino made it a feature of his soundtrack for 1994's *Pulp Fiction*, although Honey Bunny shrieking 'Any of you fucking pricks move and I'll execute every motherfuckin' last one of ya!' certainly had more dramatic oomph than Emperor Ming's 'Klytus, I'm bored, what plaything can you offer me today?'

Post *Flash Gordon*, other rock musicians began scoring films. Among them, Led Zeppelin's Jimmy Page for director Michael Winner's thriller *Death Wish II* and former Genesis frontman Peter Gabriel with Martin Scorsese's *The Last Temptation of Christ*.

Today, though, Queen's soundtrack lives in the shadow of Brian Blessed's catchphrase and 'Flash's Theme', the one song everybody knows. In 2016, corporate giant Proctor & Gamble used a new version in a TV ad campaign for Flash cleaning products. 'Flash! Aha! Cleans up the impossible!' trilled the session singer tasked with mimicking Freddie Mercury's falsetto.

In a 2021 interview with *Record Collector* magazine, Roger Taylor was asked if 'a little piece of him died every time the advert came on'.

'Oh, definitely, yeah. It's just awful, isn't it?' he replied. 'But at least it's not us doing it.'

40 FERRY ROAD

Buckingham Palace, circa 1970

Today, estate agents would describe 40 Ferry Road in Barnes as 'a highly desirable family residence'. With seven bedrooms, three bathrooms and two reception rooms, this London SW3 town-house is currently valued at over £3.5 million. But do its owners know that Freddie Mercury and Roger Taylor once slept in what is now one of the well-appointed reception rooms? Or that Brian May dossed down on a mattress in the other? 40 Ferry Road was once Queen's very own stately home.

When Mercury and Taylor arrived on 10 October 1969, the property was divided in two. Their landlady, Miss Scott-Allen, occupied the first floor and rented the one below. Students from Taylor's dentistry course, pre-Queen bandmates and future roadies, including John Harris of 'I'm in Love with My Car' fame, would live or crash at the house over the coming months. But it was Freddie and Roger's Liverpudlian friends Denise Craddock and Pat McConnell, students at the Maria Assumpta Teacher Training College, who officially moved in with them. Denise's letters and diaries later filled in the gaps in Queen's pre-history.

The house was almost palatial compared to most student accommodation. The parquet flooring and chintzy curtains were outdated, but there were French windows, a spacious garden, an upright piano in the living room and roses growing around the front door.

Miss Scott-Allen often grumbled about the noise, but she was more preoccupied with her next-door neighbour, the actor Sylvia Sims. 'She really didn't like Sylvia,' recalled John 'Tupp' Taylor, the bass guitarist in Mercury's early group, Ibex. 'She used to say, "Thespians are not reliable people, they're terribly second class."' She was more amenable to regular visitor Brian May. 'She had a crush on Brian,' recalled one ex-resident, 'which we used to tease him about.'

Domesticity was not high on anyone's agenda, though. The refrigerator and cupboards were frequently empty and Mercury struggled to find his share of the £25-a-month rent. For a time, Freddie and Roger had beds that folded away into the wall, affording them the opportunity for much hijinks after a night's drinking.

The Ferry Road soundtrack included the first Spooky Tooth album, the Who's *Tommy*, the first three Led Zeppelin albums, the Move's first LP, Frank Zappa's *We're Only in It for the Money*, Jimi Hendrix's first four albums (particularly *Electric Ladyland* and *Band of Gypsies*), Rod Stewart's *Gasoline Alley*, the Beatles' 'White Album' and Family's *Family Entertainment*.

May and Taylor moved out after meeting new girlfriends. Mercury did the same after beginning a relationship with Mary Austin. But it was in 40 Ferry Road's garden where he proposed the name Queen and where May first picked out the chords to 'Keep Yourself Alive'.

In 2005, Roger Taylor was asked to cast his mind back. What was Freddie Mercury like as a flatmate? 'Very tidy,' he replied, without a moment's hesitation. 'But we had no money and used to wait for his mum to send us a weekly hamper of food – and then I used to eat as much of it as I could.'

FRANK

I, Robot

In 2017, Queen + Adam Lambert celebrated the fortieth anniversary of *News of the World* with a world tour. By doing so, they brought the album's famous cover drawing back to life. A CGI image of the *News of the World* robot, nicknamed 'Frank', appeared on stage at the beginning of the show. He peered at the audience and extended his mechanical paw just as the band struck up the opening beat to 'We Will Rock You'.

In 1977, Frank's appearance earmarked *News of the World* as different from the five previous Queen albums. It was an unusually stark, strange image that reflected some of the music inside. Roger Taylor had suggested the picture. Taylor was an avid reader of science fiction and remembered seeing the robot in a magazine from his childhood.

Artist Frank Kelly Freas had drawn the machine for *The Gulf Between*, a novella by author Tom Godwin published in the October 1953 edition of *Astounding Science Fiction* magazine. Godwin's story explored the complex relationship between men and machines. In Freas's original, the robot cradled a wounded human in its hand.

Queen found Freas and asked him to recreate the work, but with the robot attempting to save Queen. 'I decided to do the drawing before listening to Queen because I thought I might hate them,' said Freas (who died in 2005). He listened to their music later and was pleasantly surprised to find he didn't.

To the outside world, though, Frank the robot looked like a monster. 'He's not a monster; he's a likable machine who is baffled,' explained Brian May. 'He holds these bloody, injured people in his palm and he doesn't know what to do with them.' But most who saw the image presumed the robot was dropping the band members to their deaths. Freddie Mercury was already bleeding out and Roger Taylor was falling into oblivion.

EMI Records also had some misgivings: they'd wanted Queen to have a band photo on the cover instead. Undeterred, however, the company created a set of extremely expensive promotional robot clocks.

Forty years later, Frank was back from the dead. As well as an appearance in the Q + AL live show, he adorned a limited-edition 'Frank Special' guitar (£995 in the UK). Brian May's fabled Red Special was repurposed with that familiar metallic silver robot face decorating the body. Frank lives on. And Queen are still his biggest fans.

'*News of the World* is my favourite Queen album cover,' said Roger Taylor in 2021, 'because it's the one everybody remembers.'

Comic-book hero: Roger Taylor with the original 'Frank' on the cover of *Astounding Science Fiction* magazine, 1977.

FREDDIE'S FUNERAL
'*All God's People*'

Daily Mirror writer Joe Haines's article was published the day after Freddie Mercury's funeral. 'With an enormous effort of will, I won't say a word about the music of Freddie Mercury,' it began, 'except that I would prefer to spend a night stark naked on an Arctic ice-cap rather than listen to it.' Haines then described Mercury as 'sheer poison, a man bent – the apt word in the circumstances – on abnormal sexual pleasures', adding that 'his private life is a revolting tale of depravity, lust and downright wickedness'.

Haines's comments attracted criticism, but quickly became tomorrow's fish-and-chip paper. His article was then rediscovered by Queen biographers and, most recently, by comic actor Matt Lucas. 'I was 17 when Freddie died and the Daily Mirror published this article,' wrote Lucas in 2019, attaching an image of Haines's original column. 'We've come a long way.'

In 1991, though, Haines's opinion illustrated the widespread ignorance and prejudice surrounding HIV and AIDS. This was partly the reason behind Mercury's decision not to share his diagnosis publicly. He didn't want any discrimination to affect his bandmates and their families. Reporters and photographers had been camped outside his home, Garden Lodge, for months. Mercury, regardless of his declining health, had become a prisoner in his own home. But an official statement about his illness was only released a few hours before he passed away on 24 November 1991. Mercury had chosen to stop taking his medication some days earlier, thereby hastening his death. The official cause was later listed as 'bronchopneumonia b. AIDS'.

However, the Queen office's handling of Mercury's funeral and the press reflected the fears and prejudice of the time. Mercury had lived at Garden Lodge with his long-term partner Jim Hutton, his chef and former lover Joe Fanelli, and his personal aide Peter Freestone. They, along with Mary Austin, had nursed him twenty-four hours a day.

The day after his death, the *Daily Mirror* splashed a front-page interview with Mercury's friend, the musician Dave Clark, who talked about how he'd been with Mercury during his final hours.

Many of the *Mirror*'s readers knew Clark as the drummer of '60s pop group the Dave Clark Five (biggest hit: 'Glad All Over'). Clark's interview was joined by one with Mary Austin. There was no mention of Hutton, Fanelli or Freestone.

In the Zoroastrian faith, funerals should take place as soon as possible after death. Mercury had requested the same. His service was held just three days later, at 10 a.m. on 27 November, at West London Crematorium in Kensal Green. It was a funeral for two people, though: Freddie Mercury, the rock star, and Farrokh Bulsara, the man he'd once been.

It was also stage-managed. Mercury's Munich friend and ex-lover Barbara Valentin was told not to attend. There was room for only one wife, Mary Austin, who travelled, along with Dave Clark, in the first funeral car. Jim Hutton travelled in another vehicle further back in the funeral cortège, accompanied by Fanelli and Freestone.

The grounds of the crematorium were filled with wreaths and bouquets – among them yellow roses from David Bowie and pink rosebuds from Elton John. Mercury's coffin was carried in to Aretha Franklin's 'You've Got a Friend'. The dichotomy between Freddie Mercury and Farrokh Bulsara soon became obvious. Freddie's parents, Bomi and Jer, had requested a traditional ceremony for their son. This involved Parsee priests reciting prayers in the ancient language of Avestan or Zend, as used in the Zoroastrian scriptures.

Mercury's Queen bandmates and many of their fellow mourners listened uncomprehendingly. 'None of us understood a word of it,' said Elton John. 'It was kind of demoralising and upsetting.' But it gave them a glimpse of the world into which their friend had been born – a long way from London, the Marquee and Jimi Hendrix. It was a world Mercury had rarely discussed with them.

Freddie made his exit to a recording of Verdi's *D'amor sull'ali rosee*, sung by his friend and musical partner Montserrat Caballé.

Celebrity photographer Richard Young had been hired by the Queen office to record the event. His pictures captured Queen and their familiars, everybody black-clad and wan-faced, gazing at the coffin, the flowers and each other; everybody still coming to terms with their loss.

In his final press statement, Mercury requested, 'I hope everyone will join me, my doctors and all those worldwide in the fight against this terrible disease.' Joe Haines's subsequent article was a blunt reminder of how far they still had to go.

It was a complex issue. The Queen organisation had handled the press surrounding Mercury's death in such a way as to deflect attention away from his sexuality. Mary Austin and Dave Clark were not the only ones who had been with him during his final hours, but both were regarded as more acceptable to newspaper readers in 1991 than Mercury's male lover and his gay friends. Hutton and Freestone would later write books challenging the official account of Mercury's final hours. Bad blood and recrimination would linger for years.

Mary Austin inherited Garden Lodge, much of Mercury's fortune and his ashes. She has never divulged where they're scattered. 'He wanted it to remain a secret and it will remain so,' she said.

Within a week of Mercury's death, Queen announced their plans to stage a concert in his memory to raise money for the fight against HIV and AIDS. The stigma surrounding the disease had failed to damage Mercury's legacy – most of Queen's fanbase didn't care or discriminate – and the re-released 'Bohemian Rhapsody' went to number one.

Mercury's parting statement was also grimly ironic. Had he contracted the disease later, medication would have been available to alleviate his suffering and even prolong his life. 'If Freddie had lived another twelve months, it could have happened,' Brian May suggested.

May was once asked whether he still had dreams about his friend. 'From time to time,' he replied, 'and, for some reason, he's always talking to me. I had one dream not long after he died where he kept saying, "You've got to be there, Brian, you've got to be there." And I woke up in a daze thinking, "Where have I got to be?"' He never found out the answer.

THE GAME

Queen versus nature

The föhn is a dry wind that blows in from the mountains of Switzerland, Austria and southern Germany. It's a natural phenomenon with an unnatural reputation. Over the centuries, this wind has been blamed for everything from mild ailments to psychotic behaviour and even suicide. In 1931, Adolf Hitler's half-niece, 'Geli' Raubal, died from a self-inflicted gunshot wound in the führer's Munich apartment. Hitler blamed her death on the föhn.

Queen arrived in Munich in summer 1979. They were living away from their loved ones and billeted in two drab, monolithic buildings: the Park Hilton hotel and its neighbouring tower block, the Arabellahaus, which housed Musicland Studios.

Brian May soon learned about the föhn. 'It blows up from Bavaria and makes people go crazy and have suicidal thoughts,' he explained. Several people had leapt to their deaths from the roof of Queen's hotel – the last thing their sensitive guitarist needed to hear.

The Game was Queen's first album of the 1980s and their first recorded in Munich. It marked the beginning of a love/hate relationship with the city and a major change in the way they made records. 'Musically, Munich was great,' said May. 'Emotionally, less so.'

When Queen first came to Germany, they were still on a tax year out. The Jazz Tour had just ended in Japan, but the album hadn't sold as well as *News of the World*. Musicland (owned by musician Giorgio Moroder) and its resident producer, Reinhold Mack, came highly recommended. Mack had recently engineered ELO's hit albums *A New World Record* and *Out of the Blue*. Queen hoped a new environment and Mack's Midas touch might rejuvenate them.

Straight away, Mack started pushing Queen out of their comfort zone. He told them that their recent work sounded 'a little stiff' and they needed more spontaneity. He introduced the idea of splicing together different edits – 'dropping in', as it was called – instead of redoing every backing track whenever someone made a mistake. At first, they resisted. 'We laughed, "Don't be silly!"' said May. But the results were immediate and effective.

Queen's next hit single, 'Crazy Little Thing Called Love', was recorded in hours rather than days. Released in October 1979, it was a huge hit in Britain and America. In keeping with this stripped-down approach, Queen booked the eighteen-date Crazy Tour, visiting clubs and small theatres around the UK. Having played only a few British shows the previous year, these intimate winter gigs were sold as a 'thank you' to their fans. While there was something marvellously incongruous about a band of Queen's stature playing Tiffany's nightclub in Croydon, it was also a logistical nightmare.

Queen had been touring with a gargantuan, red, white and green lighting rig, nicknamed the 'Pizza Oven'. Its heat was such that Roger Taylor, perched on his drum podium, claimed it was burning his scalp. However, the crew had to drill two enormous holes in the ceiling of London's Lyceum to accommodate the rig and it wouldn't even fit in the Tottenham Mayfair. Queen's tour manager, Gerry Stickells, later collapsed backstage with nervous exhaustion. Queen had broken him.

They returned to Musicland in February 1980 with new material, ideas and instruments. After years of resisting, Taylor had purchased an Oberheim OB-X synthesiser. Queen had broken their 'no synths' rule and would never look back.

There's a case to be made for *The Game* as Queen's first pop album. Its Elvis homage 'Crazy Little Thing Called Love' and its dancefloor hit 'Another One Bites the Dust' compound this theory all by themselves. It's important to remember how left-field John Deacon's disco song was considered at the time. Even today, May and Taylor disagree over how they initially reacted to it. But the lightness and clarity of both singles informed the rest of the album.

Underneath it all, 'Play the Game' was a workaday power ballad. But there wasn't a wasted note or harmony. Mercury sang about his most recent lover, a motorcycle courier named Tony Bastin. Freddie showered him with gifts, but later discovered Tony had been unfaithful while the band were on tour. Revenge was bitter-sweet. Mercury flew Tony out to join Queen in North Carolina, told him the relationship was over and then put him on the next flight home. Bastin didn't even have time to unpack his bags.

Mercury's tortuous love life crept into his third song on the album, too. The throwaway 'Don't Try Suicide' wasn't inspired by the deadly föhn, but by Freddie's ex-boyfriend, David Minns. Apparently, Minns had taken an overdose after Mercury ordered him to leave their flat. 'In my honour, he wrote "Don't Try Suicide", [with the lyric] "Nobody gives a damn",' said Minns in 1992. 'How sweet of him.'

Elsewhere, 'Another One Bites the Dust' gave John Deacon a free pass for 'Need Your Love Tonight', his tilt at the skinny-tied power pop that was haring up the American charts in 1980 thanks to bands such as Blondie and the Knack.

Roger Taylor's contributions fully embraced the notion of a new Queen. 'Rock It (Prime Jive)' suggested a jaunty reboot of Chris Montez's '60s hit 'Let's Dance'. It was basic and elemental, with hokey lyrics about the power of rock 'n' roll. But it worked. Two versions were recorded: one with Mercury singing lead; the other with Taylor. After a heated discussion, Mack dropped Mercury's introductory vocal on to Taylor's vocal track. Taylor's second song, 'Coming Soon', was another vogueish stab at new wave. 'I think we were functioning well as a group,' Taylor said. '*The Game* was a good time for Queen.'

That just left Brian May, who was trying to find his place in this new music. It wasn't easy. After another blazing row with his bandmates, he ended up roaming Englischer Garten, a large public park in the heart of Munich. 'I was walking around thinking, "This is over, I'm never going to do this again,"' he said. 'But then you get back in there . . .'

May was frustrated about not having more of his songs on the record. He'd already suggested that they make *The Game* a concept album, but had been shouted down as 'a pretentious fart'. He was also drinking too much. They all were.

Queen had been introduced to an exclusive Munich nightclub called the Sugar Shack. It had an endless supply of Russian vodka and an amazing sound system. Queen started bringing tracks to the club to gauge how they sounded on the dancefloor. Deacon's 'Another One Bites the Dust' was a perfect fit. Some of Brian's songs, less so.

May rose to the challenge by writing *The Game*'s spare, rhythmic 'Dragon Attack'. The song grew out of a drunken, after-hours jam. But, while Mack pushed for speed and spontaneity, May found it hard knowing when to stop. 'I was always the one still sat there in the studio at three o'clock in the morning,' he admitted.

Both 'Sail Away Sweet Sister' and 'Save Me' had a reflective air. May wrote 'Save Me' about a friend 'whose relationship is totally fucked up'. But it's hard not to wonder whether it was partly autobiographical – they were heartfelt songs, but the only ones that sounded like they came from an earlier Queen album.

The Game turned up in record shops in June 1980. After two heraldic crests, one dead-eyed robot and *Jazz*'s concentric circles, the band themselves finally appeared on an album sleeve. 'Play the Game', 'Another One Bites the Dust' and 'Save Me' would all become hits and, soon after its release, *The Game* was at number one in the UK and America. 'I remember we outsold the new Rolling Stones record,' said Taylor, 'and I remember being terribly pleased about that.'

Queen finally went home, leaving behind a trail of empty vodka bottles and an astronomical black hole in the Sugar Shack's bar takings. But they would be back in Munich soon enough. Even the evil föhn blowing in from Bavaria couldn't keep them away.

GROSE, MIKE
Queen's bass player, no. 1

Mike Grose, Queen's original bass guitarist, died in May 2019. He was often asked to talk about his time with Queen and usually refused. 'I've said all I've got to say,' was his standard reply. Grose granted the occasional interview in later years, but one could understand his reticence. Being called the 'Pete Best of Queen' by music magazine *Q* hardly helped.

Like Roger Taylor, Mike Grose was a Cornishman. 'I first heard him in a band called the Individuals when we were both still at school,' said Taylor. 'He always sounded huge.' Grose went on to play briefly with Taylor's group the Reaction and once understudied for Tim Staffell in Smile, making him the obvious choice to replace Staffell when Smile folded in June 1970. Besides being what Brian May called 'a massive and monolithic' bass player, Grose also had a van and a Marshall amp – useful accessories for any new group.

That summer, Mike Grose moved to London and into 40 Ferry Road. He was present in the group's first publicity shots and recalled listening to Freddie Mercury pitching their new name: 'I said, "Queen? Are you sure, Freddie?" In those days, it was risky . . .'

Grose only played four shows with the band: their debut at Truro City Hall; two at Imperial College; and one, his last, at PJ's Club, Truro.

The day after the PJ's date, Roger Taylor threw a twenty-first birthday party at his parents' house in Cornwall. When the rest of Queen were about to drive back to London, Grose told them that he was staying behind. Unlike Pete Best, he wasn't fired; he chose to quit. In Cornwall, he'd got used to having a day job, playing gigs in the evenings and earning money. In London, his bandmates were either students or working at Kensington Market, meaning Grose spent his days alone at Ferry Road 'with sod all to do' and very little money with which to do it.

'I thought they were a great band. I truly mean that,' he said in 2011. 'But I was twenty-two and it was five years before they broke through properly. You're twenty-seven and that's part of your life gone. I also missed Cornwall.'

Mike Grose remained in his home county, played the occasional gig and worked in his family's haulage business in St Austell for the rest of his life. He was still a director of N. J. Grose Ltd when he passed away.

'The liaison didn't work out,' said Brian May after learning of Grose's death. 'But we owe Mike gratitude for helping us take those first steps.'

'HAMMER TO FALL'

Queen ban the bomb

Before enrolling at Imperial College in autumn 1965, Brian May took a holiday job at the Guided Weapons research centre in his native Feltham. His tasks included feeding numbers into arcane mechanical calculators 'until smoke started to pour out of them', but the work also presented him with a moral dilemma. 'I wasn't sure how I felt about weapons research then,' he said in 1998. 'But I know I'd have a problem with it now.'

May hadn't forgotten the 1962 Cuban Missile Crisis. As a teenager, he'd held his breath, along with the rest of the world, as the US and the Soviet Union teetered on the brink of nuclear war. The crisis only amplified his existing fears about nuclear Armageddon. 'I used to have dreams night after night where I saw the flash and the mushroom cloud,' he said.

May channelled some of his worries into Queen's 1984 single 'Hammer to Fall'. At the time, the US and the Soviet Union were engaged in a Cold War of espionage and attrition and, as the song goes, everyone was still living 'in the shadow of the mushroom cloud'.

'The song is more about life and death in general,' clarified May in 2004. 'How it comes to us all and does not discriminate.'

But, in contrary Queen style, its nagging hook takes the sting out of lyrics threatening the arrival of an arbitrary grim reaper. 'Hammer to Fall' is a jolly-sounding knees-up – so jolly, in fact, that Queen played it at Live Aid.

'Hammer to Fall' was a top-fifteen hit in Britain, but flatlined in America. In 2017, it was revived for an episode of US sci-fi thriller series *Stranger Things*. On the show, set in 1984, Queen's flop was paired with topical hits by glam-rockers Ratt and Bon Jovi.

'It's a good, loud rock song,' said Roger Taylor in 2011. Or, as a drunk Freddie Mercury once declared on stage at Auckland's Mount Smart Stadium in 1985, it's 'one for all you heavy-metal fans to have a good jerk-off to!'

THE HECTICS

Whatever happened to Freddie Mercury's first group?

On the evening of 29 October 1979, Freddie Mercury was at home in London watching the first episode of new TV comedy *Only When I Laugh*. The show was built around the flimsy premise of three male patients with indeterminate health issues billeted together in a hospital ward. It paired a dour working-class Geordie, played by *Likely Lad* James Bolam, with Peter Bowles's silk dressing-gowned southerner. In the bed between them was their naive young sidekick, played by Christopher Strauli.

One of the supporting cast was Derrick Branche, Mercury's old schoolfriend from India and the guitarist in his first musical group, the Hectics. Branche played Gupte, a staff nurse whose

role largely involved dashing in and out of the ward looking exas-
perated. 'I wish I was back in Delhi,' he grumbled at one point. 'I
could open a restaurant . . .'

In one scene, James Bolam's character refers to Gupte as
'Gandhi'; in another, as 'Gunga Din'. According to a mutual
friend, Mercury's reaction to these racial stereotypes was less than
favourable. However, roles for Asian actors were scarce in the
'70s and they were invariably typecast. That same year, Derrick
Branche played a Papua New Guinean terrorist and an Arab
sheik. Gupte remained in *Only When I Laugh* for three series; his
character disappeared following the 1981 Christmas special.

Like Mercury, Derrick Branche arrived in Britain in the
mid-'60s hoping for a life in showbusiness. In 1958, aged twelve,
both boys took their first steps with the Hectics, a group of aspiring
Elvis Presleys at St Peter's School in Panchgani.

The movie *Bohemian Rhapsody* skipped over Mercury's life in
India. But then so did Mercury himself. Only once in an interview
did he discuss his childhood in any detail. 'My parents were very
strict,' he divulged. 'They thought boarding school would do me
good. So, when I was about seven, I was put in one in India for a
while.' He never publicly discussed the Hectics.

The group's line-up was completed by friends of Mercury and
Branche from Ashlin House dormitory: Victory Rana, Farang
Irani and band founder Bruce Murray. Mercury commandeered
the school's upright piano; Rana chose the drums; Branche played
guitar and harmonica; and Irani built a homemade tea-chest
bass. 'I had the good looks and the charm, so I sang,' said Bruce
Murray.

Listening to western pop music wasn't encouraged at St
Peter's, but the boys found their fix on Radio Ceylon. Their
heroes, Elvis, Little Richard, Ricky Nelson and Fats Domino, were
all played on the station's *Binaca Hit Parade*, a weekly programme
sponsored by India's leading toothpaste brand. It was their little

glimpse of a glamorous showbiz world far away from the foothills of Maharashtra.

'We started the group mainly to impress girls,' said Murray. His strategy paid off. The Hectics' appearances at functions and fetes allowed them to mix with pupils from a neighbouring girls' school. Their young female admirers clapped and screamed 'as if we were the Beatles or something', said Farang Irani. Over time, their setlists included the Coasters' 'Yakety Yak', Elvis's 'The Girl of My Best Friend', Bill Haley & His Comets' 'Rock Around the Clock' and Jim Reeves's 'Ramona'.

'But I don't remember Freddie being any kind of showman,' said Irani, who was photographed performing with one foot on top of his tea-chest bass like he was preparing to stage-dive. As much as he enjoyed playing, Mercury was happy to let Bruce Murray front the group. Freddie was self-conscious about his protruding front teeth. His school nickname was 'Bucky' and, when he smiled, he instinctively put a hand over his mouth – a habit he never lost.

Where Mercury excelled, though, was as a musician. 'None of us were any good except him,' insisted Murray. 'If we heard a new song on the *Binaca Hit Parade* and liked it, Freddie would quickly learn the chords and teach us.'

The Hectics continued to indulge their pop-star fantasies until their time at St Peter's came to an end in summer 1962. Only Farang Irani remained in India, working in his family's restaurant in Mumbai. He later opened his own diner, the Bounty Sizzlers, in Pune and launched the Freddie Mercury Indian School Experience, a sightseeing excursion for tourists. He died in 2018.

Drummer Victory Rana's life took a different turn. In 1966, he joined the Nepalese army as a cadet. He later attended Sandhurst, the UK's world-famous royal military academy, before graduating from the US Army War College in Carlisle, Pennsylvania. Rana's distinguished service record saw him achieve the rank of major-general in the Nepalese army. In 1999, Kofi Annan, UN secretary-general at the time, appointed Rana force commander of the United Nations Peacekeeping Force in Cyprus. His last assignment before retiring was as the Nepalese ambassador to Myanmar.

Rana was the only one of the Hectics unaware that his school-mate had become 'Freddie Mercury, rock star'. After Mercury's death in 1991, Rana was astounded when a friend sent him a magazine article. 'It was only then I learned his whole story,' said Rana in 2016. 'I went out and bought a couple of CDs.'

Mercury didn't reappear fully in the lives of Bruce Murray or Derrick Branche until October 1974 when they both saw him on *Top of the Pops*. A few weeks later, Murray, who was working as a minicab driver in south London, went to the Rainbow Theatre where Queen were playing. After the show, he found himself peering at his old schoolfriend through a limousine window. 'What the fuck are you doing here?' asked an astonished Mercury. The two went to a club in Berkeley Square where they talked for the first time since leaving India.

For a while, Mercury started booking his old lead singer to drive him to showbiz functions. But Murray had some reserva-tions. 'I took him to one and the host was Elton John. Fred asked me to come in, but I didn't want to seem like a hanger-on.'

Murray last saw Freddie Mercury in America in December 1977. Bruce had gone to visit his mother, who was now living in Las Vegas. During Bruce's stay, Queen played the city's Aladdin Centre concert hall and casino. 'I went backstage and Fred seemed genuinely pleased to see me. We spoke for a few minutes and then he was gone,' Murray said. 'Our lives had changed.'

In time, Murray returned to the music business, playing in pub bands, running a music shop and managing his son-in-law's group, the Quireboys. Always gracious and willing to talk about his schoolfriend, Murray was asked his opinion of the *Bohemian*

Rhapsody biopic. 'I thought it was fantastic,' he replied. 'Some of the sequences weren't quite right, but, hey, it's a movie . . .'

Meanwhile, Derrick Branche went on to play a drug dealer in the 1985 movie *My Beautiful Laundrette*, an acclaimed drama exploring race, culture and politics in Thatcher-era Britain. He was last spotted on British TV as a sexually frustrated Cuban priest, with a Freddie-style 'tache, in the comedy series *Father Ted*. Branche then returned to India and has lived in Goa ever since.

In 2016, the culture journalist Anvar Alikhan tracked down three of the four surviving Hectics for an article commemorating what would have been Mercury's seventieth birthday. He asked to speak to Derrick Branche via a third party and later received a message back: 'Freddie was a lovely man, highly talented, fun-loving and a good friend,' Branche wrote. 'But I don't like to talk about anybody, dead or alive.'

HENDRIX, JIMI
Pop idol

Queen loved Jimi Hendrix. But none of them loved Jimi Hendrix as much as Freddie Mercury. 'Jimi Hendrix was my idol,' he once said. 'I would scour the country to see him.' Freddie's trips across Britain in pursuit of Jimi passed into Queen folklore. Roger Taylor claims Mercury saw him 'fourteen nights in a row in different pubs around the country'.

The obsession started in December 1966 when the Jimi Hendrix Experience released their first single, 'Hey Joe'. The sound was loose and heavy and, above all else, free. Most British rock guitarists took a scholarly approach to their craft. Hendrix played his instrument down on his knees, behind his head, with his teeth and between his thighs. He was as commanding a showman as he was a musician.

There was perhaps another attraction for a young immigrant in 1960s London: Hendrix's mixed African-American, Irish and Cherokee heritage. He was a black musician conquering a white-dominated rock world. 'He was living out everything I wanted to be,' said Mercury, who first saw his hero at London's Blaises on 21 December 1966 and then at the Marquee the following month. He was on a roll . . .

Hendrix never actually played fourteen pubs in a row, but he performed in cinemas and theatres across the country in spring 1967. Mercury's art-school friends remember him disappearing 'to go to see Hendrix' and returning days later. This led to a showdown with college principal James Drew, who, rather than expel Freddie, allowed him to change course from fashion to graphic design the following term.

The move did little to quell Freddie's obsession. Mercury compared Hendrix to the abstract expressionist painter Jackson Pollock, imagining his guitar solos like wild splashes of colour on a canvas. Just a burst of his hit 'Purple Haze' on the radio in the art studio was enough to get Freddie on his feet, mouthing the lyrics and 'playing' a T-square (left-handed, like Jimi).

Rosemary Pearson, Mercury's girlfriend at the time, recalled how the couple could be walking down a street when Freddie would start crooning Hendrix's 'Have You Ever Been (To Electric Ladyland)'. 'Just hearing it in my head makes me feel like a pagoda gyrating in the sky!' he told her. 'And, in an instant, he was off, moving like a whirling dervish,' she said.

Brian May had his first Hendrix experience on 29 January 1967 at London's Savile Theatre. He had mixed feelings: 'I'd put a lot of work into playing guitar. But Hendrix came along and destroyed everyone. When I saw him, I felt excited, overwhelmed and also completely deflated.'

A month later, May, who was on the student entertainment committee at Imperial College, booked Hendrix to play for £1,000, though he didn't quite manage to speak to his hero: 'Jimi came out of the dressing room and said, "Where's the stage, man?" We just pointed, starstruck.' By that point, May's band-mates had nicknamed him 'Brimi' in Jimi's honour.

Hendrix caused a similar stir in Roger Taylor's life. On 25 April, the drummer and his friends skived off school early and made the trip from Truro to Bristol to see their idol. Soon after, the Reaction were playing 'Foxy Lady' and Taylor's bass drum was decorated with a painting of his new hero.

A shared appreciation of Hendrix was one of the bonds that drew the members of Queen together. In summer 1970, May visited Mercury at his parents' house shortly after they'd formed the group. There was a photo of Jimi pinned to a mirror and drawings of him scattered around Freddie's bedroom.

Mercury put on Hendrix's second album, *Axis: Bold as Love*. 'He goes, "Brian, Brian, Brian, listen, listen, listen." And I go, "Yes, it's Jimi Hendrix."' May recalled. 'And he goes, "No, no, listen to what they do in the production."' Mercury was fascinated by the way the guitar panned from speaker to speaker. 'This is the kind of thing we have to do,' he told May. 'This is what we're gonna do.'

Later, Freddie put his art-school thesis up for sale on the stall he and Roger ran at Kensington Market. 'The whole thing was based on Hendrix,' Taylor said. 'There were some beautiful things in there. He'd written out the lyrics to "Third Stone from the Sun".' It sold for a pittance, but 'would probably be worth thousands now'.

Hendrix died on 18 September 1970 at his girlfriend's flat in the Samarkand Hotel on Lansdowne Crescent, barely a couple of miles from Queen's stamping ground. Queen were rehearsing at Imperial College that evening. They played 'Stone Free', 'Voodoo Chile' and 'Foxy Lady' and Mercury and Taylor closed their market stall as 'a mark of respect' the next day.

In June 2020, readers of *Total Guitar* magazine voted Brian May the world's number-one guitarist, with Hendrix at number two. 'I'm absolutely speechless, deeply touched,' Brimi wrote. 'But Jimi is, of course, my number one. To me, he's still something superhuman. It's like he really did come from an alien planet and I will never know how he did what he did.'

HERBST, CHRISTIAN

Professor of Queen

In 2016, the Austrian voice scientist Professor Christian Herbst and a team of researchers published a study titled 'Freddie Mercury: Acoustic Analysis of Speaking Fundamental Frequency, Vibrato and Subharmonics'. Herbst was fascinated by Mercury's vocal technique and wanted 'to arrive at more empirically based insights into [his] voice production and singing style'.

Herbst's researchers analysed six recordings of Mercury's speaking voice from interviews conducted between 1984 and '87 and twenty-eight different vocal performances. They also hired a singer to mimic Mercury's vocals and filmed his larynx with a high-speed endoscopic camera.

They made several discoveries. Apparently, Mercury sung his lowest recorded note on 'Don't Try Suicide' and his highest on 'All God's People' and 'Hang on in There'. After listening to 'Seaside Rendezvous', 'Love of My Life', 'Keep Passing the Open Windows' and 'Teo Torriatte (Let Us Cling Together)', they deduced that his familiar vocal characteristics were achieved by blending higher and lower registers (known as 'chest' and 'falsetto') and by switching easily between 'breathy' and 'pressed' phonation.

The study also revealed that Mercury had a baritone speaking voice. His duet partner, opera singer Montserrat Caballé, once asked Mercury if he'd sing a baritone/soprano duet with her. He refused, claiming his audience only knew him as a tenor and 'wouldn't recognise my voice'.

Musicians who performed with Mercury early in his career recalled his 'strange vibrato', with Roger Taylor comparing him to a 'powerful bleating sheep'. Herbst's team discovered that the main component of Mercury's vocal fingerprint was his vibrato technique. 'Typically, an opera singer's vibrato has a frequency of about 5.5–6 Hz,' said Herbst. 'Freddie Mercury's is higher and also more irregular.' They offered the line 'Goodbye, everybody, I got to go' in 'Bohemian Rhapsody' as a good example.

Mercury also used intentional distortion. An endoscopic camera recorded 4,000 frames per second of the hired singer's larynx. By impersonating Mercury's vibrato, he revealed that Freddie used tissue structures in his throat, known as ventricular folds. These were rarely used in classical singing, but popularly used in Tuvan throat singing, as practised by the indigenous peoples of Tuva, Mongolia and Siberia.

'Freddie always had a unique way of singing,' said Roger Taylor. 'He never really sounded like anybody else.' Christian Herbst and his team finally discovered why.

HOT SPACE
Queen's worst album?

There's a great scene three minutes into the video for Queen's single 'Body Language'. Until that point, the song's shimmying bassline has been paired with shadowy images of black lingerie and bare flesh. Then the band flicker into view. When the camera reaches Roger Taylor, he raises his eyebrows. The gesture only lasts for a second, but says so much. Asked about the song and video years later, Taylor replied, 'Not a bad record – but it wasn't really us, was it?'

'Body Language' was the first single from Queen's tenth studio album, *Hot Space*. It's always divided opinion. 'It was an experiment,' said Brian May. 'We got sidetracked,' said Taylor. 'A disappointment,' said John Deacon. 'Only a bloody record,' said Freddie Mercury . . .

While *The Game* had brought the band a new fanbase, Queen were now ten years old (veterans by '80s pop standards) and had four distinct musical personalities fighting to be heard. 'I could never get more than two songs on a Queen album,' Taylor said. 'So I wanted to be selfish and have the palette to myself.' In April 1981, Taylor released his debut solo record, *Fun in Space*. It was only a modest hit, but this was the first time a member of Queen had stepped away from the mothership.

Queen could now afford to experiment. With an annual salary of £700,000 each, they'd just been declared Britain's highest-paid company directors in *The Guinness Book of Records*. They'd also bought Montreux's Mountain Studios. Queen spent several weeks recording new songs at Mountain in summer 1981. Among them was 'Cool Cat', written and performed by Mercury and John Deacon without the others. Its sleepy soul and Al Green-style falsetto was left-field even by Queen's standards.

David Bowie, who was also at Mountain recording for the *Cat People* film soundtrack, sang backing vocals on the song. It became the catalyst for the 'Under Pressure' duet, although Bowie's domineering presence upset Queen's delicate balance of egos. 'Under Pressure' outshone everything else on the finished album and became a big hit. But, like the rest of Hot Space, it was an artistic struggle from beginning to end.

Work resumed in January 1982 in Munich. Queen were committed to exploring new ideas, though they disagreed about how far they should go. Mercury wanted them to make the kind of dance music he heard in clubs. Deacon, buoyed by 'Another One Bites the Dust', agreed. Taylor was cautious and May fretted about where he fitted in. Co-producer Mack was there to referee.

Mercury stripped everything back on 'Body Language', including the lyrics, which barely made it past 'Give me . . . your body'. This was not the tongue-twisting 'pedagogues', 'tatterdemalions' and 'junketers' of 'The Fairy Feller's Master-Stroke'. But the video, directed by *Flash Gordon*'s Mike Hodges, showed more female than male flesh. 'It was cloaked in a heterosexual veneer,' suggested Brian May. 'But, in his private life, Freddie was immersed in the gay world and I think the people around him were waiting for him to do something like this.'

By 'the people', he meant Paul Prenter, Mercury's personal manager. Prenter was busy convincing the singer that he didn't need Queen any more and that rock music and May's guitar-playing especially were old-fashioned. 'Prenter wanted our music to sound like you'd just walked into a gay bar,' said Taylor. 'And I didn't.'

'But Freddie was a true extremist,' said May. 'He'd get an idea in his head and take it to the nth degree.' Mercury's 'Staying Power' (working title: 'Fucking Power') was another hymn to lust, with horn parts arranged by R&B royalty Arif Mardin, who'd produced hits for Aretha Franklin and the Bee Gees. Mardin's 'hot and spacey horns' replaced May's guitar.

This wasn't an isolated incident. John Deacon informed Brian that he didn't want him playing on his songs any more. 'On that album, we abandoned most of the methods that we'd grown to love and trust,' said May. 'Some of it was quite painful.'

Deacon played rhythm guitar on his song 'Back Chat'. May wanted to add a solo, but Deacon refused to let him. May eventually got his way to the benefit of the finished track. Although Mercury's jive-talking outro ('You been givin' me the runaround? Yes, ah have!') made the teeth itch.

Roger Taylor found the middle ground, borrowing wartime leader Winston Churchill's saying for his punchy-sounding 'Action This Day'. His other contribution – the superior 'Calling All Girls' – also featured its composer, rather than Brian, playing guitar.

Once again, Queen were living miles away from home in a self-imposed bubble: the Hilton Hotel; Musicland; the Sugar Shack disco; and Mercury's favourite club, Henderson's. Their support network were roadies, barmaids, dealers, clubbers and Mack. Queen's new songs were played through the Sugar Shack's sound system and then dissected. Was it hot enough? Was it spacey enough? . . .

Most days, work started later and later. Everybody was hungover and sleep-deprived, tempers frayed and band members walked out. Mercury hated being in the studio and wanted to sing his parts quickly so he could get back to the clubs. Mack, meanwhile, tried to impose order. His wife, Ingrid, was due to give birth and he started to measure the gestation of *Hot Space* against her pregnancy.

Meanwhile, Brian May's songs suggested he'd had his nose pressed to the studio glass for too long. On 'Dancer', he soloed cathartically over a strident groove and the sound of a Hilton Hotel receptionist's wake-up call: *'Guten Morgen, sie wünschten, geweckt zu werden . . .'*

In December 1980, John Lennon had been murdered by an obsessed fan. In his last interview with *Rolling Stone*, Lennon said how much he liked 'Crazy Little Thing Called Love'. In response, May wrote 'Put Out the Fire' – a plea for peace, love and handgun control – and recorded his solo drunk. Mercury responded with the Beatles soundalike 'Life Is Real (Song for Lennon)', his only nod to the 'old' Queen.

May's final contribution was the ballad 'Las Palabras de Amor (The Words of Love)', a sort of 'Teo Torriate (Let Us Cling Together)', but inspired by Queen's new South American fanbase rather than the Japanese. 'Las Palabras de Amor' marked Queen's final appearance in person on *Top of the Pops*. Mercury and Taylor wore evening dress. Freddie looked bored; Roger looked like he'd come straight from a Champagne breakfast; and a downcast Brian May sat behind a piano looking like earnest music student Bruno Martelli from the new TV show *Fame*.

Ingrid Mack gave birth to a boy, John Frederick, in March 1982. *Hot Space* popped out soon after. Then, just before the album's release, Bowie insisted his backing vocals be removed from 'Cool Cat'. Apparently, they weren't good enough. A Bowie-less version was used, but meant *Hot Space* wasn't released until May, by which time Queen were touring Europe performing songs nobody had heard before. When some at Frankfurt's Festhalle booed Mercury's introduction to a new track, he dropped his guard: 'If you don't wanna hear it, fucking go home!'

The *Hot Space* songs acquired a new dimension on stage, though. 'Brian had to insert himself,' suggested Taylor. May did so, with powerful consequences, especially on 'Staying Power' and the problematic 'Back Chat'.

Meanwhile, some critics warmed to the album. Essentially, the less Queen sounded like Queen, the more the press liked them. 'Hot Space shows more imagination than tripe like Jazz,' suggested one reviewer. However, the album's sales failed to match those of The Game. Hot Space went into the top five at home, but didn't even make the American top twenty. On their US tour, Queen's new songs received a noticeably lukewarm response.

At first, Queen presented a united front. In May, they appeared on the BBC's Nationwide show, sat on chairs like schoolboys outside host/headteacher Sue Cook's office. Mercury nervously smoked a cigarette and insisted Queen's new direction 'was not really new at all'.

Within twelve months, though, May was telling interviewers that Hot Space was 'a step too far', while Taylor applied his 'not really us' statement to the album as well as to 'Body Language'. In recent times, however, Taylor has reserved his ire for the LP sleeve. It was supposed to resemble a Motown Records cover, 'but it came out looking absolute shit', he grumbled.

Hot Space is now commonly regarded as a rock folly – a regular in magazine lists of the 'Ten Crap Albums by Great Bands' variety. Unfairly so. Seven months after Hot Space came Queen fan Michael Jackson's Thriller. Comparisons between the two are glaringly obvious. But Queen were too closely identified as a rock band to get away with 'Staying Power', a song one could imagine Jackson and his producer, Quincy Jones, reworking into a hit. 'I make no apologies for Hot Space,' said Brian May this century. 'We all came out of it much wiser.'

For some, though, Hot Space will forever be the soundtrack of Queen ripping themselves apart: of John Deacon refusing to allow a guitar solo; of Bohemian Rhapsody's whispering pantomime villain, Paul Prenter; and of Brian May crashed out on a hotel bed, possibly still wearing last night's jeans and white clogs, groaning at his wake-up call, 'Guten Morgen . . .' etc.

'You can hear it on the record,' May said. 'We all lost our minds and sacrificed ourselves to the gods of excess.' At the time, he offered a hollow laugh. But he was only half joking.

In a funk: Freddie Mercury and Roger Taylor on 1982's problematic Hot Space Tour.

HYDE PARK

Queen's free homecoming

The laundry van ferried its precious cargo – the members of Queen – into the backstage area at London's Hyde Park. It was 18 September 1976 and the group were about to do something they wouldn't do again until Live Aid: play a concert for free.

The doors swung open and Freddie Mercury emerged. He cast a questioning eye around the VIP enclosure, didn't recognise anybody and then unleashed a torrent of abuse. 'Fuck off, you fucking liggers!' he shouted at everyone within earshot before flouncing off to his dressing room.

It was a disappointing start. Queen hadn't played the UK since winter 1975. 'And we weren't sure if we were acceptable in England,' said Brian May. Queen had taken a break from making *A Day at the Races* and booked three shows – in Edinburgh, Cardiff and Hyde Park. The London date also marked the sixth anniversary of Jimi Hendrix's death. The free gig was Queen's way of honouring their hero and doing some vital self-promotion.

The Hyde Park show was organised by Virgin Records boss Richard Branson, who offered customers in his shops 60 pence off *A Night at the Opera*. Queen headlined above Elton John's duet partner Kiki Dee, Virgin's resident hippy guitarist Steve Hillage, and a Liverpudlian funk group called Supercharge, whose guitarist, Les Karski, had known Mercury at art college.

'I saw Freddie at Hyde Park,' said Karski. 'I also met him backstage and didn't recognise him.' Such was the singer's transformation, Karski only discovered Freddie Mercury was Fred Bulsara when he heard about his death years later.

Between 150,000 and 200,000 people showed up at the park. Among them was 'Jesus', Queen's eccentric superfan, carrying an upright vacuum cleaner. Kiki Dee sang 'Don't Go Breaking My Heart' to a life-size cut-out of Elton, and Steve Hillage preached peace and good vibes until a scuffle broke out in the audience. 'Stop fucking fighting!' he shouted.

Queen arrived on stage to the opera section from 'Bohemian Rhapsody'. Their motto was 'Blind 'em, deafen 'em and leave 'em wanting more.' At Hyde Park, they achieved all three. Queen rattled through 'Ogre Battle', 'Sweet Lady' and 'Flick of the Wrist' with, in the words of their most famous song, plenty of thunder-bolts and lightning.

Halfway through the show, as though he'd gone from a kung-fu bout to a ballet class, Mercury swapped his billowing boiler suit for a slash-neck satin one-piece. Due to a police curfew, Queen were only supposed to play for an hour, yet they over-ran by thirty minutes and found uniformed officers waiting in the wings when they came off stage.

Mercury was furious when they informed him that he'd be arrested if Queen played an encore. However, standing there with his eye make-up smeared, wearing a ballet dancer's catsuit, he also didn't fancy spending the night in a cell at Kensington police station.

Besides, Queen's work was done. They'd reminded Great Britain of their existence, thanked the nation for its patience and celebrated a musical idol. 'It was one of the most significant gigs of our career,' said Brian May.

IBEX AND WRECKAGE

Freddie goes to Liverpool

The sparse audience for the lunchtime gig at Bolton's Octagon Theatre were scattered across circular pews facing the stage. It was Friday 23 August 1969 and Farrokh 'Freddie' Bulsara – the man who would become Freddie Mercury – was making his live debut with his new group, Ibex. He'd convinced the trio that they needed him as lead singer. 'But I don't think Freddie had sung lead vocals on stage before,' said the band's ex-guitarist, Mike Bersin.

This probably explains why Mercury had his back to the audience for the first half of their opening number, Elvis's 'Jail-house Rock'. He soon overcame his nerves, though. The following afternoon, Ibex performed at an open-air festival in nearby Queen's Park. 'I was used to playing solos with my eyes shut, but now there's a singer on his knees holding the mic stand up at me,' marvelled Bersin. In the space of twelve hours, Mercury had transformed from a shy novice to an assured performer. Live Aid was sixteen years in the future, but Freddie was already gearing up for it in a municipal park in Bolton.

Mercury rarely discussed his early groups in interviews, prefer-ring people to believe he'd emerged fully formed in Queen. But he hustled his way into the music business, driven by his determination to achieve something similar to his friends in Smile.

Smile's social scene revolved around Imperial College, the nearby Kensington Tavern pub and the Maria Assumpta Teacher Training College, where various Smile members had girlfriends. Also studying there was a student from the north-west named Pat McConnell. On 31 July, she celebrated her twenty-first birthday at the Kensington. Among her friends were a Liverpudlian three-piece, Ibex, who'd come to London for the summer holidays hoping to find gigs and a record deal.

Mercury and all of Smile were also at the Kensington. After the pub closed, the party moved on to Pat McConnell's flat where Smile gave an impromptu performance with a little help from their friend. 'My impression was Freddie wanted to be in that band [Smile], but they didn't need him at the time,' said Bersin. Within days, he'd joined Ibex instead. 'He told us, "I'm a singer, but I haven't got a band." He was very sure of himself.'

Like Smile, Ibex idolised Cream and the Jimi Hendrix Experience. But Led Zeppelin's recent first album had demonstrated what a power trio with an equally powerful lead singer could achieve. Not that he was quite up there with Zeppelin's Robert Plant yet. 'Freddie always wanted to sing higher, but he didn't have the power in his voice,' said Bersin.

Undeterred, Mercury and Bersin started writing songs. Many of them changed from week to week or gig to gig. Mercury was also an exotic creature to these self-confessed 'rough and ready' teenagers from Merseyside. Every night, they'd watch, astonished, as he meticulously folded his clothes over the back of a chair before going to bed.

On 9 September, Mercury played his third Ibex gig at the Sink club in Liverpool. Their roadie, Geoff Higgins, recorded thirty minutes of the show, but his tape ran out before capturing Brian May and Roger Taylor joining the band for the encore. Mercury can be heard struggling gamely through the Beatles' 'Rain' and Ten Years After's 'We're Going Home', compensating for his vocal shortcomings with what May later called 'the will and the charisma and the passion'.

A few weeks later, he went to see Led Zeppelin at the Lyceum and returned bursting with more ideas. The first was to change Ibex's name to Wreckage. An ibex was a wild goat; wreckage alluded to the remains of the burning airship on the cover of Led Zeppelin's first album. Mercury proposed the change of name to each of his bandmates in turn, pretending that the others had already agreed. They hadn't, but he'd had the new name stencilled onto their equipment anyway.

Ibex's drummer, Mick 'Miffer' Smith, didn't stick around and was replaced by Richard Thompson from Brian May's old group, 1984. Wreckage were launched with a gig at Ealing Art College on 26 October. A surviving setlist includes the Mercury/Bersin originals 'Cancer on My Mind', 'Vagabond Outcast' and 'Blag-A-Blues'. 'They were crap,' said one eyewitness. 'The only good bit was when Freddie lay on his back, took the microphone off the stand and dangled it down his throat while wailing. Anything to get the audience's attention.'

'We went to see Fred with his new group,' recalled May. 'You could hardly keep up with him. He was being very ebullient and making a big noise and we didn't quite know what to make of it.'

Wreckage are believed to have played their final gig at Twickenham Rugby Club on 26 November. There was no great falling out; they simply had real lives to go back to. 'I had a place at art college in Liverpool,' said Bersin, 'but Freddie wanted to keep it going. He didn't have any money, but he still paid for me to get the train down to London. But I wasn't that focused on music and the overwhelming reality is that the band wouldn't have made it.'

Tales from Mercury's pre-Queen life emerged gradually in the years after his death. Some are untrue but continue to circulate nevertheless. Geoff Higgins claimed that Mercury lived for several weeks at his family's pub, the Dovedale Towers, on Liverpool's Penny Lane in late 1969. 'Freddie made brief visits to Liverpool, but he never lived there,' countered one of Mercury's other Liverpudlian associates.

The myth continues, though. 'The man who would go on to become Freddie Mercury lived in what is now our events space from 1969 to 1970,' the Dovedale's current operations manager told the *Liverpool Echo* in 2019. After all, John Lennon and Paul McCartney played the Dovedale with their pre-Beatles group, the Quarrymen, so why not have the lead singer of Queen living there as well?

In 1998, Richard Thompson sold a 1969 recording of a Wreckage rehearsal at Christie's auction house. One song from the session, 'Green', later appeared on Freddie's solo box set, *Never Boring*.

The song is ramshackle and off-the-cuff and Mercury only sounds like 'Freddie Mercury' for a split second. The snippet of recorded conversation before the song starts is more revealing. 'Listen, don't forget, after the two verses, you'll be doing the same thing,' fusses Mercury as his bandmates mumble inaudibly. Despite his inexperience, he sounded like a rock star in waiting.

'I'M IN LOVE WITH MY CAR'

The most expensive B-side in the world

'Money may be vulgar, but it's wonderful,' said Freddie Mercury. Few Queen songs illustrate this better than 'I'm in Love with

My Car'. It made its composer, Roger Taylor, a lot of money –
and the rest of Queen never let him forget it.

Taylor presented the song for 1975's *A Night at the Opera*. Brian
May's initial reaction was 'You are joking, aren't you? "I'm in
Love with My Car"?' Taylor insisted he wasn't joking, but said he
had written the song about Queen's soundman, boy racer John
Harris, and John's beloved Triumph TR4.

'Roger will tell you it was written about someone else, but we
both know the truth,' insisted May in 2008. The title and swagger
fitted Taylor's petrol-head playboy image and it was his Alfa Romeo
that can be heard belching exhaust fumes in the song's big finale.

'I'm in Love with My Car' was accepted for the album, but
some claim Taylor went to extraordinary lengths to have it as the
B-side to 'Bohemian Rhapsody'. 'He locked himself in the tape
closet at SARM [Studios] and said he wouldn't come out until
they agreed to put it on,' said Roy Thomas Baker.

Neither Taylor nor May have confirmed or denied this. But an
argument about the song was included in the *Bohemian Rhapsody*
film. '"With my hand on your grease gun"?' sneers Gwilym
Lee's 'Brian', quoting the lyrics. 'It's a metaphor!' protests Ben
Hardy's 'Roger', who then threatens to throw a coffee-maker at
his smirking bandmates.

The B-sides to Queen's first four singles had been split
between Mercury and May. Perhaps Taylor had seen Freddie
arriving at the studio loaded with shopping bags – the spoils of
another spending blitz on the King's Road – and was jealous.
Whether he did lock himself in a tape closet or not, Taylor's
'automobile song' (as May later called it) became the flipside of
'Bohemian Rhapsody'.

This meant Taylor earned the same royalties as Mercury did
for the A-side. The rest of Queen had accepted that 'Bohemian
Rhapsody' was Freddie's creation and that he would earn accordingly, but their drummer's success off the back of the record

skewed the group dynamic. Taylor was suddenly wealthier than May and Deacon and bought himself a nice house in Fulham and another nice car to celebrate. 'The financial side of things can get terribly divisive,' he admitted.

'There was contention for years,' concurred May. 'A lot of terrible injustices take place over songwriting, especially B-sides.' Whatever misgivings the rest of Queen had about the song, they threw everything they could at it. Guitars and harmony vocals piled up on top of each other as their drummer huskily serenaded 'the machine of a dream' over a rolling 6/8 waltz.

'With my hand on your grease gun' is not the greatest lyric in the Queen canon. But the braggadocio of 'I'm in Love with My Car' signposted the way for later statement songs like 'We Will Rock You', 'We Are the Champions' and 'I Want It All'. Its title alone is guaranteed to provoke scorn or admiration, but always a reaction.

IMPERIAL COLLEGE

School of rock, no. 2

In August 2007, Brian May finally submitted his PhD thesis and received his doctorate from Imperial College. It had been a long time coming. May had begun work on 'A Survey of Radial Velocities in the Zodiacal Dust Cloud' thirty-seven years earlier. Then Queen took over his life. But, with the band inactive at the time, May resumed his studies in 2007. 'I came back to Imperial and checked my identity at the door,' he said. 'I was not a rock star.'

Brian May first enrolled at Imperial College, South Kensington, to study physics and mathematics in 1965. He'd been a top-stream student at Hampton Grammar School and many believed he was destined for a life in academia. However, May brought his guitar to college and joined the student union's entertainment committee. The Union Concert Hall was also on the capital's gig circuit and May's school group, 1984, played at the venue in May 1967 – on the same night as Jimi Hendrix.

The following year, May started a new group, Smile, with Roger Taylor. Imperial's jazz practice room became their rehearsal space and they opened for Pink Floyd in the Concert Hall in October 1968.

By then, May had passed his degree and received his BSc from the Queen Mother in a graduation ceremony at the Royal Albert Hall. May then signed up for a four-year post-graduate PhD in astrophysics. In the meantime, Smile turned into Queen and played their first official gig at Imperial in July 1970. They would perform at the college several times over the next three years. During this period, the battle between Brian the academic and Brian the rock guitarist began in earnest. In September 1972, with his PhD thesis one last push from completion, May walked away from Imperial to focus on Queen. His tutors and parents were devastated.

May always considered his PhD unfinished business, though, hence his decision to start studying again. In May 2008, May returned to the Royal Albert Hall for his post-graduate ceremony. Taller, older and more famous than his fellow graduates, May received a noticeably loud cheer when he went up to collect his certificate.

Four years later, May was filmed outside Imperial for the TV documentary *Queen: Days of Our Lives*. 'I was happy but very lonely here,' he said. 'Our little clique from physics would sit there and eat our sandwiches and over there sat the clique from biology. I was totally in love with this girl from biology and I never ever talked to her.' Instead, he wrote a song, 'White Queen (As It Began)', which was partly about the biology student who got away.

'I would say to anyone here now: make sure you realise your personal potential,' said May, looking wistful. 'It's about more than academic success; it's also about finding yourself – and I didn't find myself quick enough.' For a moment, Dr Brian May, with his scarf, winter coat and untamed hair, looked like the academic he could so easily have become.

A couple of dons: Roger Taylor and Brian May unveiling a
blue plaque at Imperial College, 2013.

INNUENDO

The final curtain

One evening, Queen were having dinner in Montreux when Freddie Mercury showed Brian May his foot. 'Tragically, there was very little left of it,' wrote May in 2017. Mercury was very sick and AIDS had left his body covered in lesions, with one foot especially affected.

'Freddie said, "Oh, Brian, I'm sorry if I've upset you by showing you that." And I said, "I'm not upset, Freddie, except to realise you have to put up with all this terrible pain."'

It was in this moment that May realised how little time his friend had left. Neither Brian nor Roger Taylor have ever told interviewers precisely when Mercury informed them he had AIDS. They both guessed the truth, but the singer chose not to disclose his condition for some time.

Mercury's doctors apparently suggested he wouldn't live to see the release of Queen's thirteenth album, *The Miracle*, in May 1989, so Mercury asked the band to keep making music for as long he was able to. Queen started their follow-up album, *Innuendo*, before its predecessor had even been released.

Queen holed up in Montreux's Mountain Studios in early 1989 with co-producer David Richards. They were far away from prying eyes and the British press. The band worked for three weeks at a time, with a fortnight's break in between. Several songs from sessions for *The Miracle* were revisited; others came out of long jams in the studio. Everything was once again credited to Queen. After years of squabbling over writing credits, they'd reached a state of harmonious democracy – or harmonious by Queen's standards.

'I know it's hard for people to believe, but it was actually a happy time,' said May. Mercury was terminally ill, but it hadn't affected his sense of humour. 'He was laughing and joking,' confirmed Taylor. 'He didn't want pity, didn't want anybody feeling sorry for him.'

There was something liberating about *Innuendo*. It was like all bets were off, though Queen's business sense hadn't deserted them and the album included five future hits. The album's title track and first single was originally a Mercury/Taylor creation. On 'Innuendo', Queen fused elements of Led Zeppelin's grand-sounding 'Kashmir' with Ravel's *Boléro* and Beethoven's Fifth. Even Mercury's opening 'ooh, ooh's were straight out of Zeppelin singer Robert Plant's vocal guidebook, though Plant later sang the song at the Freddie Mercury Tribute Concert and famously hashed it up. 'Innuendo' also breaks off halfway through for a flamenco guitar interlude reminiscent of the instrumental break in Fleetwood Mac's 'Oh Well'.

The involvement of Yes's Steve Howe in the song was another nod to the past. Smile and Queen had both opened for Yes in a previous life. Howe was producing an album at Mountain when he ran into Mercury in the hallway. He listened to 'Innuendo' and was surprised when Brian May asked him to play on it. 'They all chimed in: "We want some crazy Spanish guitar flying around over the top. Improvise!"' recalled Howe. 'After a couple of hours, I thought, "I've bitten off more than I can chew here." But they said, "That's great. That's what we wanted."'

Some months later, Howe was on a ferry to the Netherlands when he was approached by a pair of Queen fans en route to a fan-club event. His long, illustrious career with Yes was of little interest to them: 'They said, "You're Steve Howe. You're on 'Innuendo'."'

While 'Innuendo' suggested biblical pestilence and whole continents being swallowed by the ocean, Queen immediately diffused the drama with its follow-up single, 'I'm Going Slightly Mad'. Its accompanying video showed the band larking about in comedy hats and masks, with an extra lumbering about in a gorilla suit. Mercury wore a wig and several layers of padding to disguise how thin he'd become.

Freddie and his friend, the singer and actor Peter Straker, stayed up all night composing witty lyrics such as 'I'm knitting with only one needle'. But there was something melancholy about it all. Mercury's mental faculties were deteriorating and he was now experiencing blackouts. His vocal performance was peerless, though, as he theatrically rolled his 'r' on 'unravelling fast' like a dying man mocking his condition.

May had composed 'Headlong', a route-one rocker, for his next solo album, but it became *Innuendo*'s third single. 'Sometimes it's painful to give the baby away,' he admitted. It was sold with a performance video in which Queen tried to turn back the clock. It worked – almost. In one scene, Mercury played his sawn-off mic stand like a guitar. In another, he dropped to his knees about to do a press-up, seemingly defying anyone who dared question his health.

Innuendo's last two singles addressed Queen's situation indirectly. Taylor's 'These Are the Days of Our Lives' was a delicate pop song; May's 'The Show Must Go On' a Hollywood blockbuster of a ballad. Both touched on the issues their composers weren't allowed to discuss in public.

As with most Queen albums after 1980, the singles overshadowed the rest of the album. This was a blessing in the case of 'Delilah' – Mercury's love song to his favourite cat. The track included a guitar solo in which May imitated a feline 'miaow', presumably under great duress. 'Not Fred's best work,' understated Taylor.

Freddie's other contributions swung from the contemplative ballad 'Don't Try So Hard' to the duet 'Bijou', on which May played the verses and Mercury sang in place of where the guitar solo would normally have been. He also provided the curious gospel-meets-fairground waltz of 'All God's People' and the howling heavy metal of 'The Hitman'.

Innuendo was completed by Taylor's 'Ride the Wild Wind' and May's 'I Can't Live with You'. Taylor's song suggested incidental music from a car-chase movie. Think: sullenly handsome male lead tools his muscle car down a long strip of desert road. Though the song didn't quite make it into fourth gear, it was redeemed by a peppy guitar solo. 'I Can't Live with You' was another of May's token rockers/tortured love songs. The Red Special helped convey his angst and suggested that life with ex-soap star Anita Dobson wasn't hearts and flowers all the time.

Innuendo was preceded by its title track in January 1991. 'It's a bit of a risk,' said May, 'but you either win it all or lose it all.' 'Innuendo', Queen's least commercial single since 'Bohemian Rhapsody', went to number one in the UK. The album would also become Queen's third UK chart-topper in a row. But the band couldn't tour. 'Freddie finds it hard, physically and mentally,' said May at the time, toeing the party line. 'A frontman bears a lot of the pressure.'

Meanwhile, Queen's management had negotiated them out of their American deal with Capitol Records and on to a brand-new label. Hollywood Records were rumoured to have paid £10 million for Queen – an extraordinary amount for a group who hadn't had an American top-twenty album or top-ten single since 1980 and whose lead singer refused to give interviews or tour.

When *Innuendo* peaked at number thirty in the US chart, Hollywood's business decision seemed flawed. Yet the label had also acquired the rights to Queen's back catalogue, which, with the growing popularity of the compact disc, would allow Hollywood to repackage Queen's music in a new format.

Years later, Hollywood Records' president, Peter Paterno, discussed the deal in greater detail, claiming that the label's chief executive, Michael Eisner, had been opposed to signing Queen based on their poor US sales and rumours about Mercury's health. Eisner even wanted to include a clause in the contract regarding what would happen if Mercury died – to which Paterno responded, 'If he does, as morbid as that sounds, that sells records, too.'

Freddie Mercury's death was fast approaching, but his commercial afterlife was about to begin.

ISLEWORTH POLYTECHNIC
School of rock, no. 3

Farrokh Bulsara – the boy who would become Freddie Mercury – made his first appearance on stage since leaving India, in December 1964. He played a Cypriot porter in Isleworth Polytechnic's Christmas production of Arnold Wesker's *The Kitchen*. Bulsara was an eighteen-year-old art foundation student who'd recently left his native Zanzibar. He had joined Isleworth Poly in September that year.

Now part of the West Thames College campus, the original polytechnic building on London Road housed a diverse mix of English, Greek, Middle Eastern and Asian students. Friends remember Bulsara in his first term wearing what appeared to be a maroon school blazer with gold piping. His trousers were a little too short and he still had his hair fashioned in a quiff while everyone else was trying to look like the Beatles.

He told other students to call him 'Fred', played the piano in the college common room (his rendition of the Beach Boys'

'I Get Around' was fondly remembered decades later) and joined his friends for trips to Eel Pie Island, where he saw Long John Baldry's band perform with a young Rod Stewart on vocals.

In June 1965, one of the students brought an 8-milimetre cine camera to college. He silently filmed Fred and his acquaintances marching around the car park and laughing and chatting. Bulsara was still wearing the blazer and self-consciously covered his teeth with his top lip. The film was put up for auction at Bonhams in 2006.

Among Bulsara's earliest Isleworth friends was an art student named Patrick Connolly. 'I liked Fred because he was sensitive and caring and not as jack-the-lad as some of the other students,' Connolly said. 'Fred wasn't so good as an actor, but he joined the choir and loved anything to do with singing.'

Connolly visited the Bulsaras' family home in Feltham. He'd sit at the piano with Fred, listening to him sing, while Jer Bulsara brought them tea. 'Fred used to talk about Zanzibar and I had a feeling he was a bit lonely. He was still finding himself.'

In 1966, Fred tried to start his own musical group. He and Connolly designed posters advertising an audition and plastered them across the polytechnic and neighbouring schools. Around forty musicians turned up on the day. 'I remember Fred being very organised and he knew what he wanted: "You can come in, you stand there. You play. No, that's not the way to do it."' But the auditions never went any further.

Both students needed to concentrate on their exams. Mercury's A-level project was a painting of the crucifixion scene. He'd managed to paint the crucifix, but Jesus and the Roman soldiers were proving a problem. 'He just couldn't paint the figures,' said Connolly, who secretly painted them for him. Bulsara passed his A-level and enrolled at Ealing Art College in autumn 1966; Connolly took up a place at Saint Martin's School of Art. The pair lost touch.

Then, one day, Connolly was walking by Claridge's in London's West End when his old friend came running out and invited him in for afternoon tea. Connolly didn't listen to pop music and didn't know Queen. He sat there marvelling at the former Fred Bulsara, now with long hair and painted fingernails. 'I told him I had no idea,' said Connolly. 'No idea at all.'

Mercury started laughing. 'Oh, Patrick,' he sighed. 'You're the only one who doesn't know.'

The two men finished their tea and went their separate ways. Mercury became a global rock star; Connolly went on to become the dean of Croydon Art College and a wildlife artist. Sadly, Fred Bulsara's biblical A-level artwork, created with a little help from his friend, was never seen again.

'IT'S A HARD LIFE'

Queen's worst video

Bring up the subject of Queen's videos in an interview and Roger Taylor always mentions 'It's a Hard Life'. 'Not my favourite,' he'll say, usually while stroking his beard and wincing.

Yet it started so well. 'It's a Hard Life' was released as a single in July 1984. Freddie Mercury's ballad addressed his struggle to find a lasting relationship. 'Freddie was desperately unhappy in love,' said Brian May, who helped write the lyrics and adored the song, which is partly why he and the rest of Queen were so disappointed by the video.

The song's opening bars borrowed a melody from 'Vesti la giubba' – an aria sung by a broken-hearted clown in the Italian opera *Pagliacci*. The story gave video director Tim Pope a jumping-off point, but his imagination soon ran wild.

Pope created a gilded fantasy palace at Munich's ARRI Film Studios. It was a riot of Baroque, Renaissance and Tudor styles, with touches of Shakespeare's *A Midsummer Night's Dream* and painter Richard Dadd's *The Fairy Feller's Master-Stroke*.

Freddie emerged on set in a dazzlingly bright red one-piece, decorated with fourteen eyes across the torso, wrists and crotch, plus a flurry of feathers and antennae. 'He looked like a giant Mediterranean prawn,' said an appalled Taylor.

A cast of exotic-looking extras bustled around him: women in ballgowns with birds' heads; men dressed as insects; a transvestite ballerina and Mercury's Munich 'wife', Barbara Valentin, flashing her cleavage on a balcony.

Mercury played a spurned lover, too heartbroken to enjoy the surrounding excess. But, despite the personal lyrics, he played it for laughs. 'Fred was being ironic,' suggested May. 'But it became a joke within a joke.'

After a minute and a half of managing to stay off camera, Taylor and John Deacon reluctantly sloped into view, both wearing tights and Elizabethan ruffs. Deacon, who was clad in silver, resembled the bastard love child of Sir Walter Raleigh and the Tin Man from *The Wizard of Oz*. For reasons never explained, he also carried a unicorn's head under one arm. Taylor's mortified expression remains a particular highlight. That and a continuity error in which he briefly appeared wearing baseball boots with his period costume.

Brian May made his grand entrance last, carrying a dead-head skeleton guitar. 'I was the bringer of death,' he explained. Queen all came together for the final sequence, but even Mercury looked uncomfortable. He'd injured his right knee fooling around in a nightclub and was in plaster from thigh to ankle beneath the prawn suit. In the final scene, Freddie can be seen sitting down on the staircase, unable to fully bend the damaged limb.

'I think we look more stupid in that video than anyone has looked in a video ever' are Roger Taylor's last words on the matter.

'IT'S LATE'

Queen's greatest non-hits, no. 2

Brian May once said that he was 'screwed up about sex'. He blamed this on marrying his first wife, Chrissie Mullen, at the start of Queen's adventures: 'It excluded me from being wildly promiscuous, but, emotionally, I became utterly out of control.' These feelings crept into his writing, portraying May as a most self-questioning rock star.

'It's Late', from 1977's *News of the World*, was a postcard from the road in three parts: Brian at home with his partner; Brian in a hotel room with a woman who was not his partner, but with whom he's in love; and, finally, Brian back home again, feeling guilty. 'I think it's about all sorts of experiences I had,' he admitted.

At almost six and a half minutes in length, 'It's Late' is about thirty seconds too long, but the song is salvaged by a great, swinging guitar riff. It sounds like Queen imitating macho blues-rockers Bad Company, until those face-shredding harmonies pin the listener to the wall. It was also an opportunity for May to showcase some of that fancy two-handed 'tapping' later popu-larised by guitarist Eddie Van Halen.

'It's Late' was released in Japan and the US, where it sank without trace, while 'Spread Your Wings' was chosen instead of it as a single in the UK. Queen + Adam Lambert took a valiant stab at the song again in 2017 before admitting defeat. Brian May's romantic misdemeanour then went back in its box.

'I WANT TO BREAK FREE'

A classic pop video dissected

'This was the most fun we ever had making a video.'
— Roger Taylor, 2002

0:01 Opening shot of rooftops in the Harehills district of Leeds, Yorkshire. (Mimics the credits of TV soap *Coronation Street*.)

0:11 Brian May's bedside teamaker starts brewing his first cup. (In real life, Brian likes his milky.)

0:15 First glimpse of Brian, face smeared with night cream and hair in rollers, à la *Coronation Street* charlady Hilda Ogden.

0:19 Camera pans across the outside of the Queen family's fictional residence. (In real life: 41 Dorset Mount, Harehills, Leeds.)

0:21 Brian gets out of bed. Viewers ponder whether Eric Clapton or Jimmy Page would sit, legs apart, wearing a pink nightdress and fluffy rabbit slippers.

0:25 First glimpse of the vacuum cleaner. Camera pans up to reveal a suspiciously hairy forearm. (According to Freddie Mercury's friend Barbara Valentin, the one time the singer tried to vacuum her apartment, he ripped a plug socket off the wall.)

0:29 First glimpse of Freddie, paying homage to *Coronation Street* barmaid Bet Lynch: black wig; pink earrings; pink sleeveless sweater; black leather mini-skirt; black stockings; fake breasts. (Bet Lynch was blonde, but Freddie rejected the idea of a blond wig as being 'too silly'.)

0:31 John Deacon appears on the sofa reading the *Daily Mirror*. His black hat and dress suggest *Coronation Street*'s vintage battle-axe Ena Sharples crossed with 'Grandma' from the *Daily Express*'s *Giles Family* cartoon strip. John never leaves his seat during the drag scenes. (He wrote the song and presumably had special privileges.)

0:39 Camera shows the back view of a slender, black-stockinged figure wiggling their bottom while washing up in the kitchen: 'God knows I've fallen in love . . .'

0:56 Back to Freddie, bra strap hanging down, hogging the camera with his winking and vacuum-cleaner thrusting. John's *Daily Mirror* back-page headline is revealed: 'They Never Had It So Good'. (This was a famous political slogan of 1950s prime minister Harold Macmillan.)

1:06 The big reveal: Roger Taylor dressed as a schoolgirl with pigtails and a straw boater. Many men watching have an inner existential crisis. (Roger and the video's director, David Mallet, also pretended to be having an affair when Mallet's fiancée arrived on set. She didn't know it was Taylor in drag.)

1:14 Freddie opens a cupboard door; viewers enter a parallel universe in which a non-cross-dressing Queen are now surrounded by coal miners with Davy lamps on their hats. (Certainly topical: striking miners and their union boss, Arthur Scargill, were rarely out of the news in 1984.)

1:44 A shirtless Freddie emerges from some sort of cave into some sort of fairy-tale glade. (Viewers wonder if they've changed channels by mistake – and where is Roger?)

2:16 Freddie reappears, now clean-shaven, blowing panpipes and wearing a catsuit like ballet dancer Nijinsky in *L'Après-midi* *d'un faune.* (He'd waited seventeen years to recreate this scene after seeing it in a book at Ealing Art College.)

2:41 Freddie collapses face down into a bunch of grapes and starts eating them. One of his five a day, at least . . .

2:51 The famous ballet sequence: Freddie is carried over the dancers' heads before rolling himself across their writhing torsos. (Viewers wonder which episode of *Coronation Street* this was from.)

3:10 Freddie disappears in a puff of smoke with the Royal Ballet's principal, Bryony Brind. (Queen later donated an undisclosed sum to the chosen charity of ex-Royal Ballet choreographer Kenneth Macmillan after he complained that the video's ballet sequence was too similar to one of his from *The Rite of Spring*.)

3:15 Back in the house; back in drag. Normal service resumes . . .

3:18 Freddie double-skips through the doorway between the kitchen and the living room, ensuring he's off camera for the shortest time possible.

3:30 Freddie polishes his bandmates with a feather duster. Brian is reading *Home Chat* magazine; Roger is doing his homework. The front-page headline on John's newspaper reads: 'Rock 'n' Roll Earl Weds the Typist'. (This refers to the July 1957 wedding of the Earl of Wharncliffe, who played drums in a jazz group.)

3:47 Freddie climbs the stairs, twerking, flashing his stocking tops and dusting the bannister.

3:57 Back to Queen's fantasy coal mine.

4:00 Individual shot of Roger, now a man again. (Subtext: don't worry, girls.)

4:02 Individual shot of Brian, sans rollers and nightie.

4:03 Individual shot of John, finally off the sofa and no longer dressed as an old woman.

4:05 Freddie bids farewell as the coal miners sway back and forth around him. (Which one is Arthur Scargill?)

JACKSON, MICHAEL

A less than thrilling collaboration

In spring 1983, Michael Jackson and Freddie Mercury recorded three songs together. Jackson's recent album, *Thriller*, had sold 30 million copies in America alone and would deliver seven hit singles. Queen had just started recording *The Works*, but Jackson's sales hadn't gone unnoticed by Mercury, who was preparing tracks for his first solo album, *Mr Bad Guy*.

Jackson and Mercury had been mutually admiring each other for years. Queen always credited the Jacksons with suggesting they release 'Another One Bites the Dust' as a single. But Freddie's admiration of Michael went back further. Friends remember him raving about the Jackson 5's 1969 single 'I Want You Back' when everyone else was obsessed with *Tommy* and *Led Zeppelin II*.

In early 1983, Jackson invited Mercury to his home studio in Encino, California. Accounts vary as to what exactly happened, but Mercury's former personal assistant, Peter Freestone, recalled the encounter in remarkable detail in his 2001 book, *Freddie Mercury: An Intimate Memoir*. The Encino property – the forerunner of Jackson's Neverland ranch – was manned by security staff and designed to cater to Jackson's every whim. There was a recording studio, a video library and a room filled with arcade games, but Mercury was shocked to discover that Jackson slept on a mattress on the floor, rather than a bed.

'Why?' he asked.

'I prefer to be closer to the earth,' Jackson replied.

In 1987, Paul Prenter, Mercury's ex-personal manager, sold a story to *The Sun* in which he claimed that Jackson abandoned the session after catching Mercury snorting cocaine. There is no mention of this in Freestone's account – only that, after a couple of hours, Mercury was gasping for a cigarette. Jackson allowed him to smoke, but didn't own an ash tray, so Freddie had to use the lid of a jam jar.

Freestone also recounted how Jackson insisted on showing them his pet llama and how Freddie's jeans and white boots became covered in dirt from the animal's enclosure. 'Freddie picked his way as daintily as he could on tiptoe, shrieking at the horror of the mud bath,' Freestone wrote.

'The Llama Story' has become Queen folklore, but with some adjustments. According to band manager Jim 'Miami' Beach, Mercury telephoned him mortified about Jackson bringing the animal into the studio: 'He said, "You've got to get me out of here. I'm recording with a llama. I've had enough."'

But apparently Mercury told his friend and trusted journalist David Wigg that it was Jackson's pet chimpanzee, Bubbles, who caused a problem. 'Freddie got very angry because Michael made Bubbles sit between them,' said Wigg, 'and he would turn to the chimp between takes and ask, "Don't you think that was lovely?" or "Do you think we should do that again?" After a few days, Freddie just exploded: "I'm not performing with a fucking chimp sitting next to me each night."' Peter Freestone omits any mention of a llama or chimpanzee interrupting the recording session, but the accounts of Beach and Wigg make much better stories than his, regardless of their veracity.

Either way, the two pop stars worked on three songs: Jackson's 'Victory' and 'State of Shock' and Mercury's 'There Must Be More to Life Than This', which Queen had recorded an unused version of for *Hot Space*. The recordings were never completed, but, according to Roger Taylor, neither drugs nor animals were the problem: 'We had to go back to London, so Freddie and Michael never finished what they were working on.'

On the drive home that afternoon, Freestone recalled Mercury's giggling comments about Jackson's house: 'All that money and no taste, dear. What a waste.' The two musicians went their separate ways, with Jackson later moving to Neverland and become ever-more reclusive. 'Michael simply retreated into his own little world,' grumbled Mercury. 'We used to have great fun going to clubs together, but now he won't come out of his fortress. It's very sad.'

There was another reason for Mercury's disgruntlement. In 1984, 'Victory' and 'State of Shock' appeared on the Jackson 5's comeback album, *Victory*, with Mick Jagger's vocals replacing Mercury's on the latter song. 'State of Shock' was a strident rocker that echoed Jackson's dance-rock crossover hit 'Beat It' in spirit, if not sales; it would have been a welcome addition to *Hot Space*.

'Fred came out of it all a little upset,' divulged Brian May. 'Some of the stuff he did with Michael got taken over by the Jacksons and he lost out.' Some in the Queen camp suggested that Mercury was passed over for Jagger because *Hot Space* had flopped and Mercury's camp image had alienated Queen's fanbase.

A spurned Mercury re-recorded 'There Must Be More to Life Than This' as a torchy piano ballad on *Mr Bad Guy*. 'It's a song about people who are lonely,' he said in 1985. 'Michael Jackson happened to hear it and, if it had worked out diary-wise, we would have done it together. But I wanted it on this album, so I did it without his help.'

The Mercury/Jackson version eventually surfaced in 2014. Queen's backing track was added, giving them something new on which to hang the *Queen Forever* compilation. Michael Jackson had died suddenly in 2009 and the song's release had come after much protracted haggling with the singer's estate. 'It was like wading through glue,' a weary-sounding Roger Taylor remarked.

Apparently, Mercury still kept a close eye on Michael Jackson's career, even after the snub. In 1987, Jackson finally released *Thriller*'s long-awaited follow-up, *Bad*. 'Do you know what?' Mercury posed to Brian May. 'We should call our next one *Good*.'

'Not one of Fred's better ideas,' said the guitarist.

JAZZ

Queen versus the taxman

Roy Thomas Baker paced up and down Super Bear Studios. The carpet that had recently covered the polished marble floor was lying in rolls outside, next to Queen's drums, guitars, pianos, gongs – the lot.

It was summer 1978 and Baker was co-producing Queen's new album, *Jazz*. They'd started work in Switzerland and were finishing at Super Bear, near Nice in the south of France. Baker had decided that the studio didn't sound sufficiently 'live', so the crew had been instructed to remove the carpet plus all the gear they'd just loaded in. After some deliberation, however, Baker decided that the room sounded 'too live', so he insisted that the crew refit the carpet and bring everything back in again. This was Queen's world now. Nothing was too much trouble to help them make the best record, but nothing was ever quite good enough either.

Two songs on *Jazz* best illustrate the differences between the band members at this time. One is Brian May's 'Leaving Home Ain't Easy'; the other is Freddie Mercury's 'Don't Stop Me Now'. While May sings about the emotional stress of leaving his family behind to be a rock star, Mercury sounds like he's loving everything that being a rock star entails.

By now, Queen had broken America with *News of the World*, 'We Will Rock You' and 'We Are the Champions'. But, at the beginning of 1978, they parted company with manager John Reid and set up Queen Productions Ltd with lawyer Jim Beach. One of Beach's first suggestions was for Queen to leave the UK.

The British government had just passed a top tax rate of 83 per cent on earned income and 98 per cent on unearned income. Like Led Zeppelin and the Rolling Stones before them, Queen became tax exiles, which meant spending fewer than 183 days a year at home. They filled the time by touring Europe, the States and the Far East – and making *Jazz*.

Queen and their entourage arrived at Mountain Studios, Montreux, in July 1978. A returning Roy Thomas Baker was even more confident than before, having just made hit records for the Cars. There were other changes within the camp, too. Mike Stone – Queen's long-serving unofficial co-producer – was gone, replaced by Baker's engineer, Geoff Workman. 'Mike was an amazing, talented guy,' said May, 'but he had a fond relationship with drink.' Also absent was John Harris Queen's long-serving road manager/sound engineer. 'He succumbed to a mystery illness,' said May. *Jazz* was dedicated to Harris.

Mountain Studios was situated in the Montreux casino. *Jazz*'s inside sleeve photo showed Queen in the 'Salon' – their cordoned-off studio/HQ. To the left of the picture was May's bespoke guitar booth, draped with sound-proofing sheepskin rugs; to the right, a fancy new electronic drum kit. Deacon is seen leaning on a gong, Taylor coolly ignoring the camera, May waving and Mercury stretched out on top of his Steinway like a lioness in the Serengeti.

Real life had split Queen into two lifestyle camps. Mercury, who had recently come out as a gay man, was – in the words of one friend – 'making up for lost time'. Roger Taylor, meanwhile, had left his long-term girlfriend, Jo Morris, and was in a new relationship with record company PA Dominique Beyrand.

By contrast, Brian May's wife, Chrissie, had just given birth to their son, James, while John and Veronica Deacon now had a second child, Michael. Stashed in the back of the roadies' vans, alongside guitars and amps, were packets of nappies and kids' soft toys. 'I don't think we were much of a group at that time,' said Roger Taylor.

Montreux was a picture-postcard town, but the after-hours entertainment was limited. The crew found a hospitable English-style pub, while Baker, Workman and others became regulars at the Hungaria – a late-night strip club. 'We'd stop work at 11 p.m. every night, go there and then come back to the studio after,' Baker recalled.

After several weeks at Mountain Studios, final overdubbing and mixing took place at Super Bear (once the crew had negotiated the 40-foot trailer of equipment through little Alpine villages and treacherous mountain passes). This transient lifestyle was reducing Queen's tax bill, but it felt like they were making an album while on tour.

A sense of disconnection ran through *Jazz*. The songs were often inspired, but rarely sat well together. The double A-side 'Bicycle Race'/'Fat Bottomed Girls' captured the record at its contrary best. Mercury's homage to the Tour de France boggled the mind with its barbershop quartet harmonies and trilling bells, while May's counterpart song had an irresistible hook and a title that provoked scorn even in the '70s.

'We lost some of our audience there,' May admitted, still sounding surprised in 2008. 'They said, "How could you do it? It doesn't go with your spiritual side." But my answer is: the physical side is just as much a part of the person as the spiritual side.'

Between them, Mercury and May composed *Jazz*'s strongest songs. On 'Let Me Entertain You', Mercury sang about being an old diva prepared to shed blood for his audience, though the lyrics alluded to his personal life: 'The S and M attraction, we've got the pleasure chest . . . If you dig the New York scene, we'll have a son-of-a-bitch of a time.'

New York had become Mercury's playground. He had an apartment there and would spend many lost weekends flitting between its gay clubs and bars. The singer's hedonism inspired the other *Jazz* single, 'Don't Stop Me Now'. In 1978, though, Queen's fanbase were largely ignorant of which highs Mercury was singing about. His drug habits and sexual tastes weren't really discussed in teen magazine *Look-in* or even in the *NME*.

Mercury sounded high on life throughout most of *Jazz*. On the opener, 'Mustapha', he mangled the English, Arabic and Persian alphabets and even threw in some invented words. 'It is complete gibberish,' he explained helpfully. 'Mustapha' had a breathless quality that reappeared in May's 'Dead on Time' – a song whose stop/start rhythm and noisy thunderbolt were provided by an electrical storm and credited as 'Courtesy of God' in the LP sleeve note.

Mercury only really calmed down on the ballad 'Jealousy', while May insisted on singing 'Leaving Home Ain't Easy' because the song was so personal to him. Elsewhere, though, May and Taylor fell out over Brian's New Orleans jazz curio, 'Dreamer's Ball'. Taylor disliked the song and Mercury intervened. 'Freddie was very pragmatic,' said May. 'If he saw a situation arising between me and Roger, he would find a compromise.'

Queen in luxurious exile: the band with Roy Thomas Baker (far right)

at the press conference launch for their *Jazz* album, New Orleans, 1978.

However, Taylor reserved his strongest criticism for his own material – the funk-rock crossover 'Fun It' and the drearily downbeat 'More of That Jazz'. 'My songs were very patchy,' he admitted. 'Not my best work, frankly.'

Queen's bass player had similar misgivings about the whole thing. Mercury did the best he could with Deacon's slight 'If You Can't Beat Them' and 'In Only Seven Days', but it wasn't enough. '*Jazz* is an album I dislike,' said Deacon.

So what went wrong?

Taylor blamed his songs and Baker's co-production: 'I don't think it really worked with Roy; my drums sounded tinny.'

'It was a strange mixture,' concurred May. '*Jazz* was a very European-sounding record.'

The LP also came with a free poster showing the naked female cyclists from the 'Bicycle Race' music video. It seemed a bit tacky even then. Meanwhile, *The Sun* reported on *Jazz*'s Bacchanalian launch party under the headline 'Way Down Yonder in Nude Orleans', featuring a photo of Mercury autographing a woman's bare behind. 'We're excessive,' said May, 'in a harmless way.' But he didn't sound too sure.

Released in November 1978, *Jazz* went to number two in Britain and number six in America, despite some of the worst reviews of their career. 'Queen may be the first truly fascist rock band,' suggested one critic. 'If you have deaf relatives, buy this as a Christmas present,' suggested another.

Today, *Jazz* sounds like Queen on the cusp of change. One minute, they're toasting their fame, wealth and singer's sex life while autographing bum cheeks; the next, they're second-guessing themselves. *Jazz* mirrors the environment in which it was made: it sounds like everyone has too much money, but can't afford to go home.

'JESUS'

The strange tale of Queen's holy man

On 8 January 2021, William Jellett – known to many British gig-goers as 'Jesus' – died in his sleep at a London hospital. He was seventy-two. His family broke the news online, prompting a stream of reminiscences on social media. It seemed that anyone who had attended a concert or festival over the past half-century had a 'Jesus' story.

Jellett had attended a Queen show at Wembley Arena in 1980, but his relationship with the group already predated this event by a decade. Seated at the end of a row with his flowery shirt, DIY haircut and thinning pate, he seemed to come from another era. Later, he was reprimanded by a steward for dancing in the aisle and then left before the end of the concert.

Yet William 'Jesus' Jellett was a Zelig-like presence at most concerts in the 1980s. He was always spotted at the Hammersmith Odeon and the Marquee, often stripped to the waist and usually jiggling from foot to foot with a complete lack of self-awareness. Sometimes he even shook a tambourine or maracas.

Though Jellett seemed to disappear from gigs in the early 1990s, he still made some surprise appearances, including turning up on the front cover of *Surrender* – an album by dance duo the Chemical Brothers. The original photo had been taken at Kensington's Olympia more than twenty years before.

Then, in 2007, music photographer Mick Rock published his book, *Classic Queen*. Rock had befriended the group early on and among his many commissions were the covers of *Queen II* and *Sheer Heart Attack*. In the book is a photo taken at Queen's Imperial College gig in July 1971: Freddie Mercury stands centre-stage singing to a topless fan who appears lost in reverie, arms raised upwards and eyes closed. It was 'Jesus'.

Queen's first album also included a song called 'Jesus', written by Mercury and performed live in 1971. Were they playing it when Jellett's picture was taken, hence his excitement? The song always seemed like an anomaly. Queen never identified themselves as a Christian group and, though Mercury was irreligious, he'd been baptised into the Zoroastrian faith, not Christianity. Zoroastrians believe in one supreme deity and five holy immortals. Jesus doesn't get a look-in.

However, Mercury always loved a good drama and the Bible provided plenty. Themes of conflict, heaven and hell ran through several early Freddie compositions, including 'Great King Rat', 'Liar' and 'Mad the Swine' – a track left off Queen's debut mainly because his fellow bandmates didn't want another religious song on the record.

The Tim Rice/Andrew Lloyd-Webber musical *Jesus Christ Superstar* was a likely inspiration, too, having opened in theatres in 1971. Queen's 'Jesus' certainly starts off sounding like a showtune. It's also a masterclass in brevity. Freddie has the son of God healing lepers as early as the first verse.

Meanwhile, more information about Queen's messianic superfan started to emerge. William Jellett was born in Poole, Dorset, in 1948 and spent some time in a children's home. In the '60s, he became a fixture at London's underground clubs, including UFO and Middle Earth. His great inspiration was the Crazy World of Arthur Brown, whose frontman – the eponymous Arthur – performed a Shiva-like dance with a crown of burning petrol on his head.

In 1969, Jellett was caught on camera gyrating at free concerts by Blind Faith and the Rolling Stones in London's Hyde Park. It was there where DJ/compère Jeff Dexter publicly anointed him 'Jesus' over the PA. With his long hair and state of undress, Jellett was the perfect hippy waif; his photo was guaranteed to raise the hackles of broadsheet readers convinced that Britain had gone to seed since the abolition of National Service.

Those who knew Jellett in the early '70s recall him working as an office cleaner and living a frugal life. He shunned material possessions (once chopping up a perfectly good pair of shoes to make open-toed sandals) and was a devout vegetarian.

But Jellett had his demons. After 1970, he told anyone who'd listen that he was the reincarnation of Jesus and that the self-inflicted scratches and blisters on his palms were stigmata. He also spread his message further afield at Speakers' Corner – the open-air forum in Hyde Park – where he stood on a milk crate holding up placards and declared himself the son of God.

In 1974, Jellett was photographed cavorting stark naked to Hawkwind at the Windsor Festival. Two years later, he was spotted again when the Sex Pistols played the Nashville Rooms. In summer '76, he showed up at Queen's concert in Hyde Park carrying an upright vacuum cleaner. Nobody knows why.

In 2000, Jellett returned to Speakers' Corner and handed out flyers explaining his absence during the '90s. Reading between the garbled lines, it seemed he had been experiencing depression or mental health issues. Apparently, his milk crate was now decorated with pictures of Queen LP covers. A website article later revealed that 'Jesus' was living in sheltered accommodation in Shepherd's Bush. He remained there until his health declined and he was admitted to hospital.

After the news of Jellett's passing, Mick Rock's photograph of Freddie Mercury and his superfan reappeared online. It showed a man who believed he was the messiah with a master showman who acted as though he were. For a brief moment, both lived again.

'KEEP YOURSELF ALIVE'

Queen's first song

Composer Brian May considers 'Keep Yourself Alive' to be 'Queen's first proper song'. May first played it to his bandmates on acoustic guitar in the garden of their Barnes flat. It sounded like something new, rather than an existing piece by May and Taylor's previous group, Smile. The lyrics also explored its writer's state of mind: 'It's sort of saying, "Is there more to life than this?"'

'Keep Yourself Alive' was among the tracks recorded at Queen's first ever session in December 1971. Smile had previously recorded at De Lane Lea Studios in London's Kingsway, so May phoned studio engineer Terry Yeadon to tell him that he'd now formed Queen. It was perfect timing: De Lane Lea had a new facility in Wembley and Yeadon needed a group to test the rooms. Queen's payment would be a professionally recorded demo.

Queen dutifully dragged their equipment from one studio to another to test the soundproofing and the mixing desk. Once the tape was running, Mercury preened as though on stage and was even reprimanded for singing off mic. But, at the end of it all, Queen walked away with master tapes for five songs: 'Liar',

'Jesus', 'Great King Rat', 'The Night Comes Down' and 'Keep Yourself Alive'.

The song was later mixed and remixed several times during the Trident Studio sessions for *Queen* and it has driven Brian May to distraction ever since. 'The mix has never been right,' he said as recently as 2017. But the song managed to cram every facet of Queen's sound into its three minutes and forty-seven seconds, making it a mini showcase for the group.

It was also one of the songs that helped Queen land a record contract with EMI. But it wasn't a hit when released as a single on 6 July 1973. 'It didn't get played much on the radio, apart from in Japan,' said May. 'We kept getting told, "It takes too long to happen, boys. It's more than half a minute before you get to the first vocal."'

This was a shame as Queen went to great trouble to record two promo videos for 'Keep Yourself Alive'. They rejected the first, but accepted the second, albeit with reservations. Mercury had shaved off his fulsome chest hair before filming and loathed the results. Queen also rejected a set of press pictures for the same reason. Later, after nature had taken its course, Mercury was accused by one critic of wearing a chest wig. 'Poor Freddie was furious,' said May.

Mercury's shaved chest aside, the video for 'Keep Yourself Alive' captures the essence of Queen in summer 1973. They may have had holes in their shoes and no money for the bus ride home, but they performed as though they were already headlining an arena. A month later, Queen embarked on their first support tour with glam-rockers Mott the Hoople. Mott's signature song, 'All the Way from Memphis', included the line 'you look like a star but you're still on the dole'. It could have been written about their lowly opening act.

KENSINGTON MARKET

Freddie Mercury, salesman of the year

One afternoon, Slade's unassuming bass guitarist Jim Lea was wandering around Kensington Market. It was August 1972; Slade were Britain's biggest pop group and their new single, 'Mama Weer All Crazee Now', had just gone to number one.

Lots of pop stars shopped at the chichi market on London's Kensington High Street. Lea, however, preferred to go about his business unnoticed. If he did get recognised, he'd tell people he was a motorcycle scrambler 'who happened to look like that bloke from Slade'. But Lea hadn't reckoned on Freddie Mercury.

'All of a sudden, this guy came up to me in the market,' Lea recalled. 'He said, "I recognise you; you're Jim Lea from Slade. I want to be famous like you."' Lea realised that the motorcycle scrambler line wasn't going to work on this guy. 'I said, "Look, mate, sorry – I've only come in here to buy something stupid to wear on *Top of the Pops*."'

Freddie stopped talking. He looked crestfallen and stared at the floor. 'It freaked me out a bit,' said Lea. 'I felt sorry for him, so we had a chat and I gave him some advice. Queen hadn't taken off then and I had no idea who he was.'

Kensington Market opened in 1967 and closed its doors for good in 2000. By then, its clientele were tourists ticking off another London landmark or die-hards from the last surviving youth cults. It was a different story in 1970, though, when penniless students Freddie Mercury and Roger Taylor started working there. Back then, the basement and ground floors were teeming with clothes stalls and even Jimmy Choo – the Freddie Mercury of cobblers – once dealt his wares at the market.

Unfortunately, Mercury and Taylor were billeted in a narrow, unlovely passageway on the first floor that was mostly populated by antiques dealers. Most customers rarely ventured upstairs to what stall holders nicknamed 'Death Row'.

Mercury and Taylor rented a 10-foot-square space for £10 a week, paid for out of Roger's student grant. To begin with, the pair sold antiques and art, including Mercury's Jimi Hendrix-themed dissertation and pieces by his fellow students. But they struggled.

Over time, though, more clothes stalls appeared on the first floor, squeezing the antiques dealers out, and the clientele changed accordingly. Musicians, actors, models and showbiz movers and shakers started going upstairs – not that Mercury and Taylor had much to offer them.

'When we ran out of art, we got into old Edwardian clothes,' said Taylor. The pair scavenged items from rag traders and charity shops. Soon, the front bedroom of their Barnes flat was filled with bags of musty-smelling garments. 'The most dreadful tat, absolute rags,' recalled Brian May.

Anything and everything – from an ancient cricket umpire's blazer to a threadbare feather boa – was considered stock. Mercury ripped the arms of an old lady's rain mac and passed it off as a cape, while a fashion student friend turned a pair of discarded curtains into a fancy velvet jacket.

In one apocryphal story, Mercury sold Taylor's leather jacket on the stall so he could pay for a cab home. An alternative version has the drummer flogging Mercury's jacket instead. This is the version Brian May recalls. Taylor claims he can't remember. 'But you'd never leave Fred in charge of the money,' he said. 'Bloody hell, no! That would have been an absolute disaster. Freddie took care of the . . . er . . . artistic side.'

While their rival traders were quick to predict fashion trends, Mercury and Taylor just scraped by. They couldn't compete.

Scottish musician-turned-shoemaker Alan Mair rented the stall opposite and watched the pair's faltering progress. 'Freddie and Roger never cut the mustard, but they were nice guys,' he said.

After eighteen months, Taylor was tired of being a salesman and needed to concentrate on his studies. Mercury closed their stall and went to work for Mair. 'I was selling a lot of boots by then and had a workshop and staff,' Mair explained. 'I asked Freddie to look after my stall. He had to open up at ten and often I'd find out he hadn't shown up until eleven. On Saturdays, we'd have a queue of people waiting outside. But I always trusted him.'

The boot stall also allowed the nascent Freddie Mercury to be seen and heard. He even gave out the market's public phone box number to friends and contacts at record companies. Jim Lea wasn't the only pop star he asked for advice from either. Freddie interrogated David Bowie while attempting to sell him a pair of stack heels and cornered Yes's bass guitarist, Chris Squire, on more than one occasion. 'He was a character, someone you saw around all the time,' said Squire. 'I was shocked when I realised the same guy was the lead singer of Queen.'

Alan Mair was also shocked. In September 1970, he saw Queen play a sparsely attended gig at the nearby College of Estate Management. 'It wasn't very good,' he said. 'Freddie sang sharp and was a bit awkward on stage. He wasn't rhythmic.' Two and a half years later, Mair switched on the radio and heard 'Seven Seas of Rhye'. 'I couldn't believe it; my jaw dropped. Then Freddie told me he was turning professional.'

When Mercury finally parted company with Kensington Market, Alan's stall started opening on time and the nearby phone box stopped ringing with calls 'for Freddie'. The next time Mair bumped into his ex-employee was a few years later. Unfortunately, Mercury was high on cocaine and acting the superstar. 'I thought he was a bit too into himself,' Mair complained.

The two didn't meet again until June 1980. Mair was playing bass with new-wave group the Only Ones, who were opening for the Who at the LA Forum. Queen were in town and Mair spotted Mercury wafting around the backstage area, surrounded by his minions. Alan deliberately looked away.

Minutes later, as he was on his way to the Only Ones' tour bus, Mair heard footsteps and a familiar voice: 'Alan! Alan!' He stopped and turned. It was Freddie. 'He asked why I'd walked away from him and said, "Was it because I was such a cunt last time I saw you?" I said, "Yes, Freddie, it is and you were."' Mercury burst out laughing.

Back in London, Freddie invited his old boss over to his new house, Garden Lodge – an eight-bedroom, neo-Georgian property a few minutes' drive from Kensington Market. 'It was nice to see him; he was like the old Freddie again,' said Mair. Mercury's wish had come true and he was now even more famous than Slade's Jim Lea.

KEYBOARD PLAYERS
Queen's hired help

Morgan Fisher
Length of service: April 1982–June 1982

Mott the Hoople's ex-keyboard player, Morgan Fisher, was the first outside musician Queen ever took on tour. He'd met the band when they supported Mott in 1973 and hadn't been impressed. 'No, I was not a big Queen fan,' he admitted. 'They were a bit too frantic for me.' Fisher left Mott the Hoople and then quit the music business entirely in 1980. 'I'd had enough and headed off to India to meditate.'

The following year, Fisher was living in Belgium and running out of money. 'So I sent letters to my friends in England, including Brian May, saying I was looking for work.' The Queen office responded with a telegram, a box of Queen albums and a ticket to LA where Queen were auditioning keyboard players for the Hot Space Tour. Fisher was up against Roger Powell of American prog-rockers Utopia, but it was his association with Queen's heroes Mott the Hoople that secured him the gig.

Fisher joined Queen for a two-month European tour, beginning in April 1982. He'd been a heavy drinker and something of a court jester in his Mott days 'and I think that was the Morgan Fisher Queen were expecting', he said. 'Now I was meditating every day instead of getting pissed.' The road crew, aware of Fisher's interest in meditation and his time spent in India, started playing jokes on him. One night, he walked on stage to see an arrow chalked next to his keyboards pointing to the word 'East'.

'I played the music professionally, but there was something about me that Queen were uncomfortable with,' he said. 'So that made me uncomfortable.' Fisher played his final Queen gig at the Milton Keynes Bowl in June 1982. He can be seen in the film *Queen on Fire* wearing a puce jumpsuit and playing Freddie Mercury's piano on 'Crazy Little Thing Called Love'.

Fisher went on holiday expecting to rejoin the group for their American dates. Instead, he received a telegram telling him that Queen no longer required a keyboard player. 'I had cassettes of the songs – I piled them up on the floor and jumped on them,' he confessed. 'They were too embarrassed to say, "Morgan, something's not right, we'd rather get somebody else."' Within days, Queen had replaced Fisher with Fred Mandel.

Fred Mandel

Length of service: July 1982–January 1984

Canadian session musician Fred Mandel had been recommended to Queen by their ex-producer Roy Thomas Baker. In summer 1982, Mandel was summoned to Queen's LA office to meet tour manager Gerry Stickells. 'We talked for two minutes and then he said, "Oh, you'll do,"' recalled Mandel. 'I said, "Don't you want to hear me play?" Gerry said, "No, I just wanted to make sure you're okay to hang out with."'

The following Sunday, Mandel (nicknamed 'Fred 2' as Mercury was 'Fred 1') was rehearsing with Queen for a show at the 70,000-seater Montreal Forum on Wednesday. Mandel's resourcefulness ('I'd learned how to play a new synthesiser in a week') quickly made him an invaluable sideman.

In 1983, he joined Queen at the Record Plant in Los Angeles to help record *The Works*. Mandel played on 'Man on the Prowl', 'Hammer to Fall', 'Radio Ga Ga' and 'I Want to Break Free'.

He later played on Mercury's 1985 solo album, *Mr Bad Guy*, before leaving the Queen mothership to tour with Supertramp and Elton John. 'Queen were a formidable force,' he said, looking back. 'A lot of their stuff sounds deceptively simple, but it's pretty complex. Freddie was a great pianist, too. I still have trouble playing "Bohemian Rhapsody".'

Spike Edney

Length of service: August 1984–present day

By summer 1984, musician Spike Edney's CV included touring stints with the Boomtown Rats, Duran Duran and Edwin Starr's band, as well as playing trombone for Dexys Midnight Runners. When Roger Taylor's drum tech, Chris 'Crystal' Taylor, told him about the Queen job, Edney was working as the resident pianist in the West End nightclub Stringfellows.

He was asked to bring his passport to the Queen office and was then given a plane ticket to Munich for the following Monday: 'I said, "What if they don't like me?" And they said, "Then, on Tuesday, you fly back."'

Edney's first night in Munich ended with him knocking back Champagne in Roger Taylor's hotel suite until 6 a.m. on Tuesday. He'd passed the audition and remained with Queen for the rest of their touring days. Unlike his predecessors, Edney was more visible on stage and was allowed to play rhythm guitar during 'Hammer to Fall'. He worked with Taylor and Brian May on their solo projects and resumed his duties on the Queen + Paul Rodgers Tour in 2005.

In 2009, Edney saw *American Idol* contestant Adam Lambert sing Led Zeppelin's 'Whole Lotta Love' on TV. He was so impressed that he emailed Roger Taylor about it. Two years later, Edney was playing keyboards on the first of several Queen + Adam Lambert tours.

Today, Edney's only regret is that people don't always believe he played with Queen at Live Aid. 'There's a nanosecond when you see me,' he said, referring to the TV footage, 'but not one single camera shot.'

'KILLER QUEEN'

Queen's most regal-sounding hit

It was 1974 and Queen were having dinner together at Rock-field Studios in Monmouthshire. The band and producer Roy

Thomas Baker had been working on 'Killer Queen' in one of the old livestock farm's converted barns. 'We did take after take after take,' recalled Roger Taylor. 'Over and over again to get it just right.'

Freddie Mercury wasn't known for his patience. When Baker insisted they return to the studio for one more go, he flatly refused. 'No, dear, I'm done,' he protested, planting his elbows on the table. When all efforts to persuade him failed, Queen's roadies lifted Mercury's chair and carried the little princeling, complaining all the way, back to his domain.

The results justified the pain when 'Killer Queen' became Queen's first big hit (number two in the UK, number twelve in the States and top twenty around Europe). But it was also the first sign that the group wouldn't be pigeonholed. 'It was a radical departure,' said Brian May. 'It wasn't rock like people expected us to be.'

Mercury said he wrote 'Killer Queen' about 'a high-class call girl'. Its spicy lyrics reference perfume from Paris, caviar and Moët & Chandon, evoking a jet-set lifestyle. But the delicate melody and graceful rhythm suggested aristocrats gliding around the floor at an eighteenth-century masquerade ball.

'It was so incredibly well crafted,' said an admiring Roger Taylor. Every finger click in the intro, every jangling note of the deliberately off-kilter 'tack' piano, that single triangle chime at the 0:56 mark – 'My God, the attention to detail Freddie put into that song.'

Above all, 'Killer Queen' sounded regal. But the whole thing was an exercise in power and restraint, especially May's spare guitar solo. During the *Sheer Heart Attack* sessions, May was hospitalised with a stomach ulcer and underwent an operation. In hospital, he heard a tape of 'Killer Queen' in progress. 'I can't take any great credit for that song as I was incapacitated,' he explained. 'But I came out of hospital and was very horrible to Fred as I thought the backing vocals were abrasive.' May rejoined the others in the studio for take after take until the background voices were perfect.

On 11 October 1974, Queen flickered into view on TV screens across the country as millions tuned in to *Top of the Pops*. Among the viewers were some of Mercury's old schoolfriends from India, now living in the UK. Many hadn't set eyes on him for years. They squinted at Queen's lead singer, preening into the camera lens in his feathery fur blouson, and collectively gasped: 'Oh my God, that's Fred Bulsara.'

A KIND OF MAGIC
The pop album

The four inflatable members of Queen floated above the audience at Wembley Stadium. It was June 1986 and the cartoon of the band on the cover of their new album, *A Kind of Magic*, had suddenly come to life. The helium-filled Roger Taylor gurned like a Cheshire Cat, while the blow-up Brian May resembled a musclebound Frankenstein's monster.

It was all going well until Freddie Mercury's wire snapped. Up he shot towards Wembley's famous twin towers. Up, up and out of the stadium. It was twenty-eight years before Freddie's blimp was seen in public again.

Mercury's disappearing act could have been a metaphor for his relationship with Queen, but it would have been commercial suicide for him to leave the group in real life, especially when Live Aid had taken their *Greatest Hits* and *The Works* back into the UK top ten the previous year.

There were other factors to consider, too. Mercury's solo album, *Mr Bad Guy*, had arrived in spring 1985 after a rumoured $6 million advance and nearly two years in the making. Solo Freddie was an underwhelming mix of teary ballads and dance-floor pop, neither cutting-edge enough for hardcore clubbers nor immediate enough for *Smash Hits* readers. Freddie Mercury without Queen didn't really work.

'When you lose the brand, people aren't interested,' said Roger Taylor years later. 'That's why even Freddie's solo albums and certainly mine aren't going to break any sales records.' Taylor suffered the same fate when his second solo LP, 1984's *Strange Frontier*, failed to reach beyond Queen's most faithful subjects.

In 1985, the brand kept Queen together. After Live Aid, they seemed untouchable. Just like *The Works*, their twelfth studio album, *A Kind of Magic*, developed from a movie soundtrack. Russell Mulcahy had previously made videos for Duran Duran and had directed the cult horror pic *Razorback*. His latest film, *Highlander*, was a time-travelling swashbuckler starring Sean Connery and brooding French pin-up Christophe Lambert. It contained romance, death, heartache and sword fights. Queen were an obvious choice (though Mulcahy later admitted he'd approached wordy prog-rockers Marillion first). 'I showed Queen twenty minutes of cut film, about six or seven different scenes,' he said. 'I thought we'd get one song out of them, but we got the message back that they all wanted to write a song.'

Queen spent seven months, starting in September 1985, recording at their usual haunts – Montreux's Mountain Studios and Munich's Musicland. Mercury and John Deacon worked in Munich with co-producer Mack; Taylor and May with Moun-tain's resident engineer David Richards. Mack was disappointed: 'Everybody was off working on their own things; it wasn't the four of them together any more.'

Composer/arranger Michael Kamen was in charge of the soundtrack. Queen delivered him six original songs and then decided to use the same material for their own new record. The songs were reworked – and sometimes taken apart and rebuilt – to fit both purposes. For example, the original version of Roger Taylor's 'A Kind of Magic' was markedly different. 'But Freddie said, "You bugger off and I'll make it a hit,"' revealed Brian May.

Mercury put a dance beat underneath the track, bumped up the bassline and made a feature of the guitar fill. Taylor returned after a week in Los Angeles to discover that he'd actually written a top-five single. 'We were knowingly making a pop record,' he said. 'Before, we weren't recording songs specifically because we thought they'd be hits. That all changed with *A Kind of Magic*.'

Brian May struck gold with 'Who Wants to Live Forever'. He liked writing songs with deep meaning and this came to him while watching *Highlander*'s film rushes. In one scene, Christophe Lambert's immortal hero cradles his dying lover in his arms. 'It opened the floodgates in me,' said May, whose marriage was breaking up at the time. He conceived the song so quickly that he was already humming its melody to manager Jim Beach in the car home.

'Who Wants to Live Forever' was perfect for *Highlander*'s death scene, but it worked just as well without the visuals. A big, sweeping ballad (co-starring the National Philharmonic Orchestra), it didn't stint on the drama but never lapsed into histrionics either. 'I think it's one of the best songs Brian ever wrote,' said Taylor.

The song was a minor hit in 1986, but has grown in popularity since, albeit with a morbid subtext. In 2010, a digital TV station poll placed Brian's weepie at number five in a list of the most popular funeral songs (the top spot went to Robbie Williams' 'Angels').

The rest of *A Kind of Magic* struggled to live up to those two songs, though. John Deacon's role suggested a Trojan horse, subverting Queen from the inside. His 'One Year of Love' was an orchestrated waltz with a sax solo by session ace Steve Gregory (of George Michael's 'Careless Whisper' fame). It was Queen pre-empting Whitney Houston's slow-dance power ballads and it's easy to imagine Brian May's pained expression during the first playback.

While Deacon's bandmates were busy making solo records, he'd bought himself a new Porsche. In spring '85, he was pulled over by the police while driving it home from a Phil Collins after-show party. Deacon was breathalysed, found to be over the limit and later fined. In response, Taylor slipped the lyric 'Don't drink and drive my car / Don't get breathalysed' into his song 'Don't Lose Your Head'. It was a brief flicker of gallows humour in an otherwise doomy electro-rocker with singer-songwriter Joan Armatrading on backing vocals.

After more than ten years as an insular unit, Queen declared an open-door policy on *A Kind of Magic*. This led to contributions from Joan Armatrading, Steve Gregory, members of the National Philharmonic Orchestra, string arranger Lynton Naiff and Queen's touring keyboard player Spike Edney.

Highlander also gave Brian May the chance to play guitar hero. Mercury, Deacon and even Russell Mulcahy disliked 'Gimme the Prize (Kurgan's Theme)', but the film demanded some squalling heavy metal. Meanwhile, Mercury's 'Princes of the Universe' was full of noise and grand gestures.

Having fulfilled their soundtrack duties, Queen needed three more songs to complete their album. The post-Live Aid hit 'One Vision' was dusted off, while Deacon and Mercury composed 'Pain Is So Close to Pleasure' and the top-twenty hit 'Friends Will Be Friends'. On the former, the pair indulged their Motown fantasies. This was Queen doing Diana Ross & the Supremes. 'It's a very unusual song for us,' offered May diplomatically. If a computer were programmed to write a

Queen single, it would come up with 'Friends Will Be Friends'. Sentimental lyric? Yes. Arm-waving chorus? Yes. Pealing guitar solo? Yes. The video even showed Queen performing to adoring fan-club members – just as they'd done for 'We Are the Champions'.

Finally, for the album's front cover, *Highlander*'s visual effects guru Roger Chiasson reimagined Queen as superheroes in *Miami Vice*-style suits. It looked dreadful, but this was the mid-'80s. Two years later, Chiasson helped animate *Who Framed Roger Rabbit*.

Russell Mulcahy and Queen both had a good 1986. *Highlander* grossed nearly $13 million globally and *A Kind of Magic* reached number one in Britain and made the top ten around Europe. *Highlander* and Queen were a good fit. 'People hate *Highlander* because it's cheesy, bombastic and absurd,' suggests film review website Rotten Tomatoes. 'And people love it for the same reasons.' They could be describing Queen.

The post-Live Aid effect was strong everywhere except the States. *A Kind of Magic* didn't even reach the top fifty there. A handful of American dates were scheduled, but Mercury apparently refused to go. 'Because things didn't sell so well in America, there were always other places for us to play,' said May. It had become a vicious cycle, though.

Instead, Queen returned to Wembley Stadium – the scene of their Live Aid victory – and released their big blow-up dolls. In June 2014, Brian May posted a photo on his website of the missing Freddie. He'd floated 45 miles and ended up in a family's back garden in Leigh-on-Sea, Essex. 'Nobody has seen this wonderful piece of ephemera since 1986,' said May. It was a reminder of a time when Queen could do no wrong.

KNEBWORTH
Freddie's last stand

In February 1986, Neville Keighley – a 26-year-old singer-songwriter calling himself Belouis Some – had his first top-twenty hit with the snappy funk-pop song 'Imagination'. Soon after, Belouis talked his way on to Queen's Magic Tour.

Both acts were signed to EMI/Parlophone and both were due to perform at the Montreux Golden Rose Pop Festival in May. When Belouis discovered that he and Queen were both staying in the same hotel, he roamed the corridors until he found them. 'I wanted to tell them it was a great idea to have me on their tour,' he said in 2019. 'I said I was new and fresh and they needed me, which they all thought was very funny.'

Perhaps Queen found his self-confidence familiar or even appealing. After the festival, Freddie Mercury had Belouis added to Queen's list of opening acts. Belouis opened three shows for the group – in Manchester, Paris and Knebworth Park.

Knebworth was a last-minute addition. In July, Queen sold out two nights at Wembley Stadium and discovered that the venue wasn't available for any more. Instead, they booked the grounds of David Lytton-Cobbold's fifteenth-century stately home in Hertfordshire for 9 August.

Knebworth Park was steeped in music history. Ten years earlier, the Rolling Stones had arrived on stage several hours late after discovering Keith Richards comatose in one of Lytton-Cobbold's spare bedrooms. Knebworth had also hosted Led Zeppelin's last British shows in 1979. Keith Richards made an appearance on their bill, too (this time, with his side-project group the New Barbarians), but had to be rocked out of his backstage trailer by Zeppelin's man-mountain manager, Peter Grant, after refusing to go on stage.

When Queen performed there, nobody woke up in a strange bed or had to be tipped out of a caravan, but the gig was significant nevertheless. Knebworth would be Freddie Mercury's last ever on-stage performance with Queen. The park's official capacity was 120,000, but as many as 200,00 showed up for Queen, making it the biggest UK show the band had ever played.

Outdoor shows in the 1980s were notable for aerial bottle fights – a trend started at the Reading and Castle Donington music festivals. True to form, the sky at Knebworth filled with plastic flagons of suspicious-looking liquids, thrown with great force and velocity. It was like watching the Red Arrows, but with bottles of urine instead of planes.

Promoter Harvey Goldsmith – a man who always resembled an angry maths teacher – appeared on stage and demanded that the audience stop throwing things. Unfortunately for Belouis Some, nobody listened to Goldsmith and debris continued to rain down on him and his poor backing band, especially during the aptly titled song 'Target Practice'. Belouis carried on regardless. 'It was a good day,' he insisted in 2019, his confidence still high more than thirty years later.

Peace broke out when the second support act, bedenimed '70s survivors Status Quo, arrived. Like Queen, Quo were also enjoying an Indian summer after Live Aid and had enough hits to keep the partisan crowd onside. Halfway through, though, they were interrupted by Queen's two-helicopter arrival.

The choppers – one emblazoned with Queen insignia – buzzed overhead to deafening cheers. Both took too long to complete their journeys; it was as though Queen were enjoying being applauded in the middle of Status Quo's set.

Vogueish Scottish rockers Big Country followed. Being another guitar band with hits helped their cause, even though their guitars sounded like bagpipes. But, as the sun started to set, the audience became impatient for the main event. There was an uneasy atmosphere, too. A disturbing rumour spread through the audience and turned out to be true: a 21-year-old male had been stabbed to death during Status Quo's set. In a bizarre twist, the following day's newspapers also reported how a woman had given birth at Knebworth. (In 2012, Queen put out an online request for the baby to come forward. Some wags joked that the band were only trying to identify the baby in order to make it pay for its Knebworth ticket, since it had technically gained free admission on the day.)

At last, it was time for the headliners. Queen were seen loitering in the wings as Bryan Adams' 'Run to You' faded into the intro of 'One Vision'. Queen's show was one long victory lap: 'Under Pressure' and 'Another One Bites the Dust' were pin-sharp; a new song, 'Who Wants to Live Forever', was eerie and strange – and even Brian May's guitar solo was tolerable.

As the whiff of fried batter from the fish-and-chip van wafted over the throng, Mercury cantered across Queen's gigantic stage like a prize racehorse. In between songs, he gulped down mouthfuls of lager, thanked 'all you fuckers out there' and promised 'to throw my cunt around even more than I've already done'. He also denied rumours that Queen were splitting up. 'We're not that stupid,' he huffed.

'We didn't know it would be the last time, but you might say there was an inkling,' Roger Taylor said. 'Freddie was saying, "Oh God, I can't do this any more." But then he used to say that on every tour. This one was no different.'

Brian May also recalled an incident backstage in Spain a week before Knebworth: 'John Deacon and Freddie were having a minor disagreement and Freddie said, "Well, I won't always be here to do this." We thought maybe it was just a stage he was going through and I put it out of my mind.'

None of this was apparent to the 200,000 people in the crowd. But, at the end of 'Radio Ga Ga', Deacon took off his bass and flung it, headstock first, at his amp. 'I don't know why,' said ex-road manager Peter 'Ratty' Hince. 'John was pretty strange on that tour. He was behaving out of character and I think he'd had enough.' Apparently, Deacon apologised to Hince (who retuned the instrument) and then rejoined the rest of Queen for the encores.

During 'We Are the Champions', Mercury reappeared from the wings modelling his crown and ermine robes. 'Thank you, you beautiful people, you have been tremendous,' he said as the show closed. 'You've been a really special audience, thank you very much, thank you, goodnight, sweet dreams, we love you.'

The backstage area was set up with funfair rides for the after-show party. None of Queen stayed behind for the carousel, though. Instead, the two helicopters whisked them away, over the rippling sea of humanity and back to London. It was the end – even if none of Queen knew that at the time.

In summer 2019, Belouis Some returned from the pop wilderness to perform at three Let's Rock 80s festivals around the UK. Fortunately, nobody threw anything at him. When an interviewer later asked him to name his favourite Queen song, Belouis replied 'We Are the Champions'. He was still as reassuringly confident as ever.

LAMBERT, ADAM

The understudy's tale

Adam Lambert's appearance in *Bohemian Rhapsody* only lasts for thirty seconds. But it couldn't be more self-referential. Queen's guest vocalist plays a truck driver who entices Rami Malek's 'Freddie Mercury' into a public lavatory for sex. While Lambert is unrecognisable, it's evidence of Queen's willingness to have fun with their story. After all, he couldn't have taken the role without Brian May and Roger Taylor's approval.

Lambert is the reality-TV singer who won the true-life equivalent of Willy Wonka's golden ticket. He's not Freddie Mercury, as he has gently reminded audiences every night on tour since 2012. But, with Mercury gone, it's impossible to imagine Queen performing their songs with anybody else.

Adam Lambert was born in Indianapolis on 29 January 1982, just as Queen were squabbling over their *Hot Space* album in Munich. His first Queen experience was hearing 'Bohemian Rhapsody' in the movie *Wayne's World*, aged eleven. 'When we got home that night, my dad showed me some Queen albums.'

Adam had been performing in youth theatre since the age of nine. After quitting university, he took a job on a cruise ship, followed by a three-year run in the *Wizard of Oz*-spin-off musical, *Wicked*. Lambert was a working performer: he sung on sessions and demos and even briefly fronted a rock band – whatever paid the rent.

In 2009, he auditioned for the TV talent show *American Idol* with a performance of 'Bohemian Rhapsody'. He survived the show's weekly culls and first came onto Queen's radar when their keyboard player Spike Edney spotted Adam and emailed Taylor. Lambert had a remarkable vocal range, but was also a natural performer – self-assured and exuberantly camp. When photos of him kissing another man appeared online during the season's run, he brushed off the homophobic criticism. What did they expect? He was openly gay.

In May that year, Taylor and May appeared on *American Idol*, accompanying Lambert and fellow contestant Kris Allen on 'We Are the Champions'. Allen won the show, but Lambert was asked to work with Queen. 'I was performing "We Are the Champions" and I did a little vocal run and Brian looked at me like, "Oh,"' Lambert recalled. 'I did something a bit different to the original melody and I think he got a kick out of it.'

'It was really blindingly obvious there was chemistry,' May concurred. 'Even Freddie would have been gobsmacked at his range.'

At the time, Queen's collaboration with Paul Rodgers had just ended and May and Taylor were cautious about working with another new singer. 'We thought we were done after Paul,' admitted May. 'We thought, "That's it, we had our little revival and now it's over."'

The clincher was Lambert's voice and showmanship. Rodgers would only sing particular Queen songs; Lambert would sing anything. Rodgers was coolly reserved on stage; Lambert was a diva. Regardless of his predecessor's strengths or weaknesses, he was a natural fit. 'Our songs are big and theatrical,' Taylor told the author. 'Adam's not trying to be Freddie, but he's closer to Freddie and that's what we need.'

It was a baptism of fire. Queen + Adam Lambert made their concert debut in June 2012, playing to half a million people in Kiev's central square. Ten days later, Lambert split his trousers on stage at London's Hammersmith Apollo. He was the perfect man for the job.

Lambert was thirty when he started performing with Queen. He had a parallel solo career and wasn't weighed down by the band's legacy. He'd watched videos of Mercury, but still performed the songs his way. Every night, he told audiences he was only there because Freddie Mercury wasn't. Every time Mercury's recorded voice rang out or his image appeared on the screen, Lambert looked like he was as much of a fan as the audience.

Q + AL's subsequent tours saw them filling arenas across Europe, Australia and North America. Lambert commanded the stage in black ostrich feathers, black leather and a black diamanté choker, his showmanship increasing with each new run. 'He is like a sort of camp Elvis,' said Taylor admiringly.

The irony of winning over the States with a gay singer wasn't lost on the band. America had struggled with Mercury's image and Queen's comedy transvestism in the '80s. 'It was so narrow-minded,' grumbled the drummer. 'MTV wouldn't play us. It was all fucking Whitesnake.'

Lambert even believes that his sexuality has enabled Queen's audience to accept him. 'I think it helps people understand me,' he said. 'Maybe it creates a framework to understand my sense of humour or put me into a category similar to Freddie.'

So far, though, Q + AL have resisted the temptation to record new music. 'It's been discussed, but I don't know if we will,' said May. 'I don't want Queen to become a museum piece, but right now the show is a celebration of our recorded works – and it really works.'

Rather than trying to replace the irreplaceable, 'Madame Lambert' (as May calls him) has found his own sweet spot a few feet to the left – and in Christian Louboutin silver-studded ankle boots. It's working so far.

LARRY LUREX AND THE VOLES FROM VENUS

Queen by any other name

The producer Robin Geoffrey Cable, who died in January 2020, was never famous or even infamous. Yet those who worked with Cable at Trident Studios in the early '70s remember him being 'a sound wizard' and having 'the best ears in the business'. Robin Geoffrey Cable also produced Queen's first unofficial single.

In autumn 1972, Cable was tinkering with a cover version of the Beach Boys' hit 'I Can Hear Music'. The song was co-written by Phil Spector – Cable's crazed production hero – and Cable was obsessed with reproducing Spector's signature 'Wall of Sound'.

Queen were making their first album at the time, which meant they were often loitering around Trident waiting for a studio to become vacant. Cable was impressed by Freddie Mercury and asked the singer to moonlight on his 'I Can Hear Music' cover. It took Freddie all of ten minutes to start trying to take over the project. Next thing, Brian May was playing a guitar solo and Roger Taylor was shaking a tambourine and maracas. (John Deacon was nowhere to be found, though.)

Mercury returned alone to sing the B-side: a cover of Gerry Goffin and Carole King's 'Goin' Back' – previously a hit for the

Byrds and Dusty Springfield, among others. This time, May and Taylor were replaced by session musicians.

Cable achieved a fair replica of Spector's panoramic sound on 'I Can See Music'. He sped up Mercury's voice to make him sound younger, more feminine and more like Spector's protégées the Ronettes, who'd recorded the original.

Three-quarters of Queen had just recorded their debut single without meaning to, but it was shelved until the band signed with EMI. Queen's first official single, 'Keep Yourself Alive', was due for release in June 1973, so Cable invented a pseudonym for their secret project: Larry Lurex and the Voles from Venus. The name was inspired by the now-disgraced glam-rocker Gary Glitter and David Bowie's alien support band, the Spiders from Mars.

The band name was handwritten on an early acetate, but later abbreviated to just 'Larry Lurex' on the final record, which snuck out two weeks before 'Keep Yourself Alive'. Despite *Record Mirror* enthusing about Larry's 'high-pitched voice going like the clappers', the single sank without trace.

Robin Geoffrey Cable would revive his Phil Spector sound for the song 'Funny How Love Is' on *Queen II*. He would also engineer records for Carly Simon and Dana Gillespie before suffering a life-changing car accident. Cable lost some brain function and experienced short-term memory loss after that; it was months before he could remember any of the artists he'd worked with.

Cable eventually resumed his production career, but never worked with Queen again. Larry Lurex (with or without the Voles from Venus) was soon forgotten. But copies of his one single still float around online record shops – a permanent reminder of Queen before Queen.

LENNON, JOHN

Queen's favourite Beatle

In spring 2021, Brian May and Roger Taylor were asked: 'If you could collaborate with any musician, alive or dead, who would it be?' Both answered 'John Lennon'. Like most musicians of their generation, Queen owed much to the Beatles. But, by the time Queen came together, the Fab Four were going their separate ways.

In December 1970, Lennon released his first solo LP, *John Lennon/Plastic Ono Band*. It made a lasting impression on Taylor. 'I loved that album,' he said. 'It was raw and brave.' Not all of Queen agreed. 'I remember having a heated discussion with John Deacon about Lennon versus Paul McCartney; John was a great fan of solo McCartney.' Taylor sounded slightly appalled. 'McCartney's solo album *Ram* had come out and I remember John loved it,' he recalled. 'John's tastes were just different.'

Almost ten years later, Lennon praised Queen in *Rolling Stone* magazine. He said their recent hit, 'Crazy Little Thing Called Love', had inspired him to start making music again.

Lennon's return to music was all too brief: he was murdered in December 1980. For their next album, *Hot Space*, Queen recorded 'Put Out the Fire' and 'Life Is Real (Song for Lennon)' in honour of the late Beatle. 'I would never like to put myself on a par with John Lennon,' said Mercury, 'because he was the greatest.'

No mention was made, though, of the time John Lennon turned down Queen. It was 1973 and Queen's handlers at Trident Studios were pitching them to every record company in town, including the Beatles' boutique label, Apple. Tony Bramwell – the Beatles' childhood friend and an Apple employee – recalled playing Queen to John Lennon. 'It's dreadful,' Lennon told him. 'Rubbish.'

In his 2005 memoir, *Magical Mystery Tours*, Bramwell explained that Lennon deemed most music 'rubbish' unless it was made by his girlfriend, Yoko Ono. 'I liked the sound of Queen's music and persisted a little,' Bramwell wrote. 'If John had been more positive, I would have given the other Beatles a listen, but, once you got a negative from one Beatle, you didn't pursue it.'

Bramwell and Brian May later became neighbours in west London. 'I used to chat to Brian while he was mowing his back lawn,' wrote Bramwell. 'About a year after this, "Killer Queen" went massive. "You should have signed us, Tone," was all Brian said. "I wish we had," I said ruefully.'

LIVE AID

A world-class performance in three acts

ACT I

Before the show

In the movie *Bohemian Rhapsody*, Queen, who have been split up, agree to reunite for Live Aid and, prior to the concert, Freddie Mercury tells his bandmates that he has contracted AIDS. In real life, however, Queen had recently completed the last leg of their The Works Tour and, if Freddie was already sick, he hadn't told the band. By then, though, he wasn't telling them very much anyway.

'Our personal relationships had all suffered,' said Brian May. 'Freddie had stepped so far away I thought we might not get him back. He became estranged for a while.'

Bob Geldof, the Boomtown Rats' singer-turned-philanthropist, was raising funds for famine-stricken Africa. In 1984, he'd persuaded, cajoled and emotionally blackmailed more than thirty pop stars into performing on the Band Aid charity single, 'Do They Know It's Christmas?'. Queen were noticeably absent and claimed not to have been asked. 'I don't know if they would have had me on the record,' said Mercury. 'I'm a bit old.'

The next phase of Geldof's campaign involved staging two simultaneous concerts – one at London's Wembley Stadium and the other at Philadelphia's JFK Stadium – on 15 July the following year. The shows were to be beamed via satellite to over fifty nations, where viewers were urged to make donations by telephone. Geldof needed big stars. After some persuading, Queen finally agreed.

'We definitely hesitated about doing Live Aid,' admitted May. 'Not just Freddie. We had to consider whether we were in good enough shape to do it. It would have been easier not to do it as the chances of making fools of ourselves were so big.'

Later, a BBC interviewer asked Queen if they were appearing because it was a charitable cause or because they didn't want to miss out. 'A bit of both,' Mercury replied.

Queen were determined not to be upstaged. The line-up at Wembley included Dire Straits, Phil Collins, Spandau Ballet, the Who, U2, Paul McCartney and Queen's old sparring partner, David Bowie. Over in Philadelphia, there was Bob Dylan, random Rolling Stones and a re-formed Led Zeppelin.

Each act was given twenty minutes and ordered not to over-run. There would be a clock and a traffic-light system on stage. If the light turned red, the power was pulled. Queen booked three days of intense rehearsals, beginning on July 10, at London's Shaw Theatre. They fought over the contents of the setlist, then used alarm clocks to pare it down to the allotted time. There would be

70,000 people at Wembley Stadium and an estimated 1.9 billion watching around the world. These people wanted hits.

The Wembley Stadium concert began at noon with the Coldstream Guards piping royal guests Prince Charles and Princess Diana to their seats. Sat behind were fellow royals, May and Taylor, in chic pastel-coloured suits. Neither Mercury nor Deacon met the royal couple: Deacon, pleading shyness, sent a Queen roadie instead, while Mercury, who was supposedly suffering with a throat infection, told everyone he was there against doctor's orders.

Others remember him being in fine fettle, though. 'I knew Freddie, but not that well,' said Francis Rossi, Status Quo's guitarist. 'We were joking around at Wembley; I said something a bit rude and he got me around the neck in a headlock. I could not move and he was like, "Hello, darling." I felt like we'd finally bonded.'

Later, U2's Bono recalled meeting Queen's frontman for the first time at Live Aid: 'Freddie pulled me aside and said, "Oh, Bono. Is it Bo-No or Bon-O?" I told him, "It's Bon-O." I was up against a wall and he put his hand on the wall and was talking to me like he was chatting up a chick. I thought, "Wow, this guy's really camp." It hadn't dawned on me.'

The good weather and general goodwill ensured that nobody died a dreadful death on stage, apart from Adam Ant, who played his new single instead of any hits.

Dire Straits finished their two-song set at around 6.20 p.m., but the audience started to flag during the twenty-minute lull that followed. Queen's timing was perfect. Finally, comic actors Mel Smith and Griff Rhys Jones sidled on stage dressed as policemen. A couple of minutes of comedy riffing ensued – featuring jokes about the noise, 'boogie-woogie music' and the 'elderly Status Quo' – before the pair stood to attention and saluted: 'Her majesty . . . Queen!'

ACT II

The show, as seen minute-by-minute on the BBC

0:01 Queen arrive stage left. Freddie, trotting like a show pony, does the clenched-fist-arm movement thing that makes him look like he's punching somebody over his left shoulder.

0:34 Freddie strikes up the piano intro to 'Bohemian Rhapsody'. (There are six Pepsi-branded cups of water and two plastic pints of lager on top of the Steinway.)

1:27 Freddie blows a kiss. But to whom?

2:19 Brian starts the guitar solo. (His white shirt looks freshly ironed.)

2:42 Big scrubbing power chord as 'Bohemian Rhapsody' is cut short. Roadie Peter 'Ratty' Hince hands Freddie his sawn-off mic stand.

2:44 'Radio Ga Ga' commences. Freddie skip-walks stage right, finger-clicking and pointing. His right leg starts twitching.

3:17 Lots of hand gestures and close-ups of Freddie's teeth. Viewers discuss the provenance of the studded leather strap across his right bicep. That right leg is still going . . .

4:04 Panoramic view from behind the drum riser. A girl in a black Queen T-shirt is on her friend's shoulders; she knows all the words.

4:16 Unseen but heard, Roger's backing vocal comes through loud and clear: 'You've had your time, you've had your power . . .'

4:23 First shot of the audience doing the synchronised handclap as seen in the 'Radio Ga Ga' video.

4:32 John 'sings' the chorus into the microphone and hops on one foot before bobbing back to the drum riser.

5:00 Freddie performs from the step above the photo pit. A St John's Ambulance man, stage right, is seen grinning.

5:39 Big close-up of Brian. (A few creases in his shirt now.)

5:48 The famous synchronised handclap shot.

6:22 Freddie (in clenched-fist, opera-singer pose): 'Still loves . . .'

6:26 Freddie (does a suggestive tongue movement): ' . . . yooooooou.' He then drops to one knee and throws his head back like Dionysus waiting to be fed grapes.

6:46 Wild applause, beaming smiles. Brian takes a bow.

6:54 Freddie starts the call-and-response game with the audience: 'Ay-oh . . .'

7:05 A long, sustained 'ayyyyyy' lasting six seconds.

7:26 The game's over: 'Awriiiiight . . .'

7:35 'Hey, hey, hey, "Hammer to Fall".' (A surprise song choice in hindsight, given it missed the UK top ten the previous summer.)

7:43 Freddie starts dancing with a cameraman, pouting and 'playing' the mic stand.

8:25 Freddie grabs the cameraman's camera, sings into it and fluffs the lyric.

10:12 Freddie wields the mic stand like a golf club.

10:36 Freddie promenades with the mic stand draped across his shoulders like a towel, as though emerging from a sauna.

11:02 Everybody watching realises just how long Brian's guitar solo is going on for.

11:20 Freddie makes a cheeky masturbatory gesture with the mic.

11:27 Freddie bends over and points his arse at the audience. (He's wearing stonewashed pale-blue Wranglers – fashionable in 1985.)

11:30 'Give it to me one more time!'

11:45 'Ratty' hands Freddie an electric guitar.

12:05 Freddie speaks: 'This next song is only dedicated to beautiful people here tonight. That means all of you. Thank you for coming along and making this a great occasion.'

12:24 'Crazy Little Thing Called Love' kicks off.

13:18 Viewers realise how much better and harder the song is live than on record as Freddie gives it the 'full Elvis': 'She leaves me in a cool, cool sweat . . .'

14:02 Freddie conducts a mass singalong for the chorus.

14:11 Spike Edney, Queen's usually off-stage keyboard player, suddenly appears, clapping along. He's been playing the song all along on Freddie's piano, but isn't shown on TV until now. 'Who is that guy?' viewers ask.

14:14 Roger: 'Ready, Freddie!'

14:42 Freddie: 'Take it, Brian!'

15:40 Freddie raises his guitar like an axe; viewers wonder if he'll do a 'Pete Townshend', but he dangles it down his back instead.

16:05 Intro to 'We Will Rock You' commences. Mass handclaps.

16:32 The audience takes over the vocal. Camera reappearance of the fan in the black Queen T-shirt, still on her friend's shoulders.

17:20 Freddie returns to the piano for 'We Are the Champions'.

18:09 Slight crack in his voice on the word 'fighting'.

18:11 Panoramic audience shot of everyone swaying, even those in the bad seats at the back.

19:09 Freddie off the piano stool and centre-stage.

19:46 Freddie singing again on the step below the stage.

20:19 Freddie blows another kiss to the world.

20:45 A final twirl of the mic stand and an arm wave before 'conducting' the last note. Job done.

ACT III
The aftermath

Bob Geldof's strongest memory of Queen's Live Aid performance is finishing a phone call with an Arab businessman (who'd just donated £1 million) and realising how much noisier the band were than everybody else. None of the acts had been given sound-checks, but Queen's engineer, James 'Trip' Khalaf, had snuck out and set the sound limiters on the PA before their set. Queen were officially the loudest band of the day.

Backstage, immediately after the show, Mercury polished off the first of several vodkas and basked in the effusive praise of his peers and rivals. 'There was a lot of "Oh, darling, you were wonderful!"' recalled one. It took a while for Queen to process what had happened, though. 'There was a point during "We Are the Champions" when I looked up and the audience was swaying as one, like a field of wheat,' reminisced Taylor. 'That was when I thought, "Oh, okay, maybe we got away with this."'

Queen weren't done yet – Mercury and May returned to the stage later. Introduced by actor John Hurt of *The Naked Civil Servant* and *The Elephant Man* fame, the duo played an acoustic ballad, 'Is This the World We Created . . .?', written as a response to news footage of poverty and famine in Africa. Their performance came and went in the blink of an eye.

Closing act Paul McCartney's showstopping 'Let It Be' was followed by an all-star grand finale of 'Do They Know It's Christmas?'. Sting, Wham!, Elton John, Alison Moyet and sundry members of the Who and Spandau Ballet crowded and jostled around a bedraggled Bob Geldof. It had been a very long day.

Happy and glorious: Queen

take a bow, Live Aid, 1985.

Taylor appeared briefly on camera alongside Status Quo guitarist Rick Parfitt, who appeared unable to keep his eyes open. Not to be outdone by any young upstarts, Mercury, now wearing a bright red vest, inched closer towards the centre of the stage, grabbing Bono's shoulder to get nearer to the mic and cuddling up to Wham!'s Andrew Ridgeley.

Later, the party continued back at Mercury's Kensington pied-à-terre. John Hurt recalled video tapes of the Wembley and Philadelphia shows being played, accompanied by humorous, bitchy commentary from Mercury: 'Just look at them waddling across the stage.' An off-key Duran Duran, an under-rehearsed Led Zeppelin and a raddled-looking Bob Dylan (flanked by an even more raddled-looking Keith Richards and Ronnie Wood) were reminders of how superior Queen's performance had been.

At some point in the small hours, a bleary-eyed Roger Taylor turned to his dear friend. 'Do you know what, Fred?' he slurred. 'I think we were really, really good today.'

LIVE ALBUMS

Freddie Mercury's greatest on-stage ad-libs,
as heard on record

'Thank you, you lovely darlings, have you all got your black fingernails?'

– Live at the Rainbow '74

'Do you like my claws? They're a present from the devil himself.'

– Live at the Rainbow '74

'Hey, you buggers can sing higher than I can, I tell ya!
– Live Killers

'This is called Brighton Rockshhhhhh.'
– Live Killers

'You can take all your clothes off, too, if you like, doesn't matter. Fuck off.'
– Queen Rock Montreal

'There are some beauties here tonight, I can tell you.'
– Queen on Fire

'I have three words to say: fat, bottomed, giiirrrllls!'
– Queen on Fire

'This shitty guitar never plays the chords I want it to play. It only knows three chords.'
– Live at Wembley Stadium '86

'Give us the right key, fuck's sake.'
– Live at Wembley Stadium '86

'Thank you, you beautiful people. Goodnight, God bless.'
– Live at Wembley Stadium '86

LYNYRD SKYNYRD

An uncivil war

One-upmanship and competition exists between all groups on the road. But few aggravated each other as much as Queen and US southern rockers Lynyrd Skynyrd. In November 1974, the two acts began a European tour together in Gothenburg – and nearly came to blows.

Queen were coming off the back of their hit 'Killer Queen', while Skynyrd had just conquered the US with 'Sweet Home Alabama' – their rooting-tooting homage to that deep-southern state 'where the skies are so blue' etc. The two groups headlined on alternate nights, but it was a mismatched bill. In one corner, Freddie Mercury in his satin leotard and chainmail glove; in the other, Skynyrd with their cowboy hats, confederate flag backdrop and – what Roger Taylor called – 'fifty fucking guitarists' (in reality: three).

The drummer has hinted at a conspiracy, claiming that Skynyrd's label, MCA, paid people in the audience to hold up banners reading, 'Queen Suck!' and 'Queen Shit!'. One show at Munich's Brienner Theater was especially fraught. The audience largely comprised drunk GIs from the nearby McGraw Kaserne US military base, who spent most of Queen's set 'yee-haw'ing and clamouring for 'Sweet Home Alabama'.

The two bands were at loggerheads off stage, too. 'Skynyrd weren't fun; they were very aggressive,' Taylor suggested. 'And no one was allowed to touch their confederate flag. I thought, "Fuck that! I'd like to cut it up with a pair of scissors."' The warring factions parted company in Hamburg, never to cross paths again. As Taylor put it, 'Skynyrd couldn't believe that four nancy boys caked in make-up had given them a run for their money.'

MACK, REINHOLD

The producer's tale

There's a fleeting glimpse of Queen's producer Reinhold Mack in the video for 'One Vision'. He appears briefly behind the mixing desk in Munich's Musicland Studios with a concerned look on his face. You sense that this may have been his default setting. Mack had plenty of cause for concern: besides co-producing five Queen albums, including *Hot Space*, he also tried to referee 'Under Pressure', the band's duet with David Bowie.

Mack was Queen's co-producer, conscience, confidant, umpire, whipping boy and dear friend, especially to Freddie Mercury and John Deacon. So dear, in fact, that Mack's third son was named John Frederick after his two Queenly godfathers.

Mack did his greatest work at Musicland – a facility owned by the Italian dance producer Giorgio Moroder. In the mid-'70s Mack worked as a sound engineer and co-producer for Deep Purple, the Rolling Stones, ELO and one of Brian May's favourite guitar players, Rory Gallagher.

Queen booked their first sessions at Musicland in summer 1979. Mack was in Los Angeles at the time, but Moroder suggested he fly back immediately. When Mack turned up in

Munich, there was no sign of Queen. He booked himself on a plane back to LA, only to receive another call from Moroder soon after. Queen had finally arrived and needed a producer. Mack booked another flight . . .

Mercury's reputation for being difficult preceded him. On the day, though, Mack encountered a painfully shy man, incongruously dressed in a Hawaiian shirt and matching flowery shorts. 'I expected the worst, but Fred was gentle and helpful,' he recalled. He'd also written a new song, 'Crazy Little Thing Called Love', and wanted to record it as quickly as possible, 'before Brian turns up'.

It was Mack's first experience of the sometimes strained relationship between the four band members. 'They were very resistant to change,' he said. 'My forté was working fast, whereas they worked slow, especially Brian. My attitude was "Give it a shot and, if you don't like it, we'll change it." And, all of a sudden, they liked it.'

Mack taught Queen about speed and spontaneity. 'Never two notes played if one would do,' said May, who namechecked the producer in the lyrics for 'Dragon Attack'. Mack's relationship with Queen peaked during 1982's troublesome *Hot Space*. His wife, Ingrid, was expecting their third child and famously said, 'I think it's easier being pregnant for nine months and giving birth than getting this album done.' As a joke, Ingrid suggested that, if the baby were born before *Hot Space* was finished, all four members of Queen could be godfathers.

Their son's arrival did beat *Hot Space*'s by a fortnight, but only Mercury and Deacon received the honour. On the day of the birth, Freddie sent his personal assistant out to buy as many flowers as he could. A Munich florist's entire stock was then delivered to Ingrid's maternity ward.

Although Mercury threw himself into Munich's wild club scene, Mack and his family offered the Queen frontman an escape and a change of pace. 'With us, he could be ordinary,' explained

Mack. 'He could sit around, read the newspapers, go shopping. I think we provided him with a family of his own.'

Mercury spent Christmases with the Macks and doted on his godson, showering him with gifts, including enormous teddy bears and an eerily lifelike rocking horse. 'I was often scared of his presents because they were just supersized,' said John Frederick Mack in 2014, 'but he spoiled the shit out of me.'

Mercury and Mack drifted apart when Mercury stopped living in Munich. After Freddie became ill, he retreated even further. 'He put up a safety barrier for us as a family,' suggested Mack. 'He wanted to preserve the memories we had and not see him go through his transformation.'

Mack left his mark on the albums he helped produce for Queen, though – the speed, the spontaneity, the use of one note instead of two – and, as Brian May once said, 'He took us into uncharted territory.'

MADE IN HEAVEN
Freddie Mercury's epitaph

In November 1995, BBC Radio 1 refused to add Queen's new single, 'Let Me Live', to its playlist. The station was trying to attract a younger demographic and considered Queen too old. It was the era of Britpop, *Loaded* magazine and the first stirrings of 'Cool Britannia'. Radio 1's subsequent rebrand saw seasoned presenters fired or falling on their swords. It was a difficult time to be a DJ or rock star in your mid-to-late forties. And a difficult time to be in Queen.

'Let Me Live' was one of thirteen songs on Queen's new 'old' album, *Made in Heaven*. Parts of these songs dated back as far as 1980 and some were Freddie Mercury's final recordings from May 1991. Everything was diligently woven together by Queen and Mountain Studios' co-producer David Richards. *Made in Heaven* was inspired, mawkish, sad, shameless and occasionally eerie.

Freddie Mercury recorded two Queen albums (1989's *The Miracle* and '91's *Innuendo*) while he was terminally ill. He persuaded his bandmates to keep on working and was brutally unsentimental. 'He told us, "Get me to sing anything – write me anything and I will sing it – and I will leave you as much as I possibly can,"' said Brian May. 'He was adamant this material should be released.'

This approach suggested quality over quantity, though. Roger Taylor and John Deacon began tinkering with the material as early as 1992. Brian May, who was away touring his latest solo album, *Back to the Light*, was not best pleased. 'Roger and John became impatient with me and started working on the tapes,' May said. 'I didn't want this stuff to go out without my involvement, so I took the tapes off them and spent months putting it all back together.'

Taylor's memory differs. 'I was the one driving it to begin with,' he said. 'Brian, particularly, was reluctant. But, when we heard Freddie's voice coming back to us from the control room, it made all the difference.' May later admitted it was unsettling to hear Mercury talking in between takes – his jokes, his laughter, the chink of ice in his vodka glass . . .

Whatever ravages Mercury's illness had inflicted upon him, his voice was unaffected. 'It's a Beautiful Day' revived Mercury's vocals and piano from Munich 1980. It was a peerless performance: Freddie extolling the beauty of nature – 'The sun is shining / I feel good' – like Julie Andrews gambolling through the Alps at the start of *The Sound of Music*. But it was only a few seconds of prime Mercury spun into a 2:34-minute song with a long instrumental intro and outro. The song was later reprised with a thumping backing track.

Queen's earlier solo projects also provided them with valuable source material. 'Made in Heaven' and 'I Was Born to Love You' (both from Mercury's 1985 solo LP, *Mr Bad Guy*) became Queen songs with the careful application of walloping drums and bell-like guitar solos.

Taylor had originally pitched his song 'Heaven for Everyone' to Queen in 1987. They didn't bite, so instead he recorded two versions – one with him singing lead vocal and one with Mercury – for his side project, the Cross. 'I think Fred and I got through a bottle of vodka that day,' he recalled. 'When you get Freddie Mercury to sing something you've sung, you realise your limits and how much further he could take it.' May, Deacon and Taylor reworked the song for *Made in Heaven* and Freddie's final Elvis-inflected 'for ever-won' drove Roger's point home.

The gospel song 'Let Me Live', from 1983, was daring and jolly, but the female backing voices almost turned it into a parody. Somewhere in the vaults is a version with Rod Stewart singing, recorded at a jam session during *The Works*. John Deacon's 'My Life Has Been Saved' was another '80s curio, with its lyrics asking for peace and understanding in an uncertain world – again, salvaged by Mercury's voice.

These were songs about living and dying sung by a man with a death sentence hanging over him. Never more so than in the case of May's plangent ballad 'Too Much Love Will Kill You', first performed at the Freddie Mercury Tribute Concert. 'It wasn't about AIDS,' he insisted. 'But I felt it was the best way of expressing myself.' May had wanted the song on *The Miracle*, but, after a publishing dispute with his collaborators Frank Musker and Elizabeth Lamers (aka songwriting duo World Goes Around), it wasn't included.

Made in Heaven offered its most revealing glimpse of Mercury's final months on two tracks from the *Innuendo* sessions. Mercury wrote the lyrics to 'A Winter's Tale' – all swans, seagulls and 'silky moons' – while gazing at Lake Geneva from his Montreux villa. 'It was Freddie's last bit of songwriting,' said May. 'He knew he didn't have long and was singing about the beauty of the world. But it's not maudlin. After he died, I decided nobody else could touch it – until Roger and I decided to bring it to a natural conclusion.'

From the same sessions came Mercury's final recording, 'Mother Love'. 'Mama, please let me back inside,' he sings over burbling bass and a spooked-sounding drum machine. 'It's the last utterance of Freddie in the studio,' revealed the song's co-writer, May, whose wounded lead vocal on the fourth verse suggested he was singing from a foetal crouch.

In fact, the whole of 'Mother Love' could be Queen stretched out on their respective psychiatrists' couches. The coda sampled Mercury's call-and-response game ('Ay-oh!') from Wembley Stadium, a snatch of Larry Lurex's 'Goin' Back', split-seconds of every Queen song ever (though who can tell?), and a baby crying. It was utterly shameless and utterly Queen.

Really, *Made in Heaven* should have ended there. Instead, Queen conjured up three more 'songs'. There was 'Yeah' (a four-second sample of Mercury's voice lifted from the 1980 track, 'Don't Try Suicide') and '13' (a sample of random vocals looped over an instrumental backing track), though the wildest card was 'You Don't Fool Me'. Queen later confessed that there was no song to begin with; they just created the modish dance track between them, using Mercury's disembodied voice. It sounded like something drifting out of a Balearic nightclub at 2 a.m. and became a number-one hit in Italy. 'I remember skiing and being on top of the mountain,' said Taylor, 'and there was a little hut with a guy in it, working the lift, and there it was, belting out. We pieced it together from scraps really.'

Taylor's comment could have applied to most of *Made in Heaven*. Queen's so-called final album was released in November 1995 with a picture of Irena Sedlecká's Freddie statue on the cover. Queen's late singer quickly proved immune to BBC bans when the album reached number one in ten countries, including the UK. 'The Queen chapter should now be closed,' said Brian May at the time. But *Made in Heaven* would be a premature epitaph.

MADISON SQUARE GARDEN
Father to son

Brian May's father, Harold, passed away on 2 June 1991. By then, he'd long accepted his son's chosen profession – but it hadn't been easy. It wasn't until 1977, after a Queen show at New York's Madison Square Garden, that Harold and Brian finally made their peace.

Harold May was serving in the RAF when he met Brian's mother, Ruth. After they married, he worked as an electronics engineer, turned the family's spare bedroom into a workshop and hand-built their first TV set.

Harold was also musical – he played piano and a George Formby-style banjo-ukulele. In 1963, he and Brian famously constructed the Red Special guitar from an abandoned fireplace and other household objects. It was a father-and-son bonding exercise that took them over a year to complete.

It was Brian's decision to abandon his PhD and turn professional with Queen that ruined the pair's relationship. Harold had worked hard so that his son could pursue an education. 'And now my dad thought I was throwing it away to become a pop star – or a failure,' Brian said.

Harold also struggled with his son's life choices, including Brian moving in with his girlfriend, Chrissie Mullen, before they were married. In 2014, Brian addressed the wider impact of their estrangement in his book *Brian May's Red Special*. 'Mum was caught in the middle,' he wrote. 'She had what in those days was called a nervous breakdown because she was trying to stay close to us and we were diametrically opposed.' It was after Ruth May was taken to hospital that father and son tried to make amends.

While working as a radar engineer, Harold had helped design the blind landing equipment for Concorde, but was never able to afford to fly on the supersonic jet. In December 1977, when Queen were midway through a North American tour, Brian arranged to fly his parents out to New York by Concorde. 'I also put them up at the Ritz hotel and told them to order room service,' he said. 'I wanted to show my dad I'd made it.'

Later, Harold and Ruth sat in the audience at the 20,000-seater Madison Square Garden. They watched their son playing the songs he'd written for Queen and marvelled at the spectacle of his friend, Freddie, promenading around the stage in jester's tights.

Backstage, after the show, Harold May quietly grabbed his son's hand, shook it and said, 'Okay, I get it now.'

MARX, GROUCHO

Queen's favourite wise-ass

One Saturday night in summer 1975, Roy Thomas Baker invited Queen to his place for dinner and a movie. Queen and their co-producer had spent a fractious day at Rockfield Studios and needed some light relief. Baker had a rented house nearby with a new-fangled video tape recorder.

After dinner, Baker put on a VHS of the Marx Brothers' wise-cracking 1935 comedy, *A Night at the Opera*. According to Roger Taylor, he and Freddie Mercury looked at each other halfway through and suggested it would be a great title for Queen's next album. Everybody agreed.

A year after *A Night at the Opera*, Queen, who were just about to release their fifth LP, *A Day at the Races*, received a telex from a 'Dr Hugo Z. Hackenbush'. Hackenbush was the name of Groucho Marx's character in the brothers' movie *A Day at the Races*.

'I understand that you have a new album coming out called *A Day at the Races*,' the telex began. 'That, as you undoubtedly know, happens to be the name of one of the Marx Brothers' more successful film outings.' Groucho, aged eighty-five at the time, then went on to reveal that his 'stereo listening these days is pretty much restricted to hearing aids in both ears', before adding, 'I know that you are very successful recording artists. Could it, by any chance, be your sage choice of album titles?'

In March 1977, Queen played the LA Forum and Groucho invited them to his Hollywood home for lunch. 'We all went except for John, who chickened out,' recalled Taylor. Marx made a grand entrance with a young, attractive woman on his arm, whom he introduced as his nurse. She was then joined by a young, attractive female pianist. Groucho entertained the Queen party by singing some of his greatest hits, including his 1939 signature song, 'Lydia the Tattooed Lady', and one of his later, post-war compositions, 'Omaha, Nebraska'.

When he was done, Marx insisted his guests reciprocate: 'Ya singers! Fuckin' sing!'

Queen declined as they didn't have any instruments, but Marx produced a Spanish guitar. So began one of the strangest performances of Queen's career: huddled together singing Brian May's "39' – a song about a man who gets trapped in a space-time continuum – for the doyen of great American comics. Groucho died five months later.

The story doesn't end there, though. According to one EMI insider, Queen asked Groucho if they could call their next album *Duck Soup*, after another Marx Brothers movie. He refused, but mischievously suggested, 'I would like it to be named after my next movie instead: *The Rolling Stones' Greatest Hits*.' Fact or fiction, it's the perfect ending.

MAY, BRIAN

The guitarist's tale

Brian May's hotel aliases in Queen:
Brian Manley, Chris Mullens

Brian May's answers in a *People* magazine interview, 1974:

My idea of beauty:
The smallest imperfection in a perfect face

My favourite flower:
Rose

My favourite colour:
Deep blue

My favourite place:
Home

My greatest happiness:
The promise of the future

My greatest misery:
Losing people

My favourite amusement:
Making things – anything

My favourite hero/heroine:
Jimi Hendrix

My present state of mind:
A little sad, but hopeful

My motto:
'Give'

Five things the rest of Queen have said about Brian May:

Freddie Mercury:
'Never in my wildest dreams would I have imagined someone like Brian would be a rock 'n' roller.'

Roger Taylor:
'Brian is one of the most eccentric people I have ever met.'

Freddie Mercury:
'Brian and I fight every time we're in the same room.'

Roger Taylor:
'We've had a long, up-and-down relationship. But we're brothers from another mother.'

Freddie Mercury:
'Brian takes his time being nice to people. He's too much of a gentleman.'

Sometime in the 1970s, John 'Jag' Garnham went to see Queen in concert. As schoolboys, Jag and Brian May had played together in a group called 1984. May's subsequent transformation surprised his former bandmate.

'Brian was rushing to the front of the stage doing that Pete Townshend windmilling arm thing,' Garnham recalled in 2009. 'And I was thinking, "This is not the same person I know." I was never sure whether it was a role he was playing or he'd made a real change.'

There are two Brian Mays, then: Brian the rock star and Brian the studious schoolboy who used to take his homemade telescope on family holidays to Sidmouth. You sense that the schoolboy Brian is still in there somewhere.

Brian Harold May, born on 19 July 1947, was the only child of electronics engineer and Ministry of Aviation draughtsman Harold and his wife, Ruth. The family home was 6 Walsham Road, Feltham, in west London. Harold also played piano and banjo and bought his son a Spanish guitar for his seventh birthday. Brian soon combined his love of music with his love of science by listening to Buddy Holly on pirate radio through a pair of German submarine headphones plugged into a homemade crystal set.

In 1962, father and son approached the making of Brian's signature Red Special guitar like an engineering project. The instrument also offered shy Brian a protective shield. 'Along with my shyness was a great loneliness,' he later told *The Guardian*. 'I was an only child and always looking for that thing that can get rid of the loneliness. I went to a boys' school and was totally afraid of girls. On stage, I could be some kind of hero.'

When his first girlfriend broke his heart in 1965, May moped around Imperial College listening to Smokey Robinson's 'Tracks of My Tears'. He has since described himself at this time as a diligent student, but lacking confidence and obsessed with music.

May arrived at his signature sound by studying the collected works of James Burton, Eric Clapton, Jimi Hendrix and Irish bluesman Rory Gallagher. May even used to wait for Gallagher outside the Marquee club's dressing room. Years later, Gallagher remembered the lanky youth with the helmet of curly hair, asking questions like, 'How do you make your guitar sound like that?'

Gallagher told May that he used a Vox AC30 amp and a Rangemaster Treble Booster. May then went to a Soho guitar shop and tried out both devices. It was like someone had waved a magic wand: 'I plugged my homemade guitar in and the sound was there.'

By then, Roger Taylor had breezed into May's life and helped him form Smile. 'The first time I heard Brian pick up the electric guitar, I thought, "This guy has the touch,"' said Taylor. 'I'd never heard anyone play like he did.'

Soon after came Freddie Mercury, bursting with bold ideas and even bolder stage clothes. 'Freddie had a vision for me,' said May. 'In the very early days, he said, "You are what I want – you are my Jimi Hendrix – and we will do this thing." I think he had more belief in me than I had.'

May's musicianship was exceptional, but his showmanship lagged behind. Elektra Records' Jac Holzman saw Queen at the Marquee in 1973. He told them that May and Deacon needed to show off more. 'Tell the guitarist to make it look harder,' he said. 'Kids like to think it's Beethoven.'

Mercury later wrote to Holzman advising him of their progress. 'Both Brian and John have recently excelled themselves in their performance and presentation,' he said. 'You'll be pleased to know that they don't make it look so easy any more.'

Queen's subsequent success colours the picture, but it took a huge leap of faith for May to turn professional in summer 1972. Everyone in Queen took a chance, but May, who was still completing his PhD, took the biggest chance of all.

His decision damaged his relationship with his parents for several years, while the chaos of touring life challenged May's need for comfort and order. He was homesick and then physically sick on Queen's first American tour in 1974.

But May would adjust to it over time by plotting Queen's global adventures like a school homework assignment. 'Brian Manley', aka 'Chris Mullens', acquired a map of the US and customised it with flight details and travel times. He kept ticket stubs from every show and matchbooks from every hotel. Come the mid-'70s, May was already indulging his passion for stereoscopic photography (a technique that makes two-dimensional images appear three-dimensional) and seeking out stereoscopic card dealers in every city.

Recently, May has talked fondly of Queen's penurious early days. Brian and his future first wife, Chrissie Mullen, started out renting a bedsit in Earl's Court. They cooked on a single gas ring and shared a bathroom with strangers. 'It was probably the happiest time of my life,' May said, though this is difficult to believe.

Then again, Mercury and Taylor were always Queen's best rock stars, spending their royalties on flash cars and flashier houses before they could even afford to. In contrast, the Mays resided in a modest property in Barnes until the bigger royalties arrived.

Fame and money didn't bring Brian happiness, though. 'It's not an easy life,' he insisted. 'This is going to sound like a spoiled pop star, but it has its own stresses. You're exposing yourself to the public; you're putting yourself at the risk of looking stupid. You're fighting various battles with the rest of the band, the organisation around you.'

When he wasn't arguing, May helped to define Queen's sound with the unique noise created by the Red Special and a sixpence for a plectrum. His songs sometimes suggest a battle between art and science or between heart and brain. For example, ''39', from *A Night at the Opera*, was a campfire singalong inspired by the works of spiritual poet and author Hermann Hesse, while the dizzying detail of 'The Prophet's Song' made it the prog-rock equivalent of a Heath Robinson invention.

May was Queen's biggest heavy-rock fan. But his songs – 'Keep Yourself Alive', 'Tie Your Mother Down', 'It's Late', 'We Will Rock You' etc. – rarely succumbed to macho posturing, despite some bragging lyrics. May was always too sensitive for that. He also rates his subtle solo on 'Killer Queen' as his favourite.

As big and boastful as Queen became, Brian still sounded a bit like his teenage self: good at maths; rubbish with girls. Listen to his fragile supporting vocal on 'I Want It All' or his lead vocal on 'Leaving Home Ain't Easy'. His voice matches his answer to the *People* magazine question 'What is your present state of mind?': 'A little sad, but hopeful'.

His mindset extended beyond the music. May is the only '70s rock star on the planet more likely to have been jonesing for stereographic cards than cocaine. 'I've never taken anything stronger than an aspirin,' he said, 'and I don't even like taking that.' Like the rest of Queen, though, he nearly drowned in vodka during their wild years in Munich and landed himself into some emotional trouble, too.

'I became utterly out of control,' he said. 'Needy for that one-to-one reinforcement, feelings of love and discovery. That's what I became addicted to.' Ultimately, this addiction cost him his marriage to Chrissie (the mother of his three children) and would impact his relationship with his second wife, Anita Dobson, too.

The 1990s were a difficult time for Brian. Harold May and Freddie Mercury died within months of each other. He had a hit single, 'Driven by You', shortly after Mercury's death, but it was a pyrrhic victory. (Freddie, who told him to release it, had joked that, if he passed away, 'it would be good for business'.)

May toured with his own Brian May Band, sometimes as an opening act in arenas he'd once headlined with Queen. His 1998 solo album, *Another World*, was full of big songs with big guitars and self-questioning, even self-pitying lyrics: 'It's a hard business to make it on your own,' he sang. Was he talking about his personal life? Or life without Queen? Or both?

'Truthfully, I'd love someone to come up to me and say, "I love your new album," rather than, "How do you do that guitar effect on *A Night at the Opera*?"' May admitted in 1998. 'I'd like to be viewed as something alive and relevant and not some fossil.'

In this century, though, May has become a household-name rock star; Britain's go-to guitar hero. His distinctive image has helped. 'Sometimes I wish I had a paper bag over my head and people just listened to the music,' he once grumbled. 'I do think I'm in danger of becoming a prisoner of my own hair.'

In 2002, May spoke openly about the depression he'd experienced following Mercury's death and the end of his first marriage. After having suicidal thoughts, he checked into Cottonwood Tucson, a clinic in Arizona, for therapy. 'I have a depressive personality,' he has since said. 'I don't think you get cured of being a depressive; you just learn to deal with it. And I have dealt with it for many years.'

May has busied himself with various non-musical projects and worthy causes. Besides completing his PhD thesis and gaining his doctorate, he's co-authored books about astronomy and is a high-profile advocate for animal rights. His country pile is in an official hedgehog-friendly village and, in 2012, he purchased 63 hectares of Dorset woodland (May's Wood) in which he planted 100,000 trees.

May has been a keen horticulturist since the '70s, sometimes gardening at odd hours. Ex-Queen roadie Peter Hince delivered equipment to May's house one night and was shocked when the guitarist answered the door with a torch in his hand and twigs in his hair: 'Brian had been out in the dark attending to his beloved plants and trees.'

Britain's go-to guitar hero: Brian May, 1976.

In May 2020, May told his social media followers that he was in hospital after tearing his buttock muscles 'in a moment of over-enthusiastic gardening'. Jokes followed about Spinal Tap's fictitious drummer, John 'Stumpy' Pepys, who'd died in a bizarre gardening accident.

A few weeks later, May revealed that he'd had a heart attack after his gardening mishap. He was diagnosed with arterial disease and had stents inserted into three blocked arteries. The trouble didn't end there, though. May later suffered a stomach haemorrhage after reacting badly to prescribed drugs. He posted photos from his hospital bed on Instagram, giving a thumbs-up with an IV drip in his hand. 'I'm grateful to be alive,' he said.

As Queen's last men standing, May and Taylor's relationship has come under deep scrutiny in recent times. They're one of rock's greatest odd couples. There's Brian, the vegan animal lover and self-proclaimed 'poor little rich bastard'; then there's Roger, the game-shooting, Rolls-Royce-driving, unapologetically wealthy rock star.

But they make it work by making it all about the music. 'When you walk out on that stage, you feel alive,' May once said. No longer a fossil or a prisoner of his own hair, he's still doing the 'windmilling Pete Townshend arm thing' and making the audience believe it's Beethoven.

MERCURY, FREDDIE

The singer's tale

Freddie Mercury's hotel alias in Queen:
Alfred Mason

Freddie Mercury's answers in a *People* magazine interview, 1974:

My idea of beauty:
Face-pack

My favourite flower:
Rose

My favourite colour:
Black

My favourite place:
London

My closest friend:
My cats

My greatest happiness:
Audience participation

My favourite amusement:
My manager

My favourite song and composer:
'House Burning Down'/Jimi Hendrix

My favourite name:
Rapunzel

Five things the rest of Queen have said about Freddie Mercury:

Brian May:
'There was always that element of self-parody in Freddie.'

Roger Taylor:
'I think he'll be remembered as this great, slightly self-mocking showman.'

John Deacon:
'There is no point carrying on. It's impossible to replace Freddie.'

Roger Taylor:
'He was a mystery. I'm not sure anybody really knew him.'

In 1970, Freddie Mercury tried to join the real world by getting a regular job. Newly graduated from Ealing Art College, he received a commission from the Austin Knight advertising agency on London's Chancery Lane. His old flatmates remember him drawing a corset for a women's underwear ad.

Others recall the future rock star illustrating a children's science-fiction story and a book about First World War aircraft. He also designed Queen's original logo, based around the band members' respective star signs. But Freddie was easily distracted, too. He was always ready to put down his pencil and talk about Jimi Hendrix, listen to Led Zeppelin or mess around with his hair.

Mercury never took these things very seriously. One art-school assignment required students to create advertising slogans for a fictitious product; Mercury jokily proposed some kind of genital cream.

'I'm sure his slogan was "Add lacquer to your knacker",' recalled an amused Brian May years later.

'Yes, "Add lustre to your cluster",' replied a laughing Roger Taylor.

Even after Queen signed a record deal, Mercury lived in fear of conventional employment. He'd catch the number-nine bus from Kensington High Street and sit in the same seat (top deck, front left) on his way to Queen's management's office in Soho. He'd watch ordinary people, bustling like worker ants on the pavement, and shudder. 'I don't know what I'm going to do if this band doesn't take off,' he'd tell whichever friend or bandmate he was travelling with. 'I don't want to end up working in an art studio.'

Today, it's entirely possible to imagine Dr Brian May as a university lecturer, but Freddie Mercury was born to be Freddie Mercury. In reality, though, he was Farrokh Bulsara, born in Zanzibar City on 5 September 1946 to father Bomi, a high-court cashier at the British Colonial Office, and mother Jer. The Bulsaras were Parsi Indian; their ancestors had lived in what was once Persia (now Iran) before fleeing when the Arabs conquered the country in the seventh century. Many headed south to Zanzibar; others to the Indian subcontinent.

One of the earliest photographs of Mercury shows him sitting upright in his pram with his stony-faced nanny, or 'ayah', watching over him. Mercury surrounded himself with ayahs for most of his life, except later they were personal dressers, bag-carriers and aides. In Queen, Mercury was dependent on others (he'd never catch a plane on his own, for example), but he also had a self-reliant streak, instilled in him from an early age.

Freddie was sent away to boarding school in Mumbai at the age of eight. The voyage from Zanzibar to India took ten days and he travelled with only a couple of other pupils for company. They filled their time playing table tennis – back and forth, hour upon hour, day after day. . .

Many years later, Mercury challenged Thin Lizzy guitarist Scott Gorham to a game at London's Olympic Studios. One match turned into a 'best of five' tournament, rock star against rock star. 'I thought, "Woah! Fuck! This isn't happening!"' recalled former school champion Gorham, who leapt for the ping-pong ball, bat flailing and hair flying. 'We were trying to psych one another out, trying out different spins, shit talking.' Gorham won, but only just.

Mercury spent eight years at St Peter's School in Panchgani, near Mumbai. 'Accomplished boxer, good singer, outstanding pianist, unbeatable table tennis player, thoroughly mediocre cross-country runner,' read his 1959 school report. He helped start a group, the Hectics, and became their pianist and arranger. He would listen to the new Elvis or Fats Domino single on the radio and teach the other band members the chords. The job of lead singer went to his more outgoing classmate, though.

In January 1964, Zanzibar's sultanate was overthrown in a violent uprising. As an employee of the British consulate, Bomi Bulsara was in danger. Mercury later told a college friend that the rebels threatened to execute his father.

The family left Zanzibar with a pair of suitcases and the clothes they were wearing. They arrived in England in spring. Bomi found work as an accountant and the Bulsaras settled at 22 Gladstone Avenue, Feltham – an unprepossessing suburb of west London. Today, there's an English Heritage blue plaque on the wall of the house and a 'Hollywood Walk of Fame'-style memorial star for Freddie on Feltham High Street.

Those who met Mercury at the time remember a softly spoken boy, a little adrift in a new country, but determined to fit in. He asked his new friends to call him 'Fred' or 'Freddie' and told his parents that he wasn't bright enough to become a doctor and wanted to study art. Attending Ealing Art College allowed him to embrace pop culture. It was full of other wannabe musicians.

The metamorphosis from Farrokh Bulsara to Freddie Mercury had begun. Studying graphic design was quickly superseded by the thrill of seeing Jimi Hendrix. By 1969, the gauche ex-boarding school boy had become a fashionista in knotted silk scarves. He was telling everyone that he was going to be a pop star.

Freddie's first girlfriend was an art student named Rosemary Pearson. He took her for tea in the college canteen after discovering she'd been to a filming of *Top of the Pops*. 'He confided to me that it was his secret ambition to perform on that show,' wrote Rosemary (now known as Rose Rose) in their memoir, *Life, Art and Freddie Mercury*.

To achieve this, though, he had to find a group. His college friend, Tim Staffell, was singing and playing bass in Smile alongside Brian May and Roger Taylor. Freddie wanted to join them, but the option wasn't available. Instead, he discovered a Liverpudlian group called Ibex and talked his way into becoming their singer. Rosemary remembers literally stitching Freddie into a pair of homemade trousers before an Ibex show in Merseyside.

But his showmanship and dress sense was ahead of his vocal prowess. Today, May and Taylor politely acknowledge Mercury's shortcomings without tarnishing the legend. In less guarded moments, both have admitted that, as much as they adored their friend, they didn't take him too seriously at first.

However, when Smile broke up in 1970, Mercury put them back together again in his image. May and Taylor had spent two and a half years getting nowhere, but Mercury had ideas about presentation and showmanship. Now they listened. 'Freddie was a blagger,' Taylor said. 'He had this enormous drive and charm, though. I think in his mind he was always plotting to join up with us. It just took us a while to realise it.'

He was already a star in his own mind, too. Freddie drifted between friends' flats and sofas and the stall he ran with Taylor at Kensington Market. He was impoverished but immaculate and kept his one pair of white trousers in pristine condition by pressing them under whatever mattress or cushions he was sleeping on. His white boots were spotless, but, when he put his feet up, his friends noticed holes in the soles.

Changing his name to 'Freddie Mercury' helped him visualise his dream. He adopted a new persona in the same way that preacher's son Vincent Furnier turned himself into shock-rocker Alice Cooper or a group of disparate New Yorkers painted their faces to become Kiss. 'Mercury isn't my real name, dear,' he teased journalists. 'I changed it from Pluto.'

Over time, he also learned how to harness the power in his voice. 'He became a singer by sheer force of will,' said Taylor. 'He was a product of his own enormous energy – a tribute to the idea that, if you believe in something hard enough, you can make it happen.'

Like most aspects of his life, Mercury was rarely forthcoming about his musical training. He studied piano up to grade four and insisted he couldn't sight-read ('I play by ear, dear'), though he could also be disingenuous.

'Freddie was a unique pianist and didn't realise how good he was,' said May. 'His playing was very percussive and rhythmic – like a metronome, but with feeling. Amazing fingers. He also had this very attacking, staccato way of playing guitar.'

It's audible on songs as diverse as 'The Fairy Feller's Master-Stroke' and 'Crazy Little Thing Called Love', but there was a restlessness to his writing. It was like his musical brain was sometimes moving too fast for his mouth and fingers. No two Freddie songs – be they 'Seven Seas of Rhye' or 'Killer Queen', 'Bohemian Rhapsody' or 'We Are the Champions' – ever sounded the same.

His influences zigzagged between the Who and the Jackson 5, Led Zeppelin and Liza Minnelli. There were no boundaries or limits. He also wasn't defined by what was deemed hip in '70s rock circles. He had no problem being schlocky, sentimental and overly obvious. It's also no wonder Queen's music is used in so many TV adverts; the chorus of 'We Are the Champions' sounds like an advertising jingle.

At the same time, Mercury's songs could also be wonderfully strange. In the pantheon of peculiar '70s pop hits, few are more peculiar than 'Bicycle Race'. 'Most of us worry whether we're pleasing people or not,' said Brian May. 'But Freddie had the ability to think, "No, I'm pleasing myself and I'm going to do what I want to do."'

Rosemary Pearson once described Mercury's mindset like so: 'Feel the fear and do it anyway.'

'He taught me to ignore notions of personal limitations,' she wrote. 'To never accept prosaic conventions, to keep on moving forward and never be demeaned by the negativity of others.'

Mercury's single-mindedness also meant casualties. Rosemary believed Freddie was bisexual long before they broke up, but it wasn't until 1976 that he came out to his then-'wife', Mary Austin. Though there was a great emotional fall-out, the two stayed friends for the rest of Freddie's life.

Brian May believes that these battles were reflected in his songs 'Lily of the Valley' and 'Love of My Life'. Before then, he'd disguised his feelings. Writing about fairies, ogres and 'lords and lady preachers' etc. was 'a convenient way for him to freely express his emotions, but not make them too naked'.

Mercury was similarly fearless with his image. His plunging V-neck one-pieces and minuscule glittery shorts were considered brave even in the androgynous '70s. 'I was aghast at the nerve he showed,' said Taylor. 'But really I had to stand back and admire the brass neck. Just thinking, "Christ, I would never have had the nerve to go on stage wearing a ballet outfit."'

When the money came, Mercury embraced the trappings of stardom with great gusto. He acquired a chauffeured Rolls-Royce Silver Shadow, a Kensington pied-à-terre and an expensive cocaine habit. Underneath, though, he was still insecure about his sexuality, his background, his protruding teeth . . .

'So he built this armour around himself,' explained May, which often entailed goading the music press. 'Is this man a prat?' asked the *NME* in 1977. At times, yes.

'He was very, very shy and that shyness could be interpreted as aloofness,' admitted Taylor. 'Freddie also thought it was sensible not to be too available, which was probably a very good idea.'

While it was sometimes an act, there were still arrogant gestures and genuine tantrums. Mercury once arrived on stage in New York, sprayed the front row with Champagne and called them cunts. Backstage in Sydney, he smashed a hand mirror over his personal manager's head. 'I seem to have created a monster,' he once said. 'But I'm not like that really.'

In the studio, though, he was willing to compromise, putting himself between bickering siblings May and Taylor like a boxing referee. 'He was very good at mediating,' said Brian. 'People don't expect that of Freddie because all they see is the diva he was on stage.'

As the years passed, Mercury's image, eccentricities and tastes changed. Ballerina Freddie turned into moustachioed, macho Freddie. Like John Deacon, he also started smoking cigarettes in his thirties, 'though he never learned how to hold them properly', says one Queen associate.

On Queen's problematic *Hot Space* album, Mercury dived headlong into R&B and dance music, but Queen's audience refused to join him. Undeterred, he signed a solo deal with CBS and made another album, 1985's *Mr Bad Guy*, in a similar vein. It bombed. So much so that CBS president Walter Yetnikoff later described it as 'the worst deal I ever made'.

'Freddie loved Michael Jackson's *Off the Wall*,' explained Taylor, 'and loved the idea of doing an album like that. But I don't think he really wanted to go solo; it's just that he got a lot of money from CBS. When it came down to actually doing a solo album, he did miss us. He used to ring me up and I'd have to fly to Munich to do his backing vocals.'

Mercury didn't dwell on *Mr Bad Guy*'s failure. Instead, he went back to Queen and made a number-one album, *A Kind of Magic*. Then, to confound expectations, he had a solo hit with a cover of the Platters' 'The Great Pretender' (as apt a song as any), followed by another left-field hit, 'Barcelona', with the

Spanish opera star Montserrat Caballé. No boundaries, no limits and no fear.

'He had no masterplan,' wrote Peter Freestone, Mercury's former personal assistant. 'He wouldn't have had the patience for long-term planning and strategies. His life and work was a progression, one thing leading from another.'

Queen's performance at Live Aid also illustrates a crucial aspect of the Freddie Mercury persona: humour. There's none of the cheek-sucking earnestness displayed by some of his contemporaries. He has a big, goofy grin on his face from the moment he canters on to the stage. 'He always had a twinkle in his eye,' said May.

On stage, Mercury was always in control; off stage, less so. There were many ex-boyfriends and ex-lovers and as many fights and bust-ups. He even played the Milton Keynes Bowl in summer 1982 with a bleeding wound in the webbing between his thumb and forefinger – his partner had bitten his hand during a row before-hand. 'Freddie could be too trusting,' said one Queen familiar, 'and some men took advantage of that.' Many believe that he was happy with partner Jim Hutton in his final years, though.

After his HIV diagnosis in 1987, Mercury kept his private life private, but he was pursued by the tabloid press until his death on 24 November 1991. 'I've lived a life that's full,' he once said, 'and, if I'm dead tomorrow, I don't give a damn. I've done it all.'

He bequeathed his London townhouse, Garden Lodge, and most of his royalties to Mary Austin, as well as £500,000 each to Hutton, Freestone and fellow carer Joe Fanelli. But there would be arguments and recrimination in the years ahead. With Mercury gone, the Queen organisation weren't as accommodating towards his friends, including Mary, as they had been during his lifetime.

Mercury once described his songs as disposable. 'Like Bic razors,' he said, 'people can discard them like a used tissue afterwards.' His music hasn't been used to advertise razors or tissues – yet – but Mercury's afterlife has proved lucrative for the estate and the band.

Who wants to live forever: the immortal Freddie Mercury, 1976.

The image of 'Alfred Mason' is currently preserved through T-shirts, figurines, official clip-on replica moustaches and Mercury Phoenix Trust face masks (all available from Queen's online store).

Freddie Mercury made it to forty-five years old without having to take a proper job in an art studio. Today, he enjoys the rare distinction of being one of the few rock stars instantly recognisable by his silhouette. It's almost as though he drew his own logo in the art-school studio in 1970.

THE MIRACLE

Queen in love

It only happened a couple of times, but it was an irritation. It was February 1988, Roger Taylor's side group, the Cross, were playing live and Cadbury Flake bars were being thrown on stage. The reason: newspapers had just run a story about Taylor's affair with model Deborah Leng, the 'Cadbury Flake girl' from the famously suggestive TV ads.

The pair had met the previous year and were now a couple. But, in the meantime, Taylor had married Dominique Beyrand – his long-term partner and the mother of his two children – to secure their finances. The marriage lasted just twenty-four days before Roger left. 'It's a complicated situation,' he understatedly told the *Daily Mail*. And now chocolate bars were landing at his feet while he performed.

The drummer wasn't the only one having his private life splashed across the papers. The press were still pursuing Freddie Mercury as rumours about his health escalated. Meanwhile, Brian

May and actor Anita Dobson's relationship was under scrutiny as May was still married to his first wife. John Deacon just kept his head down, skiing in Biarritz usually. All this emotional drama was played out on Queen's thirteenth album.

The Miracle was Queen back together after a long, mutually agreed hiatus. In the words of estranged couples everywhere: they'd been 'on a break'. 'We hadn't split up,' insisted Taylor, 'but we had taken the decision to spend some time apart.'

However, nobody had been idle in the seventeen months between the end of the Magic Tour and the start of Queen's work on *The Miracle* in January 1988. Mercury had managed two hit singles (each so dissimilar to the other that it was difficult to believe they came from the same musician): 'Barcelona' – a duet with opera star Montserrat Caballé – and a campy cover of the Platters' 'The Great Pretender'. Brian May oversaw Anita Dobson's solo LP and produced the spoof heavy-metal band Bad News (featuring comic actors Adrian Edmondson and Rik Mayall). Their album's deliberately hopeless cover of 'Bohemian Rhapsody' was a talking point. 'But Freddie saw the humour,' said Brian.

John Deacon also detoured into comedy. He co-produced and played on the top-five hit 'Stutter Rap' – a hip-hop pastiche by Morris Minor and the Majors (featuring TV comic actor Tony Hawks). Taylor went a step further and formed the Cross, indulging his rock-star fantasies by becoming their lead singer. The Cross's debut album, *Shove It*, had Mercury singing on one song, 'Heaven for Everyone', and May playing on another, but it didn't chart. The upside was that Taylor met his Flake girl on a video shoot for the single 'Cowboys and Indians'.

There was one fundamental difference with *The Miracle*. Prior to recording, Queen agreed to divide the songwriting credits four ways. 'We made a decision we should have made fifteen years ago,' said May at the time. 'It also helps when we choose singles because it's difficult to be dispassionate about a song that's purely of your own making.'

Thirty years on, May felt differently. 'There were moments where all of us thought we'd given too much away,' he admitted. 'If it comes up about who wrote, say, "I Want It All", I'll say, "Yes, that's me." Then I have to remember, "Oh, hang on. It says 'Queen' in the credits." If I'm being honest, there is still a bit of that.'

The sessions began with each member presenting their demos, some thirty in total, at London's Olympic Studios. These were then turned into Queen songs at Town House and Montreux's Mountain Studios, with co-producer David Richards mediating. While there were artistic disagreements, everybody had a financial interest in every track.

Taylor's songs, 'Breakthru' and 'The Invisible Man', reinforced the positives of this new arrangement. Neither song was that far removed from the overprocessed heavy pop he was doing with the Cross, but Queen gave the songs character. During 'The Invisible Man' (inspired by Victorian sci-fi author H. G. Wells's novel), Taylor shouted out Mercury's name before he began singing. Mercury then announced John Deacon and Brian May as the song progressed. The message: this was a group effort.

Meanwhile, Mercury grafted a gospel vocal from one of his unreleased songs, 'A New Life Is Born', onto the intro of the pacey, cod-hard rocker 'Breakthru'. 'I wrote "The Invisible Man" and "Breakthru" very deliberately to be hits,' Taylor said. 'We wanted to stay relevant in the '90s.' It worked: both singles later went into the top twenty.

Brian's May's 'I Want It All' was *The Miracle*'s first hit. With a bold riff and a bolder lyric (the title was one of Anita Dobson's sayings), it was another of what Taylor called 'Queen's statement songs'. But it was destined never to be played live with Mercury.

Director David Mallet's performance video was carefully shot to disguise Freddie's condition. He'd lost weight and grown a beard to hide the Kaposi's sarcoma marks on his jaw. 'Fred was really very sick,' admitted May. 'You can't tell from the video, but he found some of it a struggle.'

The nature of Mercury's disease was such that he looked healthier in the promo for the follow-up, 'Breakthru'. In the video, he joined his bandmates on top of a steam train, haring through the Cambridgeshire countryside. Deborah Leng also made an appearance, marching down the track in a short black skirt and dramatic eye make-up. May later said that the whole song was a metaphor for Taylor 'breaking through to the next chapter in his life'.

One of Taylor's other songs, the mid-tempo '80s rocker 'Hijack My Heart', suggested the same. It didn't make the album, but instead became the B-side of 'The Invisible Man'. In the song, Roger huskily serenaded a girl in a sports car, whose smile 'zapped me right between the eyes'. Queen's resident playboy sounded like a lovestruck teenager – and a bit like Rod Stewart, too.

The rest of *The Miracle* skittered between loud rock, machine-tooled ballads and Deacon and Mercury's random oddities. The pair's 'Rain Must Fall' was a bouncy soul number of the kind heard in '80s rom-coms – perhaps during a scene in which two young lovers drink rum punch and dance self-consciously on a Caribbean beach. 'My Baby Does Me' moved the same story along – the couple are now having sex in the overwater bungalow while Brian May plays a solo on the balcony outside.

As a contrast, the double whammy of 'Party' and 'Khashoggi's Ship' were a sweetener to Queen's neglected rocker fanbase. The latter was a leadfooted bump-and-grind track inspired by billion-aire arms dealer Adnan Khashoggi's monied lifestyle. 'We read about that kind of society life – the parties on the ship, the excess,' said May in 1989. 'We feel that we've touched on those areas at some time. We've been through it.'

May's song, 'Scandal', was a frustrated commentary on his and Mercury's recent run-ins with the press (May's children had apparently learned of his affair with Anita Dobson through the papers). With its soupy production and percolating synths, the song was also endemic of the album's overall sound.

The Miracle might sound dated now because of the technology used, but it was more of a piece than its predecessor, *A Kind of Magic*. Its title track and 'Was It All Worth It' suggested the band casting a rueful eye over the past and wondering whether they still had a future. 'The Miracle' was schlocky and obvious, with Mercury celebrating the Taj Mahal, Jimi Hendrix and a cup of tea, before wishing for world peace. 'It's a brave concept,' said May. 'Because you're talking about a man who knows he has a death sentence hanging over him.'

The video for 'The Miracle' had the band played by 'mini-me' actors. The four young boys, dressed in curly wigs, harlequin suits and stick-on moustaches, were then joined on stage by the real members of Queen. Viewers couldn't help noticing how Freddie's yellow bolero jacket hung off him in a way it never did in 1986.

The opening lyric to 'Was It All Worth It' was surprisingly candid, considering Mercury's condition. 'What is there left for me to do in my life?' he announced. Then the wall came back up as he told Queen's Kensington Market rags-to-riches story with some wincing rhymes ('We bought a drum kit / We blew our own trumpet') over one of the album's best riffs. For a band eager to stay relevant, this song suggested the end was nigh.

Not that Queen would admit it. Their audience had stuck with them this far, so why spoil the party? *The Miracle* was released in May 1989. Its cover image – of the band's four faces merged together via the computer software Quantel Paintbox – compounded the impression of Queen reunited.

The album reached number one in the UK and several European countries, as well as producing five UK top-thirty hits. It only made number twenty-four in the US and any chance Queen had of winning over America disappeared entirely with the announcement that they would not be touring anywhere. 'I don't think a 42-year-old man should be running around in a leotard,' joked Mercury, deflecting an awkward question with humour.

Mercury insisted his illness be kept secret, so it fell to May and Taylor to promote the album and reassure the world that their lead singer was fine, but just didn't want to tour. The strain of hiding the truth was tough. 'I think it took its toll on all of us,' admitted May years later. Queen had a huge hit album, but were already on borrowed time. That *The Miracle* happened at all now seems miraculous in itself.

MITCHELL, BARRY

Queen bass player, no. 2

The dressing room of the old Marquee club on London's Wardour Street was notorious for graffiti. Almost every inch of the wall and ceiling was covered in band names, random obscenities and insults between rival musicians. Somewhere in the midst of it all was the name 'Barry Mitchell'. Queen's second bass guitarist remembers autographing the wall on 8 January 1971 – the first time he played the Marquee.

Barry Mitchell grew up in Harrow, north-west London. By 1970, he'd been performing in groups for five years. (The line-up of one of these groups included Alan Parsons, who'd later engineer Pink Floyd's *The Dark Side of the Moon* and launch prog-rockers the Alan Parsons Project.) None lasted, though. That summer, Mitchell was employed at Sopers department store in Harrow, where he met a friend of Roger Taylor's, named Roger Crossley, who was up from Cornwall for the holidays. Crossley told Mitchell that his friend's band, Queen, needed a bassist (as Mike Grose had just left). Phone numbers were exchanged and Roger Taylor asked Mitchell to audition.

Barry made his Queen debut at London's Imperial College on 23 August. It was a private gig for friends and the bassist's lasting memory of the night is watching Freddie Mercury teasing his hair with heated tongs before going on stage. 'I'd never seen a guy use heated tongs before,' he laughed. 'Freddie was a bit of a puzzle, but very sweet. Brian was fantastically nice and Roger was a bit of a lad.'

Mitchell played eleven gigs with Queen, including four in Merseyside. 'A couple of colleges and a derelict church,' he recalled. There was also a date at Liverpool's fabled Cavern Club on 31 October. (It was 'such a thrill to stand on the same stage as the Beatles'.) However, by Christmas, it seemed to Barry that Queen weren't going anywhere.

There were musical differences, too. 'Hendrix was the big connection for all of us,' he said. 'I remember rehearsing the night he died and we just played Hendrix songs. But Queen's own songs were a bit airy-fairy for me. I also thought Freddie was the weakest link. He didn't have the command of his voice then. None of us could have foreseen what he became. I also wanted to do something more soulful, something with a brass section.'

Mitchell played his final Queen gig on 9 January 1971, supporting Kevin Ayers and Genesis at Ewell Technical College. 'We parted ways and it was all amicable,' he insisted. 'Though I remember Freddie's girlfriend, Mary Austin, trying to talk me out of it.'

Barry later joined a hard-rock band called Tiger: 'But nothing happened with them, so I sold my gear and gave it all up.' By 1974, he was working in the Ealing branch of electrical retailers Dixons. ('One day, John Deacon came in to buy a plug . . .') A year later, Mitchell saw the video for 'Bohemian Rhapsody' blaring out of a TV set in the shop: 'I told my co-workers, "Hey, I used to be in that band!" But I don't know if they believed me.'

Like Mike Grose, Mitchell moved on with his life and didn't dine out on his time in Queen. It wasn't always easy. 'At first, Queen still weren't my cup of tea,' he said. 'I saw them again at Imperial College and with Mott the Hoople, but they really came of age at Live Aid, didn't they?'

In 1988, the Marquee club in Wardour Street was demolished, turning Barry Mitchell's graffitied autograph to dust. It was like his past life with Queen had been erased. Then, eight years later, *Q* magazine ran an article mentioning ex-Smile man Tim Staffell. Mitchell wrote a letter to the magazine adding further information. It was seen by Jim Jenkins, the writer and co-founder of the Queen fan club, who contacted *Q* asking to be put in touch with the elusive Barry Mitchell. 'Until then, I didn't talk about it,' said Mitchell. 'But, if I'm honest, it bugged me a little that Queen didn't talk about the early guys.'

Queen's second bassist had come out of hiding. However, there weren't any photographs of him with the group, which was an issue when a Sunday newspaper wanted to run an interview. 'It meant the article never came out,' he said. 'But I remember Brian had a new camera when we played the Cavern and he spent the whole journey in the Transit looking through the lens. I'm sure Brian has photos.'

After being outed, Mitchell became a regular guest at Queen fan-club conventions. In 2018, he was interviewed at the 'Freddie for a Day' charity event in Paris. 'Why did I leave the band?' he pondered. 'In hindsight, it seems foolish, but, when I was with them, they weren't the band they became.'

'Had you stayed, would you have continued with Queen + Adam Lambert or retired like John Deacon?' asked the interviewer.

'I agree with John's decision,' Mitchell replied emphatically. 'If that had been me, I'd have taken that decision, too. Retire gracefully and count your money.'

MOTT THE HOOPLE

Queen's fairy godfathers

In 2019, Brian May joined re-formed rock veterans Mott the Hoople for their encore at the Shepherd's Bush Empire. Four decades earlier, Mott had adopted a rookie Queen as their support act. Queen never forget the lessons learned. 'With Mott the Hoople I was conscious we were in the presence of something great,' said May. 'Something to breathe in.'

Queen met Mott the Hoople in October 1973, a month before their first tour of British theatres and town halls. Mott's biggest cheerleader, David Bowie, had written their hit single, 'All the Young Dudes'. Against all expectations, Mott had become pop stars after years of hard graft and modest sales.

Mott the Hoople were also a people's band; they had little time for airs and graces and hifalutin progressive rock. Neither Mott nor their road crew had seen anything like Queen when they arrived for their first rehearsal. Everyone else at London's Manticore Studios was dressed for the grim British winter, but Queen were in their satin stage clothes. According to one Mott roadie, the general consensus was that Freddie Mercury was 'a bit of a wally'.

Queen's management had paid the headliners £3,000 to get their band on the tour. For a support act, Queen were certainly precocious, hustling Mott the Hoople's crew for more stage space and a drum riser of their own. Mott bristled at their demands, but Queen were too good to be dismissed. The groups travelled on the same bus and soon bonded.

'Brian May was a very intelligent man,' said Ian Hunter, Mott's lead singer, 'and Fred had so much confidence it was funny. I don't think he even knew he was funny, which made it even funnier. In his head, he was a star already, but he was also rather needy.'

As good as Queen were, Mott had the hits. Their grand finale, 'All the Way From Memphis', was a guaranteed crowd-pleaser. 'We picked up a lot from them about stagecraft and how to connect with an audience,' said May. 'It was a true education. We took some of their tricks and started using them.'

Mercury, though, found it frustrating being second on the bill. 'The most traumatic experience of my life,' he half-joked later.

The following April, Queen joined Mott the Hoople for their inaugural US tour. The seasoned headliners ensured their young charges sampled everything America and the road had to offer. They boozed the night away with bawdy singer Bette Midler and a coterie of drag queens, and Freddie once passed out, hungover, in a plate of breakfast eggs. In Boston, Brian went on stage drunk after guzzling bourbon with guitarist Joe Perry from opening act Aerosmith. In New Orleans, he fell head over heels for a girl mysteriously known as 'Peaches'.

Mott the Hoople were a glam-rock group in as much as they wore stack-heeled boots and their guitarist Ariel Bender had a thatch of dyed silver hair. But their music was anthemic pop and bluesy rock 'n' roll. It went down well everywhere. Queen's more frenetic sound and dandy fashions proved a harder sell. 'The problem with Queen at the time was that they were very stiff where everybody else was very sloppy,' suggested Hunter.

There was another obstacle, too: the name. Waitresses in truck-stop diners peered quizzically at Mercury in his ruinously tight trousers and asked whether all the band were queens 'or just him'. At the time, he was still in a relationship with girlfriend Mary Austin.

One night, after a show, Hunter found Mercury pacing up and down, upset about the audience's lukewarm reaction. 'I said, "It's a big country, Fred. You've got to go around three or four times before it happens. It's not like England where you can conquer it in a day."'

'Even then, Ian was the sage old man of rock 'n' roll,' recalled Brian May. On the road, Queen were sharing rooms and were only allowed to make calls home from their manager's hotel suite. May missed his old life. 'I said to Ian, "I am finding it difficult." And he looked at me and said, "Brian, if you are the kind of person who needs his home stuff around you, then you are in the wrong job."'

When the tour reached New York for a six-night run at the Uris Theatre, Queen's provocative name and image finally paid off. The theatre lobby swarmed with exotically dressed creatures. At the box office, local glam-rockers Kiss talked their way onto the guest list.

'We thought we were unusual,' said May, 'but a lot of the people who came were surprising, even to us – a lot of transvestite artists, the New York Dolls and Andy Warhol – people who were creative in a way that seemed to trash everything that had come before.'

But Queen's American adventure was rudely cut short when May contracted hepatitis. The band flew home and Mott carried on without them. The apprentices acknowledged their masters on *Sheer Heart Attack*, with May including the lyric 'Down in the city, just Hoople and me' in his song 'Now I'm Here'.

Not long after, Ian Hunter left Mott the Hoople and began a solo career. Mott struggled on for a time before conceding defeat. Unlike some of their devotees, they never became huge stars, but, in years to come, the Clash and the Sex Pistols would join David Bowie and Queen in paying lip service to the band.

'I was happy when Queen got huge,' said 81-year-old Ian Hunter in 2020. 'I loved Fred. He was the real thing. When I see Roger or I see Brian now, it's like seeing two younger brothers.'

MOUSTACHE

Hair apparent

Roger Taylor's favourite comment about Freddie Mercury's facial hair goes like this: 'It's funny how he got more press out of growing a moustache than he would have done walking naked down Oxford Street.' Good point. Mercury's 'tache has survived its owner's demise. In 2019, *Men's Health* magazine voted it number twenty-one in 'The 40 Best Moustaches of All Time', just ahead of fellow pop royalty Lionel Richie, though some way behind Mexican artist Frida Kahlo.

Freddie first acquired his divisive accessory in Munich, spring 1980. 'I love it,' he told everybody at Musicland Studios. But he was in the minority. The moustache completed his 'Castro clone' look. This slang expression (named after San Francisco's gay-friendly Castro district) was applied to homosexual men who exaggerated their traditional masculinity with moustaches, short hair and plaid shirts. Mercury had been adopting elements of this image for the preceding two years.

However, the moustache also reflected his love of vintage movie-star glamour, including matinee idol Clark Gable (number sixteen in the *Men's Health* moustache poll). Later, Freddie hired the veteran photographer George Hurrell, who'd worked with Gable and other Hollywood stars, to shoot Queen for the cover of *The Works*.

The moustache was publicly unveiled in May 1980 in the video for Queen's new single, 'Play the Game'. Disgruntled fans began sending packets of razors to the group's office. 'A man grows a moustache? Big deal,' huffed Taylor. Razors were also thrown on stage during Queen's next US tour. 'Do you boys like this moustache?' Mercury teased the audience. 'I don't give a fuck.'

Today, Queen's music is one big amorphous collection of songs. In the early '80s, though, the state of their singer's top lip was a marker post. For some, there was the music Queen made before Freddie's moustache and the music they made after.

The facial hair remained for most of the decade, but disappeared briefly for some scenes in the video for 1984's 'I Want to Break Free'. Queen historian Jim Jenkins was an extra at the shoot and complimented Mercury on being clean-shaven. 'I said, "Oh, we've got our old Freddie back – you might write some decent songs again." He glared; I went cold. If looks could kill . . .'

NEW ORLEANS

The most debauched party of all time?

Queen's most infamous soirée was held on Halloween night 1978 at the Fairmont Hotel in New Orleans. Its bacchanalian excess has become music-biz folklore, but even Queen aren't entirely sure what happened.

EMI Records hired the Californian music PR firm Gibson & Stromberg to organise the event. It would be held after Queen's show at the New Orleans Municipal Auditorium to celebrate the release of their new album, *Jazz*. Although later described in *Interview* magazine as 'Saturday Night in Sodom', the party actually took place on a Tuesday.

Gibson & Stromberg were told that invitees would include eighty journalists and fifty-two EMI managing directors from around the world – and these people expected decadence. 'I was instructed to find anyone offbeat who might bring a little colour to proceedings,' said boss Bob Gibson (who died in 2020).

Gibson chose the Fairmont on Roosevelt Avenue. It had been built for the 1894 Mardi Gras and was close to the vibrant French Quarter. His team spent three days auditioning more than fifty acts from clubs and bars, many on the city's world-famous

Bourbon Street. The good, the bad, the ugly and the bizarre beat a path to the hotel. Gibson vetted strippers of every conceivable shape and size, dancers, drag queens, jugglers, snake charmers and contortionists. But he apparently drew the line at one whose act consisted solely of biting the heads off live chickens. Another unsubstantiated rumour claimed an auditionee offered to decapitate herself with a chainsaw for $100,000 – presumably she would have to have been paid up front.

The Fairmont's Imperial Ballroom was decorated with dozens of rented dead trees to create a skeletal forest in keeping with Halloween. Queen made their grand entrance on the stroke of midnight, piped into the room by the New Orleans Olympia Brass Band. Unlike their hired entertainers, the band looked remarkably ordinary. Mercury's partywear included a plaid shirt twinned with braces; John Deacon wore a woolly tank-top – the kind a young boy might receive from a maiden aunt at Christmas.

As many as 500 guests mingled among the dead wood, quaffing gratis Champagne and sampling from banquet tables heaving under the weight of meat and seafood. Beyond this point, though, is where legend takes over.

There was certainly nudity. EMI's Japanese label reps were fascinated by the strippers, and Bob Gibson remembered doling out wads of cash 'so they could do the traditional thing of putting money in the G-string'. One *Rolling Stone* journalist insisted he saw a naked woman 'smoking' a cigarette from her private parts. Another reporter claims the smoker was Samoan and weighed 'at least 300lbs'.

'There were women doing strange things with their anatomies,' confirmed Brian May. Some accounts also include naked mud wrestlers, but sources claim they actually came later, after Queen's 1982 Madison Square Garden concert.

And then there were the dwarves . . .

'As they enter the hotel, guests are greeted by hermaphrodite dwarves serving cocaine from trays strapped to their heads,' wrote Jon Wilde in *Uncut* magazine in 2005. 'The coke has been specially imported from Bolivia and quality-checked by Mercury.'

Most accounts eschew any reference to the dwarves' sex, Bolivia or quality checks. Sometimes it was said that the cocaine was carried around in bowls, but both trays and bowls would have been problematic: how were they strapped to the dwarves' heads? Were they, essentially, hats, the tops of which were filled with cocaine? In one story, the dwarves also offered oral sex, kneeling down to allow the recipient to snort the drug at the same time as being pleasured. In another, the dwarves were naked, which scotches a further rumour that they were carrying straws in the top pockets of their jackets with which to snort the drug.

Brian May was asked about cocaine-dispensing dwarves in the 2011 *Days of Our Lives* documentary. 'Oh, I don't know,' he replied. Roger Taylor, though, recalled seeing 'one man of restricted growth' at the party, but he was not carrying drugs. Instead, he was employed to lie on a table, covered completely in cold cuts and sliced meats 'so you couldn't see him'. Whenever a guest approached the table, he shook his body and the smorgasbord wobbled.

'The dwarves with cocaine never happened,' Taylor said in 2008. 'Well, I never saw it. Actually, it could have been true.'

'The dwarves and cocaine is a myth,' he insisted ten years later. 'Actually, we were probably responsible for exaggerating that story ourselves.'

According to legend, the Fairmont party cost EMI $200,000. Not necessarily money well spent. One company insider said that the band complained the party was 'too contrived'. Freddie Mercury wanted 'real decadence, and this was pretend'.

Too late. Queen had created a monster. Like the apocryphal tale of the Who's Keith Moon driving a Rolls-Royce/Cadillac into a hotel swimming pool, Queen's cocaine-bearing dwarves became a universal symbol of '70s rock excess. It will never go away.

What goes around comes back around, though, and with uncomfortable consequences. In 2013, Sacha Baron Cohen – the actor due to play Freddie before Rami Malek – quit *Bohemian Rhapsody*, complaining the script was too sanitised. So what did he want? 'Sacha wanted dwarves with cocaine on their heads,' admitted Roger Taylor.

NEWS OF THE WORLD

Queen versus the robot

Taylor Hawkins – the blond-haired, perma-grinning Foo Fighters drummer – is one of the world's biggest Queen aficionados. Interviews about his band's new album can easily be derailed just by saying the words 'Roger Taylor'. In a 2005 interview, a casual mention of Queen's drummer set his half-namesake off down the rabbit hole.

Hawkins explained how Queen's *News of the World* – particularly the album's 'We Will Rock You' – is inextricably linked to his childhood. It was a sunny afternoon in 1977 and six-year-old Taylor was in his parents' car, cruising back to their home in Laguna Beach, California. The family had been to the cinema to see the latest remake of the classic monster movie *King Kong*.

Suddenly, 'We Will Rock You' came on the car radio. 'Somehow, in my mind, there was now a correlation between

King Kong and the sound of Roger Taylor's drums,' explained Hawkins. 'Somehow they fitted so well with the image of this monster stomping through the city that I couldn't separate the two.' Later, upon seeing *News of the World*'s cover plastered across record store windows, the link between music and monster was further compounded. Except now a giant robot joined a giant ape in Hawkins' impressionable young mind.

After five albums of ornate, fiddly hard rock, *News of the World* came as a shock. Its predecessor, *A Day at the Races*, had sold in droves, but no more than *A Night at the Opera*. Queen were forever in competition with themselves and decided on a radical overhaul. 'We were bored, restless and needed to strip the music back,' said Roger Taylor.

News of the World was recorded between July and September 1977 at Wessex Studios – a converted church building in Highbury, north London – with Queen's trusted engineer Mike Stone co-producing. The idea was to record quickly, spontaneously and without multiple overdubs.

But *News of the World* was also the first Queen album on which its four writers sounded like they were wrestling each other. Not just tussling either, but rolling around on the floor. Its opening salvo – Brian May's 'We Will Rock You' – and Freddie Mercury's 'We Are the Champions' demonstrated the yin and yang. But the real battle began later.

The Sex Pistols paid a visit to Wessex while Queen were working. Thus ensued a mildly awkward encounter between two pop groups with radically opposing hairstyles. Taylor's 'Sheer Heart Attack' suggested Queen snubbing their noses at these young punks, but he'd started composing the song three years before the meeting.

No two songs here sounded alike, though. May's 'All Dead, All Dead' and his bluesy, one-take 'Sleeping on the Sidewalk' were at loggerheads with Taylor's self-sung, punchy-sounding 'Fight from the Inside' (Guns N' Roses' Slash later named that song's guitar riff one of his all-time favourites). Meanwhile, John Deacon's 'Spread Your Wings' is the greatest Queen anthem never to have been a hit, while 'It's Late' contains one of Brian May's finest, if often overlooked, guitar riffs.

There's no bigger contrast, though, than the one between Deacon's quirky samba 'Who Needs You' and Mercury's 'Get Down, Make Love'. 'I give you meat,' declares Freddie on the latter, 'I suck your mind.' This was Mercury reinterpreting the sounds he heard in New York's gay clubs: a heady mix of dance music and sex. Brian May used an Eventide Harmonizer (a sound-effects processor) to conjure up what he called 'an erotic interlude' in the middle of the song. It was like the breathless orgasm in Led Zeppelin's 'Whole Lotta Love', but with what sounded like copulating robots rather than Robert Plant.

'Get Down, Make Love' was exhumed for Queen + Adam Lambert's 2017 European tour. It was sometimes greeted by shuffling feet and confused whispers: 'What's this? Do you know this one? I hope they play "Crazy Little Thing Called Love" . . .'

Queen's pared-back approach worked. Trailered by the double A-side 'We Will Rock You'/'We Are the Champions', *News of the World* arrived in October and became a top-five hit in Britain and America. Nobody at EMI liked the cover, though. 'Oh God, it was awful,' one ex-employee complained. 'We'd been trying for ages to get Queen to put their own picture on a sleeve.'

Instead, at sci-fi fan Roger Taylor's behest, Queen had commissioned Frank Kelly Freas – once known as the 'dean of science-fiction artists' – to draw the artwork. Queen wanted a recreation of Freas's robot from a 1953 edition of *Astounding Science Fiction* magazine. They nicknamed the automaton 'Frank'.

In 2006, an all-grown-up Taylor Hawkins fulfilled his boyhood dream and played 'We Will Rock You' live with Queen + Paul Rodgers. It sounded like King Kong's footsteps and he looked like the happiest drummer in the world.

NICKNAMES

What Queen called each other

Freddie Mercury:
'Melina', after the Greek actor, singer and political activist Melina Mercouri.

Brian May:
'Maggie', after Rod Stewart's 1971 hit 'Maggie May'.

Roger Taylor:
'Liz', after movie icon Elizabeth Taylor (later famous for shouting, 'Use a condom!' during her speech at the Freddie Mercury Tribute Concert).

John Deacon:
'Deaky', from his surname; 'Ostrich', because 'he was like a bird who stays quiet until it finally lays a perfect egg'; 'Birdman', after the 1962 prison movie *Birdman of Alcatraz* (which dramatises the incarceration of shaven-headed murderer Robert Franklin Stroud), because he cut his hair short in 1978.

A NIGHT AT THE OPERA AND A DAY AT THE RACES

Two albums, one vision

Queen went to the races on 16 October 1976. Manager John Reid and EMI Records had sponsored '*A Day at the Races* Hurdle' at Kempton Park Racecourse to celebrate Queen's forthcoming fifth album. The band sipped Champagne, studied the form and placed bets, but they were mainly there to be seen.

There are photographs from that day. Freddie Mercury in a crimson velvet blouson and sunglasses sits between John Reid and Mary Austin. Behind him is Roger Taylor and his girlfriend Jo Morris. The drummer's hair looks freshly blond, he's modelling a rabbit-fur coat and looks like a glam-rock bookmaker. In the row behind him is Brian May, wearing a dark suit and tie beside his new wife, Chrissie Mullen. Finally, to May's left, stands John Deacon, peering at a race sheet and looking distinctly unstarry in double denim.

The photographs capture a moment in time. *A Day at the Races* would be a number-one hit before Christmas, just like its predecessor, *A Night at the Opera*. Queen were about to enter their most imperial and imperious phase.

The two albums arrived just over a year apart. Both were named after Marx Brothers movies and both looked alike. Even Queen consider *A Night at the Opera* and *A Day at the Races* to be their unofficial double album. 'I wish in some ways we'd put them out at the same time,' said May. 'We regard them as twins.'

The albums also chart the most dramatic arc in Queen's music and fortunes. After six weeks of rehearsals at Ridge Farm Studios in Surrey and at an old manor house in Herefordshire, Queen arrived at Monmouthshire's Rockfield Studios in August 1975.

They began *A Night at the Opera* not knowing if they were even going to stay together. Queen were in dispute with their old boss, Norman Sheffield, and had been forced to cancel a US tour. As a result, they were almost bankrupt. 'I think we had 1,500 quid between us,' said Taylor. 'If the next album hadn't worked, it would have been the end of Queen.'

Reid and Queen's lawyer, Jim Beach, cleared up the contractual mess, leaving the band and co-producer Roy Thomas Baker free to do as they pleased. It was oddly empowering. They'd reined themselves in on *Sheer Heart Attack*, but they'd show no such restraint on *A Night at the Opera*. Any hits would be strictly on Queen's terms.

The opening, 'Death on Two Legs (Dedicated to . . .)', was the musical equivalent of beating up Sheffield in a back alley. The lyrics cost Queen dearly with an out-of-court libel settlement. According to folklore, Mercury sang it with such force that he ruptured the blood vessels in his throat or his ears (depending on who's telling the story). But, surprisingly, it's the only angry-sounding song on the album.

The scope of Queen's imagination was apparent in the first five tracks alone. After 'Death on Two Legs' came 'Lazing on a Sunday Afternoon', with Mercury sounding like a pre-war big-band singer, crooning through a megaphone (actually a microphone fed through headphones wedged inside a tin can). Then there was Taylor's auto-erotic 'I'm in Love with My Car'. His bandmates weren't convinced by the tongue-in-cheek lyrics, but the drummer railroaded his song onto the album and, later, onto the B-side of 'Bohemian Rhapsody'.

John Deacon composed 'You're My Best Friend' for his wife, Veronica. It had taken until now for Queen's bass player to feel confident with his writing. He'd been the last to join the band and had worked hard to find his place among three different yet similarly forceful characters. The song would become Queen's first American top-twenty hit.

On his sci-fi folk song ''39', Brian May sang about a father who leaves his family, falls into a time warp and returns home to discover they've all aged 100 years. It was a metaphor for how discombobulated he felt after touring overseas. 'You're swept away, you're nowhere near your family, you're in a hotel room on the other side of the world, you live in this strange bubble,' he grumbled.

After such a rich five courses, the standard blues-rock song 'Sweet Lady' and another retro pastiche, 'Seaside Rendezvous' (with Taylor's voice impersonating brass and woodwind), came up wanting. But *A Night at the Opera*'s second act upped the ante even further.

Apparently, Mercury barely drew breath at Rockfield – his mind racing, his fingers clicking, his mouth issuing instructions. It intimidated Brian May. 'I remember listening to all the stuff Freddie was pounding out very confidently and I wasn't feeling very confident.' May's masterpiece, 'The Prophet's Song', was eight minutes and twenty-three seconds long. It drove its composer to distraction. 'I was struggling to get these riffs in my head into shape,' he said. 'I was tearing my hair out because the song was just out of reach.'

Brian had experienced vivid, disturbing dreams since child-hood and the inspiration for his prophet 'on a moonlit stair' also arrived while he was asleep. 'Marc Bolan was an elf, so it was perfectly acceptable' is the get-out-of-jail-free card Roger Taylor cites in response to Queen's early lyrical excess. That could apply here, though the song's ghostly a cappella mid-section provides a contrast. 'My challenge on *A Night at the Opera* was to make sure every song still sounded like Queen,' said Roy Thomas Baker. Not easy when one song alone could go through so many stylistic shifts.

On May's final composition, 'Good Company', he meticu-lously recreated the sound of a trad-jazz band on guitar. There was a reason for all this: May and Mercury both listened to the BBC radio show *Children's Favourites*, which played vintage novelty songs and comedy records. May was also smitten with the Temperance Seven – an ensemble of Chelsea art students who'd mixed trad jazz with surreal humour. 'There was a lot of stuff from my childhood waiting to get out,' he said. 'I was deeply influenced by how the Temperance Seven arranged their stuff harmonically.'

But it was one parody too far and not everyone was a fan. 'Oh no!' groaned Taylor. 'It was Led Zeppelin, the Who and Hendrix all the way [for me].' However, this juxtaposition of the conventional (Zeppelin, the Who, Hendrix) and the unconventional (trad jazz, music hall, a cappella) drove everything on both *A Night at the Opera* and *A Day at the Races*. For every screaming electric guitar, there was also a harp, a Japanese toy koto, a double bass, Roger Taylor trying to sound like a tuba . . .

Mercury's last two songs on the album – 'Love of My Life' and 'Bohemian Rhapsody' – symbolised this better than anything else on the LP. 'Love of My Life' was a mournful ballad written for Mary Austin at around the point Mercury began a new relationship with record company executive David Minns. Was the song a farewell to Mary? Or was he serenading Minns?

'There are no hidden messages in our songs, except for some of Brian's,' said Mercury, before giving a little more away: 'My songs are commercial love songs. I write songs like that because basically what I feel very strongly about is love and emotion.'

'Fred was good at hiding things,' confirmed May. 'But I know a lot of what was going on and there's a lot of depth in his songs. Even the light stuff and the humour had an undercurrent.'

'Bohemian Rhapsody' was no exception. What Taylor called 'Fred's symphonic prog doodah' was pieced together between Rockfield, Scorpio Sound and SARM Studios, among other venues. Tape ops and engineers recalled fourteen- and fifteen-hour shifts, with Mercury barely moving from the mixing desk.

The song had layers upon layers, but all those 'Galileo!'s diverted attention away from any deeper meaning. 'There is a lot of auto-biography in the way Freddie wrote it,' said May. 'I think he was pouring his heart out.'

A Night at the Opera ended with the British national anthem. Queen were penniless but clearly hadn't lost their sense of humour. During a press playback at Roundhouse Studios, Mercury leapt to his feet as May's arrangement of 'God Save the Queen' peeled out. 'Stand up, you cunts!' he told the critics slouched around him.

Mercury also heard something on the album that he wasn't happy with. Once the playback was done, the tapes were spirited away for more tinkering. *A Night at the Opera* had been recorded over four months in seven studios and cost approximately £40,000, prompting a rumour that it was the most expensive album ever made. The exaggeration suited Queen, especially as Mercury was now telling the world that these were 'the finest songs ever written'.

Thirteen months later, *A Day at the Races* began where *A Night at the Opera* left off. Play them back to back and the final drum beat of 'God Save the Queen' segues perfectly into the opening gong roll of 'Tie Your Mother Down'.

However, Queen's world had changed in between. They'd topped the UK charts and had reached the US top ten with both the album and 'Bohemian Rhapsody'. In May 1976, they toasted their newfound fame at London's Dorchester Hotel, where 'Bohemian Rhapsody' scooped an Ivor Novello Award for Best Selling British Record.

There'd also been a change of personnel. Baker's contract with the band had expired, so Queen produced *A Day at the Races* themselves. 'We'd taught ourselves what to do in the studio and one didn't really need the services of a producer,' claimed a bold-sounding John Deacon. However, engineer Mike Stone was retained and, according to May, 'had his hands all over the faders'.

Work began in July at Manor House Studios, Oxfordshire, and finished four months later in the cutting room at New York's Sterling Sound. The studio became Queen's fifth member. Every note, riff and harmony was tweaked, polished and finessed, ensuring *A Day at the Races* sounded even more expensive than its predecessor.

It also felt like Freddie Mercury's album more than the others'. He contributed four of its ten songs, but they dominated the final work. Even the daftly risqué lyrics of 'Tie Your Mother Down' sounded like they'd been written specifically with Mercury in mind. Freddie's love life drove much of his writing, too. The ballad 'You Take My Breath Away' was composed for David Minns (and had Mercury multi-tracking his voice to create a choir of Freds), while the title 'Good Old-Fashioned Lover Boy' was Minns' jokey description of his pop-star boyfriend.

Mercury was supposedly smitten with Minns, whom he'd met at Rod's, a club on the King's Road, in 1975. Decades later, Minns published some of the pair's correspondence. 'My dearest, precious cherub, I thought I'd finally get it together and write you my first little card,' began one postcard from Mercury. Another saw Mercury apologising for his behaviour on one occasion. 'My dearest, I'm sorry about last night,' it read, 'but that's because I'm a dreadful tart.'

John Reid, Queen's manager, was the subject of 'The Millionaire Waltz' – the one piece on the album that came close to the pomp and melodrama of 'Bohemian Rhapsody'. Brian May's 'Long Away' and Deacon's 'You and I' sounded like they were trying to bring the singer back down to earth, while Taylor's 'Drowse' suggested it was written on a sun lounger during the UK's hottest summer in over a century. 'It was borne out of personal feelings of indolence,' Taylor admitted.

Queen achieved the perfect balance on 'Somebody to Love'. Having ticked Tamla Motown, novelty pop and trad jazz off the list, why not gospel? The song demonstrated the band's unerring ability to zone in on a musical genre, examine its component parts and then rework it to their own ends. But, while Mercury sounded smitten on 'You Take My Breath Away', he sounded bereft on this track. His love life was never easy. 'Sometimes the messages in Fred's songs did get buried,' said Taylor. 'But a song like "Somebody to Love" really did come from his heart.'

While a bigger contemporary hit than 'Don't Stop Me Now', 'Somebody to Love' would enjoy a similar revival after Mercury's death. In 1993, the version George Michael sang with Queen at the Freddie Mercury Tribute Concert went to number one in the UK. Later, a waddle of emperor penguins performed it on an ice floe in the animated kids' movie *Happy Feet*.

The parallels with *A Day at the Races'* twin were obvious, though. If 'The Millionaire Waltz' was 'Bohemian Rhapsody', 'You and I' was 'You're My Best Friend' and 'Good Old-Fashioned Lover Boy' was 'Lazing on a Sunday Afternoon', then Brian May's 'White Man' was 'The Prophet's Song'.

Whereas Mercury's compositions all suggested a carefree rock star cradling a glass of Moët while singing, 'White Man' – the album's heaviest song – was an earnest critique of how early European settlers had subjugated Native Americans. The LP bowed out with May's 'Teo Torriatte (Let Us Cling Together)', an anthemic love letter to Japan that suited Mercury better than 'White Man', even when he had to sing some verses in Japanese.

A Day at the Races was another number-one hit and returned Queen to the American top five. But it had its critics. 'I thought it reeked of sequel,' was Roy Thomas Baker's bitchy assessment.

'The fact one came out after another is a shame because it was looked on as a follow-up,' admitted May.

A royal family: Queen with their wives, girlfriends and handlers

t the launch of *A Day at the Races*, Kempton Park Racecourse, 1976.

'I think it's a better-sounding album than *A Night at the Opera*,' said Taylor. 'Maybe the material wasn't quite as good. But is it overproduced? No, not at all. Well, maybe a bit.'

Early on, Brian May admitted that Queen wanted *A Night at the Opera* to be considered their version of the Beatles' *Sgt Pepper's Lonely Hearts Club Band*: 'I know it's a cliché to say that, but it's true.' Like *Sgt Pepper* in the 1960s, *Opera* and *Races* changed the way rock music was recorded in the 1970s; both albums pioneered the use of the studio almost as an additional instrument.

While die-hards may disagree, one Queen album is regarded more fondly than the other in the wider world. In 2006, BBC Radio 2 listeners put *A Night at the Opera* at number nine and *A Day at the Races* at number sixty-seven in the 'Top 100 Albums' poll. (Inevitably, *Sgt Pepper* was number one.)

That day, though, at Kempton Park Racecourse, the four Queens ruled the world. They all placed bets without telling each other who they'd backed. When jockey John Francomb romped to victory on Lanzarote and bagged the £300 prize money, they realised they'd all bet on the same horse. Queen would rarely be quite so in tune with each other again.

1984

Brian May predicts the future

Britain in the 1950s was full of great possibilities, but also lingering fears. Adolf Hitler was dead, but the threat of the atomic bomb loomed large. *Nineteen Eighty-Four* – George Orwell's post-war novel about a dystopian society – fired the imaginations of those born into this uncertain world. It was the perfect name, then, for serious-minded schoolboy Brian May's first band.

In summer 1964, sixteen-year-old Brian and his Hampton Grammar School friend Dave Dilloway decided to start a band. 'Brian used to teach me guitar chords in our German lessons,' Dilloway said in 2009. 'I had a fretboard drawn on my forearm. I'd slide up my cuff and ask, "Which one is that?" The joke is Brian passed German O-level and I failed. He was a clever sod.'

The boys also wiled away their lunch hours dreaming up band names; other contenders included the Mind Boggles. They settled on 1984 and the group began as May, bassist Dilloway, vocalist Tim Staffell (later of Smile), bassist/rhythm guitarist John 'Jag' Garnham and pianist John Sanger. Hampton Grammar was short of drummers, so they placed an ad in the window of Albert's Music Shop in Twickenham. One drummer answered: Richard Thompson. He would later play in Freddie Mercury's early group, Wreckage.

Some considered pop music a threat to the nation's morals and way of life. Not so Mr Conisbee, a local scout leader, who organised the Whitton Beat Club. For a small fee, aspiring pop groups were permitted to use a network of local schools for rehearsals. 1984 were given the run of Chase Bridge Primary School, next to Twickenham RFC.

Brian May and 1984 supposedly made their debut on 28 October 1964 at St Mary's Church Hall, Twickenham. It was a youth-club dance and they played numbers by Sam & Dave, Otis Redding and Little Richard. A week later, they did it all again at Richmond County School for Girls. When John Sanger ducked out to concentrate on his studies, 1984 continued as a five-piece. More gigs followed in the New Year around Putney, Shepperton and once as far out as Henley-on-Thames.

They were a disparate bunch with different tastes: Staffell and Garnham gravitated towards Chuck Berry, the Rolling Stones and soul music; May and Dilloway loved the Beatles. Brian would sing lead vocals on 'Yesterday', 'which went down especially well with the girls'. Later, May would become smitten with Jimi Hendrix and Cream. 1984's setlists changed to keep up with the shifting times and tastes of both band and audience. For a while, they even flirted with the idea of composing a rock opera based on George Orwell's novel.

They were different characters, too. 'Tim and Richard were the loosest personalities and "Jag" was in it for a bit of fun,' recalled Dilloway. 'But Brian was serious-minded. He was never the life and soul.'

'Being on stage playing was infinitely preferable than being in the audience wondering whether I should ask someone to dance,' admitted May.

Before long, though, there were exams to be passed, so 1984 were temporarily put on hold. In autumn '65, May enrolled at Imperial College, Staffell at Ealing Art College, and Dilloway to study electronics, first at Southampton University, then at Twickenham College of Technology.

1984 continued to rehearse via letters and tapes, with Staffell and May hustling occasional gigs at their new colleges. Dilloway remembered meeting Freddie Mercury for the first time at Ealing Art College. 'Fred would get into 1984 gigs for free by being a roadie. He liked the scene and was mad about Hendrix. I never even knew he could sing until I heard Queen.'

When a group of electronics students needed a band with whom to practise their engineering skills, Dilloway suggested 1984. In March 1967, the group recorded a dozen songs at Thames Television's Broom Lane Studios. Among them was an original May/Staffell composition, 'Step On Me'. Today, it sounds a bit like Queen before Queen.

Six months later, 1984 won a Battle of the Bands contest, sponsored by Scotch Tape, at Croydon's Top Rank Club. It earned them a news story and a photograph in *Melody Maker*. 'We were just having fun,' said Dilloway. 'But it was never a serious thing for most of us.'

1984 came to a natural end soon after. They played their final gig at Kensington's Olympia on the morning of 23 December 1967. Christmas on Earth Continued was billed as an 'all night long' concert, starting on 22 December. It featured Pink Floyd, the Jimi Hendrix Experience and the Move, and 1984 didn't make it on stage until dawn: 'We were mediocre and very loud and there wasn't a lot of audience.'

After the show, the band discovered that their money had been stolen from the dressing room and their vehicles towed away. They had to walk from the Olympia to Hammersmith car pound, still wearing eye make-up and their Carnaby Street stage clobber. May and Staffell drifted away soon after to form Smile; Dilloway and Garnham kept 1984 going as a covers act for the next few years, before day jobs and family life took precedence.

In 1990, Brian May reunited with his school bandmates for a barbecue in the back garden of Dave's bungalow near Weybridge, Surrey. Dilloway still had May's Spanish guitar from their Hampton Grammar days: 'I gave it to Brian and he sat there with a Guinness, strumming away. I said, "Do you want it back?" He said, "Yes, please."'

Dave Dilloway passed away in 2011. 'Honestly, I didn't know Brian May wanted to set the world on fire,' he confided. 'I wasn't dedicated enough to earn my living from music. But I have no regrets.'

'If I could have joined any band, it would have been Deep Purple, Fairport Convention . . . or Queen,' he said finally. 'I often think how many people must have seen Brian in those little clubs we played, completely unaware he would later become Brian May of Queen.'

Future shock: Brian May (second right) with his 1984 bandmates (from left)
Richard Thompson, Tim Staffell and John 'Jag' Garnham, 1964.

'NO SYNTHESISERS!'

Queen's guide to life, 1973–80

The sleeve for *Queen II* contains the following message: 'And
nobody played synthesizer . . . again.' It was a sly dig at the
music press, specifically *Melody Maker*, whose review of Queen's

debut praised their 'great use of synthesiser'. The band had made a point of mentioning 'no synthesisers' on the LP's sleeve, but nobody noticed. 'It was all guitar and that got up our noses quite a lot,' grumbled Roger Taylor. 'We were a bit put off by the early synthesisers.' So much so that Queen included the following messages on their next three albums: 'No synthesizers' (*Sheer Heart Attack*); 'No synthesisers!' (*A Night at the Opera*) and 'No synths!' (*A Day at the Races*).

Queen then stopped mentioning the 's' word until 1980's *The Game*. By that point, they'd embraced the new technology. 'This album includes the first appearance of a synthesiser (an Oberheim OB-X) on a Queen album,' declared the sleevenote. In fact, the first sound heard on the record was the Oberheim OB-X, whistling away, like a *Doctor Who* kettle on 'Play the Game'.

'I'm afraid that was my fault,' said Taylor, who'd invested in the hot-off-the-production-line keyboard and was enthralled by its possibilities. 'I also showed it to Fred and immediately he said, "Oh, this is good, dear."' Queen's 'no synthesisers' rule was abandoned from here on.

'ONE VISION'

The song about Live Aid that wasn't actually
about Live Aid

At the end of Queen's The Works Tour, the band planned to take the remainder of the year and the whole of 1986 off. Then came July 1985's Live Aid victory. Six weeks later, Freddie Mercury rang the others insisting they start work again. This spontaneous recording session gave Queen an unexpected hit.

'One Vision' was recorded in September at Munich's Musicland Studios and credited to the whole group (though John Deacon was late to the sessions, so may have had less to do with the composition). The original lyrics, partly inspired by civil rights activist Martin Luther King Jr's 1963 speech, were written by Roger Taylor. King's words 'I have a dream' found their way into the finished song, but Mercury threw out or rewrote many of Taylor's other lyrics, including the line 'one God-damned religion'.

The song's inclusive, peace-to-all-mankind message was yoked to a big Brian May riff and daubed with programmed drum patterns and backwards-masked vocals. It was flashy '80s heavy rock with a pop chorus and its genesis was caught on camera. Queen had allowed the Austrian film-makers Rudi Dolezal and Hannes Rossacher, aka the 'Torpedo Twins', to film Queen's every move for a forthcoming documentary. 'I thought they'd never bloody go away,' admitted Taylor.

But the pair's footage of Queen recording 'One Vision' (later seen in the song's promo video and in *The Magic Years* documentary) showed the band bickering, joking and ad-libbing the lyrics. 'One dump, one turd, two tits, John Deacon!' sings Mercury. 'One heart, one soul, one sex position, one swift, one frog, one clap, one chicken . . .'

A gag line even made it onto the final mix: the words 'fried chicken' instead of 'one vision' at the very end of the song. 'You can't take these things too seriously,' warned Taylor. 'It's only a pop record.'

'One Vision' was released in November. The accompanying press release claimed it was inspired by Live Aid. Critics, who hadn't forgotten or forgiven Queen's Sun City faux pas, savaged them for cashing in on Bob Geldof's charity bonanza. 'Some public relations person got the wrong end of the stick,' grumbled Taylor. 'I went absolutely bananas.'

The song was a top-ten UK hit, appeared on the soundtrack to goofy action movie *Iron Eagle* and was promoted to show-opener on Queen's 1986 tour. Besides capturing the band at work in the studio, the original promo also included a recreation of the famous 'four heads' shot from the *Queen II* cover and 'Bohemian Rhapsody' – but now with considerably less hair and an additional moustache.

THE OPPOSITION

The first sighting of Queen's invisible man

Whatever happened to Jenny and Charmaine? In 1967, these two Leicestershire teenagers were go-go dancers with John Deacon's group the Opposition. As the band rattled through the hits, the girls shimmied away on the side of the stage at glamorous venues like Kirby Lane Community Centre. 'Anything to create some interest, to stop the band being stale,' said bandleader and ex-keyboard player Richard Young.

While his Queen bandmates dominated their early groups, Deacon seems to have drifted, almost ghost-like, through the Opposition. 'He was a shy, unassuming kid,' recalled Young. 'You really never would have guessed . . .'

Future piano-shop owner Richard formed the Opposition in 1965. 'My parents sent me to private school, but I left with no qualifications to join my dad's business,' he explained. 'I lived in Oadby and met John Deacon and [Opposition drummer] Nigel Bullen at our local park. We were all interested in music and groups.'

Despite his youth, Young knew what he wanted. 'There was a lot of competition in Leicester at the time. It was the Beatles era. There would be a full page of venues and bands playing in our local paper. I was working in my dad's business and had the money to finance the group. I wanted us to be the best around.'

When Young decided that the Opposition's bass player wasn't good enough, he fired him, and Deacon switched from guitar to bass. Young bought the instrument – an EKO bass – at Cox's music shop and John paid him back in instalments. 'John was a good rhythm player,' he said. 'I always thought he was the most musical in the group.'

Young was also tough on himself. After deciding he wasn't good enough to sing lead vocals and play guitar, he switched to keyboards. The teenager's drive and ambition paid off. The Opposition's gig sheet filled with dates at youth clubs, church halls and ballrooms, playing the same top-forty hits as Brian May and Roger Taylor's school groups. But Deacon's mother, Molly, forbade him to play pubs, so Young sometimes had to find an understudy.

Besides being his first experience of playing music, Deacon learned another valuable lesson: the power of silence. 'Easy Deacon', as his bandmates called him, had an unflappable manner, in contrast to the drama going on around him. The Opposition's lead singer, Pete 'Pedro' Bartholomew, was fired by Young for fooling about too much on stage. But Deacon wouldn't be pushed around either and flatly refused to wear stage clothes he didn't like. It was a good grounding for life in Queen.

The group's setlist and shifting line-ups charted the changes in pop music. One summer it was all Tamla Motown and go-go dancers; the next, covers of the Animals and the Zombies. In early 1967, the band earned a mention in the *Leicester Mercury*: the Opposition were finalists in the Midlands Beat Championships. But the planned final was cancelled after the promoter disappeared with the money. Maybe Deacon never forgot, but he was famous for his attention to detail when it came to Queen's finances.

The Opposition changed their name to the New Opposition, then back to the Opposition and then, finally, to the Art. In 1969, they recorded a self-financed single at a studio in Wellingborough, but nobody, not even Richard Young, has a copy. 'I lived and breathed the band, probably to the detriment of my job,' he admitted in 2010. 'Most of my waking hours were spent thinking about the band and the next step up the ladder.'

That summer, the Opposition came to an end and Deacon moved to London to study electronics. Young remained at his father's business for almost a decade, before spending twenty-five years as a working musician in Europe and the US.

He never saw Queen ('I wasn't particularly moved by their music – very well executed, though') and rarely spoke to John Deacon after the 1970s. 'It's still strange to think one of the members of my first group made it. Not just big, but mega, mega big.'

In 1995, Queen biographer Mark Hodkinson tracked down Jenny, one of the Opposition's go-go dancers. 'What was John Deacon like back then?' he asked.

'Oh, he never said a word,' she replied. 'He never said anything, never spoke. You're talking about a completely unremarkable character.'

PENGUINS

A royal bird

There's a photograph of Queen taken in Freddie Mercury's flat in 1973. It was for their first single, 'Keep Yourself Alive'. John Deacon is wearing two-tone platform shoes and Mercury has shaved his chest. There's also a tiny model penguin perched on the arm of Brian May's chair.

Brian and this great aquatic bird have history. In summer 1971, Queen attended a fancy-dress party thrown by one of their friends. May came as a penguin. He'd approached the making of his costume with the same scientific rigour as the building of his Red Special.

'Brian had the most amazing penguin mask that actually worked,' recalled one partygoer. 'When he spoke, the beak opened and closed.' There are photos of Brian and his working beak on the back cover of *Queen*.

'Do you have a particular thing for penguins?' a writer from *Circus* magazine asked him later.

'Yeah, I like penguins,' May replied. 'They are very stylish.'

In 1975, Smile's ex-keyboard player, Chris Smith, visited May at his west London flat after Queen's first visit to Japan. They'd sold out everywhere and had been deluged with gifts. 'He took me into this room and it was full of toy penguins the fans had sent him,' said Smith. 'Everything from tiny penguins to 6-foot penguins, which took up three-quarters of the room.'

It was a poignant moment. Queen had been greeted in Japan like the Beatles at the height of Beatlemania. But they were penniless. Brian had all the penguins he could want – and more – but still couldn't afford to move out of his dire basement flat. 'He said, "I've got no money,"' recalled Smith, 'and took me into the bathroom and there was all this fungus on the walls.'

Penguins still featured in May's life after he became a famous rock star. Namely, in the video for Queen's 1991 single 'I'm Going Slightly Mad'. The song, typical of Mercury's gallows humour, gently addressed his declining mental faculties. Freddie dressed as a Charlie Chaplin-style clown; John wore a jester's hat; Roger had a boiling kettle on his head; and Brian reappeared with his fully functioning penguin beak, presumably intact from that fancy-dress party.

Real penguins followed Brian on set, like he was an avian Pied Piper. During the shoot, two of the birds were placed on a couch next to the band. One quickly released a plume of shit, which ran down the seat between Mercury and Taylor. 'Roger, what have you done?' tittered Freddie, jumping to his feet. Meanwhile, its mate sat quietly next to Brian May, clearly at ease with Queen's resident Doctor Dolittle.

PRENTER, PAUL
Mr Bad Guy

Every great drama needs a villain – and *Bohemian Rhapsody* was no exception. Before Queen's biopic, it's doubtful many beyond the band's inner circle and a handful of journalists knew about Paul Prenter. But *Bohemian Rhapsody* turned Freddie Mercury's personal manager into a movie villain.

The reality was more complex. Belfast-born Prenter had been a DJ in Northern Ireland before moving to London and joining Queen manager John Reid's organisation. Prenter started working as a personal assistant to Queen in 1977. 'I first remember him when we were touring the States with Thin Lizzy,' said Queen's former road manager Peter 'Ratty' Hince. 'He was running around getting everybody pizzas.'

To begin with, Pete Brown had handled Queen's day-to-day business. Brown was highly respected and an expert at dealing with Mercury's airs and graces. But, when Brown left, Prenter started handling Queen's daily management. Prenter (nicknamed 'Trixie') was also gay and quickly became Mercury's confidant and an enthusiastic drinking and drugging partner. The movie suggested that Mercury and Prenter were once lovers, but others deny this.

The arrangement with the band worked well for a time. 'Prenter was relatively professional,' recalled Hince, 'and he understood the problems we had on the road. But he could easily turn. He was fickle and he had a big axe to grind.'

But Prenter committed the cardinal sin of trying to interfere with the music. 'Prenter had different interests,' producer Mack recalled. 'He had an influence on Freddie. They were both into R&B and disco, going to the clubs, so you had Prenter telling Freddie that Queen were old-fashioned and didn't need guitars.'

The funk-influenced *Hot Space* album challenged the idea of Queen as a rock group. But it didn't sell as well as their previous records and damaged their reputation in the States. Queen later discovered Prenter had refused interview requests and snubbed American promoters, often without Mercury knowing. 'He didn't have Queen's best interests at heart,' suggested Brian May. 'He prioritised Freddie and trampled over other people.'

Today, 'Don't Stop Me Now' is Queen's universal party anthem. A decade ago, May was telling interviewers that he didn't care for its lyrics as they referred to Mercury's self-destructive life-style. Prenter was widely blamed for encouraging this hedonism with his own behaviour.

'Paul's capacity for sex and drugs and alcohol was phenom-enal,' Peter Hince remarked. Once, in Munich, Prenter informed Mercury that his cocaine had been stolen by a hotel maid and replaced with salt. In fact, Prenter was just trying to disguise the fact that he'd snorted all of Mercury's stash himself.

Writer Lesley-Ann Jones's book *Freddie Mercury: The Definitive Biography* contains a scene in which Prenter and Mercury behave like jaded emperors at a Roman orgy. Jones interviewed a former male prostitute who had sex with Mercury in Rio during Queen's 1985 visit. 'First we drank and then snorted some cocaine,' he told her. 'Next, we'd shed our clothes and enter Freddie's room, where he would greet us, wearing just his dressing gown. Freddie engaged in sexual activity with each in turn, in front of the others.'

Apparently, Prenter remained clothed during this encounter and watched the action. When Mercury grew weary of the men, Prenter paid them off and kicked them out. The scene was absent from the film, but *Bohemian Rhapsody* compounded the idea that Prenter led Mercury astray. In 1985, though, Mercury was thirty-nine years old and arguably more than capable of making his own decisions about what drugs to take and whom to have sex with. His great weakness was actually his misguided loyalty – as he would soon learn to his cost.

When Queen dispensed of Prenter's services, Freddie took him on as his personal manager and paid him out of his own pocket. Then Prenter threw a party at Freddie's London flat while the singer was away. Furniture and wallpaper was damaged and Mercury fired him – at which point, Prenter started issuing threats.

In 1984, Mercury's former chauffeur had sold a story to *The Sun* claiming that Freddie was spending £1,000 a week on cocaine and vodka. In May 1987, Prenter went to the same newspaper, who paid him £32,000 for several days' worth of stories. He supplied photos of Mercury with former boyfriends (just a handful of the 'hundreds of homosexuals' the frontman had supposedly had sex with); he claimed that Michael Jackson had caught Freddie snorting cocaine through a $100 bill; he revealed that two of Mercury's ex-lovers had died of AIDS and that Freddie was terrified he'd be next; and he also outed Irish hairdresser Jim Hutton as Mercury's live-in lover.

Until now, Mercury had always deflected questions about his sexuality with jokes, telling interviewers he was 'as gay as a daffodil, dear' etc. In fact, Mercury had just discovered that he was HIV-positive, making Prenter's story an even greater betrayal.

Prenter called Mercury to justify his actions, but Freddie refused to speak to him. The two men never spoke again. Prenter died of AIDS-related health issues in August 1991, just three months before Mercury. For some years, Brian May refused to name him in interviews, referring to Prenter only as 'the guy that looked after Fred'. After *Bohemian Rhapsody*, this was no longer possible.

Actor Allen Leech's portrayal of the scheming Ulsterman upset Prenter's family so much that they talked to the *Daily Mail* about it. In a May 2019 story, the family criticised the film's blurring of fact and fiction and its 'Disney movie' portrayal of Paul as the story's archvillain.

They also insisted that Mercury would be appalled by how Prenter was treated in *Bohemian Rhapsody* and claimed that their relative had only sold his stories to *The Sun* in 1987 because Queen 'had let him down' and 'he was very hurt'.

'Paul was no saint,' said Gerard, his brother, 'but he was a kind and generous person and not the villain the film makes him out to be. The film is all about burnishing the image of the mediocrities that are left behind.' Queen declined to comment.

QUEEN

The most impatient-sounding LP in the world

The Star café at 22 Great Chapel Street has been a Soho institution since its owners served their first beverage in 1933. In summer 1972, Queen became a fixture in the Star, making cups of coffee last for hours. If they were feeling rich and reckless, they'd have a drink in the Ship pub on nearby Wardour Street instead. Other customers came and went as Soho bustled around them, but Queen sat around, waiting, until it was time to go to work.

Queen recorded their first album in the early hours at Trident Studios in St Anne's Court. The band had previously signed a deal with its owners, brothers Norman and Barry Sheffield. There were positives to this: the brothers' company, Trident Audio Productions, allowed Queen to use their 24-track, state-of-the-art studio and financed the record. But Trident now owned Queen's song publishing, their management, the lot . . .

This conflict of interest eventually destroyed their working relationship. But, in 1972, the Trident deal meant Queen could make an album. The caveat was that they could only use the studio at night when it wasn't booked by the likes of Paul

McCartney and Elton John. Queen were often given the deathly graveyard shift of 1 a.m. to 7 a.m. – 'when the cleaners came in', said Brian May.

Among the studio's other clients that summer was ex-Velvet Underground frontman Lou Reed. His second solo album, *Transformer*, was being produced by David Bowie. Queen had been in limbo for some time – off the road and concentrating on writing songs and finessing their stage act. They were also juggling the band with PhDs, degrees and market-stall day jobs. In the meantime, Bowie and others had zoomed past them and started having hits. Some evenings, Queen watched their nemesis coming down the stairs at Trident as they were going up.

Queen's first album is a product of its environment. It's restless and frantic and sounds like a band throwing everything into the mix in the hope that something sticks. Queen were allocated producer John Anthony – a former DJ at London's Speakeasy and a Mercury Records A&R man who'd previously considered signing Smile. But, when Anthony passed out in the studio and was diagnosed with Epstein–Barr virus, another of Trident's in-house producers, Roy Thomas Baker, took over.

Queen also insisted on co-producing. The album was essentially their live show; they wanted a live-sounding record and demanded that Roger Taylor's kit be moved out of the drum booth and into the middle of the studio. The staff insisted that this wasn't Trident's way of working and, if the usual way was good enough for Paul McCartney, it should be good enough for Queen.

Listening now to Queen's version of the old Smile number 'Doing All Right', 'Liar' (the album's best riff, bar none) and 'Son and Daughter', with its mish-mash of paint-stripping harmonies and orchestral guitars, you can almost hear a waspish Freddie Mercury squabbling with his co-producers (while surreptitiously undoing the top button on his tight trousers before sitting down).

You can almost smell the coffee breath and see the bleary, bloodshot eyes. When they weren't recording or arguing, Queen watched the covert movements of Soho's prostitutes and clients from the studio window. It was a bit of welcome light relief.

Roy Thomas Baker matched Mercury for campness and grandiosity. He gushingly told Queen they were going to be superstars, but also pushed them to try harder, take after take: 'Not good enough, dearie, try again.' But they pushed themselves just as hard. May and Baker spent hours making Brian's guitar sound like every other instrument in an orchestra, hence the line 'and nobody played synthesiser' in the sleevenotes. 'We put it on as a joke at first,' said Mercury, 'but it turned out to be a good idea because we even managed to fool [BBC Radio DJ] John Peel. He said something in a review about there being a good use of Moog and it was just multi-tracked guitar.'

'Great King Rat' and 'My Fairy King' could broadly be described as sci-fi/fantasy songs. As Taylor often points out, Mercury rarely read a book, but managed to create an imaginary world in which 'horses are born with eagle's wings'. 'It was part of the zeitgeist,' he explained, though the album's biggest anomaly, 'Jesus', still sounds like Mercury forced it onto the LP against the band's wishes. Meanwhile, Taylor's debut Queen song and lead vocal, 'Modern Times Rock 'n' Roll', was aptly described in *Rolling Stone* magazine as 'remarkably reminiscent of [Led Zeppelin's] "Communication Breakdown"'.

Nobody could quite agree on how anything should sound. So much so that Queen used a previous version of 'The Night Comes Down', recorded for a test disc at the inferior De Lane Lea Studios, instead of the Trident mix. A recuperated John Anthony also returned in Baker's absence and insisted they remix the whole LP. '"Keep Yourself Alive" sounded like it had been done at four in the morning, especially Roger's drums,' Anthony complained. Which it probably had been.

Working alongside them was 21-year-old runner and assistant engineer Mike Stone. Stone impressed them all and it was his mix of 'Keep Yourself Alive' that made it onto the final album. But Queen were still tinkering with the LP in January 1973 until Trident ordered them to step away from the mixing desk.

Queen's Trident-appointed manager, Jack Nelson, then tried to sell the finished LP to a record company. He was met with widespread disinterest and occasional hostility. 'Queen? Are these guys homos?' asked one A&R man. It also didn't help that Trident had initially tried to sell Queen as part of a package, along with debut albums by two of their other clients: ex-Rare Bird vocalist Mark Ashton and Irish singer-songwriter Eugene Wallace.

Finally, EMI said yes. Queen signed to the great British institution in spring 1973. In another precocious move, they railroaded EMI's art department into accepting their cover proposal: a Mercury-designed band logo and a photograph of the singer on stage, 'looking like a figurehead on the prow of a ship', said May.

Queen was released on 13 July 1973, a year after the band had started work on it. Taylor was listed in the credits by his full name, hyphenated to read 'Roger Meddows-Taylor', which made him sound like a home-counties Conservative MP, while John Deacon became Deacon John, apparently 'to make him sound more interesting'. 'Deacon never said a word,' John Anthony recalled. 'Just stood there at the back, going along with it all.'

The LP's back-cover montage of photos captured the innocence and naivete of the times, though. Mercury and May laboured over the collage, cutting up the pictures and sticking them all onto a piece of plywood, which was photographed and reproduced on the sleeve as a standalone piece of art. Some of these images had been taken two years before at a friend's twenty-first fancy-dress birthday party. There was Freddie with his cat, car-mad roadie John Harris, Roger with a flower in his mouth, Freddie eating grapes, Roger dressed as the Mad Hatter, and the whole band posing at Mercury and Mary Austin's Victoria Road flat.

'Keep Yourself Alive' became a modest hit, but *Queen* struggled to reach the UK top fifty. In the band members' minds, though, the album was already obsolete. They were forging ahead with new songs and ideas. 'Queen wanted the world,' said one band familiar, 'and they wanted it no later than Friday teatime.'

QUEEN ELIZABETH II

When their majesties met Her Majesty

Queen first met a version of the Queen at London's Café Royal in 1974. It was Queen Elizabeth II lookalike Jeanette Charles, who presented them with silver discs to celebrate 100,000 sales of their second album. It wasn't until 3 June 2002 that the band came close to the real thing.

Queen were invited to appear at the Party at the Palace concert to commemorate Her Majesty the Queen's Golden Jubilee. The televised show from Buckingham Palace would feature performances by Shirley Bassey, Brian Wilson, Paul McCartney, Rod Stewart and Elton John. The only wild card in the line-up was Ozzy Osbourne, who'd recently become a national treasure after starring in his own reality-TV show.

Queen later performed 'Radio Ga Ga', 'We Will Rock You' and 'We Are the Champions' with the cast of the newly opened *We Will Rock You* jukebox musical. But the only bit anyone remembers now is the opening ceremony.

The celebrations began with the British national anthem, performed by Queen and members of the Royal Academy of Music Symphony Orchestra. Roger Taylor kept his feet and drum kit on the ground, but some 200 million TV viewers, plus an estimated 1 million people lining the Mall, watched Brian May cranking out 'God Save the Queen' from the roof of Buckingham Palace.

At the time, May called the performance a 'symbol for my generation', but it seems to have become even more significant to him recently. 'It was riveting and it was terrifying and it changed me as a person,' he said in 2020. 'But it's one of those times where you face the fear and you're never quite the same again after it.'

Three years after his rooftop performance, Brian was back at the palace. In March 2005, he attended an event honouring the British music industry and lined up for a royal audience with fellow guitar heroes Jimmy Page, Jeff Beck and Eric Clapton.

'Very pleased to meet you,' May said to the Queen. 'I have an apology to make for making so much noise on your roof, ma'am.'

'Oh, it was you? Yes,' she replied. Long pause. 'It seemed . . . quite . . . quite alarming.'

'The only alarming thing was how big a fool I'd have made of myself if it was wrong,' May replied. 'It wasn't about falling off. It was a thrill.'

The Queen looked bemused and moved down the line to Jimmy Page.

'Are you also a guitarist?' she said.

'Yes,' Page replied. Another long pause.

May jumped in to fill the dead air: 'Jimmy's a hero of mine.'

'Hello, ma'am': Queen with Queen impersonator Jeanette Charles,
Café Royal, London, 1974.

QUEEN II

The Yes album

Queen and Yes had history. Queen once supported Britain's artiest progressive rockers at Kingston Polytechnic in March 1971. Yes's LPs *The Yes Album* and *Fragile* had been pored over and analysed by Queen during many late-night listening parties.

Comparisons had since been made between the two acts. The *NME*'s waspish appraisal of *Queen* likened Freddie Mercury's vocals to Yes singer Jon Anderson's 'cosmic castrato'. 'You just know six months ago these guys were plugging away at the old effete glam bullseye,' griped *NME* writer Nick Kent. 'Just like a year before that they were probably trying to play like Yes.'

By the early 1970s, most rock groups also wanted to make an 'important work' – a concept album rather than a collection of random songs. In December 1973, Yes upped the ante further with *Tales from Topographic Oceans* – a four-sided LP based on the teachings of an Indian guru, Paramahansa Yogananda. It was too much for Roger Taylor. 'I liked Yes,' he said. 'But *Tales from Topographic Bollocks* or whatever – all a bit too proggy for me. But John Deacon liked it. John really liked Yes.'

While Yes were introducing their fanbase to a yogi master, Queen were recording *Queen II* at Trident Studios. The sessions lasted from August 1973 until February '74. Their debut hadn't sold particularly well, but Queen insisted on equal rights and were now recording during daylight hours. The production was split between the band, Roy Thomas Baker and another Trident alumni, Robin Geoffrey Cable. Why have one pair of hands on the mixing desk when you could have six?

If Queen ever tried to make a Yes album, it would sound like *Queen II* (but with a side helping of Led Zeppelin *IV* and the Who's *Tommy*). The delay between finishing their debut and releasing it meant that, by the time the group returned to the studio, they were bursting with new ideas. 'On *Queen II*, we went berserk,' admitted Brian May. 'Suddenly, we were able to wield all the power and the skills we'd learned and we had the indulgence of a little bit of money and more time to put them into the operation.'

There wasn't a concept, per se, but *Queen II* aspires to be an important work. 'Side White' and 'Side Black' pitch their respective writers, May and Freddie Mercury, as opposing forces: light versus shade; even good versus evil. It certainly gives an impression of synergy, as though one composer's songs are complementing the other's.

Unlike Yes, Queen didn't have a keyboard player, but they did have Brian May's one-man guitar orchestra: his Red Special manages to sound like a trumpet fanfare on 'Procession' and like the London Philharmonic on 'Father to Son'. At this time, May and his father, Harold, were estranged over Brian's decision to pursue music for a living. The lyrics of 'Father to Son' hint at the generational divide, but suggest a baton being passed from a monarch to his heir.

There's also a romantic relationship flitting, ghost-like and unrequited, through most of 'Side White'. May later revealed his inspiration for 'White Queen (As It Began)'. He was reading Robert Graves's *The White Goddess* and was struck by the poet's idea of a universal female deity. But May was also hopelessly smitten with a biology student at Imperial College, though he 'never ever had the courage to speak to her'. Instead, he wrote the song.

Roger Taylor, meanwhile, snuck onto the end of the first side. His and May's contrasting approaches are writ large here. Brian's folky love song 'Some Day One Day' is rudely upended by Roger's swaggering 'The Loser in the End'. 'Mama's got a problem, she don't know what to do,' rasps Taylor – a caution to mothers everywhere to let their male offspring sow their wild oats. While May sounds insecure about life, love and the world in general, Taylor couldn't sound any more assured.

Mercury's 'Side Black' turns everything upside down. The opening 'Ogre Battle' is a swashbuckling tale of warring giants with 'mighty tongues' living inside 'a two-way mirror mountain'. 'It was of its time,' suggested a diplomatic Taylor. Mercury wrote the song on guitar, playing it 'like a small, nervy animal', recalled May. Brian, like other guitarists who'd worked with Freddie, noted the frontman's choice of unconventional chords. 'He forced me into finding ways of doing things that made unusual sounds,' May said.

'The Fairy Feller's Master-Stroke' was another deep dive into the singer's obsessions – namely, Victorian artist Richard Dadd's painting of the same name. Dadd died in Broadmoor Hospital, where he'd been detained indefinitely after murdering his father. The song is crammed with detail and Rococo flourishes, but barely lasts two and a half minutes.

'Side Black' is full of ideas, but a few of them overstay their welcome. The brief ballad 'Nevermore' (reputedly a love song for Mary Austin) could have been a full piece in its own right, but instead it's used as a segue between 'The Fairy Feller' and 'The March of the Black Queen'. Parts of the latter song's intro suggest the music to a silent horror movie, as though Mercury were sat in a cinema orchestra pit hammering the keyboard with his black-painted fingernails. It also showcases more of what Taylor called 'Freddie's gestures'. These were ambiguous lyrics and free-wheeling wordplay intended to create an atmosphere. The black queen is joined by blue powder monkeys and water babies 'singing in a lily pool delight'. It plays like a prog-rock nursery rhyme.

The song was reworked and overdubbed so many times that the tape became transparent and even broke in two. It was salvaged and made it onto the album – but only just. It also wouldn't be the last time that Queen's ambition ran up against '70s studio technology. And only Queen could follow such gothic melodrama with 'Funny How Love Is', on which they're miraculously transformed into the Beach Boys, with Robin Geoffrey Cable striving to recreate producer Phil Spector's 'Wall of Sound'.

Queen II's closing 'Seven Seas of Rhye' is the album's only pop song. The band's EMI paymasters must have breathed a big sigh of relief on hearing this track during the first playback. Nothing else would have had a chance of getting played on the radio.

Mercury's pièce de résistance was the LP cover. He hired his friend, photographer Mick Rock, to shoot the band for the inner and outer gatefold sleeves. 'Freddie and I shared the same tastes,' said Rock. 'Oscar Wilde, Aubrey Beardsley, the decadence that was around at the time . . .'

Rock's photographs look like how 'The March of the Black Queen' sounds. The white-clad band are preserved on the white inside sleeve, with Mercury peering coyly over the top of a fur stole. It's all very mannered and majestic. But it's the front-cover photograph that has become Queen's most famous image.

In the run-up to the shoot, Mercury excitedly showed his bandmates pictures of Hollywood royalty Marlene Dietrich. The black-and-white portraits of her had been taken for director Josef von Sternberg's 1932 Chinese Civil War drama, *Shanghai Express*. Mercury was smitten by Dietrich's imperious pose and wanted to recreate it on the cover. 'Honestly, I thought it might be a bit pretentious,' admitted May. But Mercury would not be swayed.

On the day, all four band members committed to the idea. But none committed to it with such conviction as their lead singer. With his black eyes, folded arms and delicate fingers splayed, Mercury dominated the picture. Little wonder, then, that director Bruce Gowers revisited the idea for the 'Bohemian Rhapsody' video a year later.

In Queen's minds, they were already untouchable superstars, but the National Union of Mineworkers soon disabused them of this notion. Due to the union's ongoing strike action, the government imposed a 'three-day week' on non-essential electricity use. From 1 January until early March 1974, working hours in offices and factories were reduced, pubs were closed and, for a time, Britain's three TV channels stopped broadcasting at 10.30 p.m.

Vinyl-pressing factories were subject to these restrictions, so *Queen II*'s production was put on hold. After normal service resumed, John Deacon discovered that his name had once again been listed on the sleeve as 'Deacon John'. The joke had only been funny the first time, so the sleeve had to be reprinted.

Queen II was finally released on 8 March 1974 – the day after government restrictions were lifted. Buoyed by the success of 'Seven Seas of Rhye', the album eventually reached number five in the UK, but was roundly panned in the press. *Rolling Stone* magazine's critique was especially harsh. 'It has none of the wit and sophistication of Genesis,' they suggested, 'but has appropriated the most irritating elements of Yes.'

The normally bullish Roger Taylor admitted to being so stung by the reviews that he began to question his own judgement: 'I thought, "Christ, are they right?"' He took the album back to his Earl's Court flat and listened to it again. And again. Then decided the critics were definitely wrong.

If it was any consolation, John Deacon's beloved *Tales from Topographic Oceans* experienced a similar drubbing. 'Cohesion is lost to the gods of self-indulgence,' complained *Melody Maker*.

Later that year, a teen magazine asked Deacon to name his favourite album of all time. Forget Yes; '*Queen II*,' he replied.

He wasn't alone. 'One of my personal favourites will always be *Queen II*,' said Brian May, 'because it was such a giant leap at the time. It was the biggest single leap Queen ever made.'

'RADIO GA GA'

Queen's great dance move

'Radio Ga Ga' is the essence of Queen: clever and shameless. Its lyrics celebrated a golden age of radio at a time when music videos were conquering the world. Queen then sold the song with a world-conquering music video. Its title was an in-joke that most would have rejected as too self-indulgent, but Queen turned it into the USP of one of their greatest hits.

Roger Taylor sketched out the song at Los Angeles' Record Plant studios in summer 1983. Taylor later said it would have been impossible to have composed 'Radio Ga Ga' on a guitar. He used a drum machine and a synthesiser instead. At first, Brian May worked with him on the song, but they then went their separate ways: Taylor stuck with 'Radio Ga Ga'; May finished *The Works*' 'Machines (Or "Back to Humans")'.

That same summer, New Order, Heaven 17 and even old hands Genesis were in the UK charts with synthesiser-driven pop songs. Queen joined the club. They'd done it before with disco, gospel and rock 'n' roll; they could do it again now – and better than most.

The title came first, inspired by Felix, the toddler son of Taylor and his French partner Dominique. The story goes that the boy uttered the words 'radio caca' ('caca' being French slang for excrement) while the radio was playing. His amused père interpreted this as an indictment of the music. It struck a chord. Taylor's 'Modern Times Rock 'n' Roll' from *Queen* had complained about 'a worn-out rock 'n' roll scene'; he was now ready to get stuck in again.

Taylor's lyrics talked about how radio had been a friend during his adolescence and denounced the fact that, in the modern world, 'we watch the shows . . . and hardly need to use our ears'. Queen knew they couldn't call the song 'Radio Caca', but Mercury insisted on singing those words anyway.

Then came the telex. In October 1983, Jim Mazza, president of Capitol Records, heard an early version of the track and sent a message to the Queen office. Mazza explained the radio industry's fears about the dominance of music videos and suggested that Queen amend their lyrics so that the song became 'a supportive endorsement of radio's future, rather than a prediction of its demise'.

Capitol had paid a lot of money for Queen and expected them to compromise. The band have never said how much they changed the lyrics, if at all, but the final words did end up contradicting themselves. 'You've had your time, you've had your power' does not suggest a medium that is 'yet to have your finest hour'.

According to Mercury, Taylor took a break from the sessions and gave the singer carte blanche to do as he wished with the song. 'Roger had the ideas all together,' Mercury explained. 'But I felt there were some construction elements that were wrong. I virtually took the song over.'

Fred Mandel – Queen's touring keyboard player and session musician – also contributed. 'I helped with the arrangement and put together some synth stuff,' he said. 'I also played a bass part, which John Deacon borrowed some of the concepts from.'

'Radio Ga Ga' was released as a single in January 1984. Regardless of who had a hand in its creation, it was credited to Roger Taylor alone and gave him his first UK top-five hit since 1975's 'I'm in Love with My Car' (on the B-side of 'Bohemian Rhapsody').

Despite Jim Mazza's fears, the single started to receive airplay in the US. Then Capitol fired their independent pluggers during an industry-wide investigation into payola. Partly as a result, 'Radio Ga Ga' and *The Works* tanked in America.

It was different in Britain, though, where DJs loved songs about radio, regardless of the lyrics. The Buggles' 'Video Killed the Radio Star' had been all over the airwaves in summer 1979, despite predicting the death of the medium. Now it was the turn of 'Radio Ga Ga'. The song included all of Queen's signature moves: massive chorus; infuriating hook; talking-point title. The only thing missing was a solo, but May's simple slide guitar fill did the trick.

As good as the song was, director David Mallet's video gave 'Radio Ga Ga' the final push. Mallet's film cost an eye-watering £110,000. The irony wasn't lost on Queen, but they knew what was needed to sell records. At the time, the band were working with producer Giorgio Moroder on yet another film sound-track – this one was a restored version of Fritz Lang's pre-war sci-fi drama, *Metropolis*. Though the soundtrack later became a Mercury solo project, Queen were allowed to use Lang's footage in their video.

Metropolis's smoke-bellowing factories, churning machinery and worker drones brought a bleak undercurrent to Mallet's video. His story began with a gas-mask-wearing wartime family switching on the radio and being transported to a futuristic world in which Queen zoomed around in a flying car. Taylor pretended to drive (with his foot up on the dashboard); Mercury sang; May and Deacon sat in the back. You almost expected one of them to ask, 'Are we there yet?' Around the 3:15 mark, Taylor struggled not to laugh and Mercury looked a bit tipsy. He had a supply of vodka and tonic stashed in the car's footwell during filming.

Halfway through the video, Queen reappeared on a clunky space-age set at Pinewood Studios. Apparently, they were now playing revolutionary leaders, 'making a very Eva Peron-like heroic appearance on stage in front of the "proles", who were being encouraged to revolt', explained May.

Queen's 'proles' comprised 500 extras, mostly from the band's fan club. The film's most famous scene showed Queen conducting their obedient servants through a synchronised salute and double handclap on the chorus (though it was actually a single clap repeated electronically on the record). This 'Simon says' routine was meant to illustrate how radio's 'ga ga' and 'goo goo' had turned us all into unquestioning robots. Some critics, however, later compared it to a Nazi Party rally. 'Arrogant nonsense,' huffed the *NME*.

'I'm still shocked,' groaned May two decades later. 'People thought we were really trying to be dictators.'

None of this criticism mattered when Queen walked on stage at Live Aid the following year. They played 'Radio Ga Ga' and watched, astonished, as 72,000 people mimicked the video's salute and double handclap. Queen had achieved something that Hendrix, Led Zeppelin and the Who never had: a personalised dance move.

From that day onwards, no live performance of 'Radio Ga Ga' would be complete without this semaphore. Maybe the Buggles were right: video had killed the radio star. But radio's loss was Roger Taylor's gain.

RAINBOW THEATRE
Queen versus the Who

In 2014, Roger Taylor listened to a forty-year-old recording of Queen at London's Rainbow Theatre. 'I thought, "My God, we really made a good noise, didn't we?"' he remarked. The *Live at the Rainbow '74* album (and accompanying DVD) was the latest addition to the growing list of Queen live albums. But this one was special and long overdue.

Queen's March and November 1974 dates were intended to be captured on a live album at the time. The November shows had also been filmed. Then Queen's management problems and Brian May's ill health, among other issues, resulted in the LP being shelved. For some years after, a half-hour edit circulated at cinemas as a supporting film to Pink Floyd's *The Wall* or *Jaws 2*.

Queen made their Rainbow Theatre debut on 31 March 1974. Other smaller dates on their gig sheet included the Isle of Man's Palace Lido and the Croydon Greyhound. 'When our promoter, Mel Bush, suggested the Rainbow for the last night of the tour, we looked at him as if to say, "Are you sure? Can we fill it?"' said Brian May.

The Rainbow was a major step up for Queen. Formerly known as the Finsbury Park Astoria, the 3,500-capacity theatre had history. Freddie Mercury had seen Jimi Hendrix set his guitar on fire there in 1967; the Who had played the Rainbow's opening night in November 1971; May and Taylor had watched David Bowie turn himself into Ziggy Stardust there in December 1972 . . .

Despite their reservations, Queen sold out the venue within a week.

In the hours before the show, though, Mercury's nerves crept up on him (it wasn't unheard of for the singer to throw up before a gig). This time, he picked a fight with Taylor over their stage clothes. Mercury stormed out of the soundcheck and sat sulking in the crew's van until May began teasing him over the mic: 'Freddi-iieee. Freddiiieee. Come back . . .'

Later, Queen's first producer, John Anthony, watched the show from the wings. Mercury was sporting black, Cleopatra-style eye make-up, black-painted fingernails and a white Zandra Rhodes-designed satin tunic. He prowled the stage during 'Ogre Battle' and 'Great King Rat', but dashed over to Anthony in between songs, looking flustered. 'I told him, "Calm down, Freddie, you're doing great,"' recalled the producer. 'He looked relieved and said, "Oh, thank you, Johnnypoos."'

The show was such a success that Queen returned to the Rainbow for two more sold-out nights on 19 and 20 November. By then, they'd toured America and had a top-ten hit with 'Killer Queen'. It showed. The opening scene in *Live at the Rainbow* has Queen emerging from a chauffeur-driven limo outside the theatre. Roger Taylor is wearing sunglasses even though it's pitch black outside.

On stage, the early crowd-pleasers ('Liar', 'Seven Seas of Rhye', 'Keep Yourself Alive') ran seamlessly into hot-off-the press new songs ('Flick of the Wrist' and 'Bring Back That Leroy Brown'). Every drum roll, guitar riff and three-part harmony was nailed down tight. It was, as Taylor said, 'a good noise'.

Mercury preened, posed, pouted, dashed between the piano and centre-stage, and flapped the 'wings' on his white tunic. He resembled a cross between his beloved Nijinsky and a giant swan. In between songs, he addressed the audience in a mix of public-school posh and theatrical camp: 'Right now . . . no, no, no, no . . . listen, my darlings . . .'

Mercury's appearance certainly caught the press's attention. 'Freddy [*sic*] Mercury is a rather endearing person,' noted Philip Norman in his review for *The Times*. 'Curveting and prancing to display a bottom small even by the attenuated standards of rock music.'

'Freddie was famous in those days among the girls for having a vanishingly small bum,' confirmed May.

Backstage afterwards, record company bosses, band members and promoters cheered as Champagne corks popped and plumes of Dom Pérignon showered the walls. Everyone raised a glass to a great night. But Queen's greatest accolade was still to come.

March of the black queen: performing at London's Rainbow Theatre, 1974.

Suddenly, Mercury spotted John Anthony steering a starstruck-looking teenager towards him. 'Oh, Johnnypoos, Johnnypoos,' he whispered. 'Who is this?' It was Simon Townshend – the thirteen-year-old brother of the Who's guitarist, Pete. Freddie put down his glass and shook the boy's hand. Simon looked up and grinned, before loudly announcing, 'You're better than my brother's band. Queen are much better than the Who.' In 1974, it was the greatest compliment Queen had ever received.

THE REACTION

The coronation of Queen's singing drummer

The Drummer is a statue that stands outside Truro's Hall for Cornwall – the scene of Queen's debut concert. In June 2011, Roger Taylor returned to his old hometown. The city mayor and hundreds of locals gathered to see Truro's most famous rock star unveil sculptor Tim Shaw's 15-foot rendering of a naked percussionist. 'No anatomical part of it was modelled on me,' joshed Taylor.

Roger Taylor began his musical journey at the Hall for Cornwall when it was still called Truro City Hall. He and his friend Mike Dudley were schoolboys when they joined local group Johnny Quale and the Reactions in 1965. Dudley played keyboards and then guitar; Taylor played the drums. 'Roger's favourite saying was "I'm gonna be a pop star,"' the band's ex-guitarist, Geoff Daniel, once mentioned. 'He said it all the time – it drove everybody mad – but he was absolutely right.'

Taylor made his Reactions debut on 15 March 1965 when the group competed in the Rock and Rhythm Championship at Truro City Hall. They came fourth out of fifteen, which wasn't good enough in the eyes of their new drummer. He would never settle for anything less than number one.

Local builder and Elvis uber-fan Johnny Quale (not his real name) was older than the others and already a seasoned performer on the Cornish circuit. In November 1965, Presley's new movie, *Spinout*, opened at the Truro Plaza. Quale wanted to go, but the Reactions had a booking. He refused to cancel his cinema outing, so their agent, Roger 'Sandy' Brokenshire (who also worked at local butchers Thomas Mutton & Sons), stepped in as lead singer.

Brokenshire was another veteran of the circuit and had once supported Gene Vincent. He told jokes in between numbers and hammed it up on stage in a gold lamé jacket, which was later replaced by a fur coat modelled on the one worn by Sonny Bono of Sonny & Cher. His bandmates complained that he smelled of sausages, but Brokenshire's old-school stage act worked. In March 1966, the Reactions came first in the Rock and Rhythm Championship.

Over the coming months, they played every village hall and ballroom within driving distance of Truro. Roger's mother, Winifred, even booked the band to play a Women's Institute event in a church hall in St Agnes. They were so loud, though, that some of the older women had to take their hearing aids out. Elsewhere, the Reactions opened for Gerry and the Pacemakers and the Kinks, as well as playing a fundraiser for the Truro Young Liberals and performing at a Conservative Party barbecue hosted by future deputy prime minister Michael Heseltine.

Taylor made his recording debut with the Reactions in spring 1966. Johnny Quale was making a demo and enlisted his old backing group. With time left over at the end, the Reactions recorded covers of Wilson Pickett's 'In the Midnight Hour' and James Brown's 'I Got You (I Feel Good)' for the A- and B-sides of a privately pressed single. Taylor played drums and sang lead vocals.

'I Got You' suggested a group on the cusp of change. The Reactions' saxophonist sounded like a throwback to the 1950s, but Taylor's Keith Moon-inspired drumming and rasping vocal was perfectly attuned to 1966. 'The music was changing,' said Geoff Daniel. 'Cream and Hendrix were coming . . .'

Before long, 'Sandy' Brokenshire had returned to butchery and solo gigs, and Roger Taylor had become the Reactions' lead singer. Taylor had been driving the group forward for some time: 'His drum kit literally started moving nearer and nearer to the front of the stage,' recalled Daniel.

'Those other singers all flaked away,' Taylor confirmed. 'So I ended up singing and playing drums. Yes, I admit it: my kit did end up getting nearer the front of the stage. A lot of people when they're young think, "Yeah, I want to be in a group, that's cool." But I really did want to be in a group and I really did think I was going to make it – which is absolutely ridiculous when you think back.'

Shortly after, other members left and Taylor and Dudley implemented another name change: knocking the 's' off and becoming the Reaction. To celebrate, Roger painted their new logo across the bonnet of the group's Bedford van.

Inspired by Pete Townshend's auto-destructive stage act, Roger started setting his cymbals on fire, too, and he even stripped the Taylor family's upright piano down to a shell, painted its innards with psychedelic colours and then smashed it up during 'Land of 1000 Dances'. And, as a foretaste of Queen's self-sufficiency, Taylor also fired the Reaction's agent, having realised that the band could make more money by booking gigs themselves.

Everything was going well until 11 February 1967. The Reaction were on their way to a gig in Dobwalls Village Hall in Liskeard. Taylor had just passed his test and was driving the group's Thames Trader when they encountered fog 5 miles outside Truro. They crossed a hump-backed bridge, but didn't see a fish lorry parked up with its tail jutting out. The lorry's reflectors were too dirty to catch the oncoming van's lights, so the vehicles collided.

The Thames Trader flipped upside down and Taylor was thrown through the windscreen. Most of the passengers escaped without serious injury, but their schoolfriend and roadie, Peter Gill-Carey, suffered a punctured lung and major damage to his right arm.

The lorry had already been reported for bad parking and the police were on the scene within minutes. Gill-Carey spent the next twelve months in hospital and would never regain full movement of his right hand. While neither Gill-Carey's family nor the rest of the band blamed Taylor for the accident, it cast a huge shadow over them all.

'I was driving myself to the gig that night,' said Geoff Daniel. 'I didn't know anything about it until the police told me. At school the following Monday, the headmaster made me stand up in assembly and tell everyone what had happened.'

In 1980, Taylor answered a light-hearted questionnaire in *Flexipop!* magazine. For 'worst thing that has ever happened to me' he wrote: 'A bad car smash I had once.'

After the accident, the Reaction continued sporadically, but parental pressure, further education and day jobs soon took precedence. 'I went to university and that was the end of it for me,' said Daniel. 'That was the difference. For me, the group was a bit of fun, but Roger was so driven.'

By summer 1968, the Reaction was all over. Just before Roger began his dentistry studies in London, Winifred Taylor offered him a word of advice: 'Remember, you're not going there to play, you're there to study.' He didn't listen. The Reaction were finished, but Winifred's son was still determined to become a pop star.

RED CROSS
Queen's real first gig

Queen's performance at Live Aid defined both the band and the idea of a charity concert. But Queen's first ever gig was also for a humanitarian cause. In February 1970, Roger Taylor's mother suggested that Smile play a show in aid of the Truro Detachment of the British Red Cross Society. Scheduled for Saturday 27 June at Truro City Hall, it was promoted months ahead in the *West Briton Advertiser*: 'We invite YOU to come and DANCE!'

In the meantime, Smile split up and Taylor and Brian May regrouped with Roger's bass-playing acquaintance Mike Grose and their wannabe-singer friend Freddie Mercury. In a matter of weeks, Mercury had engineered a name change and a stylistic overhaul.

Apparently, Queen made their Truro City Hall debut in identical black T-shirts, black crushed velvet trousers and black stack-heeled boots. Earlier, Mercury had taken Mike Grose shopping on the King's Road. Grose, who wasn't quite as under-nourished as his bandmates, struggled to walk in his new trousers and ripped the crotch when sitting down on a train. However, the strides were repaired well enough to withstand Queen's debut, which Grose remembered as 'being a bit scrappy', with Freddie 'prancing about, a bit like Mick Jagger'.

'It was Freddie's first actual proper performance with us,' confirmed Taylor. 'People did not quite know what to make of the not quite fully formed Freddie, who was fairly outrageous.'

No setlist exists, but it's believed that Queen played Elvis's 'Jailhouse Rock' and Led Zeppelin's 'Communication Break-down' in addition to their own 'Son and Daughter' and 'Stone

Cold Crazy'. Some 200 people showed up at the venue (which could hold four times as many attendees) and Queen were paid £50. 'We thought we were rich,' said Taylor.

Neither the British Red Cross nor Truro City Hall (since rebranded as the Hall for Cornwall) have been acknowledged for the part they played in Queen's history. Instead, in March 2013, May and Taylor attended the unveiling of a blue plaque at London's Imperial College to commemorate 'Queen's first public performance in London' on Saturday 18 July 1970.

RED SPECIAL

How to make your own guitar like Brian May

Method:
1. Take one teenage guitar player.
2. Add one resourceful electronics engineer father.
3. Combine with one understanding mother.
4. Prepare in the spare bedroom of 6 Walsham Road, Feltham, Middlesex, between August 1963 and October 1964.
5. Play with a sixpence.

Ingredients:
    1 century-old fireplace mantel (for the neck and headstock)
    1 piece of blockboard, plus 1 piece of oak dining table (for the body)
    1 handful of household matchsticks (with which to fill any wormholes in the oak body)
    1 hardened steel knife-edge moulded into a 'V' shape (for the tremolo system)

1 bicycle saddle-bag support (to make the tremolo arm)

1 plastic knitting-needle tip (to make the tremolo arm)

2 motorcycle valve spring sets (to support the tremolo arm)

3 hand-crafted roller saddles (for the bridge)

3 Burns Tri-Sonic single-coil pick-ups

2 volume/tone knobs (can be bought from an electronics shop or handmade on a lathe at Imperial College)

6 hand-tooled aluminium bridge blocks

1 3/16-inch steel truss rod (to support the neck)

1 removable black Perspex scratch plate

1 packet of plastic shelf edging (soften in warm water to shape around the body)

24 hand-tooled frets

16 mother-of-pearl buttons for dot markers (use the most colourful button on the twenty-fourth fret)

6 machineheads

6 strings

2 bolts

2 screws

1 tin of Cascamite resin-based wood glue

Several coats of Rustins plastic coating to achieve deep mahogany-red finish

REID, JOHN

The manager's tale

In 2019, John Reid realised he couldn't hide any more. It had been twenty years since he'd retired from music management and now there were two different actors playing him in two different films:

Bohemian Rhapsody and the Elton John biopic *Rocket Man*. Suddenly, journalists wanted to ask him about his past life and loves again.

John Reid had stories to tell. Queen's ex-manager was born in Paisley, Renfrewshire, and trained as a marine engineer before coming to London in 1967. Reid didn't know anybody in the city; he only knew that he wanted to work in the music business. For a time, he sold clothes in the Knightsbridge branch of men's outfitters Austin Reed. On his way to work, he'd admire a beautiful house in nearby Montpelier Square. A few years later, he was rich enough to buy it.

In 1968, Reid became British label manager for Tamla Motown. He was ambitious and go-getting and even put out Smokey Robinson's 'The Tears of a Clown' as a single without his bosses' permission. 'They said, "Who told you you could do that?" I said, "Nobody."' When 'The Tears of a Clown' went to number one, they quickly stopped complaining.

In 1971, Reid was working for song publisher Dick James Music when he met unknown singer-songwriter Elton John. He and Elton were lovers for five years and had a manager–client relationship for twenty-seven. When Reid formed his own company, John Reid Enterprises, it was the beginning of a tempestuous, hedonistic time: he chartered a Pan Am jet to fly his family and friends to see Elton play the Dodger Stadium; he ended up in a New Zealand jail cell after a nightclub brawl; he bought himself a white Rolls-Royce because singing elf Marc Bolan told him to; and he reached millionaire status by the time he was twenty-five.

Reid was recommended to Queen by EMI chairman Sir Joseph Lockwood. He was chosen above Peter Grant (Led Zeppelin's handler) and Don Arden (Sharon Osbourne's dad). In summer 1975, Reid told Queen to go away and make a hit album while he took care of business. It was what they wanted to hear and, six months later, they came up with *A Night at the Opera*.

Reid (whose nickname was 'Beryl', after the comedy actor Beryl Reid) started managing Queen at the right time in their career. The manager and many of his staff were gay, so their organisation offered supportive security to Freddie Mercury, who was still coming to terms with his sexuality. Apparently, Mercury even asked Reid to tell the rest of Queen he was gay. They already knew. 'The visitors to Freddie's dressing room started to change from hot chicks to hot men,' said Brian May. 'It didn't matter to us. And he did say at some point, "I suppose you realise I've changed in my private life?"'

Reid encouraged Mercury to explore his sexuality, but also to recognise his worth as Queen's lead singer and as a potential solo artist. 'It went well in the beginning, but John related more to Freddie than to the rest of us,' said May.

Roger Taylor also believed that Elton was unhappy about competing with Queen. 'John was put under terrific pressure from Elton,' he said. 'We were very successful and Elton was massive at the time, but I think he felt a bit threatened.'

Reid's romance with Elton added a volatile edge to their business relationship. But Mercury was also a demanding client. He and Reid once had a row in a London restaurant and Mercury told the manager to fuck off. Reid went back to his Montpelier Square townhouse, only for a brick to come crashing through the window soon after. Reid peered through the broken glass to see Mercury in the street below. 'Don't you ever fucking leave me in a restaurant again!' he screamed.

Queen and Reid only signed a three-year contract. The group's long-term aim was always to manage themselves. Once their time was up, they split from Reid without rancour or bad blood. 'It was one of the gentlest parting of the ways I ever had,' said the manager. By way of contrast, after Elton John fired him, the two men never spoke again.

Reid left the music business following his costly bust-up with Elton and a legal spat with another client, Irish Riverdancer Michael Flatley. Then came the movies. In *Rocket Man*, Reid was portrayed by actor Richard Madden as a devious opportunist who ripped off his lover. In *Bohemian Rhapsody*, Aidan Gillen's John Reid is unceremoniously fired and dumped out of Mercury's limousine after suggesting he go solo. Both actors replicated Reid's Glaswegian burr, but that was about it. 'I don't recognise a lot of the stuff,' Reid said.

In fact, Reid and Queen signed a severance contract in 1978 in the back seat of Mercury's new Rolls-Royce, parked outside Taylor's new country pile – the spoils of Queen's success and Reid's business acumen. But the manager's legacy was perhaps best summed up in 'The Millionaire Waltz' – a song that Mercury told London's Capital Radio he wrote about Reid. 'Make me feel like a millionaire,' sang Freddie. Which is exactly what John 'Beryl' Reid did.

The millionaire waltz: Freddie Mercury with manager John Reid, 1977.

RHODES, ZANDRA
Queen's dresser

In 1970, Brian May and Roger Taylor went to see the movie *Wood-stock*. Director Michael Wadleigh's celebration of the American pop festival was a box-office hit, but Queen weren't convinced. 'There were a lot of bands getting stoned and shuffling around,' complained May.

'We loved the Who and Hendrix and thought Sly and the Family Stone were good, but the rest was crap,' added Taylor.

Musically and visually, Queen were the anti-Woodstock. 'In those days, it was fashionable to eschew an act and not be glamorous,' said May. '"Showbiz" was a dirty word. Queen wanted to be glamorous and we weren't shy about using the language of theatre.'

Mott the Hoople's Morgan Fisher – later Queen's touring keyboard player – spotted this glamour the first time he met them. 'Queen were like a Biba version of a rock band,' he said.

It was Freddie Mercury who steered Queen's image. In 1974, he hired fashion designer Zandra Rhodes to create their stage costumes. Zandra worked with unusual prints to create garments designed to accentuate form and shape and serve as an extension of the body. 'I liked the idea of people wearing living paintings,' she said. 'Like living works of art.'

Mercury, a former fashion student, understood all this. At Ealing Art College, he'd been given a book about the androgynous costumes worn by Russian dancers Diaghilev and Nijinsky for the 1912 ballet *L'Après-midi d'un faune*. Mercury camped it up by pretending to swoon over the images in the art studio, playing for laughs, but he filed the designs away for future inspiration, too. They reappeared in the video for 'I Want to Break Free'.

Zandra Rhodes wasn't the first designer to make clothes for Queen. Their friend Wendy Edmunds created several early costumes based on Mercury's sketches. These included a balletic stretch-velvet top and a satin one-piece with dainty wings on the heels and cuffs (in honour of the Roman messenger of the gods: Mercury). Wendy later recalled how good a seamster Freddie was and how he always stitched his own sequins. But, after Queen signed to EMI, Mercury decided they should pay for a new wardrobe.

Zandra Rhodes had never heard of Queen when Mercury called her studio in Paddington. She sent her assistant out to buy their latest record. When Queen arrived for their appointment, she told them to try on anything from the rails lining the room. Mercury went straight for a cape shirt in ivory silk. It was the top half of a wedding dress and had large, pleated butterfly sleeves/wings.

Mercury persuaded EMI to pay for four outfits for each of the band. Rhodes swapped ivory silk for satin and went to work. The costumes fulfilled her desire to accentuate the form and they delighted Mercury by blurring the lines between male and female.

For a time, Mercury and his pleated satin tunic were inseparable. During Queen's 1974 tour, he used it as camouflage, a mask and a stage prop, while the 'wings' became an extension of his body. Brian May also made good use of his pleated bolero jacket: when he stood in the spotlight and raised his winged arm to strike a chord, the effect was dazzling. But the outfit could be cumbersome. 'It helped that Freddie didn't have a guitar to deal with,' he said.

Apparently, John Deacon persevered with his outfit for a few dates, but Taylor abandoned his after one show. 'I think Roger thought he was being made to wear a dress,' suggested May. 'But it certainly wasn't easy to drum in.'

In June 1974, Queen featured in a *Daily Telegraph Magazine* cover story. 'Geared into the Teen Scene: Young Fashions That Mother Might Allow' showed Mercury in his tunic next to models Marianne and Louise wearing Biba and Dorothy Perkins tops. Strangely, it was Brian rather than Freddie who appeared on the magazine cover, looming menacingly over the models in a black, witchy Zandra Rhodes cape.

May's original white bolero jacket was stolen, but he wore a gold replica on Queen + Adam Lambert's 2017 tour. Mercury's original tunic is currently on show in the Montreux Museum, though Zandra Rhodes was asked to reproduce it for Rami Malek in *Bohemian Rhapsody*. In 1974, Queen's 'dresses' served an important purpose. They marked the young band out as dramatic and theatrical and light-years removed from Woodstock's stoned shufflers. 'Freddie saw the value of dress and make-up,' Rhodes later told *Vogue*. 'He was a god on stage.'

ROCK IN RIO

A boob job

There was always something terribly British about Queen. Scratch away the shiny veneer and you'd find a product of post-war England – a world of milky tea (two sugars, please), Bakelite radios and saucy seaside postcards showing fat-bottomed girls or boys . . .

Queen had embraced another great British tradition when they'd dressed as women in the video for 'I Want to Break Free'. However, Freddie Mercury would soon discover that this wasn't such a well-received trope in South America. Queen were booked to play the opening and closing nights of the ten-day Rock in Rio festival in January 1985. AC/DC, Rod Stewart, George Benson and Yes were also headlining the 250,000-capacity Barra da Tijuca stadium, but Queen were the star turn.

As Mercury had already worn some of his 'I Want to Break Free' costume on stage in Europe, he saw no reason to amend his act for Brazil. So, having conducted the audience through the synchronised handclaps of 'Radio Ga Ga', he then returned to the stage for Queen's next hit wearing a wig and a skin-tight sweater, under which he'd jammed a pair of torpedo-shaped plastic breasts.

At that point, the video for 'I Want to Break Free' had rarely been seen outside of the UK (MTV refused to broadcast it), but the song had been embraced as a protest anthem in Brazil. After two decades of military dictatorship, the country was now poised for its first democratic election since 1964, meaning that Queen – the world's most apolitical rock group – had accidentally become political.

Mercury's breasts upset and confused the audience. Contrary to press reports, Queen weren't bombarded with bottles and cans, but they were loudly booed and jeered. 'It was an anthem for freedom and the crowd thought Fred was knocking it,' said ex-roadie Peter 'Ratty' Hince. 'The papers said there was a riot, which was nonsense, but it surprised Fred. He couldn't work out what was going wrong.'

'Oh, there was no place Freddie wouldn't go,' marvelled Brian May, sounding wistful in 2019. 'Even singing with false breasts in South America.' Mercury removed the offending costume and Queen finished the show without further protest.

Mercury brushed aside the protest, just as he did all criticism. 'The trouble was, when I first tried [the fake breasts] in Brussels, some people said that, at the back of the arena, you couldn't see them unless they were twice the size of Dolly Parton's,' he explained. 'So I had to get some bigger tits. In Rio, they went a bit mad and I thought [it was because] my tits were too big for them.'

Brazil's democratic presidential elections were held on 15 January. It was an historic moment in Brazilian politics and Queen's accidental protest song acquired even greater resonance. When the band returned to headline the last night of Rock in Rio on 19 January, the breasts did not make an appearance. For once, Freddie Mercury knew when to back down.

RODGERS, PAUL

By temporary royal appointment

'There'll be no cape and probably a lack of tights,' said Paul Rodgers in February 2005. The plain-speaking Geordie had been asked how he planned to replace Freddie Mercury in Queen. Three years later, Rodgers' replies were less witty; he was heartily sick of being asked this question.

To date, the ex-Free and Bad Company vocalist is the only singer besides Mercury to record a studio album with Queen, though most, including Brian May and Roger Taylor, seem to have forgotten *The Cosmos Rocks*. Nevertheless, Queen + Paul Rodgers spent four years (on and off) touring the world together and it's debatable whether Queen would have worked with Adam Lambert were it not for this prior collaboration.

Another common question posed to Rodgers was whether he'd ever met Freddie Mercury. He recalled seeing Freddie and the band at Peter Grant's office in 1975 when Queen were seeking new management. (Led Zeppelin handler Grant also managed Rodgers' red-blooded rockers Bad Company.) 'They seemed like nice guys,' was the most Rodgers could muster.

Rodgers had actually met Mercury before, but had no reason to remember. Free had played Ealing Art College's rag ball in 1969 and ex-students remembered Fred Bulsara fluttering around the band asking them questions after the show. Queen all loved Rodgers' voice and Free's *Tons of Sobs* LP was a shared influence.

The roots of the Q + PR collaboration dated back to 1991 when May and Rodgers jammed at a guitar heroes love-in in Seville. They took it further when they performed together at the Fender Stratocaster fiftieth-anniversary concert in 2004. May then brought the idea to Taylor. 'It's been in the back of our minds to do something like this,' the drummer said. 'But Brian and I couldn't think of how to do it. Then, with Paul, it all fell into place.'

Queen's reluctance to commit to another singer was understandable. But so, too, was their frustration. They had a formidable back catalogue, but nobody to sing it. Since Mercury's death, they'd watched their contemporaries lapping the globe on lucrative reunion tours and with fewer hits than Queen.

Rodgers was a different beast to Freddie Mercury, though. His stage persona was studiedly cool and macho. Rodgers had given up alcohol for martial arts and he once appeared on the front of a Bad Company album wearing his karate ji and headband. Come the twenty-first century, he was still unnervingly trim and partial to wearing vests on stage.

After a couple of under-the-radar shows, Queen + Paul Rodgers formally launched with a UK tour in March 2005. There was a novelty factor to hearing Queen songs performed by a new singer, as well as relief that the band hadn't taken their mooted collaboration with Robbie Williams any further.

The setlist included half a dozen Free/Bad Company numbers and was weighted towards Queen's heavier songs. 'I don't fancy singing some of the more theatrical ones,' Rodgers admitted. But therein lay the problem. Rodgers was a bluesman who predominantly sang about sex and fighting. This meant that a great chunk of Queen's camp, vaudevillian songbook was off limits.

Furthermore, when Q + PR performed 'Bohemian Rhapsody', a video screen showed Mercury singing part of it at Wembley Stadium in 1986. Rodgers and the on-screen Mercury even performed the song's big finale together. Paul had a fine voice, but he couldn't compete with a dead Freddie.

Too late. The genie was out of the bottle. Offers from promoters flooded in. Q + PR graduated to playing arenas just two months after making their UK theatre debut. When they went to North America the following summer, they were filling aircraft hangars from Miami to Vancouver.

Q + PR's shortcomings began to surface when the shows became bigger. Audiences expected to hear all the hits. Where was 'Don't Stop Me Now'? What about 'Killer Queen'? The Q + PR demographic also caught the band unawares. 'The shows we did with Paul Rodgers had some quite shockingly old people there,' said Taylor later.

Still, everybody talked a good game. 'It's given us a sense of rejuvenation,' said Roger.

'Freddie is there in this music. I have nothing but admiration for the man,' insisted Paul.

But Taylor was also adamant that Q + PR shouldn't become a tribute band, so they needed new material if the collaboration were to continue. In April 2008, the band appeared on TV show *Al Murray's Happy Hour*. Comic actor Murray was a Queen fan who had instilled his love of the band into his 'Pub Landlord' character – a well-meaning but oafish Little Englander, bemused by political correctness and the French.

Q + PR performed a new song, 'C-lebrity' – a bog-standard rocker with lyrics skewering shallow popular culture. Sadly, it could have been written by the Pub Landlord. TV viewers collectively winced and wished Queen had played 'Radio Ga Ga' instead.

Queen + Paul Rodgers' *The Cosmos Rocks* was released in September that year. It was poorly promoted by EMI, sold weakly by Queen standards and did not add much to the band's setlist. Despite Taylor's fears, Q + PR had become their own tribute act. It was unavoidable.

Then, when they toured Japan and South America (previous Queen strongholds), Rodgers, who was less well-known in those countries, found himself marginalised. 'He'd become Queen's lead singer, which wasn't how it began,' said May. The two parties split at the end of the Rock the Cosmos Tour. 'It was only ever a temporary arrangement,' said Rodgers, who had a Bad Company reunion lined up.

'We got on fine with Paul,' Taylor said in 2013. 'But I'm sure he was sick to death of being asked about Freddie Mercury in every interview.'

'I'll never say a bad word about Paul,' Taylor added later. 'But, when it boils down to it, he wasn't the perfect frontman for us.' By then, though, Queen had discovered Adam Lambert. Better still, if required, Lambert would happily wear a cape and tights.

ROYAL BALLET
Freddie Mercury, dying swan

'I can't dance for shit, my dears,' claimed Freddie Mercury. But, like becoming an opera singer in the 1980s, he threw himself into the task of performing with the Royal Ballet. On 7 October 1979, Queen's singer gave the strangest performance of his career.

Mercury had been invited to dance with the Royal Ballet Company at a charity gala performance at London's Coliseum theatre. Sir Joseph Lockwood, EMI chairman, was also on the Royal Ballet's board of governors and he and Mercury moved in the same circles.

Freddie was fascinated by the world of ballet. He'd seen Rudolf Nureyev and Mikhail Baryshnikov dance and gushed about their performances: 'I was so in awe, I was like a groupie.' Contrary to rumour, though, he and Nureyev were never lovers. 'There is no way Freddie could have kept quiet about sleeping with Rudolf had he done so,' claimed ex-Royal Ballet dresser Peter Freestone, Mercury's former personal aide. 'And, anyway, neither was the other's type.'

Mercury was the Royal Ballet's second choice after another EMI artist, Kate Bush, had turned them down. Not only had Mercury performed in a catsuit modelled on an outfit worn by ballet supremo Nijinsky, he'd also talked up the dance genre in his notorious 1977 *NME* interview: 'I'm into this ballet thing,' he told them, 'and trying to put across our music in a more artistic manner than before.' So, naturally, Freddie couldn't refuse the Royal Ballet's offer.

The company's principal dancer, Wayne Eagling, oversaw days of intense rehearsals at a west London studio. Mercury showed up on the first morning wearing all the kit, but with little idea of what to do. 'It was murder,' he protested. 'After two days, I was aching in places I didn't even know I had.'

Mercury's approach to ballet was much like his style of song-writing, singing, piano- and guitar-playing. It was unique and defied convention. He was also terrified: 'It really scared me because I can't be choreographed.'

Mercury's cameo appearance was kept secret until the gala performance. On the night, he sang Queen's new single, 'Crazy Little Thing Called Love', while dancing in his leather jacket and biker's cap. Then, surrounded by his fellow dancers, he made a quick costume change before leading an orches-trated 'Bohemian Rhapsody'. Now in the Nijinsky-style catsuit, Mercury was manhandled, tossed, dangled upside down and borne aloft – all while trying to sing. It wasn't easy or wholly successful.

By the time 'Bohemian Rhapsody' thundered towards its grand finale, Mercury had slipped back into his old habits: prom-enading across the stage like it was the Hammersmith Odeon and twitching his right leg like he always did when performing with Queen. For the final vocal ('Nothing really matters . . .'), half a dozen bare-chested men delicately lifted the singer up above their heads like an offering to the gods – or like the campest rugby line-out ever.

Seated in a box at the Coliseum and trying to remain incon-spicuous throughout was Roger Taylor. 'I thought, "Oh, Fred, you brave, brave boy,"' he recalled years later. 'But there was only one person in the world who could have gotten away with it.'

'I wasn't quite Baryshnikov,' allowed Mercury. 'But I wasn't bad for an ageing beginner.' He was thirty-two years old at the time.

Crazy little thing: Freddie Mercury rehearsing with the
Royal Ballet, 1979.

RUSHDIE, SALMAN

Great Queen rumours, part 2

In 1999, Salman Rushdie published his new novel, *The Ground Beneath Her Feet*. The author had been in hiding since a *fatwā* for his execution was ordered following 1988's *The Satanic Verses* – a book widely denounced throughout the Islamic world.

However, in 1993, Rushdie briefly appeared with U2 at London's Wembley Stadium. The author stood on stage for two minutes (in front of some 70,000 people), experienced a fleeting taste of what it felt like to be a pop star and was then spirited away by his police protection officers.

U2 later wrote a song called 'The Ground Beneath Her Feet', with lyrics provided by Rushdie. His novel of the same name was essentially the Greek myth of Orpheus reimagined as a rock 'n' roll-themed fantasy. Its main characters included Ormus Cama – a Parsi Indian rock star who fronts fictional group VTO. Cama's backstory borrowed from the lives of Elvis, John Lennon and Freddie Mercury.

There were parallels between the lives of Rushdie and Mercury, too. The two men were born a year apart and, while Rushdie was growing up in Mumbai (then Bombay), Mercury was boarding at St Peter's School in neighbouring Panchgani. Both teenagers became hooked on western pop music and both moved to the UK in the early '60s. Rushdie has frequently mentioned Mercury's Indian roots and even tweeted about him in 2012: 'Farrokh Bulsara! First global Indian rock superstar! (Freddie Mercury to you.)' But he has also pointed out how rarely Mercury discussed his Indian childhood.

Since Mercury's death, India has collectively embraced the former Farrokh Bulsara's legacy. In 2006, *Time* magazine pointed out how 'Bulsara duplicated in popular music what other Indians – such as Salman Rushdie and Vikram Seth – have done in literature: taking the colonizer's art form and representing it in a manner richer and more dazzling than many Anglophones thought possible.'

Which, perhaps, is why a rumour spread through the Indian media that Mercury and Rushdie had been at school together. Some claimed that, after Mercury left St Peter's, he enrolled at Rushdie's alma mater, Cathedral School. The journalist Anvar Alikhan pursued the story, but discovered that Rushdie's family had moved to the UK in 1961, a year before Mercury left St Peter's to complete his education in Zanzibar. The two giants of Asian pop music and literature had definitely never been at school together or even met.

Then, in 2017, Rushdie claimed in an interview to have lived 100 yards away from Farrokh Bulsara in Mumbai. Once again, the dogged Alikhan explored this claim in an article for digital newspaper *Scroll*. He pointed out that Rushdie's family home near Warden Road was more than 100 yards from the Dadar Parsi Colony, where Mercury had stayed with his aunt during school holidays. In fact, it was nearly 6 miles away. 'Rushdie's childhood friends say they're mystified by the claim,' he wrote.

Perhaps Rushdie's brief taste of pop stardom with U2 had turned his head? Maybe he just wanted to feel closer to the real-life Ormus Cama? Or, perhaps, just like Freddie Mercury, he didn't want to let the truth get in the way of a good story.

'SEVEN SEAS OF RHYE'

Queen on TV

Queen's first appearance on *Top of the Pops*, performing 'Seven Seas of Rhye', was broadcast on 21 February 1974. None of the band had a television, so they trooped down to an electrical goods shop in Kensington and watched themselves on a TV set through the window. Both the song and the performance would become watershed points in their career.

'Seven Seas of Rhye' made its full appearance on *Queen II*, though a short instrumental version was also the last track on their first album. 'I think Freddie had written half the song by then,' said Roger Taylor, which would explain the ellipses following the song's first title. Queen originally intended to open *Queen II* with the full version, but later decided against it.

The finished song became a calling card for Queen's second album, cramming every facet of their sound into two minutes and forty-nine seconds of music. There was cod-classical piano, shrill harmonising, Brian May's guitar going off like a Bonfire Night rocket, and Freddie Mercury sermonising about 'lords and lady preachers'. But nobody had a clue what it was all about. 'I never understood a word of it and I don't think Freddie did really,' admitted Taylor. 'It was gestures really.'

'"Seven Seas of Rhye" is just fictitious,' said Mercury in 1977. 'It was just a figment of my imagination. At that time, I was learning about a lot of things in songwriting.'

The song was also a calculated attempt to get Queen noticed. Their first single, 'Keep Yourself Alive', had been criticised by some radio stations for taking over thirty seconds to reach the first vocal. 'We thought, "Right, we'll show them,"' said Brian May. 'On "Seven Seas of Rhye", everything deliberately happens quickly – guitars, harmonies, vocals.'

The song's closing section was another talking point: the sound of Queen and assorted friends singing the chorus to the old Edwardian music-hall standard 'I Do Like to Be Beside the Seaside' after a few drinks. It was a throwback to the novelty songs the band had heard on the radio as children. It also included a one-off outing for producer Roy Thomas Baker playing the Stylophone. This mini digital keyboard was a popular musical toy in the '70s. It sounded rather like a wasp trapped in a milk bottle and soundtracked many a Boxing Day or kids' birthday party.

The single became a hit, partly because David Bowie was offered *Top of the Pops* for his single 'Rebel Rebel' but had to turn it down due to prior commitments. EMI's head of promotion, Ronnie Fowler, suggested Queen take Bowie's place, even though they hadn't pressed 'Seven Seas of Rhye' as a 45 yet. Musicians' Union rules dictated that any artist appearing on *Top of the Pops* had to mime to a new recording of their song, but the original recording was actually played on the show.

Mercury and Taylor purportedly loathed *Top of the Pops*. 'It really wasn't a very cool show,' said the drummer, who particularly disliked using plastic cymbals during the performance. Industrial action at the BBC's White City studios also meant that Queen had to be filmed in a smaller room typically used for weather reports. 'We were trying to be big and bombastic in something the size of a living room.'

Nevertheless, they did the show and acknowledged its value. 'In those days, *Top of the Pops* helped sell records,' said May. 'It was also some sort of validation for our friends and families who'd been watching us trying to make something happen for so long.'

EMI rushed the single out to capitalise on *Top of the Pops*. But an early run of promos sent to radio stations contained a previously rejected mix. Outsiders would never have known the difference, but Mercury did the moment he heard it. He insisted that all copies be returned immediately.

The following month, Queen were back miming 'Seven Seas of Rhye' on *Top of the Pops*. This time, they'd been upgraded from the weather studio. As they'd hoped, the song became their first top-ten hit. Before too long, the band would be able to afford their own television sets.

SEX PISTOLS
'God Save the Queen'

Freddie Mercury went to the dentist for the first time in fifteen years on Wednesday 1 December 1976. In doing so, he unleashed what the *Daily Mirror* later dubbed 'The Filth and the Fury' on an unsuspecting British public. Queen were supposed to appear on the early-evening TV chat show *Today*. When they cancelled, EMI gave their spot to a new group called the Sex Pistols.

With their wan complexions, spiked hair, mohair jumpers and braying London accents, the Sex Pistols couldn't have looked and sounded less like Queen. According to the *Daily Mirror*, they were 'leaders of the new punk rock cult' and their debut single was entitled 'Anarchy in the UK'.

The show's host, Bill Grundy, struggled to hide his contempt. He proceeded to goad the group and their entourage, which included future Siouxsie and the Banshees singer, Siouxsie Sioux. They responded with a stream of insults. Thames TV viewers choked on their fish suppers as guitarist Steve Jones called Grundy 'a dirty sod, a dirty old man, a dirty bastard, a dirty fucker' and, best of all, 'a fucking rotter!'

Swearing on live television was a seismic event in '70s Britain. The next morning, the Sex Pistols were the talk of newspaper offices, factory floors and school playgrounds. Their appearance on Grundy's show was a water-cooler moment – had such a phrase been in common use at the time.

However, Queen's loss was the Sex Pistols' gain. Punk gate-crashed the mainstream, quickly clearing the way for other like-minded groups. Behind punk's cartoon aggression and anti-fashion image was a DIY musical ethic. You only needed three chords, not 180 vocal overdubs à la 'Bohemian Rhapsody'. Punk stripped away a lot of the flab and excess of '70s rock.

Queen were never a political band; they regarded most of their music as pure escapism. On 'Anarchy in the UK', the Sex Pistols' lead singer, John Lydon, aka Johnny Rotten, declared himself the 'anti-Christ'. Meanwhile, Freddie Mercury implored listeners to 'bring out the charge of the love brigade' in Queen's 'The Millionaire's Waltz'. Stylistic lines had been drawn and cultural shots fired.

Only Roger Taylor claimed to like punk. 'I used to see all the punk bands,' he said. 'But there were only two great ones: the Pistols and the Clash. Maybe the Buzzcocks. The rest were not very good.'

Queen and the Sex Pistols finally encountered each other at London's Wessex Studios in summer 1977. Queen were making *News of the World* and the Pistols were finishing their debut, *Never Mind the Bollocks, Here's the Sex Pistols*. But the great summit between the two diametrically opposed groups went off with less of a bang, more of a whimper. 'We all looked at each other with distrust to start with, but they were down-to-earth guys,' recalled Taylor. 'Apart from [bassist] Sid Vicious. He was a real thicko.'

Some months earlier, Mercury had mentioned ballet in an interview with the *NME* (which later ran under the headline 'Is this man a prat?'). At Wessex, Sid Vicious lurched into the control room and enquired whether Freddie 'was still bringing ballet to the masses'.

'I was wearing ballet pumps at the time,' Mercury reminisced. 'I called Sid Vicious "Simon Ferocious" – or something like that – and he didn't like it at all. I said, "What are you going to do about it?" He hated the fact I could speak to him like that.'

None of the other members of Queen recall this contretemps. But the Sex Pistols' engineer Bill Price later added to the story. He remembered Johnny Rotten telling him he wanted to meet Mercury and advising Rotten against it.

'Some time later, Johnny came back and said, "I've been to see Freddie." I said, "Oh, okay."' But then there was a knock on the door. Queen's co-producer Mike Stone walked in and said, 'Freddie was playing piano. One of your band members just crawled on all fours across our studio up to the side of the piano, said, "Hello, Freddie," and left on all fours. Could you make sure he doesn't do it again?'

During the *News of the World* sessions, Mercury went out and bought a car to cheer himself up. It was a Rolls-Royce Silver Shadow – about as un-punk-rock a gesture as one could make. But, secretly, punk made Queen uneasy and they responded in kind. Taylor's 'Sheer Heart Attack' was one of the stand-outs on *News of the World*. He'd started writing it three years earlier, but its furious tempo sounded very current in 1977. 'Roger said, "I want this on the album because this is my punk track,"' divulged May.

Footage exists of Queen performing the song at the Hammersmith Odeon in December 1979. John Deacon, with his shorn hair and shirt and tie, resembled a Talking Heads member, while topless Freddie Mercury ended the show by dramatically dry-humping and then pushing over a speaker stack. The following year, Queen appeared on the cover of *The Game* wearing black leather jackets. 'There will always be someone new on the scene – a new face coming after you and your success – and that challenge is good,' said Mercury.

In 2017, Brian May was a guest on Steve Jones's syndicated radio show *Jonesy's Jukebox* in Los Angeles. May was on the campaign trail for his new book, *Queen in 3-D*. Jones played 'Doing All Right' from Queen's first album, while May dreamily recalled how the two groups once shared a studio and how *Never Mind the Bollocks* . . . 'changed the world'.

While May looked like he'd been preserved in amber since 1977, Steve Jones bore little resemblance to his 22-year-old punk self. The presenter then cheerily told his listeners that, when he'd greeted his guest at the studio gates that day, May had mistaken him for a security guard.

'I had no idea who you were,' admitted Brian apologetically. 'The truth is: I don't know what the hell I'm doing. I just go where they point me. It just said "Jonesy" – I didn't know it was you. This is a genuine surprise.' He sounded distraught.

The punk wars were over. But, for a brief moment, one half-hoped Steve Jones would respond, 'What a fucking rotter!'

SHEER HEART ATTACK

The view from Brian May's hospital bed

While staying at the Parker House Hotel in downtown Boston, Brian May woke up one morning to discover he'd turned yellow. It was May 1974; Queen were touring America and the guitarist had contracted hepatitis. He'd been feeling weak for days, but blamed it on the usual rigours of the road. Earlier that year, the band had received travel vaccinations before a trip to Australia. The needle used on May wasn't sterile and his right arm became infected with gangrene. The condition was treated, but May's depleted immune system had called time on his body.

That morning, May peered into the mirror at his sickly yellow eyes and jaundiced hands, hoping it was all a trick of the light. Sadly, it wasn't. 'The doctor came in and said, "You are on the first plane home,"' May recalled. 'But I remember looking at this bowl of fruit in my hotel room. Someone had said grapefruits were really healthy. My mind was so muddled, I did wonder: if I ate all the grapefruits, would I get better?'

Back in England, May's doctors insisted on six weeks' bed rest, while his bandmates and crew were inoculated against the virus. Never one to be left out, Freddie Mercury told anyone who'd listen that he'd returned from America with a near-biblical 'plague of boils'.

May's illness was a significant setback. EMI expected a third Queen album before the end of the year and, although 'Seven Seas of Rhye' had been a British hit in February, the single bombed in America when Queen were unable to promote it. They'd lost momentum.

In July, Queen regrouped at Rockfield Studios, a residential facility in Monmouthshire, but May was still suffering. He struggled through the sessions, sometimes disappearing to throw up. One day, he passed out and was later taken to hospital. May was diagnosed with a duodenal ulcer, related to an underlying stomach condition from childhood. He underwent an operation at London's King's College Hospital and was bedridden for a further three weeks. 'It was awful,' he said. 'The band had to work on the album without me and I was convinced they'd find another guitarist.'

Instead, John Deacon played rhythm guitar and the three healthy band members would troop into the hospital every night to play Brian their latest recordings: 'Freddie – God bless him – said, "Don't worry, darling, we can't do it without you." They also deliberately made me laugh because they knew it was painful.'

The album, *Sheer Heart Attack*, was completed over a frantic three-month period, split between Trident, SARM and Wessex Studios. Desperate to remain involved, May snuck away from the hospital to play guitar. A bed was even brought into the studio so he could rest between takes. Queen routinely worked fourteen-hour days and fussed over the finer details. They had something to prove. 'It was time for Queen to have some hits,' said producer Roy Thomas Baker.

There'd been an upside to May's absence, though. For the first time, the guitarist had seen Queen from the outside. In hospital, bored and incapacitated, he'd mapped out a new song, 'Now I'm Here', and ideas for the future hit single 'Killer Queen'.

May contributed four compositions to *Sheer Heart Attack*. Two of them – 'Brighton Rock' and 'Now I'm Here' – combined gonzo hard rock with a scientific attention to detail; it was heavy metal reimagined by a part-qualified astrophysicist. These songs, plus Taylor's 'Tenement Funster', Mercury's 'Flick of the Wrist' and a reworked version of 'Stone Cold Crazy', all suggest that *Sheer Heart Attack* is Queen's 'metal' album. Or as close as they ever came to making one.

It's also a travelogue and a diary of their lives so far. 'Now I'm Here' salutes Queen's mentors Mott the Hoople and mentions 'Peaches' – a woman May had fallen for in the US who would later reappear in his life. 'Tenement Funster' portrayed Taylor as a charming playboy, upsetting his neighbours with loud music, but having 'a way with the girls on my block'.

There were also curios. John Deacon's cheery 'Misfire' sounded like something to mix piña coladas to on a Barbadian beach. It lasted less than two minutes, suggesting even its composer had grown bored of it quickly. The next track on the album, Mercury's 'Bring Back That Leroy Brown', was a music-hall pastiche with jangling piano and banjo-ukulele. Even in 2019, it was still perplexing Taylor: 'I don't even know how you describe that music. What is it?'

Elsewhere on the record, sex and money preoccupied Freddie Mercury. If Brian May is to be believed, the singer showed himself emotionally on the ballad 'Lily of the Valley': 'It's about Freddie looking at his girlfriend and realising his body needed to be somewhere else,' said May. Meanwhile, on 'Flick of the Wrist', Mercury seethed at the injustice of Queen's deal with their paymasters, Trident Audio Productions – a business arrangement hurtling towards a bitterly expensive showdown.

Released in November 1974, *Sheer Heart Attack* mostly expunged the whiff of hospital disinfectant and the rattle of bedpans. Only one song touched on poor Brian's predicament. His eerie 'She Makes Me (Stormtrooper in Stilettos)' had an anaesthetised quality and included laboured breathing and a wailing ambulance siren. The rest of the album, though, sounded fighting fit. Any fears that Queen had lost ground were also dismissed when it swept to number two in Britain and number fifteen in America.

In 2011, the *Stormtroopers in Stilettos* exhibition, containing items from every era in Queen history, opened at East London's Truman

Brewery. The exhibit for *Sheer Heart Attack* included Brian May's hospital bed. Bemused guests surrounded the artefact, pondering the significance of its horsehair blanket and paint-chipped iron bedrail. Was this the bed Brian was lying on when he dreamed up the guitar intro to 'Now I'm Here'? 'It's not the same bed, obviously,' an exhibition publicist pointed out. 'But it's very similar.' God bless the NHS.

'THE SHOW MUST GO ON'
Queen's personal therapy session

In December 2020, retail giant Amazon used an orchestral version of 'The Show Must Go On' in their seasonal ad campaign. The film told the story of a teenage ballet dancer struggling to follow her dream in the year of the pandemic. The ad didn't stint on sentimentality – it was Christmas, after all – but neither did Queen's original.

'The Show Must Go On', the final track on 1991's *Innuendo*, was released as a single six weeks before Freddie Mercury's death. It was another Queen statement song. But, unlike the humorous showboating of 'We Will Rock You' or 'We Are the Champions', this one had a serious message. At the time, Brian May wanted to change the song's title in the light of Mercury's terminal illness. Mercury wouldn't let him.

The song was a collaborative effort, but May took it over after hearing Roger Taylor and John Deacon's original chord sequence. 'I had this strange feeling it could be somehow important,' he said. 'I wanted to make some kind of monument to

Freddie.' May wrote the lyrics sat beside Mercury, but neither of them directly discussed the frontman's illness. It was all very British, very reserved: a dying man singing the lines 'I'll face it with a grin, I'm never giving in.' By that point, Mercury was so ill that reaching falsetto vocals was a struggle. But he glugged back a couple of vodkas and sang them anyway. 'He had an incredible strength and peace,' said May.

The song's foreboding intro (think: May's *Desert Island Discs* choice 'Saturn, the Bringer of Old Age' meets Pachelbel's 'Canon in D' meets the theme from *Jaws*) is just one of several moments of peerless Queen drama. Others include: the way Mercury's voice cracks on 'hold the line'; the breathy backing vocals ('learning . . . turning'); Mercury's ad-libbed Robert Plant-isms over the guitar solo; and the sonorous 'on with the show' when Queen transform themselves into a three-man Welsh male voice choir.

A more restrained band would have backed down. But restraint was never Queen's forté. The song was also cathartic. 'We were dealing with things that were hard to talk about,' said May. 'But, in the world of music, you could do it.'

The single was a modest hit in October 1991, but was re-released in the US (alongside 'Bohemian Rhapsody') after Mercury's death. It gave Queen their first American top-ten hit since 'Another One Bites the Dust'.

Mercury was too sick to make a video, so directors Rudi Dolezal and Hannes Rossacher spliced together a film of Queen through the ages. As sombre as the song was, the video's opening sequence showed Mercury dressed as a woman in 'I Want to Break Free', breasts thrust forward and moustached mouth pouting at the camera. Facing it with a grin and never giving in . . .

SMILE

Almost Queen

Brian May never forgot the pompom. The fluffy ball was attached to Freddie Mercury's wrist as a fashion accessory and used to punctuate his speech. 'Very good, Brian, very good,' Freddie used to say while flicking the pompom in May's direction. 'But why don't you present the show better?' Pompom flick. 'Why don't you dress like this?' Pompom flick.

It was some time in 1970; Brian May and Roger Taylor's Smile had just played a show and Mercury, their biggest fan/critic, was explaining how it could have been so much better. He was desperate to be their lead singer, but May and Taylor weren't sure he was up to the task. 'We'd been to see Fred sing with his own group,' said May tactfully, 'and we didn't quite know what to make of it.'

May and bassist/lead vocalist Tim Staffell had formed Smile in summer 1968 after the disbandment of their previous group, 1984. They placed an advert on the Imperial College noticeboard: 'Mitch Mitchell/Ginger Baker-style drummer wanted'. Roger Taylor, who had a friend from Cornwall studying at Imperial, replied to the ad. It was a fortuitous coincidence.

To begin with, Smile also had a keyboard player. Chris Smith was on the same graphic design course at Ealing Art College as Tim Staffell and the future Freddie Mercury. Smith only played a handful of gigs with Smile, but he witnessed their progress and their growing relationship with Mercury up close.

'Tim, Brian and I went round Roger's flat on Sinclair Road [in Kensington] to meet him,' Smith recalled. 'Roger didn't have his drums – they were still in Cornwall – but he did some singing. Tim said, "Oh, he's got a better voice than me. And he's better looking."'

Smile plotted world domination during conversations at Taylor's flat, Smith's neighbouring apartment in Addison

Gardens and the nearby Kensington Tavern. Staffell and Smith loved the blues; the latter envisaged Smile as 'a little version of the Rolling Stones'. But this was the post-psychedelic era. Progressive rock, with its wordy mini-symphonies and wheezing Mellotrons, would soon be in vogue.

Smith is certain that Smile's debut gig was supporting the Troggs at Imperial in summer 1968; the others are certain it was supporting Pink Floyd. Smith remembered Smile opening with Moby Grape's 'Can't Be So Bad', followed later by Tim Hardin's 'If I Were a Carpenter' and two Smile originals: 'Earth' and 'Step on Me'.

'Brian commanded respect,' Smith said later. 'I'd played a little bit of guitar, but I couldn't even tell what his hands were doing. We used to call the Red Special's neck the "tree trunk" – and Brian had very long fingers.'

May was ahead of the others musically, but needed to work on his image. 'He looked very much like a student,' said Smith. 'He had on a Bri-Nylon shirt and one of those knitted string ties you'd have worn in 1964. Before the gig, we all said, "You can't go on stage looking like that."'

Taylor took Brian back to his flat to change, but the only item that fitted the beanpole guitarist was Taylor's purple waistcoat. 'Roger was a bit of a dude,' observed Smith. 'I always remember he had this beautiful burgundy suit from Granny Takes a Trip with piping down the side.'

Smith went away for the summer holidays. Taylor returned to Truro and took the rest of Smile with him. They played as a three-piece at the local PJ's Club. 'And I think they rather liked being Cream,' said Smith. 'But I was thinking, "Whatever happened to Otis Redding and Muddy Waters?" Smile didn't have deep roots.'

Tim Staffell said that Smith was fired from the group. Smith disagreed. 'I left,' he insisted. 'I remember seeing Brian in the street and telling him I wasn't coming back. But the writing was probably on the wall.'

On 27 February 1969, Smile played the biggest gig of their short-lived career at London's Royal Albert Hall. It was a benefit for the National Council for the Unmarried Mother and her Child and they shared the bill with Joe Cocker, Spooky Tooth and Free (the band fronted by future Queen guest singer Paul Rodgers).

Smith and Freddie Mercury were in the audience. Mercury was also there when Smile played the Marquee and London's Revolution Club, as well as accompanying the band on trips to Truro and further dates at PJ's. 'I said to Brian and Roger, "You know Freddie is desperate to be in this band?"' laughed Smith. 'And Brian said, "No, no, Tim is the singer."'

By this point, Smile had been discovered by future Queen producer John Anthony, who helped secure them a one-off deal with Mercury Records. In April 1969, Smile released a single – 'Earth'/'Step on Me'. Staffell's 'Earth' was typical late-'60s sci-fi pop (in July that year, Smile and Mercury watched the first moon landing together at Taylor's mother's house), while 'Step on Me' was a cheery pop song, as bright and smiley as the band's toothy logo. However, the single was only released in the US and it disappeared immediately.

May and Taylor's confidence was dented. Even more so whenever they went to see Led Zeppelin. 'I felt sick,' May admitted, 'because they had done what we were trying to do, only a lot better.' Tim Staffell was not Robert Plant, though. Unlike Led Zeppelin, Smile looked at their feet when they played – something that their fashionista friend was quick to criticise. 'Freddie was the most reasonable, decent, accepting guy,' said Staffell in 2003. 'But he had many flamboyant ideas on how we should look, act and play – and no qualms about telling us in great detail.'

May and Taylor drooled over *Led Zeppelin* and the first Yes album. The sweet-toothed harmonies and staccato riff of Smile's

'Doing All Right' (a song later covered on Queen's debut and re-recorded for the *Bohemian Rhapsody* soundtrack) displayed both these musical influences. However, Staffell was growing disillusioned with the band's prog-rock direction and lack of success.

In spring 1970, Brian May took a working sabbatical at an observatory in Tenerife. When he returned, Staffell told him he was leaving Smile. May was deeply disappointed, but not entirely surprised. This was when Mercury – and his pompom – swooped in. 'Freddie said, "You're not giving up,"' recalled May. 'He said, "I'm going to be your singer and we're going to do this and this and this . . ."'

Thus, with one more flick of the wrist and the famous pompom, Freddie Mercury was in.

SOUR MILK SEA

The band Freddie Mercury broke up

Freddie Mercury had shaved his moustache and was wearing a puce-pink suit. Beside him were Roger Taylor and singer Peter Straker, both dressed as women. It was 1987 and they were all on a video shoot for Freddie's solo single *The Great Pretender*.

Watching from the wings was a member of the studio's art department named Chris Chesney. 'I was in the shadows, trying to be inconspicuous,' he said. Several years earlier, Chesney had hired Freddie Mercury to sing in his band, but their musical love affair went horribly wrong.

Mercury joined the group Sour Milk Sea in spring 1970. His previous band, Wreckage, had recently split, so he'd answered a 'vocalist wanted' ad in *Melody Maker*. Sour Milk Sea were Chris Chesney (then known as Chris Dummett), fellow guitarist Jeremy 'Rubber' Gallup, drummer Rob Tyrell and bassist Paul Milne. They played heavy progressive blues, with Chesney singing lead vocals, but 1970 was a time when mic-twirling lead singers like Paul Rodgers and Robert Plant were all the rage.

Mercury persuaded John Harris, Smile's roadie, to chauffeur him to the audition at a church hall in Dorking. 'He swept into the room, making a very grand entrance,' recalled Chesney. Within seconds of the first song, Mercury was posing and throwing shapes in front of the guitarist. His confidence far outstripped what Chesney called 'his unusual falsetto' and he passed the audition.

When Mercury phoned up about the job, though, Chesney is certain he said his name was 'Fred Bull'. Though Freddie later revealed his full surname, Bulsara, he never discussed his childhood growing up overseas: 'It was not an issue for us, but it seemed like he was always watching himself.'

At twenty-four, Mercury was six years older than the others and had a stronger personality. He pushed Sour Milk Sea to rehearse his former Wreckage songs 'FEWA (Feelings Ended Worn Away)' and 'Lover', which, for a time, included the extraordinary lyric 'the yoghurt-pushers are here' and later mutated into the early Queen song 'Liar'. Mercury's influences were eclectic. He wove Robert Plant-style tales of elves and faraway lands, but he also wanted pop harmonies. 'His chords were weird, too,' said Chesney. 'They broke all the rules. F-sharp minor to F back to A.' Sour Milk Sea recorded demos at two studios – one in Surbiton and one in London – but the tapes are long gone.

Though Chesney believes they played more, the band's known itinerary from March to April covered just three gigs: two in Chesney's hometown of Oxford and one at London's Temple club supporting Black Sabbath. Their singer's stage antics were certainly memorable, though. To keep audiences on their toes,

Mercury would whisper, 'Wank you, wank you very much,' at the end of a song, giggling at the reaction. He also insisted that the band play rock 'n' roll covers such as 'Lucille' and 'Jailhouse Rock' – a contrast to what Chesney called 'our great big pompous instrumental passages'.

However, relations within the group soured soon after Chris moved into Freddie's shared flat in Ferry Road, Barnes. Chesney embraced Mercury's bold ideas, but Gallup and Milne resented the singer's influence: '"Rubber" and the others thought Freddie and I were plotting something away from them.' In the end, it was best friends Gallup and Chesney who fell out. Mercury tried to arbitrate, but it was too little, too late.

Gallup, whose father had bankrolled the group, kept Chesney's Gibson SG and Marshall amp, leaving Chesney without any equipment. 'I wanted to start a new group with Freddie,' said Chris. 'But I had to get a job in a biscuit factory before I had enough to buy another guitar, and Freddie wasn't going to wait around for me.' Within a matter of weeks, Mercury had talked his way into becoming Smile's new lead singer. It was his fourth band in nine months and Chesney soon lost touch with 'Fred Bull'.

In 1987, though, Mercury spotted his former bandmate hiding in the corner at the video shoot. He came bounding over – 'Chris! Chris!' – and whisked Chesney away to his dressing room. Mercury demanded Champagne and vodka and chopped out two lines of cocaine. It was like being caught in the eye of a hurricane. 'But it was nice to see him again, to roll back the years,' said Chesney. When it was time to return to work, Mercury asked if Chris would play on his new solo album. 'I'll call you! I'll call you!' he said. It was the last time Chris Chesney ever spoke to Freddie Mercury.

SOUTH AMERICA
Viva Mercury!

ACT I
Starring Diego Maradona, Earth Wind & Fire and 'Doctor Death'

March 1981; Sao Paolo, Brazil: Queen's bodyguard has just shoved the barrel of his gun down John Deacon's trousers. The burly Brazilian with the greasy hair and walrus moustache is nicknamed 'Doctor Death' and his fellow security guards are known as the 'Death Squad'.

The doctor has already boasted of killing fifty people (some remember it as twelve; others, as many as 200) and throwing their corpses into a river. His automatic pistol is now jammed into Deacon's waistband – but only for a gag and a photo opportunity. 'Doctor Death' removes the weapon, laughs and saunters off. Welcome to Brazil . . .

Queen made two trips to South America in 1981 – the world's biggest rock band filling the continent's biggest football stadiums – but they were lucky to escape alive. During their time there, they came up against corruption, violence, guns, dysentery and even a possible kidnapping.

Queen's first South American tour (in February and March) took nine months of planning. Pop groups had played South America before, but never in stadiums. Some artists – such as the American funk band Earth, Wind & Fire – also found that their equipment went missing and never made it back home.

So Queen's tour manager Gerry Stickells and their business manager Jim Beach set up a production office at the Rio Sheraton Hotel in an attempt to maintain order amid chaos. This wasn't

easy, though. Gigs were scheduled, then cancelled without expla-
nation, then rescheduled, then cancelled again . . .

Queen played five shows in Argentina and two in Brazil, but
they were supposed to play at least another four. There was political capital to be made from the band's visit: General Roberto
Viola was about to become Argentina's president and thought
that inviting rock stars to the country would score points with
young Argentinians.

Queen arrived at Buenos Aires airport and were escorted
through customs by government officials. From there, their every
move was monitored by police and security guards and filmed
by local TV. The cops pulled their guns on anyone who came
too close, then posed for photos with their rock-star charges and
demanded autographs.

Queen's crew had the Herculean task of coordinating the
transportation of more than 60 tonnes of equipment into South
America from various locations, including Tokyo. The band also
had to supply 100 rolls of artificial turf with which to cover the
football stadiums' precious pitches. Fistfuls of US dollars passed
into the hands of local officials and business contacts just to get
the job done.

Queen's first two dates took place on 28 February and 1
March at Buenos Aires' José Amalfitani Stadium – the home of
Argentinian football club Vélez Sarsfield. The photographers' pit
between the stage and the audience was filled with armed soldiers.
'Who knew an AK-47 could get you backstage quicker than a
laminate?' joked tour photographer Neal Preston.

On the night, the audience knew every lyric to every song and
took over the vocals for Mercury's weepy ballad 'Love of My Life'.
American and British pop music symbolised freedom to people
living under a military dictatorship. These big anthems (and
Mercury's resemblance to a louche caballero) ensured Queen and
South America were made for each other.

Everybody wanted to meet the band. From Argentinian football star Diego Maradona, who swanned backstage in a Union Jack T-shirt, to General Roberto Viola himself. The band even attended a dinner at the presidential palace, though Roger Taylor was absent as he wanted nothing to do with the regime.

Queen played stadiums in Mar del Plata and Rosario before returning for a third night in Buenos Aires. The reaction was the same every night: passionate, tearful hysteria; mass singalongs; and an impenetrable line of armed police officers. Every Queen album was now in the Argentinian top ten and their first Buenos Aires date was broadcast to more than 20 million people across the continent. 'The fans down there were rabid,' recalled Neal Preston. 'But, when there are guys in front of the stage with submachine guns, you just do your job and try not to get shot.'

Queen were determined to play Rio de Janeiro's 81,000-capacity Maracanã Stadium, but it wasn't to be. For once, the offer of hard cash couldn't dissuade the city's governor. He refused to let a heathen rock band sully a venue reserved for sporting and religious events.

More planned dates disappeared from the schedule, leaving Queen with two weeks off before a brace of shows at Sao Paolo's Estádio do Morumbi on 20 and 21 March. The Brazilian journalist and TV host Hilton Gomes interviewed Queen after their arrival in Brazil.

Gomes worked the room: Mercury first, then Brian May. 'What about you? Er . . .?' he asked John Deacon in broken English, having clearly forgotten his name.

'John Deacon,' the bassist replied helpfully, before complaining about cancellations. He pitched hard on Queen's behalf: 'We have all our equipment here in Brazil, ready to go. We are willing to play.'

'What would you say if the show was about to start now?' Gomes asked Mercury at the end of the interview.

'We'd like you all to have a real good time,' Freddie replied, flashing a weary grin. 'It's like a Queen carnival, so enjoy yourself.'

Queen made the journey to Estádio do Morumbi in an armoured vehicle flanked by a motorcycle police escort. Once at the venue, 'Doctor Death' escorted them through the players' tunnel, on to the pitch and up to the stage. The noise of the 130,000-strong crowd made their heads spin and their hearts race. A few minutes into the show, Queen's lighting crew noticed that the extra follow spots they'd been loaned were stencilled with another band's name: Earth, Wind & Fire.

ACT II
Starring one kidnapping/arrest, several cases of dysentery and one dead president

October 1981; Mexico: Queen's promoter José Rota is in jail. Allegedly. Nobody can recall why he was arrested. Some claim he was kidnapped after Queen's concert at Monterrey's Estadio Universitario. 'A whole lot of trouble happened in Mexico that I really don't want to go into,' Brian May once divulged. Queen's management supposedly paid $25,000 in bail/ransom to have Rota released. In the words of Brian's famous song, the show must go on . . .

Queen had grossed $3.5 million on their first South American jaunt. They went back, seven months later, after being promised even more. But not for nothing was Queen's second South American tour christened 'Gluttons For Punishment'.

Queen flew into Venezuela in September for a string of shows, starting with three nights at the local sports arena in Caracas. Again, the band found themselves trailed by the media, which is how May, Deacon and Taylor ended up on a Venezuelan TV music show called *Fantastic*. Mercury flatly refused to participate.

Midway through the programme, a studio assistant ran on to announce that Venezuela's president, Rómulo Betancourt, had just died. None of Queen spoke Spanish, so they stood awkwardly in front of the cameras, trying to work out what was happening.

Then came a second announcement: Betancourt had suffered a stroke but was still alive. Forty-eight hours later, though, he really did die. The nation, including its commercial airlines and airports, shut down for a period of official mourning and Queen's remaining dates were cancelled. Once again, hard currency paid to important people somehow ensured Queen's passage out of the country. The group fled to Miami, while their crew travelled to Mexico to prepare for the next run.

Queen were expecting to play Mexico City, but their first date, on 9 October, was suddenly switched to the Estadio Universitario in Monterrey – almost a twelve-hour drive away. Queen's beleaguered crew had already been pushed to the limits of human endurance; an outbreak of food poisoning and dysentery suddenly made their task even harder.

'By now, we had become cynical and mistrusting of the people we were dealing with and the validity of this exercise,' wrote former roadie Peter Hince in his memoir, *Queen Unseen*. Hince later recalled major plumbing issues in the crew's hotel. 'When you flushed the toilet chain,' he said, 'the shit came back up through the shower.'

The stadium in Monterrey was dilapidated and, after the show, a purpose-built ramp collapsed, sending several fans tumbling into a concrete pit below. The police closed the gates and refused to let the band leave. Once again, money changed hands and Queen were allowed back to their hotel. But the authorities insisted that their gear remain on site and stationed armed guards outside the venue.

Having discovered the fate of Earth, Wind & Fire's missing lights, Queen's crew took extra precautions. They chained the guitar trunks to a lighting pod, which was then lifted into the air. After the chain motor was disconnected, a roadie took the hand-held controller back to the hotel. The precious cargo was suspended over the stage, visible yet tantalisingly out of reach to any thieves.

It was around this time that José Rota was arrested. Or kidnapped. 'There were some monstrous corruption issues,' said Roger Taylor, who still sounded scarred by the ordeal over twenty years later. Money was paid and Rota was released, only for Queen to discover that their second Monterrey show had been mysteriously cancelled.

A week later, Queen and their crew rolled into the Olympic Stadium in Puebla for two further shows. The roadies, broken and bloodied, found the venue half-derelict and strewn with debris. The 22,000-strong audience were searched on their way in and batteries were confiscated from cassette players and boom boxes to prevent bootlegging. Once inside the stadium, security guards sold the batteries back at a hugely inflated price.

Come showtime, many of the audience were wired on Tequila and mescaline. Passionate and vocal, they showed their appreciation by bombarding each other and the stage with bottles, shoes and, inevitably, batteries. '*Adiós, amigos*, you motherfuckers!' cried Mercury at the end of the show.

Queen were due to play a second Puebla date, but they wanted to cancel. While baton-wielding cops herded the audience out of the stadium like drunken sheep, Queen were sent into a tiny backstage room. There, they were forcefully persuaded by the organisers to sign a document committing them to play the show. Queen kept their promise, but then cancelled their two remaining dates in Guadalajara. They flew to New York and LA before the promoters could stop them.

For once, Queen and their management's unquestioning self-belief wasn't enough. They'd been unable to control the situation in Venezuela and Mexico and it had cost them a seven-figure sum. Queen returned to Munich, where they were recording *Hot Space*, and demanded a post-mortem meeting with Jim Beach.

Before Beach arrived, money-minded John Deacon decorated Musicland Studios with photographs of items to the value of what Queen had lost on their ill-fated trip. Everywhere their manager turned was another reminder: a luxury yacht, a luxury plane, a luxury country house . . .

I want to break free: Queen and their police escort, Argentina, 1981.

SPARKS

The band who tried to steal Brian May

One of the downsides of Queen's delayed success was their insecurity. They worried about being passed over for other groups. 'We kept an eye on any band signed around the same time as us,' said Roger Taylor. 'Roxy Music, Steve Harley's Cockney Rebel, Sparks. Especially Sparks . . .'

Art-rockers Sparks were the brainchild of Ron and Russell Mael, siblings from LA who'd moved to Britain and landed a residency at London's Marquee. In December 1972, Queen played their first show since signing with Trident, opening for Sparks at the Marquee. Russell Mael recalled Queen 'being their own roadies' and loading their gear into the club in jeans and T-shirts, before disappearing into the dressing room, changing into their rock-star finery 'and re-emerging as Queen'. On this occasion, it wasn't enough. Apparently, Elektra Records boss Jac Holzman came to the show hoping to sign Queen, but left feeling 'dreadfully disappointed'.

A year and a half later, in May '74, Sparks were speeding up the UK singles chart with 'This Town Ain't Big Enough for Both of Us', a riot of falsetto vocals and clanging power chords. It was louche, arty and strange – a bit like Queen. At the same time, Queen had just had to cancel an American tour due to Brian May contracting hepatitis and, come 1975, Queen were breaking up with Trident and in managerial limbo. 'Which was when Sparks tried to nick Brian,' grumbled Taylor.

The Mael brothers had just fired their guitarist and showed up at May's flat in Hammersmith with a job offer. 'They said, "Look, Brian, Queen isn't going anywhere, you're not going to have any more hits, but we're going to conquer the world,"' said May. 'And I said, "Thanks, but no thanks. I think I'm fine."'

'He was tempted enough to want to meet with us and discuss it,' said Russell Mael in 2017. 'Queen had done one tour of America and things weren't really happening for them. We really liked Brian's guitar-playing and thought his sensibility would work with Sparks.'

A few months after Sparks made their offer, 'Bohemian Rhapsody' was at number one. 'Brian made a good decision,' admitted Mael. 'Obviously, it really worked out for Queen.'

Years later, Queen still hadn't stopped worrying. 'I remember when we first saw U2,' Taylor reflected. 'I remember thinking, "Oh my God, we're going to have to watch out for them."'

'SPREAD YOUR WINGS'

Queen's greatest non-hits, no. 3

Every so often, a paparazzi photo of John Deacon appears in the newspapers. You see this unassuming septuagenarian and think, 'Christ, that's the guy who wrote "Another One Bites the Dust".'

John Deacon composed several great Queen songs, though not all were hits. Forty years after it came out as a single, Deaky's big power ballad was dusted off by Queen + Adam Lambert on their 2017 tour. But it's easy to see why some of the audience didn't know it. 'Spread Your Wings' missed the top thirty back in the day and hasn't been used to flog budget sofas, holidays or chocolate like other Queen hits.

This song about downtrodden Sammy itching to leave 'his dead life behind' suited the mood of its parent album, *News of the World*. The version on 1979's *Live Killers* is better because the audience join in on the chorus, though it doesn't include Freddie Mercury's occasional intro: 'This is called "Spread Your Legs".' It does, however, feature his amusing vocal inflection on the line 'Who d'ya think y'are?', which makes him sound like a

Hollywood diva who's just discovered her Champagne isn't suffi-ciently chilled. A 'Don't Stop Me Now'-style rediscovery or TV ad campaign must surely be overdue.

STAFFELL, TIM
He gave up the throne

Sometime in the 1980s, Tim Staffell was at Roger Taylor's house when he spotted an alien on the mantelpiece. It had bulging red eyes, multiple antennae and what appeared to be varicose veins in its neck. Staffell recognised the creature straight away.

'I said to Roger, "What the hell are you doing with that?" He replied, "That's the alien from the cover of my solo album *Fun in Space*."' Staffell then told him that he'd made the model years before, never knowing it was for his ex-bandmate. It was a strange moment for both men.

Tim Staffell had been Smile's singing bass guitarist. He left the band in summer 1970, after which Freddie Mercury turned them into Queen. Ever since, Staffell has been asked to discuss his famous ex-bandmates. Any reluctance to do so is understandable. After Smile, Staffell continued making music while working as a model-maker, an advertising director and a theatre-school tutor. But the question everybody always asked was: do you regret leaving Queen? Even though they weren't really Queen then.

Staffell was in the year below Brian May at Hampton Grammar School, but the two met when May spotted Staffell playing harmonica in the audience at a local gig. Soon after, he joined May's teenage band, 1984, as their lead singer. Tim had a different personality to the guitarist; he was the yin to Brian's yang. 'I was a bit more Jack the lad than him,' he once said.

While May went off to study at Imperial College, Staffell signed up for graphic design at Ealing Art College, where he befriended Freddie Mercury. It was Tim who designed Smile's twinkly toothed logo (a couple of years before the Rolling Stones' world-famous flapping tongue) and Tim who co-wrote several of Smile's songs, including 'Doing All Right' – later included on the first Queen album. But, over time, he found himself at musical loggerheads with May and Taylor. 'Tim had a strange driving force,' said May, 'which was always driving him away from us.'

Staffell left Smile and went to America for six months, where he became obsessed by blues, jazz and improvisational music. He joined a folk-pop group called Humpy Bong (formed by ex-Bee Gees drummer Colin Petersen) and made a fleeting appearance with them on *Top of the Pops*. Staffell then teamed up with Humpy Bong's bass guitarist, Jonathan Kelly, and later made music with Mott the Hoople's Morgan Fisher. He loved singing and writing songs, but considered himself a 'rubbish bass player'.

In the meantime, he watched Queen's progress with mixed feelings. 'I think, when I left, I was a stronger singer than Freddie,' he said in 2003. 'But, when I heard "Seven Seas of Rhye", I thought, "He's become really good, hasn't he?" The swine.'

Queen's ornate hard rock wasn't really to Tim's taste. He preferred nouveau bluesman Ry Cooder. Staffell was also strictly 'jeans and T-shirt'. One art-school friend recalled watching, alongside an aghast Tim, as Mercury had a fitting for his Zandra Rhodes-designed satin tunic. 'And Brian's got one, too!' Freddie declared, delightedly flapping his pleats. Staffell told his friend how relieved he was not to have to dress like that.

'Music was always my goal,' he said later. 'At the time, I had no interest in being an entertainer. It was only about playing my

340

songs. But Freddie also understood entertainment. He was about the show.'

When Staffell's musical career faltered, he applied his graphic design skills to model-making and TV special effects. It was a pragmatic decision as he was married and had a young family. This was how he wound up freelancing for a prop house and creating Roger Taylor's alien. Through most of the 1980s, Staffell worked for Clearwater Films, directing animations for products including Ski yoghurt and Birds Eye fish fingers. In 1984, Clearwater were commissioned to produce a new animated TV series called *Thomas the Tank Engine*. Staffell created the faces for many of Thomas's steam-engine friends, as well as characters including the Fat Controller.

However, Queen's post-Freddie afterlife meant that Staffell could never fully escape. Journalists and biographers always wanted to talk to him. 'Sometimes I felt very marginalised,' he admitted. 'Sometimes I still felt part of it.' On the flipside, the royalties from 'Doing All Right' were always welcome.

In December 1992, Staffell joined May and Taylor at the Marquee for a gig by Taylor's side group, the Cross. It was a one-off Smile reunion. In 2018, he went to Abbey Road Studios to re-record 'Doing All Right' for the *Bohemian Rhapsody* soundtrack. The finished article was a hybrid of new and old; of Smile and Queen; of 1969 songwriting and modern-day cinema.

Later, Staffell watched himself on the big screen. In one scene, actor Jack Roth's 'Tim' is shown leaving Smile to join Humpy Bong.

'Humpy Bong?' says an incredulous 'Brian'.

'Humpy Bong,' confirms 'Tim'. 'They're going places. They're gonna be big.'

'Humpy Bong?' repeats an incredulous 'Roger'. 'Are you joking?'

Seconds later, Rami Malek's 'Freddie' has taken the singer's place in Smile. It didn't happen like that, but Staffell worked in television long enough to understand dramatic license. When last asked if he regretted his decision to walk away from the band, he replied most graciously, 'There are times when I've regretted it, but I've never resented it.'

STATUES

Freddie Mercury's heavy metal monument

In 2014, some residents in Guildford, Surrey, noticed that an alien object had appeared on the local landscape. It was a 20-foot-high statue of Freddie Mercury in Roger Taylor's back garden. Until recently, the replica sculpture had towered over the entrance to the Dominion Theatre. Now that the Queen musical *We Will Rock You* had finished its twelve-year London run, Freddie had moved back in with his old flatmate.

The original version of the statue, fashioned in bronze by Czech-born artist Irene Sedleká, overlooks Montreux's Lake Geneva. Taylor, Brian May, opera star Montserrat Caballé and Mercury's mother and sister all attended its unveiling ceremony in November 1996. The likeness was modelled on Mercury '86: left hand grasping the wand-like microphone; right hand punching the air; mouth agape. It looked like him, but with a pinch of Tom Selleck and a soupcon of Joseph Stalin. Since then, tourists have flocked in their thousands to have their photograph taken with him. 'Freddie' even acquired a face mask when the market square was closed to public gatherings during Switzerland's Covid lockdown.

It was *We Will Rock You*'s scriptwriter, Ben Elton, who mischievously told the press that Taylor had acquired the London statue. 'Roger nicked it – literally,' he said. 'He hired a truck and just took it.'

'It was in a warehouse costing money,' clarified Taylor. 'So I just said, "Why don't they put it on a lorry and bring it here and we'll put it in the garden?"'

Taylor already had the gong heard at the end of 'Bohemian Rhapsody' gathering moss in the grounds of his mansion, so why not a replica of Queen's frontman? However, in February 2015, he was informed by Guildford Borough Council that the monument breached planning rules relating to historic houses in conservation areas. Parts of Taylor's rock-star pile dated back to the eighteenth century, possibly even earlier.

Taylor applied for retrospective planning permission, but mistakenly stated in his application that the statue was 19-foot high, not 20. Nevertheless, permission was granted for 'Freddie' to remain, on the understanding that Taylor would take the statue with him should he ever sell up. 'I thought it would be very funny to have the statue here and I think Freddie would have found it hilarious,' he told the *Daily Mirror*.

It seemed the only person not amused was Brian May. 'I think Brian was pissed off he hadn't thought of doing it himself,' laughed Taylor.

If he wished to, though, Brian could console himself with a £64.99 reproduction of the statue from Queen's online store. 'This highly collectable model is a 1/14th scale faithful reproduction of the original statue of Montreux,' reads the sales blurb. 'Made from epoxy resin and measuring 21cm high, the statue comes in a bespoke gift box and is accompanied by its own certificate of origin.'

A little silhouetto of a man: Freddie in transit, 2014.

'STONE COLD CRAZY'

Queen's greatest non-hits, no. 4

'Stone Cold Crazy' was the first song Queen ever played live, performed at Truro City Hall on Saturday 27 June 1970. There's no recording to confirm this; only the fading memories of those who were there. The song wouldn't appear on an album until *Sheer Heart Attack* four years later. Surprising, as Freddie Mercury wrote it before he was even in Queen.

'It was one of Freddie's frenetic ideas,' recalled Brian May. 'But the original was much slower.' May helped turn it into something nearer to Led Zeppelin's 'Communication Breakdown' or

Black Sabbath's 'Paranoid'. But, while Zeppelin sounded like they wanted to shag the world and Sabbath like they wanted to blow it up, Mercury is more akin to a hyperactive toddler racing around his parents' garden before heading indoors for an afternoon nap. 'I have no idea what it's about,' said May, referring to garbled lyrics about Al Capone and 'shooting people with a rubber Tommy water gun'.

Metallica's James Hetfield performed 'Stone Cold Crazy' at 1992's Freddie Mercury Tribute Concert, but changed the lyric to 'my fully loaded Tommy gun'. He used the same line in Metallica's version on their *Garage Inc.* covers album. Perhaps the original wasn't manly enough for them, but Queen didn't really do death and destruction. They were always the world's lightest heavy-metal band.

SUGAR SHACK

Queen's Saturday night fever

Roger Taylor once described the Sugar Shack as 'the hottest disco in the world'. Immortalised in the song 'Dragon Attack' ('Take me back, back to the shack'), this Munich nightclub offered Queen a refuge from the studio while also becoming an extension of that studio. The Shack played an unsung role in *The Game*, *Hot Space* and, notably, 'Another One Bites the Dust'.

The Sugar Shack was located in an anonymous-looking building at 6 Herzogspital Strasse. Its discreet door came with a hatch so staff could vet guests before entry. But nobody refused

Queen, who frequented the place so often they nicknamed it the 'office'. On an average evening, Taylor, Brian May, John Deacon, producer Reinhold Mack and assorted members of their trusty road crew, including future photographer and writer Peter 'Ratty' Hince, would attend. Freddie Mercury generally preferred Old Mrs Henderson's – a gay nightspot on Rumfordstrasse – but the club shut early, so he often joined the others at the Shack before its 4 a.m. closing time.

Queen had their favourite seating area and preferred tipple: Moskovskaya Russian vodka (easily identified by its lime-green label). 'I was a vodka-and-tonic man,' said May. 'I've never done a drug in my life.' But a staff member known as Otto was on hand to escort those patrons who did indulge in other substances to a separate room for privacy. Otto's visible scars and criminal reputation ensured nobody troubled him or his guests.

Discretion was key. What went on at the Sugar Shack stayed at the Sugar Shack. Sort of. 'It was blow heaven,' Mack recalled, using the American slang for cocaine. 'I remember the tennis player Vitas Gerulaitis and various sportsmen snorting grammes off the table. There were also girls galore and the lads were away from their respective wives and partners.'

The Sugar Shack was frequented by 'some of the most beautiful, classy, chic, friendly and accommodating girls', wrote Hince in his wryly amusing memoir, *Queen Unseen*. Like everyone else in Queen's world, the Shack's female patrons and bar staff had nicknames: 'Toucan', 'Roy Orbison', 'Belgian Airline', 'Tree', 'Brigitte Bardot', 'Mickey Mouse's Ears' etc.

The other great attraction was the music. Bernd, the DJ, rarely addressed his clientele, preferring to play back-to-back songs through an impeccable sound system. It was a revelation, especially for May. 'I remember hearing Bad Company's "Feel Like Making Love" and it sounded fantastic,' he said. 'Our songs, like

"Tie Your Mother Down", didn't sound as good because they were so dense. It made us rethink how we did backing tracks – to leave more space, to let the music breathe.'

A few days later, Queen returned with a tape of new song 'Dragon Attack', constructed from an alcohol-fuelled thirty-minute jam at Musicland Studios. It had a spare funk groove, over which May had layered several minutes of slashing guitar. 'It sounded wonderful played at the Sugar Shack.' As did Queen's hit-single-in-waiting 'Another One Bites the Dust' when taken for an early spin at the club. 'After that, we became obsessed with leaving space in our music and making songs that would sound great in the Shack.'

The party would often continue back at the Munich Hilton. The band and entourage, reunited with Mercury and any additional friends, would repair to Roger Taylor's suite for more Champagne and refreshments. 'Then we'd go to bed and get up in the afternoon and have breakfast,' marvelled May.

Queen's love affair with the club continued, with Bernd later road-testing tracks from 1982's dance-orientated *Hot Space*. By then, the club's walls were decorated with gold discs for *The Game*. However, the band's personal lives intervened shortly after, their dynamic changed and Queen pulled the plug on Munich.

Forty years on, the hottest disco in the world lives on in their memories. 'We spent vast amounts of time in the Sugar Shack,' said May, still sounding wistful in 2018. 'Hanging in there until dawn was coming up. Living in a fantasy world of vodka and barmaids and very loud rock music.' Real life must have seemed like such a comedown.

SUNBURY POP FESTIVAL

When Queen gigs went wrong, part 2

In January 1974, Queen made their first trip to Australia. They'd been booked to play two nights at the Sunbury Pop Festival on a farm near Melbourne. Pitched as the 'Aussie Woodstock', Sunbury showcased the country's most popular bands and had previously been hosted by future *Crocodile Dundee* star Paul Hogan. The decision to book Queen, though, was baffling: the band were neither Australian nor popular.

Things started to go awry on the flight over. The band had just been inoculated against smallpox and Brian May began to feel ill on the plane. He didn't know it at the time, but he'd been jabbed with a dirty needle and would contract gangrene in his right arm.

Once in Melbourne, the jetlagged group soon wilted in the stifling heat. Freddie Mercury tried to cool down with a swim in the hotel pool, but damaged his ear drum and went temporarily deaf. 'He couldn't understand what was happening and got very worried,' said May.

In true Queen style, they hired a limousine to take them to the festival and insisted that only their crew could touch their lights and equipment. Tempers frayed between Queen's roadies and the local crews. Backstage, homegrown acts Madder Lake, Skyhooks and Buster Brown (featuring future AC/DC drummer Phil Rudd) were furious at being bumped down the bill for an unknown British band.

The festival's host – musician and DJ Jim Keays – was similarly unimpressed. When it was time to introduce Queen, he described them as 'limey bastards' and 'stuck-up pommies' before dropping his trousers and underwear and mooning the audience.

Despite this less than stellar introduction, Queen managed to win over some of the 30,000-strong audience. But Keays killed any chance of an encore. 'Do you want any more from these pommie bastards or do ya want an Aussie band?' he shouted to a chorus of catcalls and boos. Before leaving the stage, Mercury grabbed the mic and declared, 'When Queen come back to Australia, we will be the biggest band in the world!'

Queen were due to perform again the following night, but they refused. The band flew home soon after – jetlagged, exhausted and demoralised, with Freddie still partially deaf and poor Brian infected with gangrene.

SUN CITY

Queen's big mistake

Queen's greatest strength was sometimes their greatest weakness. When told they shouldn't do something, they did it anyway. When this involved naming themselves Queen or releasing 'Bohemian Rhapsody' as a single, it was the right decision. But not so when it came to playing South Africa at the height of apartheid.

'Sun fucking City', as Roger Taylor later called it, was a hotel/casino complex in the state of Bophuthatswana. The state had been granted independence by the South African government and Sun City was being pitched as an African Las Vegas – a place where people could gamble freely and where the usual rules, including racial segregation, supposedly didn't apply.

In 1980, the United Nations requested all countries' sports teams, musicians, writers and actors boycott South Africa as a protest against apartheid. Bophuthatswana's independence wasn't recognised, so it was included in the boycott. Despite the ban, Sun City's owner, hotel mogul Sol Kerzner, courted the biggest names in pop with huge fees. Kerzner needed superstars to bring people to his roulette tables and slot machines. Over the next three years, Frank Sinatra, Ray Charles, Rod Stewart and Cher all played Sun City (with Sinatra pocketing $1.69 million for nine shows).

Queen were also asked to play there, but refused. Then, in spring 1984, 'Radio Ga Ga' reached number four and 'I Want to Break Free' hit number one in the South African chart. 'They were being played on black radio,' Taylor later told Irish broad-caster RTÉ. '"I Want to Break Free" is one of the unofficial anthems of the black people.'

'What? The ANC?' asked the show's host, referring to the African National Congress. Taylor mumbled a hesitant yes.

Next time Queen were offered Sun City, they said maybe. The group were adamant that they would only perform to a non-segregated audience, so they sent manager Jim Beach on a reconnaissance mission. 'He went down there to see if it was multi-racial,' Brian May told RTÉ. 'He came back satisfied it was and said we should go.'

'Queen's principal reason for playing Sun City was a very large amount of money,' admitted Beach years later.

On 5 October 1984, Queen played the first of eleven sched-uled nights at Sun City Superbowl. Then Freddie Mercury lost his voice during the third show and the rest of the gig was cancelled. A doctor arrived by private plane from Johannesburg and told Mercury that the arid climate had inflamed his vocal cords. He gave the singer a cortisone injection and told him to rest. Two further shows were cancelled and Mercury lounged about in his hotel suite knocking back vodka, regardless of the doctor's orders.

In the meantime, May attended an African music awards show in Soweto and pledged to come back later to play the local stadium with Queen. During the trip, Beach also arranged for the royalties from a specially commissioned Queen live album to be distributed to the Kutlwanong School for hearing-impaired children in Roodepoort.

Queen fulfilled eight of their eleven dates. Despite the promise of a mixed audience, they performed to a sea of non-black faces and tickets cost the equivalent of over £50 each in South African rand. Sun City was a rich, white playground.

Back in the UK, Queen faced widespread criticism from the Musicians' Union. 'Sod their rules!' Taylor told RTÉ. 'I didn't become a musician to be in their poxy union.'

May's response was more considered. 'We are totally and fundamentally opposed to apartheid,' he stressed. 'But we thought we could build bridges and make apartheid less acceptable. To my dying day, I will say we acted properly.'

May attended a meeting of the MU's General Committee, where he gave a speech outlining Queen's reasons for playing the shows. The union listened, but still imposed a hefty fine and Queen were placed on the United Nations' blacklist. Freddie Mercury – the one African member of the band – never spoke publicly about their visit.

For all their bravado, this was one argument Queen would never win. The following year, guitarist 'Little Steven' Van Zandt launched the protest group Artists United Against Apartheid. Their single, 'Sun City', saw Bob Dylan, Peter Gabriel, Hall & Oates and Joey Ramone railing against the oppressive regime. 'Queen are jerks,' Daryl Hall told the press. 'They were more than aware of what they were doing and should be called out for it.'

Queen ended 1984 with a new single: 'Thank God It's Christmas'. Perhaps its title summed up the band's feelings about the past year, but the song was quickly overtaken by Band Aid charity single 'Do They Know It's Christmas?', from which Queen were noticeably absent. That said, if this exclusion was payback for

Sun City (as some have suggested), Bob Geldof had no qualms about inviting Queen to play Live Aid the following summer.

Quite rightly, Queen were never allowed to forget their Sun City faux pas. Nevertheless, they went back and played there again, post-apartheid. In March 2005, Queen and guest vocalist Paul Rodgers performed a fundraiser at the Fancourt Country Club for former ANC leader Nelson Mandela's AIDS awareness charities. Three years later, Queen + Paul Rodgers played Mandela's ninetieth-birthday celebration in London's Hyde Park.

After more than two decades of defending Queen's decision to perform in South Africa, Roger Taylor finally relented. 'On balance, it was a mistake,' he said in 2011. But 'Sun fucking City' will haunt Queen for ever.

TAYLOR, ROGER

The drummer's tale

Roger Taylor's hotel aliases in Queen:
Roy Tanner, Rudolph de Rainbow

Roger Taylor's answers in a *People* magazine interview, 1974:

My idea of beauty:
Brigitte Bardot and her lifestyle

My favourite colour:
Black (and silver)

My closest friend:
My drum kit

My greatest happiness:
My own fulfilment

My greatest misery:
Not being eighteen for ever

My favourite amusement:
Music, music, music

My favourite song and composer:
'Voodoo Chile'/Jimi Hendrix

My present state of mind:
Chaos

My motto:
'Live and let live'

**Five things the rest of Queen have said about
Roger Taylor:**

Brian May:
'As a drummer, he's completely unique.'

Freddie Mercury:
'Roger is very rock 'n' roll.'

Brian May:
'Roger is better at being a rock star than me.'

John Deacon:
'Roger is the rock 'n' roller of the group.'

Brian May:
'He's very attractive to women apparently.'

Roger Taylor was always destined to become a member of the royal family. He was born at West Norfolk and King's Lynn General Hospital on 26 July 1949. A couple of days after his birth, Princess Elizabeth – the future Queen – formally opened the site's new maternity unit. She toured the ward and said a few words to Taylor's mother, Winifred. Perhaps Her Royal Highness even peered at newborn Roger, gurgling in his mother's arms. Seventy-one years later, she would award him an OBE for his services to music.

'We were four precocious boys' is Brian May's favourite quote about Queen, the band. For precocity, Roger Taylor ran Freddie

Mercury a close second. Taylor was never just the drummer. He sang, wrote songs and gave outspoken interviews. In the '70s and '80s, his blond locks, boyish looks and singular fashion sense made him Queen's most obvious rock star. On the band's rowdy *Live Killers* album, May introduced him like so: 'On drums and tiger-skin trousers . . .'

Taylor's father, Michael, worked for the potato marketing board in King's Lynn, but his family came from Cornwall. The Taylors moved to the Cornish cathedral town of Truro when Roger was four. He learned to play the ukulele and later started a skiffle group called the Bubbling Over Boys after seeing Lonnie Donegan on TV. 'When I got to school the next day, there was only one thing we talked about – "Did you see Lonnie?"' he recalled. Taylor had a similar epiphany a decade later when he saw Jimi Hendrix.

In 1960, Taylor won a choral scholarship to Truro Cathedral School. By then, he'd discovered the drums and was that kid obsessively tapping on the kitchen table, the school desk or any available work surface. Those living near the Taylors' bungalow on Hurland Road regularly had their evenings disrupted by Roger thrashing his kit in the garage, doors wide open. 'He was bloody noisy,' complained one neighbour.

Taylor joined a school group and, in a bid to make them sound hipper, changed their name from the Cousin Jacks (Cornish slang for tin miners) to Beat Unlimited. However, his first real band would be Johnny Quale and the Reactions (later known as just the Reaction). They were a fixture on the local dance circuit and gave Taylor his first taste of victory after winning Truro's Rock and Rhythm Championship in 1966. Taylor was more ambitious than his bandmates, though. When some of them drifted away into butchery and the building trade, Roger became the Reaction's singing drummer, parking his kit at the front of the stage. 'I wanted it more than the others,' he said.

In 1968, Taylor relocated to the capital to study dentistry at the London Hospital Medical College. Apparently, his friends at the time were baffled by this move, but Taylor's decision had less to do with wanting to be a dentist and everything to do with wanting to be in London. Within weeks of his arrival, he'd answered Brian May's 'drummer wanted' ad and formed Smile.

What did he think of May when he first met him? 'I liked his hair,' Taylor joked. 'But he really was the best guitarist I'd come across.'

May was similarly impressed: 'Roger has a certain way of making his hi-hat talk,' he said recently.

Taylor's drumming heroes included the Who's Keith Moon, the Jimi Hendrix Experience's Mitch Mitchell, and Led Zeppelin's John Bonham (listen to 'The Loser in the End' from *Queen II* as evidence).

An ex-flatmate of Taylor's once recalled having a conversation with the drummer about the perils of wisdom teeth extraction; Roger told him there were fifty-nine ways to die while having one's wisdom teeth pulled. However, despite this knowledge, he only lasted a year on the dentistry course before failing his exams. 'I wasn't serious about it,' he admitted. 'Really, I moved to London to be in a group.'

Taylor and Freddie Mercury's stint as Kensington Market stall-holders proved a rich source of comedy, but it failed to pay the rent. Taylor missed having a student grant and later signed up to study biology at North East London Polytechnic. He graduated with a BSc after Queen signed their first record deal, but told his parents he had no intention of getting 'a proper job'.

'My dad was quite supportive of Queen,' Taylor recalled. 'But my mother always thought it was a bit of a joke. I remember her once saying, "Look, Brian, you're a scientist. When are you going to give all this nonsense up?" And he said, "I wanna be a pop star," which amused her greatly.'

Taylor's middle name, Meddows, was passed down through the family. It made Roger sound grand in the liner notes for Queen's first two albums, especially when hyphenated to read 'Meddows-Taylor'. This was fitting since Taylor wanted Queen to be grander than everybody else. 'What's the point of being the second biggest band in the world?' he argued. 'We were hugely ambitious and unashamedly so.'

Taylor's talking hi-hat and rifle-crack snare helped shape Queen's sound. But he was never there just to keep time. He even squeezed one of his own compositions, 'Modern Times Rock 'n' Roll', onto *Queen I*. 'It's a bit of a thrash,' he said recently. But he kept writing. 'Tenement Funster' on *Sheer Heart Attack* was better and included several distinctive Taylor traits: earthquaking drums; punchy vocals; and lyrics celebrating his hairstyle, sex appeal and fabulous taste in footwear ('My new purple shoes been amazing the people next door').

In 1975, Taylor composed 'I'm in Love with My Car' – Queen's most lucrative B-side ever thanks to 'Bohemian Rhapsody'. Its profitability has no doubt delighted Taylor's bank manager and niggled Brian May ever since. 'So tell me, Rog,' smirks Gwilym Lee's 'Brian' in the movie. 'What is the sexiest part of a car?'

Taylor's choral scholarship also paid off, even if his BSc didn't. In the '70s, Roger's weapons-grade falsetto was Queen's not-so-secret weapon. That's him screaming 'Ahaaaaaaaa!' on 'Seven Seas of Rhye' and being 'very, very frightening' on 'Bohemian Rhapsody'. One enterprising soul has uploaded Queen's biggest hit to YouTube with Taylor's 'Galileo's etc. stripped out. It's several planets short of a solar system.

Taylor is usually portrayed as Queen's staunchest rock 'n' roller, embracing all the perks of the job: fast cars, country mansions, ocean-going yachts, extremely late nights. 'Compared to Brian, I was more attuned to that aspiration of wanting to be a rock star,' Taylor admitted.

The wider public's perception of Queen has sometimes irked him, though. 'People think of us as a mainstream pop band,' he said, 'whereas we thought of ourselves as a heavy albums band. All the hit singles we had came by accident.'

His competitive streak also meant that he never wanted Queen to be left behind musically. Taylor's noisy 'Sheer Heart Attack' pre-dated punk and livened up *News of the World*. By the time of *The Game* and *Hot Space*, Taylor was writing modish power-pop songs like 'Rock It (Prime Jive)' and 'Calling All Girls'. The last time he was asked, he said his best work was 'These Are the Days of Our Lives'.

Taylor was the first member of Queen to release a solo album – 1981's *Fun in Space*. A single, 'Future Management', dented the top fifty and Taylor even made an appearance on *Top of the Pops*, but it was merely a holiday from the mothership. As was follow-up *Strange Frontier*, which suggested an overspill of songs that Taylor couldn't get onto *The Works*.

By then, he'd written 'Radio Ga Ga' – a top-five hit in sixteen countries – and dressed up as a schoolgirl in the video for 'I Want to Break Free'. After Live Aid, Queen's profile and sales escalated. Taylor, with his Katharine Hamnett T-shirts and ruffled hairdo, was reborn as a pop star in the era of Sting and Boy George.

Taylor didn't want to give it up when Queen stopped touring after 1986, so he started a new group, the Cross, with bandmates almost twenty years younger than him. Roger was the boss and the lead singer, but also insisted he was still one of the boys. He travelled to a couple of dates in the band van before quietly going back to being chauffeured around in his Bentley.

Taylor was determined not to trade off the Queen name, though. He only played one Queen song ('I'm in Love with My Car') and refused to let promoters advertise the gigs as 'Roger Taylor and the Cross' – until they struggled to sell tickets. The

Cross made three albums of identikit '80s rock that sounded like most of the band looked: blow-dried mullets, duster coats and distressed denim. 'Even Mick Jagger has trouble selling solo records,' said Taylor ruefully.

In the movie *Bohemian Rhapsody*, Ben Hardy's 'Roger' appears with several different women by his side – sometimes more than one at the same time. It's a running gag to remind viewers of the playboy image of 'Rudolph de Rainbow'. 'I always felt it was my job to enjoy myself,' Taylor once said.

However, his private life found its way into the newspapers during Queen's difficult late '80s. In 1988, Taylor married his long-term partner Dominique Beyrand – the mother of his children Felix and Rory. They wed for financial reasons and divorced less than a month later. After this, Taylor embarked on a lengthy relationship with model Deborah Leng, with whom he fathered three children: Rufus, Tigerlily and Lola Daisy May. In 2010, Taylor married former dancer, actor and make-up artist Sarina Potgieter and, in recent times, has acquired a large tattoo on his right arm. 'My greatest misery,' Taylor told *People* magazine in 1974, is 'not being eighteen for ever'.

There's something reassuringly spirited about Queen's drummer; he still likes a fight. His 1994 solo album, *Happiness?*, included 'Dear Mr Murdoch' – a song that railed against the titular media mogul, 'with your news of the screws and your soaraway sun'. It wasn't a hit, but that didn't stop Taylor re-releasing the song during the 2011 phone-hacking scandal.

Taylor's other targets have included German fascists on 1994's 'Nazis' and the modern world in general on 2013's 'The Unblinking Eye (Everything Is Broken)'. In 1999, Taylor upset philatelists when he appeared in the background of a commemorative Freddie Mercury stamp. (Until 2005, the only living people permitted to be depicted on a stamp were members of the royal family.) 'Some old duffer complained,' he groaned.

Queen's most obvious rock star: Roger Taylor, 1976.

Taylor regularly goes to his well-appointed home studio to make new music. He releases individual tracks as and when the mood takes him. He has a system, though. If inspiration doesn't strike within the first eleven minutes, he stops and does something else. Not nine minutes, not ten, but eleven.

However, with a back catalogue as formidable as Queen's, Taylor finds himself in competition with the past. And the past won't go away. He doesn't watch a lot of television and is often surprised when his mobile phone pings with messages from friends saying they've heard another of his songs in a TV ad.

'There are two ways you can look at this,' he said. 'You can be very precious about your music and say, "No, we are not using it to advertise chocolate." Or you can want your music to be on the radio and be everywhere. I don't want Queen's music to just be on some piece of vinyl from the '70s.'

Taylor shares this philosophy with Brian May, even though they butt heads about everything else. 'What do you and Roger argue about?' a journalist recently asked Brian.

'Oh, anything and nothing,' he replied. 'A note, a tempo, a cup of coffee, a window . . .'

'The air we breathe,' concurred Roger.

But solo records come and go; Queen is for ever. 'I love making a racket in a big, loud rock band,' Taylor once said.

'TENEMENT FUNSTER'

Queen's greatest non-hits, no. 5

There's a story about Roger Taylor in Queen's early days scaling three balconies outside student accommodation in

Kensington to reach a woman he was seeing – like a gravelly voiced, blond abseiler. If Taylor's early songwriting is any indication, he had three main preoccupations: rock 'n' roll, women and motor cars.

'Tenement Funster', from 1974's *Sheer Heart Attack*, touched on the first two. Over an Aladdin Sane-era Bowie stomp, Taylor explains how his taste in loud music upsets his neighbours, but how popular he is with 'the girls on my block'. Presaging his illustrious future, the 24-year-old also divulges how he likes the good things in life, 'but most of the best things ain't free'.

'It was partly a reflection of who I was,' Taylor said. 'Cars and girls? A playboy image? Sounds alright. What's wrong with that? I'm not ashamed.' Like his later hit B-side 'I'm in Love with My Car', Taylor's upfrontness is refreshing – a nice counterpoint to Freddie Mercury's arty musings and Brian May's handwringing. 'I'll make the speed of light outta this place,' he sings, like a young man going places. 'Tenement Funster' suggests that, long before he'd made his first million, Roger Taylor was having the time of his life.

'THESE ARE THE DAYS OF OUR LIVES'

Friends will be friends

There are many great photographs of Freddie Mercury and Roger Taylor together, including pictures of them joking around on their Kensington Market stall in 1970. The pair's hijinks started early. They shared a room in their pre-Queen days and slept in two foldaway beds. 'I do remember folding Fred into the wall when he was asleep,' recalled Taylor, 'which I found hilarious and he didn't. If there was fun to be had, Freddie and I were usually involved.'

From the outside, Brian May always looked like he was worried about something and John Deacon was just John Deacon. But Queen's dandyish lead singer and drummer looked like firm friends who enjoyed the best of everything.

Taylor wrote 'These Are the Days of Our Lives' about Mercury for 1991's *Innuendo*. While May's corresponding song, 'The Show Must Go On', was moving and dramatic, Taylor's was lighter, though just as heartfelt – as befits a man who used to fold his sleeping friend into the wall.

There was nothing ambiguous about the song. Its lyrics were openly nostalgic, like Taylor had been looking through some old snapshots as he was writing it. The underlying message was: the past is a great place to visit, but you wouldn't want to live there. 'No use in sitting and thinking what you did,' sang Mercury. Taylor played congas and May provided a beautifully measured guitar solo.

Mercury didn't publicly announce he had AIDS until twenty-four hours before his death. But the video for 'These Are the Days of Our Lives' revealed his poor health. The film was shot in flattering black and white, but Mercury's shirt and waistcoat, decorated with pictures of his cats, billowed around his skinny torso. He weakly clenched his fists and shook his head, but hardly moved from the waist down.

At the end, Mercury stared down the camera and signed off with a hushed 'I still love you'.

'I can imagine it going through his head, "This would be a nice line to go out on,"' admitted Taylor.

The single was released on a double A-side with 'Bohemian Rhapsody' in December 1991 – a little over two weeks after Mercury's death. It went to number one, though Taylor said he was too numb to pay much attention.

Years later, he recalled how he'd tried to see Mercury just before he died. 'I had the phone call to say I should come now,' Taylor disclosed. But, when he was almost there, his car phone rang again. 'I was about 300 yards up the street when Peter Freestone called and said, "Don't come. He's just gone."'

Taylor pulled over on Kensington High Street to take in the news. He wasn't that far from the market stall where he and his old friend once had so much fun.

'TIE YOUR MOTHER DOWN'

Oedipal bondage anthem or teenage kicks?

'Ever tied anybody's mother down and, if so, what did you do with her?' Ralph Hobbs from Northallerton asked Brian May. It was June 1998 and the author was in May's rock-star pile asking readers' questions for the music magazine *Q*. Sadly, Brian's reply was no. But what did it all mean, then?

May started writing 'Tie Your Mother Down' in spring 1970. At the time, he was studying for his PhD and working with a group of Imperial College professors and students at the Observatorio del Teide in Tenerife. The views of the Milky Way and zodiacal dust (the subject of his thesis) were exceptionally clear over the island thanks to the lack of light pollution.

After work, May could often be found strumming his Spanish guitar on the hills overlooking Santa Cruz. 'I was on top of a mountain, playing some riffs while the sun came up, when the words to that song came into my head,' he recalled. 'To be honest, I thought it was a crap title.'

The riff was filed away and the song didn't appear on an album until 1977's *A Day at the Races*. May insisted that the phrase 'tie your mother down' was a joke without any sexual connotation. It was a song about an adolescent who craved escape from restrictive parents and other family members. May thought Queen would change the title, but Freddie Mercury wanted to keep it: 'Freddie said it meant something to him, so he knows the answer and who am I to argue?'

Meanwhile, Brian's scientific brain imagined the song's instrumental intro as the equivalent of Dutch artist M. C. Escher's painting *Relativity* (the one with the never-ending staircase). Each descending guitar part apparently fades into the octave below.

'Tie Your Mother Down' (minus the album version's Escher-esque intro) was released as a single in March 1977, but missed out on the UK top thirty. It was a bit too heavy for daytime radio, which is probably why several hard-rock groups, including Dave Grohl's Foo Fighters, have recorded versions since.

'Tie Your Mother Down' had a higher purpose, though. It became Queen's show-opener and then a staple of their live set – a song guaranteed to raise energy levels. Try the version from *Queen Rock Montreal* in 1981, complete with a closing blizzard of pyrotechnics. The song was performed over 450 times at every Queen concert between 1976 and '86 and has returned to the set during the more recent Paul Rodgers and Adam Lambert eras.

Brian May's love affair with Tenerife also continued. In 2015, he told the *Daily Telegraph* he'd like to walk up Mount Teide again. 'I did it once when I was a student, but I've had a lot of trouble with my knees,' he admitted. Queen's resident stargazer wanted to return to the place where he'd studied the cosmos, strummed his Spanish guitar and first considered tying a mother down.

TIME

Freddie Mercury, ice-cream salesman

The Dominion Theatre on London's Tottenham Court Road hosted Queen's jukebox musical, *We Will Rock You*, for eleven years. A statue of Freddie Mercury guarded the entrance throughout the show's epic run. Mercury never lived to see the musical, but, in 1986, he could have become a West End star at the very same theatre.

Mercury was great friends with the songwriter Dave Clark – once of the '60s pop group the Dave Clark Five. In April '86, Clark's latest project – the musical *Time* – opened at the Dominion. It told the story of a modern-day rock star who becomes embroiled in time-travelling intergalactic adventures, like *Doctor Who* meets *This Is Spinal Tap*. The show was notable for its cutting-edge special effects, which included a hologram of acting royalty Sir Laurence Olivier's disembodied head.

Clark offered the lead role of pop star Chris Wilder to Freddie. As boldly ambitious as Mercury was, he knew acting in a West End musical was beyond him. 'For one thing, my darling, I don't get up until 3 p.m., so I can't do matinees,' he cautioned. Instead, the job went to Cliff Richard, but Mercury did record two songs for the *Time* soundtrack: the emotive ballads 'Time Waits for No One' and 'In My Defence'.

His involvement with *Time* didn't stop there, though. On 9 April, during the interval of the show's premiere at the Dominion Theatre, Mercury suddenly appeared carrying a tray of ice creams and proceeded to promenade down the aisle offering his wares. The audience laughed and watched disbelievingly as the famous rock star casually tossed cartons of ice creams into their laps.

As one friend later observed, it would have been pointless asking Mercury to sell them. It had been so long since Freddie had handled cash that they weren't sure he'd have known what to do with it. As Mercury famously said, 'I don't give a damn about money; I just think it's for spending.'

TRIBUTE CONCERT
It's a beautiful day

ACT I
Before the show

It's 31 November 1991 and Brian May and Roger Taylor have just revealed plans to stage a concert in Freddie Mercury's memory. It's a week after the singer's death and the pair are appearing on the breakfast television show *TV-am*.

'There will be some kind of event in his name, which will be positive and hopefully raise a lot of money for charity,' says Taylor.

'It seems almost inconceivable to imagine Queen performing without Freddie as the lead vocalist,' responds *TV-am* host Kathryn Holloway.

'Yes, pretty inconceivable,' replies Taylor with a sad grin.

Three months later, Queen formally announce the Freddie Mercury Tribute Concert for AIDS Awareness at the annual BRIT Awards. It will take place at Wembley Stadium on 20 April 1992, with all proceeds to be donated to the Mercury Phoenix Trust – a new HIV/AIDS awareness charity named in Freddie's memory.

In addition to Queen performing with guest singers, the concert will feature musical contributions from other artists. The core band will be joined by keyboard player Spike Edney, Black Sabbath's Tony Iommi, and backing singers Miriam Stockley and Maggie Rider. Not everyone is as gung-ho as May and Taylor, though. John Deacon initially won't commit, so rehearsals take place with ex-Whitesnake bassist Neil Murray instead.

Madonna, Phil Collins, Michael Jackson, Aretha Franklin and Montserrat Caballé are apparently asked to perform, but can't or won't attend. However, the final line-up does include their peers Elton John, Robert Plant, George Michael and David Bowie, plus several top-tier modern rock acts. Though Freddie Mercury's record collection didn't include Metallica, Def Leppard or Guns N' Roses, these bands are Queen's loyal courtiers – the kids who gawped at the video for 'Bohemian Rhapsody' and then went on to start platinum-selling bands. They're also guaranteed to shift tickets. Additionally, bringing an air of surreal glamour to proceedings are vintage Hollywood royalty Elizabeth Taylor and Liza Minnelli.

It's a day of highs and lows, of sadness and comedy, of game-changing social awareness and career-defining performances.

ACT II
The show in twenty-seven parts

1. At approximately 6 p.m., Queen appear on stage to address the 72,000-strong audience and the half a billion people watching on TV across the globe. 'Good evening, Wembley and the world,' says May, before promising to give Freddie Mercury 'the biggest send-off in history'. Roger Taylor (wearing the inevitable sunglasses) talks about 'how AIDS affects us all' and then announces, 'John's got something to tell you.' A dignified Deacon takes the mic and sounds like a

headmaster thanking parents for coming to the school carol concert. He is no longer a rock star. He's already moved on. 'Please welcome . . . Metallica!' he half-shouts.

2. Metallica bring lots of stretch black denim and split ends. They're one of the biggest bands in the world and play three songs, though most of the audience only know the hit 'Enter Sandman'. It's a good rowdy opener. Bright red AIDS awareness flags and ribbons flutter in the breeze next to a bright-yellow inflatable banana. The message is getting through.

3. Brian May introduces his 'real friends': the Boston hair-metal band Extreme. Their Queen medley is brave, but they go over the handlebars and land face-first on the pavement during 'Bicycle Race'. (Guitarist Nuno Bettencourt later becomes Barbadian pop princess Rihanna's musical director.)

4. Roger Taylor welcomes sturdy northern rockers Def Leppard. One-armed drummer Rick Allen's customised electronic kit has been miswired, though. When he hits the snare, it 'plays' the bass drum. 'If you watch the gig, you can hear him flapping around,' admits singer Joe Elliott. Brian May joins them for 'Now I'm Here'. (It's the best moment so far.)

5. Bob Geldof plays a song nobody has ever heard and then introduces mock-rockers Spinal Tap.

6. Spinal Tap arrive wearing crowns and coronation robes. 'We've cut our set short by about thirty-five songs,' they announce sombrely. 'Freddie would have wanted it.'

7. At some point around 7.30 p.m., fellow Live Aid success story U2 appear via a shadowy satellite link singing 'Until the End of the World'. (The 72,000 audience members talk among themselves.)

8. Up pops South Africa's Mango Grove, also performing live via satellite from Johannesburg. (There is no mention of Queen playing Sun City.)

9. The presence of Guns N' Roses – the self-proclaimed 'most dangerous band in the world' – upsets some, since lead singer Axl Rose has been accused of homophobia. Campaign group ACT UP (AIDS Coalition to Unleash Power) have pushed for the band to be removed from the bill, but May has supported their inclusion: 'If we can pull in Guns N' Roses, who are normally thought to be macho and not concerned with gay issues, then we've really achieved something.' Guns N' Roses clatter through their hit 'Paradise City' and guitarist Slash's trademark top hat falls off in all the excitement. (Afterwards, bassist Duff McKagan passes out on a backstage staircase, where he remains for some time.)

10. Around 8 p.m., actor Ian McKellen (not yet a 'sir' or Gandalf) introduces Elizabeth Taylor. 'Don't worry, I'm not gonna sing,' she says, with a cool million dollars' worth of jewellery glinting on her wrists and earlobes. Taylor starts reeling off some shocking statistics. 'Each day, 5,000 people are infected with AIDS,' she begins. 'Get off!' shouts a voice from the crowd. 'I'll get off in a minute, I have something to say,' she shouts back. 'There are 70,000 people here. Look at yourselves. In two short weeks, there will be as many new infections as there are people here. Protect yourselves! Every time you have sex, use a condom. Straight sex. Gay sex. Bisexual sex. Use a condom.'

11. Video screens show footage of Freddie 'ay-oh'ing at Live Aid and other venues in the '80s. It's a crowd-pleasing moment that segues into Queen, Slash and Def Leppard's Joe Elliott performing 'Tie Your Mother Down'. Elliott is otherwise detained and only arrives on stage in time for the second verse. (Slash later claims that Elizabeth Taylor interrupted him backstage while he was putting his leather trousers on: 'I just pulled my pants up and went, "Nice to meet you."')

12. Tony Iommi and the Who's Roger Daltrey join Queen for a macho 'I Want It All' and a few seconds of 'Pinball Wizard'. (Daltrey is interviewed backstage after and mentions the Who losing their drummer Keith Moon. 'I know what they're going through, Brian, Roger and . . . er . . . John,' he sighs.)

13. Italian crooner Zucchero purrs through Queen's part-Spanish power ballad 'Las Palabras de Amor'. (Zucchero's career has peaked in the UK, but he remains a big star in Italy – so much so that a paparazzi later takes photos of him on his farm assisting his male donkey, Camillo, to breed with its female partner, Lucio. 'The guy had taken pictures of me kneeling beside the donkey with a hard-on!')

14. Gary Cherone, Extreme's lead singer, becomes overfamiliar during 'Hammer to Fall' and grabs Brian May's hair. Unforgivable. John Deacon looks embarrassed.

15. Taylor plays an extended intro to 'Stone Cold Crazy'. The sun's gone down and he's still wearing sunglasses. Freddie would have wanted it. Metallica's James Hetfield sings lead vocals, but looks and sounds uncomfortable. He also changes the lyrics.

16. Robert Plant shimmies on stage wearing an elderly relative's curtains. 'Crazy Little Thing Called Love' works; 'Innuendo' doesn't. ('I hadn't learned the words properly,' Plant later admits.)

17. Brian performs his previously unheard ballad 'Too Much Love Will Kill You': 'As I was walking over to the piano, I thought, "Should I really be doing this?"'

18. Blokey '80s pop star Paul Young does his valiant best with 'Radio Ga Ga'. He's saved by the audience's overwhelming urge to do the synchronised handclap. (In excess of 26,000 pints of lager will be sold today. This helps.)

19. 'Who Wants to Live Forever' is performed with modish R&B star Seal. His voice is powerful but understated and he gets

swamped by the song. (Roger Taylor has finally taken the glasses off. Shame.)

20. 'She came to do the housework; hopefully she's going to sing,' rasps Roger as he introduces Lisa Stansfield. She is wearing hair rollers and pushing a vacuum cleaner for a clean and tidy version of 'I Want to Break Free'.

21. Now for a histrionic 'Under Pressure', starring Eurythmic Annie Lennox and a mannequin-like David Bowie. Bowie stays around for Mott the Hoople's 'All the Young Dudes', performing with Ian Hunter and Mick Ronson. Two of Def Leppard wander on to sing backing vocals. Queen and Bowie's version of 'Heroes' is sublime; Bowie kneeling down to recite the Lord's Prayer, less so. ('I remember thinking it would have been nice if he'd warned me about that,' says Brian.)

22. George Michael performs three songs: "39', 'These Are the Days of Our Lives' (with a returning Lisa Stansfield) and 'Somebody to Love'. This third song is a showstopper, but credit is also due to the London Community Gospel Choir for supreme backing vocals. 'I was living out a childhood fantasy,' says Michael later. He and his Wham! partner, Andrew Ridgeley, used to play *A Night at the Opera* obsessively and attended Queen gigs at Alexandra Palace and Earl's Court. ('George Michael was the best on the day,' says Brian. 'There's a certain note in his voice when he did "Somebody to Love" that was pure Freddie.')

23. Elton John, looking small and boyish, gets stuck into 'Bohemian Rhapsody'. But it doesn't get going until the opera section when the video zooms across the screen: 'Magnifico-o-o-o!' etc. There's an almighty explosion and Axl Rose dances on wearing a black leather man-skirt. Elton snuggles up to him for the 'nothing really matters' finale. (It's been a tough day for Elton. He'd knocked on Axl's dressing-room door hours earlier to rehearse, but Axl's bodyguard told him that the boss

was sleeping. Elton then went into Def Leppard's dressing room for a cup of tea instead.)

24. Not content with wrestling one big Queen song, Elton tries for a second: a quavering version of 'The Show Must Go On'. ('None of us will sing these songs as well as Freddie did,' cautioned Robert Plant earlier.)

25. Axl Rose reappears in a pair of shorts that Mercury might have rejected in 1976 as 'a little tight, darling'. He then proceeds to kick his 'can all over the place' on 'We Will Rock You'.

26. 'There is one person in the world Freddie would be very proud to have stand in his footsteps,' announces Brian May breathily. 'Liza!' In the early '70s, Mercury's record collection comprised a handful of LPs: Led Zeppelin, the Beatles, Jimi Hendrix, the Who and the soundtrack to Liza Minnelli's 1972 movie, *Cabaret*.

27. Minnelli's showboating performance of 'We Are the Champions' teases every ounce of camp musical theatre from the song. The evening's previous performers reappear, arms around each other, matily swaying and not so subtly hustling for the best camera angles. (Except for Elton John, who later admitted: 'I didn't get involved in the bun-fight. It was a very moving day, but I felt kind of numbed by it. My feelings were: I'd rather it was Freddie up there than me.') As the camera pans across the stage, there, huddled around Liza Minnelli, are various members of Guns N' Roses, grinning like schoolboys and including a now-upright and fully functioning Duff McKagan.

ACT III
After the show

There's a party at Mayfair's Hard Rock Café. Limousines pull up bumper to bumper outside, discharging their famous cargo:

random Queens, Def Leppards and a diamond-laden Elizabeth Taylor. The Champagne flows and backs are slapped.

Figures are released soon after claiming that the show raised $35 million for the Mercury Phoenix Trust. Industry insiders later dispute this, saying that, with the cost of production, flights, expenses and lavish hotel accommodation, the figure is significantly less: maybe somewhere between $8 million and $12 million. Queen's people insist that the show was intended to 'raise awareness of HIV and AIDS rather than money'.

At the Hard Rock Café, though, Brian May admits to feeling numb. Queen had first talked about staging this concert the night after Freddie died and the planning had kept them preoccupied ever since.

'It was then that I realised, "That's it, it's over, it's done,"' he says later. 'What on earth do we do now?'

Last men standing: Deacon, Taylor and May,
Freddie Mercury Tribute Concert, 1992.

'UNDER PRESSURE'

Queen versus Bowie

'It was spontaneous and peculiar,' said David Bowie when asked about 'Under Pressure', his big hit single with Queen. Bowie and Freddie Mercury, of course, had history. In 1969, when Bowie played a gig at Ealing Art College, a student named Farrokh Bulsara helped build him a stage in the college refectory.

Twelve years later, the balance of power had shifted. In July 1981, while Bowie was in between hits, Queen had just topped the American chart with 'Another One Bites the Dust'. That summer, the band were at Mountain Studios, Montreux, working on what would become the following year's *Hot Space* album. Bowie was also in town recording a new song, 'Cat People (Putting Out Fire)', for a film soundtrack. He dropped by the studio and sang backing vocals on Queen's song 'Cool Cat', but it seems he couldn't stay away. 'Bowie kept popping into the studio,' said Mercury in 1985. 'And we were jamming to some of his songs and some of ours. We had a few bottles of wine and things.'

According to eyewitnesses, these 'things' included a large amount of cocaine. Not all of Queen indulged, but one of their crew was instructed to remove a gold disc from the studio wall to use as a pharmaceutical chopping board. For the next few hours, Queen and Bowie jammed to songs including Mott the Hoople's 'All the Young Dudes' and 'All the Way from Memphis' and Cream's 'NSU' and 'I Feel Free'.

For a long time, Queen insisted that only 'Under Pressure' was recorded during these sessions. However, in 2021, Roger Taylor admitted that, 'if we look in the archives, there is probably other stuff'. This 'other stuff' includes an early version of what became the Queen B-side 'I Go Crazy', with Bowie and Mercury swapping vocals from verse to verse and singing different lyrics from those on the later Queen-only recording.

Apparently, Bowie then suggested that they try to write something brand new together. Queen used the piano line from another new song, 'Feel It', but the rest of 'Under Pressure' was concocted on the spot. After creating a backing track, Bowie proposed that he and Freddie go into the vocal booth separately and sing a melody off the top of their heads without letting the other hear what they'd done first.

There's some suggestion that Bowie cheated and eavesdropped on Mercury's scatting vocal before recording his own contribution. 'Freddie was very impressed by what Bowie sang,' said producer Reinhold Mack. 'I said, "It's easy when you're standing in the doorway listening." Freddie said, "Oh, what a cunt."' But, with the wine and other things flowing and the session lasting over twenty-four hours, memories are understandably cloudy.

What isn't in dispute is how Bowie assumed control, writing most of the lyrics and recommending they dump the original title, 'People on Streets'. John Deacon also insisted it was Bowie who came up with that world-famous bassline. 'David's responsible for it. He's a talented man,' said Deacon in 1982. Bowie, meanwhile, insisted that Queen already had the bassline before he arrived.

Brian May found the whole process difficult. It was hard enough getting his way with three bandmates; now there were five people involved. 'We were all very pig-headed,' he said, 'but Bowie was probably as pig-headed as the four of us put together.'

'I got on well with Bowie and so did Freddie. But five egos in the studio could be a bit much,' confirmed Taylor.

May eventually stepped away from the song completely. Problems escalated, though, when Bowie, Mercury, Taylor and Mack attempted to mix the track at New York's Power Station. Mack was sandwiched between David and Freddie at the mixing desk, both telling him to what to do, until Taylor arrived to mediate. Then the desk malfunctioned and Mack downed tools. He didn't receive a production credit on the final song.

Muddying the waters further, rock star Jon Bon Jovi now claims that he saw Bowie and Mercury recording vocals together. At the time, the nineteen-year-old Bon Jovi was working as a gopher at the Power Station. 'Nobody believes me, but I looked through the window of Studio A and saw them. I am not mistaken,' he insisted.

Nobody seemed entirely happy with the results. Bowie even wanted to redo the whole song. 'There were continual disagreements about how it should be put out or if it should even be put out at all,' said May, who was annoyed by how under-represented he was in the final mix. Nevertheless, EMI/Capitol and Bowie's label, RCA, saw the commercial potential and 'Under Pressure' was released as a single in October 1981. Neither party appeared in the video, though, which instead featured footage of exploding tower blocks and clips from the acclaimed 1922 Soviet silent movie *Battleship Potemkin*.

'Under Pressure' gave Queen their first UK number one since 'Bohemian Rhapsody' and Bowie his first since 1980's 'Ashes to Ashes', but it barely troubled the American top thirty. However, the song did acquire a second wind almost a decade later when pop-rapper Vanilla Ice sampled the bassline and piano hook for his 1990 hit 'Ice Ice Baby'. Ice (real name: Robert Van Winkle), who'd discovered the song in his older brother's record collection, later disputed Queen and Bowie's claim of copyright infringement, arguing that he'd added an extra note to the bassline. Despite this, he was forced to settle out of court and add Queen and Bowie's names to the writing credits.

Like 'Bohemian Rhapsody', 'Under Pressure' was an unlikely pop hit. As immediate as the hook is, the song never stops sounding like Bowie and Queen locked in a musical tug of war. Sometimes Bowie gets Queen over the line; other times, it's Queen's turn. Like 'Don't Stop Me Now', it's also one of those Queen hits that has become bigger this century. In 2011, cartoon emperor penguins and elephant seals performed an a cappella version of the song in the animated comedy *Happy Feet Two*. The bassline has become so ubiquitous that the viewer was already in on the joke from the first note.

It was also the first and last time that a Mercury-fronted Queen would collaborate with another musician. What might a whole Queen and David Bowie album have sounded like? Would they have managed to complete it without blood being spilled? 'I still love "Under Pressure",' said Taylor, 'and I wish we'd done more with Bowie.'

'Looking back, I think it's a very special, significant song,' allowed May. 'But I would love to sit down quietly on my own and remix it.'

The song's significance isn't lost on Queen's fellow musicians. In 1999, Dave Grohl's Foo Fighters were about to start writing their third album. It was a daunting prospect. 'We were driving along on our way to our rehearsal studio in Virginia,' recalled drummer Taylor Hawkins. 'We had the radio playing and "Under Pressure" came on. We all sat there, silent, listening.' When it was over, Dave Grohl turned around to the rest of the band and grinned. 'Why are we even trying?' he laughed. 'Like we're going to do anything even close to that song.'

VALENTIN, BARBARA

Frau Mercury

In 1984, Freddie Mercury met and supposedly fell in love with an Austrian-born actor and model named Barbara Valentin. 'Barbara and I have formed a bond that is stronger than anything I've had with a lover for the past six years,' he told the press at the time.

His friends were shocked. Most presumed that, since splitting with Mary Austin, Mercury had zero interest in sexual relationships with women. 'But Freddie was always full of surprises,' suggested former aide Peter Freestone.

Freddie and Barbara met when Queen were working in Munich. Mercury was staying at the Stollberg Plaza apartment hotel and Valentin lived opposite. Both had seen each other around town, including at the New York Discotheque, where Freddie and his familiars held court from their own VIP section. 'Freddie and Barbara had many things in common,' said Freestone. 'Including a mutual sense of fun.'

Valentin, born Ursula Ledersteger, was six years older than Mercury and already a celebrity in her adopted Germany. Her mother had been an actor and her father a film art director.

Barbara graduated from 1960s B-movies to working for cult film-maker Rainer Werner Fassbinder, an auteur of German new cinema whose movies explored sex, love and obsession. Valentin made several films for Fassbinder – including 1975's *Fox and His Friends*, in which she played the wife of a gay antiques dealer – before the director's death from a drug overdose in 1982.

Barbara, an ebullient, vivacious blonde, was nicknamed the 'German Jayne Mansfield' and the 'Queen of Munich'. After Fassbinder's death, her acting career slowed down and her party lifestyle increased. She and Mercury were irresistibly drawn to each other. He adored her outrageousness, her open sexuality and her theatrical airs and graces. She encouraged the same behaviour in him.

'Freddie was a ball of energy; he consumed me,' said Barbara.

'Barbara fascinated me because she's got such great tits,' joked Freddie.

They spent an intense two years together. In 1984, Mercury cast her in the camply ridiculous video for Queen's 'It's a Hard Life'. Barbara can be seen wearing a feathered black ballgown and flashing her décolletage over a balcony before standing on Mercury's toe and laughing giddily. A year later, he dedicated his solo single 'Love Me Like There's No Tomorrow' to her. But did she love him?

'I was completely in love with him,' Valentin assured Mercury biographer Lesley-Ann Jones. 'And he told me he loved me. We even talked of getting married.'

The wedding never happened, but the couple bought an apartment together on Hans-Sachs Strasse in the heart of Munich's club district. Barbara also accompanied Freddie on tour with Queen, including their ill-fated trip to Sun City, and spent many nights at his London townhouse, Garden Lodge, too.

Barbara said that the couple had a sexual relationship, but she also accepted Freddie's male lovers, including his boyfriend at the time – a bullish Austrian restauranteur named Winnie Kirchberger. Cocaine-fuelled nights out sometimes even ended with Freddie and Barbara sharing a bed with one of his latest conquests.

However, Valentin always maintained that Mercury's gay life-style was 'a choice and not a biological thing'. She believed that he craved tenderness and affection, regardless of gender. When several of their friends were diagnosed with HIV, the pair curbed their behaviour, but their relationship suffered.

By 1987, speculation about Mercury's private life was rife in the German press. Mercury knew that Valentin had friends on the newspapers. There was no firm evidence, but he suspected she was selling stories. He gave up Munich, the clubs and the apartment and moved back to London. After Mercury's diagnosis, Queen and their management closed ranks and Valentin was shut out. Mercury stopped taking her calls, so she started writing letters. On a whim, she phoned to speak to him the night he died. One of Mercury's entourage told her he wasn't available. She found out about his death several hours later.

Barbara had bought a plane ticket and booked a hotel in London when she received the call telling her not to come to Mercury's funeral. She wasn't wanted. The message came via the band's management. She'd later spend several years fighting Queen's handlers to retain the rights to the Munich apartment she'd bought with Mercury.

Barbara suffered a stroke and died in February 2002. Freddie's Munich 'wife' was married three times in all, but never to him. In one of her final interviews, Barbara revealed that the two most significant men in her life had been Rainer Werner Fassbinder and Freddie Mercury.

'I think Fassbinder would have admired Freddie's talent,' she said. 'When Fassbinder died, I thought, "It's over, my career." I was lucky to meet such a strong, impulsive personality once more. Freddie was a loving and caring person.'

Vital Statistics

Queen's answers to pop magazine trivia questions, 1974–82

Measurements:

Freddie Mercury's neck size:
15 inches

John Deacon's height:
5 feet 11 inches

Brian May's weight:
10½ stone

'What is your dream?'

Brian May:
'Total understanding between people.'

Freddie Mercury:
'To remain the divine, lush creature that I am.'

John Deacon:
'Wet.'

Roger Taylor:
'To be rich, famous, happy and popular.'

Favourites:

Freddie Mercury's favourite food:
Spare ribs with onion sauce

John Deacon's favourite food:
Cheese on toast

Brian May's favourite drink:
Grapefruit juice

Freddie Mercury's favourite actress:
Mae West

Roger Taylor's favourite actor:
Jack Nicholson

Brian May's favourite film:
Women in Love

Freddie Mercury's favourite writers:
Beatrix Potter and Richard Dadd

Freddie Mercury's favourite album:
Imagine by John Lennon

'About me'

Roger Taylor's greatest ambition:
'To own Barbados.'

Freddie Mercury's ideal kind of girl:
'Outgoing and just a bit flirty.'

Brian May's other occupation:
'Inventing things.'

Roger Taylor's 'I would describe myself as . . .':
'Selfish, uncaring, vague, unpunctual and obnoxious.
A right cunt, in fact.'

WADE DEACON GRAMMAR SCHOOL FOR GIRLS

The scene of a happy accident

The Wade Deacon Grammar School for Girls and its all-male counterpart once stood next door to each other on Birchfield Road, Widnes. In 1974, these two pillars of learning amalgamated, finally soothing decades of frustrated adolescence. Before then, though, the girls' school played a small yet significant role in Queen's history.

Freddie Mercury's pre-Queen group Wreckage included several ex-Wade Deacon Boys pupils. Among them was bassist John 'Tupp' Taylor. In winter 1969, Taylor's sister, who was studying at Wade Deacon Girls, booked her brother's band to play the school's annual dance. The gig, on 24 November, was a shambles. Wreckage's PA malfunctioned, they battled persistent sound problems and Mercury's mic stand fell apart. Apparently, he was attempting to perform a dramatic move with it when the heavy circular base dropped off.

Nobody knows which Zeppelin/Hendrix cover or original composition they were playing at the time, but Richard Thompson, ex-Wreckage drummer, recalled looking up from his kit and seeing the stand break. 'From then on, Fred just used the top half of the mic stand,' he said.

Mercury immediately turned that broken piece of kit into a stage prop and rarely used a traditional microphone stand in the years that followed. 'It's my gimmick, dear,' he told anyone who asked. Sixteen years after his accident at Wade Deacon, Mercury was still using the prop at Live Aid, wielding his sawn-off mic stand like a guitar, a phallus, a sword or (appropriately, considering its origins) a headmaster's cane.

'WE ARE THE CHAMPIONS'

Queen's greatest victory lap

Freddie Mercury would have turned fifty in September 1996. He shared his birthday with his childhood friend Subash Shah. The boys grew up together in Zanzibar and attended the same boarding school in India. In 1964, Mercury's family moved to London while the Shahs found a new home in Wisconsin, Ohio. The two lost contact soon after.

Then, in September '96, Shah received a magazine article in the post from his father. It was a story celebrating Freddie Mercury and speculating what he might have been doing at fifty. 'I was stunned,' Shah confessed. 'I had no idea about his life or what he had become. I had no idea he had died.'

The last time they'd spoken, Mercury was still Farrokh Bulsara. Until the article, Shah had been oblivious to Queen and his friend's rock-star alter ego, preferring jazz to rock 'n' roll. However, as a basketball fan, he was also used to hearing 'We

Are the Champions' blasting out of the Tannoy whenever a team scored a winning hoop. 'I knew Freddie's music, but I didn't know it was him. I never made the connection until I read this article.'

'We Are the Champions' was a UK number-two hit in October 1977 and it's now difficult to remember life before the song. It's become a universal anthem, like Frank Sinatra's 'My Way', which is exactly what Mercury was aiming at. 'I suppose it could be construed as my version of ["My Way"],' he said. The lyrics share the same sentiment: triumph over adversity.

Mercury brought the song to London's Wessex Studios for *News of the World*. Like Brian May's 'We Will Rock You' (the other half of the double A-side single), the song was inspired by a Queen show. After the band left the stage at Stafford Bingley Hall in May 1977, the audience began a mass singalong of 'You'll Never Walk Alone'. 'I wanted to write something everyone could sing along to like a football chant,' said Mercury.

In 1977, Cherry Brown managed Country Cousin – a cabaret bar and restaurant in London. She was friends with Mercury and recalled him writing the song's lyrics in her flat. They reflected his rarefied lifestyle. With a chauffeured limousine on call, Mercury was living like a champion. One morning, he took them both to the perfume counter at Harrods. 'Freddie proceeded to buy me the biggest bottle of L'Air du Temps I had ever seen,' said Cherry. Then he was recognised, surrounded by Queen-loving shoppers and beat a hasty retreat. 'His driver whisked him, almost invisibly, out and away and I was left holding my huge bottle, completely alone.'

The original 'We Are the Champions' was two choruses longer than the final version, which runs to just two minutes and fifty-nine seconds. It's surprisingly short for such a big song, but it's all about the ingredients. In 2011, a team at London's Goldsmiths' College, led by music psychologist Dr Daniel Mullensiefen, declared 'We Are the Champions' the 'catchiest song in the history of pop music'. They based this on a combination of science, mathematics, frequencies of sound and cognitive psychology. Queen, said Mullensiefen, had found 'the elusive elixir of the perfect sing-along song'. Other contenders had included Swedish hair-metal group Europe's 'The Final Countdown'.

Mercury, however, described his creation as the 'most arrogant and egotistical song I've ever written', while insisting it was also 'a winning song, meant for everybody'. Queen's audience embraced the sentiment. Eight hundred of them flocked to London's New Theatre to wave scarves and sing along in an official promo video.

Others felt the same. At the EMI sales conference in autumn 1977, the team were handed Queen scarves and told to stand up and wave them when Queen's new anthem was played. The company also hired household-name sportscaster Dickie Davies to record a message for its employees. After the song, Davies' familiar face was beamed onto a screen, from where he delivered his motivational speech. 'I think we knew, right there and then, we had a hit on our hands,' recalled one ex-employee.

However, the lyrics troubled some. Brian May was shocked the first time he heard them. 'I remember saying, "You can't do this, Fred. You'll get us killed." And Freddie said, "Yes, we can."' The line 'no time for losers' particularly niggled critics, who perceived Queen as monied rock stars, out of touch with ordinary people. A review of *News of the World* in *Rolling Stone* magazine even suggested that 'We Are the Champions' and 'We Will Rock You' had the 'atmosphere of a political rally in a Leni Riefenstahl movie', referring to the wartime director famous for her Nazi propaganda films.

As is the case with many of their bandmate's songs, May and Roger Taylor have been left to explain the sentiment behind this one. 'The trouble is Freddie was great at "designer" songs,' said Taylor. '"We Are the Champions" was a designer song, designed to get people together. I think a lot of his songs were brilliantly crafted, but people often miss that.'

It also takes a certain kind of vocalist to sing it with the requisite conviction and self-confidence. Liza Minnelli was the obvious choice at the Mercury Tribute Concert and emoted to within an inch of her life. In complete contrast was Swedish animated novelty character Crazy Frog's jokey version (subtitled 'Ding a Dang Dong'), which was released as a single to accompany the 2006 FIFA World Cup.

More problematic than either, though, was May and Taylor's re-recording for the soundtrack to 2001 action movie *A Knight's Tale*. Their guest vocalist was the ex-Take That member turned chart-topping solo pop star Robbie Williams. The collaboration incensed John Deacon. Until that point, he'd not commented publicly on his ex-bandmates' musical endeavours. 'It is one of the greatest songs ever written, but I think they've ruined it,' he said of the remake.

However, the song's immortality has almost rendered criticism redundant. Just a few bars of 'We Are the Champions' played at any sporting or competitive event immediately denotes victory. No time for losers in pop's catchiest song ever.

'WE WILL ROCK YOU'
Queen's 'Happy Birthday'

Brian May once said that the greatest compliment he'd ever heard about 'We Will Rock You' was that people didn't think it had been written. 'They thought it had been there for ever, like a traditional song,' he said. 'We Will Rock You' celebrated its fortieth birthday in 2017. It was partnered with 'We Are the Champions' on a double A-side single in October 1977.

There's only one instrument on the track: Brian May's guitar (and even that takes one and half minutes to get going). The rest of the song comprises Mercury's vocals and the sound of band members, roadies and Wessex Studio staff stamping on a wooden rostrum and clapping their hands on the offbeat. Among the stampers was Betty the tea lady, who wheeled her urn between the studios at Wessex and was persuaded onto the platform to participate. The resulting noise was multi-tracked by co-producer Mike Stone until it resembled an army of robots slowly marching in time. It was as though the cover of *News of the World* had come to life.

Even in winter 1977, 'We Will Rock You' sounded like it had been around for ever. No sooner was the song recorded than Queen began tinkering with it. In October, they recorded a session for BBC DJ John Peel's *Sounds of the 70s* radio show. This included a new 'We Will Rock You' ending with an unidentified female voice reciting a passage ('The buddha rejected Brahmism and mocked at its rituals . . .') from one of Brian May's favourite novels, Herman Hesse's *Siddhartha*. Some who heard this version on a transistor radio late at night, in that netherworld between wakefulness and sleep, wondered whether they'd dreamt it. The alternative mix reappeared on Queen's 2017 *News of the World* box set.

The original video for 'We Will Rock You' was amusingly unglamorous. There were the band, wearing scarves, coats, gloves and, in Roger Taylor's case, monochrome Wellington boots, performing in the snowy grounds of Taylor's new country estate. The drummer had just bought the property but not yet received the keys. He was allowed to film in the grounds, but neither Queen nor the crew were permitted to enter the house and use the toilet.

It was so cold that Mercury kept nipping off to his parked Rolls-Royce for a restorative nip of Cognac. He was drunk by the time of filming and fluffed his lines. 'I think he eventually threw up in the rhododendrons,' recalled Taylor.

Queen liked 'We Will Rock You' so much that they were soon playing it twice in their set. They opened the show with a brief, sped-up version; then, during the second rendition, Mercury reappeared on the shoulders of a security guard dressed as Superman. He'd originally wanted a throne carried by oiled-up 'slaves', but none of the crew would oblige. On later tours, Superman became *Stars Wars* bad guy Darth Vader, until the film's creator, George Lucas, threatened legal action.

From there on, 'We Will Rock You' would be a mainstay of Queen's set. Its ubiquity has led to the song being officially sampled by more than 150 artists, ranging from Grandmaster Flash and Blondie to Nine Inch Nails and Lady Gaga. There have been numerous remixes, including re-recordings by Queen themselves with boy band 5ive and Aussie balladeer John Farnham. Over 100 cover versions are presently in circulation. These include entries by plaster-headed comic persona Frank Sidebottom, stoned rapper Snoop Dogg, and the Benzedrine Monks of Santo Domonica.

Like 'We Are the Champions', 'We Will Rock You' has also become the ultimate sports anthem. Its 'stomp, stomp, clap' rhythm and mocking lyric – 'you got mud on your face, big disgrace' – are perfect for intimidating the opposition in most competitive sports. Only one thing niggles Brian May about the song he now describes as 'my gravestone'. Apparently, at many Queen concerts, audiences tend to do three claps instead of two stomps and a clap. Consider yourselves warned.

WE WILL ROCK YOU
A big disgrace?

'I didn't think I could be with anyone who didn't like Led Zeppelin,' said Brian May once. He was talking about his second wife, Anita Dobson, and how she'd challenged his musical prejudice. 'The stuff she likes, I got dragged into by my heels,' he continued. 'The whole world of musical theatre made me feel physically ill.'

Brian's revulsion towards the genre would be sorely tested in the years ahead. On 14 May 2002, *We Will Rock You*, with music and lyrics by Queen, opened at London's Dominion Theatre. It would play to a full house for the next twelve years and go on to entertain more than 15 million theatregoers around the world.

Queen and musical theatre were always a perfect match; they just didn't know it. In the early twenty-first century, this was uncharted terrain for a rock 'n' roll group. 'It's a hurdle for me to go to any musical,' Roger Taylor said. 'I tried *Les Misérables*, and my daughter and I walked out in the interval. I thought it was the worst thing I'd ever seen and heard.'

Despite Queen's misgivings, they'd been considering the idea of their own musical for decades. 'We first talked about it in 1986, back when we were playing those last gigs,' divulged May. 'The idea came from [business manager] Jim Beach. He's always been involved with theatre.' In the early '60s, Beach had been a member of the Cambridge Footlights revue and had even played piano as part of a touring production alongside future Monty Pythons Graham Chapman and Eric Idle. 'Jim said it to us as a joke in the beginning – we never took it seriously – so I blame him.'

In 1996, Beach, May and Taylor were introduced to actor Robert De Niro at the Venice Film Festival. De Niro had a production company, Tribeca, and proposed a musical based around

Queen's songs. Various storylines were discussed, explored and declined. One idea was to tell Queen's own story, à la *Bohemian Rhapsody*, but this was firmly rejected by the band. (De Niro would later co-produce the award-winning biopic, though.)

We Will Rock You was eventually written by comedian, novelist and director Ben Elton. His irreverent, witty TV comedy *Blackadder* had been a roaring success in the '80s and he'd just worked with Andrew Lloyd Webber on a football-based musical titled *The Beautiful Game* (ominously described by *The Guardian* as 'a well-intentioned mess').

Elton pitched *We Will Rock You* as a mash-up of quasi-Arthurian legend and futuristic sci-fi – a concept not so far removed from some of Queen's early work. His story was set 300 years in the future in a totalitarian state, Planet Mall, where music has been outlawed by the despotic Globalsoft company and its tyrannical boss, Killer Queen.

The Bohemians, a band of revolutionaries led by Galileo and Scaramouche, plot to liberate Planet Mall through the power of twenty-five Queen songs. These include 'I Want to Break Free', 'Don't Stop Me Now' and, of course, the musical's title track, although 'Bohemian Rhapsody' is reduced to a singalong encore as even Elton couldn't find a way to jam its Byzantine lyrics into the narrative.

The production featured a cast of gifted young performers (Brian May went on to make records with original cast member Kerry Ellis), while the house band included Queen's keyboard player Spike Edney, sundry members of Wishbone Ash and Whitesnake, and, later, Roger Taylor's drummer son Rufus. '*We Will Rock You* is different from *Mamma Mia!*,' said Rufus's dad, citing the ABBA-based musical. 'It's more rock 'n' roll.'

But the plot was thin, the jokes were lame and Elton's attempt to shoehorn serious meaning into a musical narrative was unforgivably clumsy. As *Classic Rock* magazine pointed out, the story was remarkably similar to prog-rock trio Rush's 1976 concept album, *2112*, which is a sobering thought.

Even the show's co-producer, Robert De Niro, seemed a bit baffled. De Niro attended a press conference at the Dominion Theatre the day before opening night. He gamely posed with Brian May's Red Special like a man who'd never held a guitar before, grimacing as though he were about to break into 'You lookin' at me?'

'Do you have a favourite Queen number?' asked one reporter.

'No,' De Niro replied.

'This is your first musical production,' said another. 'How does it differ from your film production work?'

'It's a musical.'

Queen DVD producer, comedy writer and *Celebrity Mastermind* winner Rhys Thomas attended the first workshop for the show at the Leicester Square Theatre. He sat behind the Hollywood superstar.

In one scene, the rebels are tortured with lasers. 'Flash! Aha!' they scream in unison. The audience burst out laughing.

'Why are they laughing?' De Niro asked his business partner. She didn't know, so she asked the next person in the row and was told it was a line from *Flash Gordon*.

There was a long pause. Thomas listened closely.

'What's *Flash Gordon*?' De Niro replied.

The problem was always the story: it was nonsense. But it was the sort of nonsense that irked critics while playing well with the public. *We Will Rock You* received comically bad reviews ('Very, very frightening!') before proceeding to sell out every night.

The band defended Elton and the production – up to a point. 'There are some great singers in the show,' insisted Taylor in 2013. 'But the story is slightly crass. I do have an aversion to musical theatre, so it hasn't been easy, but I've learnt to live with the musical.'

What would Freddie Mercury have thought of it all?

'Oh, he would have loved it,' Taylor replied. 'But he'd have thought the statue outside the Dominion wasn't big enough.'

Taylor was right. Big statement songs like 'We Are the Champions' could have been written for a West End show. After the UK, *We Will Rock You* opened in seventeen countries, including Australia, the US, Japan and Brazil. The last 'Flash! Aha!' was uttered at the Dominion on 31 May 2014. By then, *We Will Rock You* had broken the theatre's house record for longest-running musical, previously set by high-school romance *Grease*. Pre-pandemic, it was also poised to return to the UK as a touring production in 2020.

It's also debatable whether Queen's biblical second coming with guest vocalist Adam Lambert would have been such a hit without the musical. *We Will Rock You* introduced younger listeners and an audience of theatregoers to a band who hadn't released a new record since 1995. It may also have convinced May and Taylor that nobody could perform their music better than they could.

Musical might: Ben Elton (left) and Robert De Niro (centre) with Queen at the UK press launch of *We Will Rock You*, 2002.

In the meantime, Ben Elton's second rock musical, *Tonight's the Night*, featuring the songs of Rod Stewart, opened at London's Victoria Palace Theatre in 2003. It told the story of a petrol-pump attendant who makes a Faustian pact with the devil to inhabit the soul of Rod so he can have sex with a woman he's too shy to ask out. *Tonight's the Night* ran for just twelve months.

WEMBLEY STADIUM
They think it's all over

It was during a production meeting before Queen's 1986 Magic Tour that Freddie Mercury finally crossed the line. Until then, Queen had usually indulged his outrageous ideas. But not this time.

According to James 'Trip' Khalaf, Queen's former sound engineer, Mercury told those present that he wanted a model of a huge penis and testicles suspended on a wire from the back of Wembley Stadium. Mercury would straddle the genitalia as it soared over the crowd. Then a stage curtain would part to reveal a similarly oversized pair of lips. Freddie and his cock and balls would disappear into the mouth. 'And I want a moustache over the lips!' he said finally. A deathly silence descended on the room. The idea was never mentioned again.

Instead, Mercury had to make do with four inflatable versions of Queen, as seen on the cover of their new album, *A Kind of Magic*. All four were devoid of visible genitalia. Nevertheless, from the moment Queen walked on stage during the Magic Tour, they could do no wrong. And never more so than at Wembley Stadium on 11 and 12 June 1986.

Live Aid boosted Queen's sales, but it also bolstered the appetite for stadium rock shows. Millions watched the 1985 concert on TV and wanted a similarly communal experience. Queen, Madonna, Pink Floyd and Bruce Springsteen would all reap the benefit, filling Wembley Stadium with audiences who liked their music but also craved their own personal Live Aid. The venue, with its flag-fluttering twin towers, had also hosted numerous FA Cup finals and was the site of England's historic win over Germany in the 1966 World Cup. Wembley meant victory.

The stadium held 72,000 and, initially, Queen's promoter Harvey Goldsmith was unsure whether they could sell two nights. Tickets had to be purchased by post, but both shows sold out within two postal deliveries and Queen even wanted to add a third night. 'I think we could have done four or five in all,' suggested Brian May. But Wembley wasn't available, so they booked Knebworth Park instead.

The key word here was 'big'. Queen's purpose-built stage measured 160 feet across and included two 40-foot runways. It spanned the whole of one end of the stadium and supported a $9\frac{1}{2}$-tonne lighting rig. Mick Jagger later watched Queen's show and insisted that the stage was too large. 'You'll knacker yourself out running around on that,' he warned Freddie. But Jagger was clearly taking notes. When the Rolling Stones played the stadium four years later, their stage was even bigger.

The show also included another novelty feature: a 20x30-foot video screen. Most stadium gigs at the time required the audience at the back to squint at the matchstick-sized figures on stage. Now, Mercury's white Adidas Sambas and John Deacon's canary-yellow football shorts were visible to all via Queen's giant TV. The screen nearly didn't make it, though. Two days before the first Wembley date, Queen's crew discovered the stadium's architectural plans were inaccurate. Tour manager Gerry Stickells received a frantic phone call when

Queen were playing Newcastle's St James' Park. The open screen wouldn't fit under the Wembley roof. Stickells told them to make it fit and a crane driver was paid extra to achieve the task.

Both shows were being filmed for a Channel 4 TV broadcast. Director Gavin Taylor arranged for Queen to be shot by fifteen cameras surrounding the stage and runways, plus one in a helicopter overhead. He told Mercury that he needed one song during which to change the film: 'I said to Freddie, "Is there a song in the concert you'll never use?"' Mercury airily replied, 'No, no, my dear, we should record everything.'

The first night, a Friday, was blighted by a torrential downpour, so filming was abandoned. The sun came out on Saturday and the whole show was recorded then. Brian May and Roger Taylor have since talked about feeling nervous 'because it was Wembley Stadium'. Out front, though, it didn't show. Mercury's rapport with the audience was telepathic. All it took was a raised eyebrow, a goofy grin, a twirl of the mic stand or a lengthy 'ay-oh' and 72,000 people did his bidding.

There was barely a song wasted either. 'In the Lap of the Gods . . . Revisited' was exhumed from the dark ages (1974) and greeted with as much enthusiasm as some of the band's big hits. Even their rock 'n' roll medley, containing Elvis's 'You're So Square (Baby I Don't Care)', was accepted by an audience whose parents had probably bought these songs as teenagers.

There were only two misfires: Brian's prolonged guitar solo triggered a snail-like exodus towards the burger van; then, during the encore, Queen shoehorned their recent hit, 'Friends Will Be Friends', in between 'We Will Rock You' and 'We Are the Champions'. ('It was the last thing anybody expected,' understated May.) Both were comparable to Germany's last-minute equaliser in the '66 World Cup: nerve-racking, but not detrimental to the final score.

Finally, as the national anthem boomed over the PA, Mercury promenaded back on stage in his coronation robes and delicately placed his crown on Taylor's head. Queen didn't need an airborne penis and testicles; victory was theirs.

WILLIAMS, ROBBIE

Hell hath no fury like John Deacon

It wasn't easy being Queen in the 1990s and 2000s. Brian May and Roger Taylor wanted to preserve the band's legacy without becoming museum pieces themselves. This is how they arrived at the 'Queen +' concept, which enabled them to use the brand name alongside guest vocalists.

First came the 1993 live version of 'Somebody to Love' with George Michael; then a re-recording of 'Another One Bites the Dust' with Haitian rapper and Fugees singer Wyclef Jean. Both were top-five hits.

Next was Queen's surprise appearance at the 2000 BRIT Awards, accompanying boy band 5ive on 'We Will Rock You'. Their collaborative single reached number one. It raised eyebrows among some, but Queen's music was now being discovered by an audience who weren't even born when these songs were hits the first time around.

Then came the controversial hook-up with Robbie Williams. Pop star Williams had been one-fifth of the boy band Take That before quitting in 1995. His 2000 solo album, *Sing When You're Winning*, had just topped the charts and delivered six hit singles. He was the biggest pop star in Britain, even if America had yet to succumb. That same year, Williams was approached to record 'We Are the Champions' for the soundtrack to adventure movie *A Knight's Tale*. He asked if he could do it with Queen.

Two days after his request, May, Taylor and Williams were in a studio together. 'To be in the room with real history, like proper history, just felt absolutely incredible,' said the singer.

'We did four takes and Rob came up with the goods,' recalled May, who acknowledged that Queen 'consorting with that person from Take That' was likely to upset some. It did, but this didn't stop rumours circulating that Robbie Williams was going to tour with Queen as their new lead singer.

'We talked about maybe touring America with Robbie,' revealed Roger Taylor in 2005. 'We were quite serious about it, but circumstances didn't come together. In retrospect, it wouldn't have been a good idea. I think Robbie would have struggled in the States. He's very pop and a very English cheeky chappy. Americans don't always get that. They like their rock.'

In 2020, Williams broke his silence and said that he was the one who'd turned Queen down. 'I just thought I'd save them the audacity of me even trying to step on a stage and be in the same echelon as Freddie Mercury. He's godlike and it was just too scary.' But he also added that he was playing stadiums at the time as a solo act and 'didn't want to split [the money] three ways'. In 2003, Williams sold out three nights at Knebworth (where Queen played their final UK show with Mercury), performing to a record-breaking 375,000 fans.

There was another issue to consider, too. On stage, Robbie Williams was a showboating performer whose force of personality gave him a free pass when his voice let him down. Queen + Robbie Williams' version of 'We Are the Champions' only made you realise how superior the original was.

John Deacon agreed and spoke out on the matter, as reported in *The Sun*. 'Roger and Brian got together to do the song with

Robbie Williams, but I told them I had retired,' he said. 'I didn't want to be involved with it and I'm glad. I've heard what they did and it's rubbish. I don't want to be nasty, but let's just say Robbie Williams is no Freddie Mercury. Freddie can never be replaced – and certainly not by him.'

Williams later briefly rejoined Take That, revealing how he psyched himself up before going on stage by watching Queen live videos. 'Freddie Mercury has been my friend this past week or so,' he told the *Irish Times* in 2011. As a solo turn, he has also performed 'We Will Rock You' and 'Bohemian Rhapsody', complete with Queen's original video playing during the operatic mid-section of the latter. A bold move, but one that only confirms John Deacon was right.

THE WORKS

Queen's American dream

The noise of shattering glass echoed around the pink-painted villa at 649 Stone Canyon Road, Los Angeles. There was a collective gasp from Freddie Mercury's entourage. The singer had just thrown a table through the glass doors of his rented mansion. Nobody remembers why, only that the previous tenants, George Hamilton and Elizabeth Taylor, would never have done such a thing.

It was summer 1983 and Queen were in LA making their eleventh album, *The Works*. The cost of the damages would be charged to the Queen office, just like the hundreds of dollars' worth of flowers Mercury ordered for his thirty-seventh birthday party. Soon, Queen's accountant was on the phone urging them to curb their spending. Despite the relative failure of their most recent album, *Hot Space*, Queen were still living like kings.

The final date on Queen's previous American tour had been the LA Forum on 15 September 1982. It was the last time Freddie would play the US. Mercury blamed Queen's American label Elektra for *Hot Space*'s poor sales and, when the tour finished, he told Queen's management that he'd never record for the label again.

Queen eventually paid $1 million to be released from their contract. They then signed with Capitol in the States and Mercury also bagged a one-off solo deal with CBS in the UK and Columbia in the US. Tellingly, the undisclosed advance for his solo album (*Mr Bad Guy*) was far greater than Capitol's advance for *The Works* – bad news for a group who bickered about money. 'We did hate each other for a while,' admitted Brian May.

It was the work, though, that united them. In 1983, Queen were approached to write the soundtrack for a movie adaptation of John Irving's novel *The Hotel New Hampshire* – a comic drama about a dysfunctional family. They agreed, but then discovered that the film's director, Tony Richardson, couldn't afford them. Queen carried over some of their abandoned soundtrack ideas to *The Works* instead.

Starting in August, Queen and their co-producer Mack spent eight weeks at LA's Record Plant (May had just recorded his solo *Star Fleet Project* EP at the same studio). May, Taylor and Deacon arrived with their families; Mercury was accompanied by his retinue, which soon included a barman named Vince from the Eagle club on Santa Monica Boulevard. It was a fun time: Mercury paid Michael Jackson a visit and Rod Stewart and Jeff Beck dropped by the Record Plant for a drunken late-night jam.

May brought several songs to the table. Among them was 'I Go Crazy', which Queen had recorded with David Bowie two years earlier. 'The other three hated it,' he complained, though Queen's Bowie-free version later surfaced as a B-side. May had more luck with his two blood-and-guts rockers 'Tear It Up' and 'Hammer to Fall'.

Meanwhile, 'Machines (Or "Back to Humans")' was a May/Taylor collaboration about the battle between man and machine. The lyrics about 'bytes and megachips for tea' were already dated ten minutes after they'd been recorded. Taylor also sang his vocal parts through a Roland VP-330 Vocoder. 'Some of these gadgets later ended up as very expensive coffee tables,' he admitted.

Taylor fared much better with 'Radio Ga Ga'. He recorded an early demo just messing around with a drum machine and synthesiser. It was a happy accident. 'I don't want to know anything technical,' he cautioned, 'like what the chords are called.' But he was on his way to writing a hit.

John Deacon apparently hid himself away while composing 'I Want to Break Free' and later disappeared for an impromptu holiday in Bali. 'Was John trying to tell us something with that song title?' joked Taylor. Deacon refused to let May add a guitar solo and instead insisted that Fred Mandel, Queen's touring keyboard player, provide a synthesiser solo.

Mandel was a Canadian session musician and the first outsider to play on a Queen album. He watched, listened, did as he was asked and maintained a Swiss-style neutrality during band arguments. Mandel felt uncomfortable about usurping May, but Deacon was adamant. A couple of years later, he was in a music shop looking at the latest Roland synthesiser. Among its presets was 'May sound', which duplicated the effect of the Roland Jupiter 8 that Mandel used on 'I Want to Break Free'. Roland had presumed that it was Brian May playing the solo.

As always, tempers frayed in the studio: May walked out at least once and the band members often worked in different rooms across the complex. They all contributed to each other's compositions, though, with Mercury playing a significant part in 'Radio Ga Ga' and 'I Want to Break Free'.

Apparently, Taylor went on a skiing holiday and gave Mercury permission to do what he wanted with 'Radio Ga Ga', although the credit and royalties remained with Taylor alone. 'I Want to Break Free' also came with a sole credit for Deacon, despite the fact that Mercury had worked closely with him on the vocals and had added several details.

Mercury's own compositions ranged from brilliant to throwaway to middling. The rockabilly-inspired 'Man on the Prowl' was only salvaged by Fred Mandel's fabulous honky-tonk piano. 'Keep Passing the Open Windows' was slick, machine-crafted pop with fortune-cookie lyrics ('You just gotta be strong and believe in yourself. . .'). The title was a phrase used by the *Hotel New Hampshire* family during troubled times. And it seems Mercury was in trouble.

One afternoon, he arrived at the studio upset. After sitting quietly for a time, he stood up and began shouting: 'It's okay for all of you. You have your wives and families. I can never be happy.' Road manager Peter Hince witnessed the outburst (which was recreated in *Bohemian Rhapsody*). 'I thought it was terribly sad,' Hince wrote later. 'I felt for him tremendously.'

'It's a Hard Life' put Mercury's feelings into words. It was a courtly ballad beginning with part of an aria from the nineteenth-century opera *Pagliacci* – the story of a sad, lovesick clown. *Hot Space*'s dancefloor lothario clearly craved romantic love. Mercury composed the lyrics to the album's final song, 'Is This the World We Created . . .?', after watching TV footage of the famine in Africa. But the ballad was partly written to order. 'What we didn't have was one of those "Love of My Life"-type things,' he confessed.

In October, Queen left Los Angeles to finish the record at Munich's Musicland Studios. On top of the cost of breakages and birthday flowers, Queen and their attendants had gone through nineteen rental cars and racked up an eyewatering drinks bill at a female mud-wrestling club.

The Works was finally released in February 1984. It shared its name with one of Mercury's favourite New York bars and Queen's pre-tour rallying cry: 'Give 'em the fucking works!' Veteran Tinseltown photographer George Hurrell shot the cover. He presented Queen as classic matinee idols, just as he'd once done with Humphrey Bogart and Errol Flynn. Except Mercury was wearing basketball boots and a muscle vest. *The Works* also sounded like a classic Queen LP: a rock album judiciously loaded with pop songs and ballads.

The Works went to number two and delivered four top-twenty singles in the UK, but it failed in America. Queen's problems were fourfold: Mercury's personal manager Paul Prenter; the singer's refusal to tour the States; a record industry payola scandal; and Queen's British sense of humour.

Prenter had appointed himself Mercury's mouthpiece. Unbeknown to the rest of Queen, he'd snubbed journalists and turned down interviews on his boss's behalf. It also didn't help that Mercury's ego wouldn't allow him to downsize. He wanted to wait until Queen had more hits and could sell out multiple nights at Madison Square Garden again.

Another American hit seemed unlikely, though. It was an open secret that many DJs took bribes in exchange for airplay, so an investigation into record company payola was under way. Capitol immediately suspended their freelance radio pluggers, and 'Radio Ga Ga', which had been inching up the charts, quickly disappeared.

In the end, what truly impaired *The Works* were Freddie's fake breasts and mini-skirt. Director David Mallet's video for the album's second single, 'I Want to Break Free', showed Queen dressed in drag as a spoof of the British TV soap *Coronation Street*. Two decades later, Queen fan Dave Grohl would dress as several women in the Foo Fighters' 'Learn to Fly' music video. Nobody cared then, but America was different in 1984.

While Britain was in on the joke (and sent the single to number two), MTV – the all-powerful music television network – refused to play the video. 'They absolutely hated it,' said May. 'They could not accept a rock group dressing up as women and, in America, we were still seen as a rock group.'

Queen did everything they could to promote *The Works* elsewhere, though, even performing in blacklisted Sun City. Their competitive streak was as strong as ever. But, without MTV, Queen lost out to Van Halen, Bruce Springsteen and even Culture Club – the British pop group whose androgynous frontman Boy George was now wowing America.

'Give 'em the works!': Queen performing live, 1984.

At the end of an almost-world tour, Queen returned to their families and vowed not to see each other again for at least six months. 'We hadn't broken up,' insisted Taylor. 'But we didn't really know what was coming next.' Neither Queen nor America could have predicted Live Aid.

X-RAY SPEX

Mr May, the maths teacher

In winter 1971, Brian May took a job teaching mathematics at Stockwell Manor, a large comprehensive secondary school in Brixton, south London. He was still working on his PhD and needed to earn some money as Queen were making very slow progress.

'Teaching turned into something I enjoyed, but it was very challenging,' said May. With his guitar and flowing locks, 24-year-old Brian cut a youthful dash compared to most of the staff. 'I had an advantage because I was young and could speak to the children in their own language. I tried to make maths feel fun.'

May drew on all his resources to engage his often bored and disinterested pupils. They were delighted when he used gambling odds on a horse race to illustrate probability. But not every idea was as successful. May once handed out coloured paper and scissors in a lesson about rectangles and hexagons. 'And half an hour later, ears and hands were getting cut and there was blood and paper everywhere.'

Among May's pupils was Marianne Elliott-Said, who, as 'Poly Styrene', would form the punk band X-Ray Spex. 'I was in a special maths group: underachievers,' she told writer Hugh Gulland in 2011. 'Brian was a student teacher and he used to come in with long hair and holes in his shoes and we used to tease him. I used to ask him, "Sir, are you married? Sir, if you're married, why doesn't your wife iron your shirts?" It was just a joke. He was a very good teacher.'

In September 1972, Queen's new management put them on £20-a-week wages. May's PhD thesis was close to completion and he was one step away from his doctorate. Undeterred, May put his PhD on hold and handed in his notice at Stockwell Manor. One of his fellow maths teachers took him aside and tried to dissuade him from leaving. But Queen came first.

Meanwhile, having run away from home, fifteen-year-old Marianne Elliott-Said was hitch-hiking around the country and living in squats. One night, she saw Mr May with Queen on *Top of the Pops*: 'I thought, "That looks good for a laugh."'

'Poly Styrene' went on to have two top-twenty hits with X-Ray Spex in 1978 before going solo. She last saw her old maths teacher parking his car in Soho. Mr May recognised her and made the joke before she did: 'He said, "Are you married?"'

Sadly, his ex-pupil died of breast cancer in April 2011. 'Poly Styrene RIP,' wrote May on his website, with a link to a *Guardian* obituary that quoted Marianne gleefully recalling the time she made fun of her teacher's crumpled shirts.

'YOU'RE MY BEST FRIEND'

Love and an electric piano

John Deacon's best friend in this song is his wife, Veronica. The couple met in 1971 when they were students in west London. Veronica Tetzlaff came from a Catholic family and the couple wed on 18 January 1975 at the Carmelite Priory on Kensington Church Street.

What must the devout Carmelite nuns have thought of Freddie Mercury? He made a grand entrance at the priory, arriving by stretch limo with a woman on each arm (one of them was Mary Austin) and a feather boa around his neck. One guest glimpsed Freddie from behind and thought he was the bride.

At the time, Veronica was working as a nanny and John was living in a small flat in Parsons Green. He had tried and failed to persuade Queen's management company, Trident, to advance him a deposit for a house and, after the wedding, they had granted him just two weeks off before travelling to Columbus, Ohio, for the opening night of Queen's American tour.

'You're My Best Friend' arrived ten months later on *A Night at the Opera*. Perhaps it was a delayed wedding gift or a 'thank you' to Veronica for putting up with him and Queen over the past four years. The song – a smiley-faced ditty with Beach Boys-esque harmonies and rolling electric piano – was only his second piece for Queen. 'And it was just this perfect pop song,' marvelled Brian May.

Some of Queen thought it a little too pop. 'Yes, but I wasn't opposed to it,' said Roger Taylor. 'It was lightweight, but I could see its commercial potential.'

Deacon composed the song on a Wurlitzer electric piano. While Freddie was happy to serenade Veronica (John couldn't sing), he didn't like the Wurlitzer. Ray Charles and Marvin Gaye had used one on 'What'd I Say' and 'I Heard It Through the Grapevine', but Mercury wasn't having it. 'Fred said, "An electric piano, dear? Oh, no, no, no,"' recalled Taylor. Mercury disliked the sound – 'Tinny and horrible,' he complained – so Deacon played it instead. A grand piano was later used whenever Queen performed it live.

The video for 'You're My Best Friend' was filmed in a barn at Ridge Farm in Surrey. Director Bruce Gowers had been inspired by Stanley Kubrick shooting the recent period drama *Barry Lyndon* by candlelight, so he decorated the space with 6,000 candles. It was a hot day and the additional heat from the candles made it stifling. The barn was also on a pig farm and under siege from an infestation of flies. Deaky's charming love song was undermined by buzzing insects and the prevailing whiff of dung.

In May 1976, 'You're My Best Friend' was released as the follow-up to 'Bohemian Rhapsody'. It went top ten in Britain, top twenty in America and has since been used in TV commercials to sell mobile phones and flea powder for dogs. John Deacon and his best friend are still together after almost half a century, but his Wurlitzer was never heard again.

Zanzibar

As it began

It doesn't take long to walk around the Freddie Mercury Museum in Stone Town, Zanzibar City. The exhibits don't extend much beyond photographs of Farrokh Bulsara and framed lyrics. 'Don't stop me now, I'm having such a good time,' reads one. After you've peered at the words and pictures (toddler Freddie with a garland around his neck; rock-star Freddie at Live Aid), you can buy a commemorative Freddie mug for $15.

The museum is in a building called Mercury House. 'Mercury spent parts of his childhood within this house,' states the tourist brochure. The 'parts' bit is important. Some say he was born there; some say his birthplace was another property nearby; and others insist that the Bulsaras lived a four-minute walk away at 566 Shangani Street.

Nevertheless, Mercury House on Kenyatta Street has been declared the singer's official childhood residence. Freddie isn't here to dispute this and he was never one for discussing his birthplace or his Parsi Indian background anyway. 'I was born in Zanzibar, which was part of the Commonwealth then,' he managed to tell the *NME* in the '70s. 'My father was working for the government as a civil servant. My uncle had a villa in Dar es Salaam only yards from the sea and, in the morning, I'd be woken by the servant. Clutching an orange juice, I'd literally step out onto the beach.'

Some people suggest that this anecdote about servants and orange juice may have been exaggerated. The facts, as far as we know, are that Freddie lived in Zanzibar until he was sent to boarding school in India, aged eight. He returned to the island for the occasional school holiday and came back for good in summer 1962 to try to complete his education. He never had the chance to, though.

In January 1964, the Ugandan revolutionary 'Field Marshall' John Okello overthrew Zanzibar's reigning sultan and proclaimed the island a republic. After the revolution, Zanzibar was no longer safe for the family as Freddie's father, Bomi, worked for the British governor.

Subash Shah was one of Mercury's closest friends at the time. The two boys first met on a ten-day voyage from Zanzibar to India. They'd both been enrolled at Panchgani School for Boys near Mumbai and they both returned to Zanzibar in 1962. 'Thousands of folks were killed in the revolution,' Shah said. 'Things were crazy, but Freddie and I had a routine where I'd go to his house for tea and then we'd walk around the town. But we had to be back at our homes by 7.30, which was our curfew.'

The boys talked about the uprising and their hopes for the future. By then, Mercury was daydreaming about a life away from Stone Town. He'd been given a tape recorder for his birthday, which he kept next to the radio, waiting for the BBC's late-night music programme. 'As soon as it came on, he would tape the songs,' recalled his sister, Kashmira. 'And then he would play them over and over again.' These were songs by Elvis, Little Richard, Dion, Cliff Richard . . .

In March 1964, the Bulsaras caught a plane to London and began a new life. Meanwhile, Shah won a scholarship to a college in Wisconsin. En route to Ohio, he flew to England and showed up, unannounced, at the Bulsaras' new family home in Feltham. Kashmira answered the door and told him that Freddie wasn't there.

For the next four years, Shah wrote regularly to his childhood friend: he told him about his life in America and his hopes for the future, just as they'd previously discussed during their walks around Stone Town. 'But Freddie never wrote back,' said Shah. 'Eventually, I made a pact with myself: if he doesn't respond to me by 1968, I would stop writing.' Shah never received a reply to his last letter. 'It was then I realised that he really didn't wish to be reminded of India and Zanzibar.'

'I think Freddie wanted to remain a mystery,' suggested Roger Taylor. 'He never talked publicly about Zanzibar or India. But he did talk to me about it a lot. He talked about his family and being Parsi Indian, but Freddie felt that he wasn't a part of that culture. His culture was Jimi Hendrix.'

On 21 December 1966, Farrokh Bulsara was part of the audience at Blaises nightclub in Kensington. The lights dimmed as a willowy, guitar-cradling figure with an explosive Afro loped onto the stage. It was Jimi Hendrix. Farrokh Bulsara's own cultural revolution was about to begin. Zanzibar was already in his past and Queen was his future.

'I'm not going to be a star . . .' reads another plaque outside the Freddie Mercury Museum, quoting the singer long before he'd made a record, ' . . . I'm going to be a legend.' He had it all mapped out in his head even then.

ACKNOWLEDGEMENTS

Many thanks to Pete Selby for the idea, Matthew Hamilton at the Hamilton Agency for the deal, Melissa Bond for the edit and Lora Findlay for the design.

Also, to Queen's Brian May and Roger Taylor for numerous interviews going back to 1992 and to all those ex-band members, musicians, producers, engineers and road managers who have spoken to me about Queen over the past thirty years.

Thanks, too, to the staff and writers at the music magazines *Classic Rock*, *Mojo* and *Q* (RIP) and to queenonline.com.

For more about my other books, please visit markrblake.com.

BIBLIOGRAPHY

Baker, Danny, *Going to Sea in a Sieve: The Autobiography* (Weidenfeld & Nicolson, 2012)

Blake, Mark, *Is This the Real Life?: The Untold Story Of Queen* (Aurum Press, 2010)

Bramwell, Tony with Kingsland, Rosemary, *Magical Mystery Tours: My Life with the Beatles* (Pavilion Books, 2005)

Brooks, Greg and Lupton, Simon, *Freddie Mercury: A Life, in His Own Words* (Mercury Songs, 2006)

Collins, Phil, *Not Dead Yet: The Autobiography* (Century, 2016)

Dannen, Fredric, *Hit Men: Power Brokers and Fast Money Inside the Music Business* (Vintage, 1991)

Evans, David and Minns, David, *This is the Real Life . . . Freddie Mercury: His Friends and Colleagues Pay Tribute* (Britannia Press, 1992)

Freestone, Peter with Evans, David, *Freddie Mercury: An Intimate Memoir by the Man Who Knew Him Best* (Omnibus Press, 2001)

Gunn, Jacky and Jenkins, Jim, *Queen: As It Began* (BAC Publishing, 1992)

Haring, Bruce, *Off the Charts: Ruthless Days and Reckless Nights Inside the Music Industry* (Carol Publishing, 1996)

Hince, Peter, *Queen Unseen: My Life with the Greatest Rock Band of the 20th Century* (John Blake, 2015)

Hodkinson, Mark, *Queen: The Early Years* (Omnibus Press, 1995)

Hutton, Jim with Wapshott, Tim, *Mercury and Me* (Bloomsbury Publishing, 1994)

John, Elton, *Me* (Macmillan, 2019)

Jones, Lesley-Ann, *Freddie Mercury: The Definitive Biography* (Coronet Books, 1998)

McDermott, John with Kramer, Eddie, *Hendrix: Setting the Record Straight* (Little, Brown, 1993)

May, Brian with Bradley, Simon, *Brian May's Red Special: The Story of the Home-Made Guitar That Rocked Queen and the World* (Carlton Books, 2014)

May, Brian, *Queen in 3-D* (London Stereoscopic Company, 2017)

May, Brian and Taylor, Roger in Doherty, Harry, *The Treasures of Queen* (Carlton, 2019)

Norman, Philip, *Wild Thing: The Short, Spellbinding Life of Jimi Hendrix* (Weidenfeld & Nicolson, 2020)

Purvis, Georg, *Queen: The Complete Works* (Titan Books, 2018)

Rock, Mick, *Classic Queen* (Omnibus Press, 2007)

Rose, Rose, *Life, Art and Freddie Mercury: 1968–1970* (2015)

Sheffield, Norman, *Life on Two Legs: Set the Record Straight* (Trident Management Ltd, 2013)

Sutcliffe, Phil, *Queen: The Ultimate Illustrated History of the Crown Kings of Rock* (Voyageur Press, 2009)

Trynka, Paul, *Starman: David Bowie – The Definitive Biography* (Sphere, 2011)

White, Rupert, *Queen in Cornwall* (Antenna Publications, 2011)

Yetnikoff, Walter, *Howling at the Moon: The True Story of the Mad Genius of the Music World* (Abacus, 2005)